Java™ Programming with CORBA, Second Edition

ANDREAS VOGEL

KEITH DUDDY

WILEY COMPUTER PUBLISHING

John Wiley & Sons, Inc.

New York • Chichester • Weinheim • Brisbane • Singapore • Toronto

Publisher: Robert Ipsen
Editor: Robert M. Elliott
Managing Editor: Erin Singletary
Electronic Products, Associate Editor: Mike Sosa
Text Design & Composition: North Market Street Graphics

This publication is designed to provide accurate and authoritative information in regard to the subject matter covered. It is sold with the understanding that the publisher is not engaged in professional services. If professional advice or other expert assistance is required, the services of a competent professional person should be sought.

Library of Congress Cataloging-in-Publication Data:
Vogel, Andreas, 1965–
    Java programming with CORBA / Andreas Vogel, Keith Duddy.
       p.   cm.
    Includes index.
    ISBN 0-471-24765-0 (pbk. / Online : alk. paper)
    1. Java (Computer program language)   2. CORBA (Computer architecture) I. Duddy, Keith, 1967–   . II. Title.
    QA76.73.J38V64   1998
    005.2'762—dc21   97-52089
                                               CIP

Printed in the United States of America.

10 9 8 7 6 5 4 3 2

Contents

Foreword to the First Edition

The meteoric rise of the World Wide Web (dragging along with it the 25-year-old "overnight success" of the Internet) has managed, as I write this, to mask a pertinent fact: to wit, the Web is full of trash. Given the fantastic rate at which the Web continues to grow, it is truly impossible to estimate the average number of Web pages that have any intrinsic value, but any guess of that percentage above even my own inflated shoe size is likely to be too high.

Nevertheless, there is an amazing amount of value on the Web, from deep-space photographs to dictionaries, from world histories to cinematic masterpieces. Why the paradox? The reasons are simple: posting information (regardless of utility) is inexpensive, and the Web is still primarily static. Even Web pages that boast dynamic content tend to consist of lookup mechanisms onto static databases.

The next leap of the Internet will be the wide connection of the popular, simple Web browser-user interface to personal, corporate, national and international legacies not only of data, but of services as well. These services will mirror—in fact, they will **be**, in many instances—telecommunications services, and also other computerized services, from home electronics management to intercorporate data interchange to international flows of monetary instruments. The urge to standardize on a simple, single-user interface that can be taught to the beginning user—and that can yet be accessible to the power user—is impossible to ignore.

What technological leaps are holding us back from this dream? The primary reason is the poor programming model that underlies most Web services. The server-side Common Gateway Interface, and its logical mirror client-side Common Client Interface, rely on arcane bits of programming lore to be useful. Proprietary replacements exist but, unfortunately, lose the open, portable, interoperable nature of the rest of the Web structure.

Meanwhile, great strides have been made in the related distributed-object computing realm. Systems based on Object Management Architecture (OMA) and in particular CORBA, developed by the members of the Object

Management Group, address enterprise integration issues, cross-platform portability and interoperability—but, interestingly enough, not user interfaces.

These two technologies, plus the exciting new programming language and virtual machine design named Java, provide a powerful potential solution to the elusive problem of simple interfaces to complex, distributed enterprise systems. This book presents the most comprehensive yet readable approach to understanding these three important technologies individually and in concert. Java-based CORBA extensions to Web browsers and servers—literally, the general communications devices of the future—are already in use at major banks, manufacturing companies, telecommunications utilities and health-care facilities. This important book brings us a vision of a heterogeneous, but integrated, future system based on these technologies.

Richard Mark Soley, Ph.D.
Object Management Group, Inc.
Somewhere over the Atlantic Ocean

Foreword to the Second Edition

It takes a strong will and clever foresight to write a technical book about a technology in flux. Yet in the first edition of this book, the authors focused not only on CORBA specification—quite mature at six years old—but on using CORBA from the Java language. At that point, Java itself was only a toddler (even in Internet years), and Java mapping for CORBA was still being considered for standardization. The authors ignored these seemingly pertinent facts and muddled through. And what a glorious muddle! This justly well-received book enlighted tens of thousands on the obvious value of the CORBA/Java merger. In this second edition, they use the now-standardized Java mapping for CORBA, and have expanded their coverage of the integrated layered CORBAservices. They've managed, however, to find a new limb to walk out on, and in this tome cover the evolving worlds of component software and patterns based on Java and CORBA. Not only will readers new to this world enjoy this book, but readers of the first edition will find quite a lot of value as well.

Enjoy the journey!

Richard Mark Soley
Ph.D. Chairman and Chief Executive Officer
Object Management Group, Inc.
Lexington, Massachusetts, U.S.A.

Acknowledgments

First of all, we want to thank those people who assisted us in writing this book. These are our editor at John Wiley & Sons, Robert Elliott, and his assistant Brian Calandra. Thanks also to Erin Singletary and the Wiley production team.

Thanks to Keith's employer, the Distributed Systems Technology Centre (DSTC) in Brisbane, Australia. DSTC's CEO David Barbagallo, Research Director Melfyn Lloyd, and Architecture Unit Leader Kerry Raymond have been very supportive. We owe David Jackson many thanks as he edited and proofread the whole book and very much improved its readability in terms of organization and English expression.

Andreas' colleagues at Visigenic Software have been very supportive. Special thanks go to Jonathan Weedon, George Scott, Wei Chen, Andre Srinivasan and Dale Lampson.

Several DSTC people helped us resolve technical questions. Thanks for sharing your expertise. The CORBA experts are Kerry Raymond, Douglas Kosovic, Michi Henning, and Mark Fitzpatrick. The Java experts are Ted Phelps and Tim Mansfield. Thanks also to Michael Neville and Derek Thompson, the implementers of DSTC's CORBA Trading Service product.

Gerald Vogt, a student from the University of Stuttgart, spent the second half of 1996 at the DSTC working on his Masters thesis. He worked on the Universal CORBA Client and contributed substantially to Chapter 10. He has now completed his Masters.

We acknowledge the cooperation of the OMG, and in particular Richard Soley.

We would also like to thank the many and diverse participants of the Java ORB course from which the book evolved, our customers and all the many people who contribute to CORBA-related mailing lists and news groups. Their feedback has been very helpful and all their questions have improved the content of the book.

Dorit and Meta: I'm sorry for all the weekends I sat in front of the computer working on the book instead of spending them with you.

About the Authors

Dr. Andreas Vogel is a Senior Consultant with Visigenic Software. His work is mainly focused on the architecture and design of CORBA applications and systems.

Prior to this appointment he worked as Senior Research Scientist with the Distributed Systems Technology Centre (DSTC) in Brisbane, Australia and as a Research Scientist for the University of Montreal, Canada. He has worked on various topics in the area of distributed computing including Formal Description Techniques, Distributed Middleware (DCE and CORBA), Distributed Multimedia, and Quality of Service. He regularly publishes and speaks on distributing computing topics. Andreas holds a M.Sc. and a Ph.D. in Computer Science from the Humboldt-University at Berlin, Germany.

Andreas lives with his wife Dorit Hillmann and daughter Meta Hillmann in San Francisco and enjoys cycling to the office in San Mateo.

Keith Duddy is a Senior Research Scientist with the Distributed Systems Technology Centre (DSTC). His special area of interest is CORBA and he is part-author of several adopted CORBA specifications, including the Trader and Notification Services. Keith leads CORBAnet, OMG's Internet-accessible ORB-interoperability showcase. He studied computer science at the University of Queensland. He has worked in the Australian and European computer industries as a UNIX operating systems and network programmer, and at the University of Queensland in the specification of real-time systems.

He enjoys taking and printing black-and-white photographs, red wine, trash TV, and cultural criticism. He will accept any opportunities to travel to places where he can practice his bad German (or any other language for that matter), but lives quite happily in inner Brisbane, a country town of about 1.2 million residents. He lives in a flat with long-term flat-mate Kathleen (bigk) Williamson, a few hundred meters from his partner of nine years, and fellow research scientist, Tim Mansfield.

How to Read This Book

This book introduces Java Object Request Brokers (ORBs) to an audience familiar with the basic concepts of object-oriented programming and distributed systems. It contains chapters that fall into three categories: introduction and background, tutorial, and reference.

Chapter 1 gives motivation for the use of Java ORBs. Chapter 2 is a solid introduction to CORBA. Chapter 3 is an introduction to Java. Chapter 4 gives a more detailed overview of Java ORBs.

Chapter 5 provides first examples demonstrating the basic use of Java ORBs. Chapter 8 introduces two fundamental CORBA Services, the Naming and the Trading Service, and demonstrates their use. Chapter 9 shows how to build applications with Java ORBs using a room booking example. Advanced features are explained in Chapter 10. They include the Any type and TypeCodes, the Dynamic Invocation Interface, the Tie mechanism, and applet servers. Chapter 11 explains the CORBA event service and how it relates to Java event models and the JavaBeans infoBus. Chapter 12 looks at security aspects of Java/CORBA applications, in particular in an Internet setting. It covers such important issues as how to work with firewalls, using Internet Inter-ORB Protocol (IIOP) over SSL and how to implement simple authentication and authorization mechanisms. This chapter also contains an example of a CORBA Bean. Design considerations for performance, scalability, and management of Java/CORBA applications are presented in Chapter 13.

Chapter 2 is a useful reference to the core CORBA specification. A complete overview of the mapping from IDL to Java as adopted by the OMG is given in Chapter 6. Chapter 7 documents the Java implementation of the pseudo-IDL interfaces ORB, Basic Object Adapter (BOA), and Object. Chapter 8 is also somewhat of a reference chapter since it documents the interfaces of CORBA Naming and Trading Services, as are Chapters 11 and 12 for the CORBA Event and Security Services, respectively. The Appendix on the companion website lists the source code (OMG IDL and Java) of all examples introduced throughout the book.

Besides the default approach of reading the book front to back, we suggest the following paths through the book. Beginners should read the book from Chapter 1 to Chapter 5 and then continue with Chapter 8 to the end. Chapters 6 and 7 can be used as references as needed.

Advanced programmers will have experience with Java and CORBA. They can start reading at Chapter 4, but if they have already had some exposure to Java ORBs they can go straight to Chapter 8 and continue from there to Chapter 13.

We expect that the expert will use this book as a reference only. They may also look up particular details of ORB implementations in Chapters 6 and 7, and familiarize themselves with the CORBA services using Chapters 8, 11, and 12. They will also find explanations of advanced features using Chapter 10 and scalability and performance patterns in Chapter 13.

We recommend the book for self-teaching as well as source material for training and university courses. In any case, it is recommended that users work through the examples provided. The source code can be obtained from the John Wiley & Sons website at http://www.wiley.com/compbooks/vogel. The website is organized according to chapters, and should be easy to navigate.

1

Benefits of Java
Programming with CORBA

This book brings together two of the major object models used in distributed computing: *Common Object Request Broker Architecture (CORBA)* and Java. They each introduce a different approach to distributed computing. CORBA provides an infrastructure that enables invocations of operations on objects located anywhere on a network as if they were local to the application using them. Java introduces platform-independent, low-level code, which, when integrated with World Wide Web protocols and browsers, results in what are known as *applets*. In this approach, instead of invoking a method on a remote object, the code for the class providing the method is transferred across the network, run locally, and then the method is invoked on a local object instance.

These two approaches converge when a mapping is defined from CORBA's interface definition language, *OMG IDL,* to Java. When combined with a run-time system which supports this language mapping, the result is a *Java Object Request Broker (Java ORB).* For the remainder of this chapter we discuss this combination of the two paradigms in the form of Java ORBs. We explain the advantages of Java for CORBA users and the advantages of CORBA for Java users. The relevance of Java ORBs to the Web and configuration management is also discussed. We also explain the relationship between Java Remote Method Invocation (RMI) and Java ORBs.

1 What Does Java Offer CORBA Programmers?

The main reason for using a Java language mapping of OMG IDL is to exploit the combination of features unique to the Java language:

- ♦ Portability across platforms
- ♦ Internet programming
- ♦ Object-oriented language
- ♦ Component model

1.1 Portability of Applications across Platforms

Java programs are highly portable due to the standardized byte-code representation generated by Java compilers. Wide industry support means that compilers and run-time systems for virtually any hardware platform and operating system are available. This is a significant advantage over other programming languages, in particular for client applications, since a single source code or compiled byte-code set will be usable on any platform without porting. Consequently, development and maintenance costs can be significantly reduced.

1.2 Internet Programming

The Java language binding allows implementation of CORBA clients as applets. This enables access to CORBA objects, and potentially to legacy applications wrapped into objects, using popular Web browsers. In fact, Java-enabled Web browsers are becoming the universal graphical user interface (GUI). In an enterprise the same technology can be used in intranets because the same TCP/IP protocols are used.

Although having applets that are only clients to CORBA objects is useful, applets can also implement CORBA objects. This approach is somewhat limited due to the applet sandbox model which disables applets' access to resources on the machine where they execute. This means, for example, that those objects cannot be made persistent. However, applets can provide callback interfaces so that they can respond to requests from other objects.

Call-back interfaces allow for CORBA-based push technology, for example, using the CORBA Event Service.

1.3 Friendly Object-Oriented Programming Language

Java ORBs provide the same functionality as any other ORB. The main language bindings offered by currently available ORB products are C++, C, and Smalltalk. In our experience, Java provides a cleaner approach to object-oriented programming than C++, with fewer memory management responsibilities, no pointers, a less confusing syntax, and simpler method resolution rules. Additionally, Java provides features not available in C or C++ such as automatic garbage collection, exception handling, and integrated thread support. These features are generally desirable and are particularly useful for distributed systems programming, as we shall see throughout this book.

1.4 Beans: Java's Component Model

The most recent addition to the core of the Java programming language model is Java Beans: Java's component model. The component model allows programmers to combine the functionality provided by a number of Java classes into a single component. Components can be easily put together, even by nonprogrammers, to achieve new functionality.

2 What Does CORBA Offer Java Programmers?

The Java programming language does not directly support the development of distributed applications or systems. The only way to implement distributed applications that is directly supported in Java is to use the network library classes in the package `java.net`. Those classes provide an Application Programming Interface (API) for the handling of URLs and an API to UDP/IP and TCP/IP sockets.

The URL API provides high-level access to Web resources. For example, it provides a mechanism to fetch the document specified in a URL using the protocol specifier in the URL. Hence the API provides the same approach to distributed computing as a Web browser, that is, either fetching documents from a remote server or using the Common Gateway Interface

(CGI) to invoke a program at an HTTP server that creates an HTML document on the fly. Here we outline the limitations and drawbacks of the CGI.

UDP/IP and TCP/IP sockets are relatively low-level abstractions providing access to transport protocols. The socket API does not provide distribution transparency or connection management.

The Java language binding for OMG IDL provides an application programmer with CORBA's high-level distributed object paradigm:

◆ Interfaces defined independently of implementations
◆ Access to objects implemented in other programming languages
◆ Access to objects regardless of their location (location transparency)
◆ Automatic code generation to deal with remote invocations
◆ Access to standard CORBA services and facilities

These advantages are discussed in detail in sections 2.1–2.6.

2.1   OMG IDL Defined Interfaces

OMG IDL provides a means of separating interfaces from implementations for distributed object applications. This separation is particularly useful for software engineering processes. Systems designs based on object-oriented design methodologies and tools, such as the Object Modeling Technique (OMT), Booch, or the new Unified Modeling Language (UML), can be expressed in OMG IDL. Once interfaces are specified in IDL, different teams or individuals can independently implement different parts of the system.

The separation of interface from implementation is also useful for managing software component evolution. In particular, it allows access to multiple implementations conforming to the same interface specification. Additionally, interfaces can be extended by inheritance, where derived interfaces are substitutable for base interfaces.

2.2   Programming Language Independence

CORBA supports multiple language mappings for OMG IDL so that different parts of a system or application can be implemented in different programming languages. However, all interactions in an application happen through interfaces that are specified independently of the programming language they are implemented in.

Previously, distributed applications were implemented in a particular programming language because of the availability of remote invocation libraries for that language. With CORBA the most appropriate programming language can be chosen for each object, based on the need for legacy integration, the prior experience of a development team, or the suitability of the language for implementing the object's semantics.

2.3 Location Transparency and Server Activation

Socket- or URL-based distributed applications need to address a server by specifying a host name and a port number. In contrast, CORBA provides location transparency, which means that an object is identified independently of its physical location and can potentially change its location without breaking the application. The ORB provides the necessary mechanisms for this transparency. In addition, CORBA provides mechanisms to start up services on demand. This can be controlled by various server activation policies.

2.4 Automatic Stub and Skeleton Code Generation

Distributed systems require a number of lower level and repetitious programming efforts including opening, controlling, and closing network connections; marshaling and unmarshaling of data (conversion of structured data into a programming language and architecture-independent format and back again); and setting up servers to listen for incoming requests on socket ports and forwarding them to object implementations. IDL compilers and ORB run-time systems free application programmers from these tasks. IDL compilers create representations of IDL-defined constructs such as constants, data types, and interfaces in a particular language binding, for example, C++ or Java. They also create the code to marshal and unmarshal the user-defined data types. Libraries are provided to support predefined CORBA types.

The generated code for the client side, that is, the code invoking an operation on an object, is known as stub code. The server-side generated code, which invokes the method on the implementation of that operation, is called skeleton code. The skeleton code in conjunction with the ORB provides a transparent run-time mechanism for handling incoming invocations and managing associated network connections.

2.5 Reuse of CORBA Services and Facilities

The ORB provides a means for the distribution-transparent invocation of methods on potentially remote objects. Typically, nontrivial distributed applications require additional functionality. Within the OMG these requirements have been analyzed and have led to the specification of corresponding fundamental services. These fundamental services are published with the brand CORBAservices. Examples are

- ♦ **Naming Service**—a white pages service for distributed objects
- ♦ **Trading Service**—a yellow pages service for distributed objects
- ♦ **Event Service**—an asynchronous, subscription-based messaging service
- ♦ **Transaction Service**—transaction processing for distributed objects
- ♦ **Security Service**—provides authentication, authorization, encryption, and other security features

There are specifications of higher level application-oriented services which are known as CORBAfacilities. More details on CORBAservices and CORBAfacilities can be found in Chapter 2.

2.6 Vendor Independence through ORB Interoperability and Code Portability

CORBA 2.0 and later versions of the CORBA specification define the means by which objects implemented using different ORB implementations can interoperate. These include object addressing through interoperable object references (IORs) and a hierarchy of protocols—the General Inter-ORB Protocol (GIOP) and the TCP/IP-specific Internet Inter-ORB Protocol (IIOP). This interoperability allows a certain independence from ORB vendor products. Any application developed using a CORBA 2.0 compliant ORB can integrate components developed using another interoperable ORB. The CORBA 2.0 specification in conjunction with the OMG IDL to Java mapping allows you to write applications which are portable not only across operating systems and platforms, but also across different Java ORB implementations.

3 The Web, Java, and CORBA

The progression of Web functionality from simple document fetching to more and more complex and interactive applications has followed these steps:

- ♦ Fetching HTML or other formatted documents from fixed locations
- ♦ Fetching documents from back-end systems, such as databases, using the CGI

◆ Building interactive systems using HTML forms and CGI
◆ Using Java script to increase GUI capabilities
◆ Using Java applets to provide client-side functionality

The Web now supports interactive applications. However, there is one thing lacking in these approaches: GUI capabilities combined with remote invocations.

3.1 Overcoming Problems in Current Web Applications

The functionality provided by HTML to create GUIs is not sufficient for commercial applications when judged side by side with applications written for Windows, Macintosh OS, or Motif. Java provides a package known as `java.awt` that matches the functionality of these systems.

The interactivity of HTML-based interfaces is provided mostly through the CGI or similar proprietary interfaces defined by certain Web server products. This enables the execution of programs on the server side. Unfortunately the CGI has a number of limitations and drawbacks:

Stateless clients. A typical CGI-based application, as illustrated in Figure 1.1, works in a two-phase cycle. A client has some state which can be changed by data entered into a form or as a result of state changes in the server. The client in this case is a sequence of HTML pages where each page is created as the result of a CGI

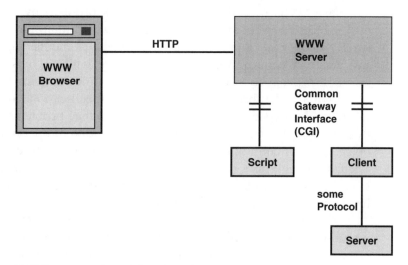

FIGURE 1.1 CGI-based distributed applications.

call. Hence all client state information has to be passed to a program behind the CGI. The only way to do this is by encoding it into the URL.

Non-type-safe interaction. Writing a client as a sequence of HTML pages and URLs is an extremely tedious task and has great potential for errors. Data transferred from client to server must be encoded in the URL string which must be parsed each time a new CGI call is received.

Performance bottlenecks. There are a number of performance bottlenecks in the CGI-based approach. Usually there is some scripting language program that glues the application-specific program and the CGI together. As a result of an invocation a complete HTML page is returned to the client side (including all the hidden state and GUI information). These HTML documents contain a lot of repeated text and formatting data that remains unchanged since the last client action. The amount of unchanged HTML often outweighs the amount of actual data produced by the application program by an order of magnitude.

HTTP, the most popular protocol of the Web protocol suite, is not very efficient. The major performance bottleneck occurs because multiple connections can be created by loading a single URL, and the connection management creates a significant performance overhead. Furthermore, the CGI will start a new operating system process each time an application processes a user input, and any server-side state must be read from persistent storage or communicated from another process.

Java ORBs overcome the statelessness problem by having continuously executing client and server programs which maintain their own state variables. Clients contain their own graphical elements, supported by the Java Abstract Window Toolkit (AWT) package, which avoids the downloading of HTML tags to format the display each time an action takes place.

CORBA's IDL provides typed interface specifications, overcoming the problem of untyped interaction. The performance problems are overcome by the ORB infrastructure allowing the invocation of operations on remote objects, which communicate only the data they need for each interaction. The ORB maintains a network connection between client and server, keeping a reasonable trade-off between lowering connection establishment overhead and freeing idle network resources.

The CORBA approach to Web-based distributed applications is gaining more and more support within the computer industry. For example, Netscape's browsers and servers contain support for Java ORBs based on Visigenic's Visibroker for Java.

3.2   Thin Clients and Configuration Management

Since HTML-based clients are a sequence of stateless HTML pages down-loaded every time from a server, they are considered to be *null clients*. At the other extreme is the case of an applet that executes in the browser without any outside communications or access to local data and contains all the application logic. In between there are a variety of options.

A *thin client* provides a complete GUI and keeps some state information. However, all the application logic and data is kept at the server. Thin clients overcome the limitations of null clients because they contain state and some application logic. They are relatively small in size and can be downloaded quickly over the network.

Thin clients can also overcome a major problem caused by software updates and their distribution. A typical distributed system could have a rel-atively small number of servers while the client front ends would number in the hundreds or thousands. When updating the software a new version of the client has to be shipped and installed on each of the client machines. This is a tedious, time-consuming, and high-cost task.

An applet client has the potential to overcome this problem. The ship-ping and installation process is automatically done by a Web browser. Caching mechanisms of today are rather simple. However, it would be pos-sible to implement a caching mechanism based on version numbers of applets. That would make the whole configuration process more effective since a client applet is only downloaded when the cached version is older than the one on the server.

Similar means are available for Java applications, for example, with Marimba's product Castanet. Castanet allows Java programs to check with their (remote) code base to see if there have been any code changes. If so, the application will be updated automatically by downloading changes in the byte code.

4   *Java ORBs and Java RMI*

Java's Remote Method Invocation (RMI) has been an alternative approach to enabling the invocation of methods on remote Java objects. The major differences between RMI and Java ORBs are

- ♦ RMI provides call-by-value mechanisms for Java objects. For example, RMI lets you send a Hashtable object from one Java machine to another.
- ♦ RMI uses its own proprietary protocol.
- ♦ RMI is a Java-only solution.

Java ORBs and RMI have been viewed as competing technologies. However, in mid-1997 Sun Microsystems announced that RMI will support CORBA's Internet protocol, IIOP. Additionally the OMG aligned its object-by-value specification so that it is fully compatible with RMI. Now RMI acts as a specialized Java ORB implementation that hides the use and creation of OMG IDL from the programmer. However, at the time of writing, it is not clear how RMI will support IDL and hence how RMI-based components can be integrated into other CORBA applications.

2

CORBA Overview

This chapter contains detailed information, from a CORBA application developer's perspective, about the OMG and the architecture documents and specifications it has produced. Section 1 is an overview of the history, goals, organizational structure, and processes of the OMG. It provides descriptions of all the committees, task forces, and special interest groups within the consortium.

Section 2 is a detailed summary of the contents of the Object Management Architecture Guide, and includes the changes made to the OMA since the third revision in mid-1995. There are two main topics in this section, the Core Object Model (section 2.2) and the OMA Reference Architecture (section 2.3).

The third, and longest, section summarizes the CORBA 2.1 specification. This section attempts to balance conciseness and detail, and covers all of the content of the July 1995 *Common Object Request Broker: Architecture and Specification* document that is relevant to ORB users while briefly introducing the material relevant to ORB implementers. The major topics covered include the CORBA Object Model (section 3.2), The Object Request Broker Structure (section 3.3), OMG IDL (section 3.4), ORB and Object

Interfaces (section 3.5), Basic Object Adapter (section 3.6), Portable Object Adapter (section 3.7), other language mappings (section 3.8), Interoperability Architecture (section 3.9), TypeCode, Any, and Dynamic Any (section 3.10), Dynamic Invocation and Dynamic Skeleton Interfaces (section 3.11), and Interface Repository (section 3.12).

1 The Object Management Group

The Object Management Group (OMG) is the world's largest computer industry consortium, with over 750 members in 1997. It is a nonprofit organization that began in 1989 with eight members: 3Com, American Airlines, Canon, Data General, Hewlett-Packard, Philips Telecommunications N.V., Sun Microsystems, and Unisys. The organization remains fairly small, and does not develop any technology or specifications itself. It provides a structure whereby its members specify technology and then produce commercial implementations that comply with those specifications. The OMG's processes emphasize cooperation, compromise, and agreement rather than choosing one member's solution over another's.

1.1 OMG's Goals

The goals of the OMG are promotion of the object-oriented approach to software engineering, and development of a common architectural framework for writing distributed object-oriented applications based on interface specifications for the objects in the application.

1.2 The Organizational Structure of OMG

The OMG Board administers the organization and ratifies the activities of the other groups within the OMG. Most positions in the OMG are unpaid and are held by representatives of member companies.

The technical group of the OMG are overseen by the Architecture Board (AB), whose members are experienced system architects. The AB is elected by the OMG membership. It reviews all technology proposals and specifications for consistency and conformance with the Object Management Architecture (OMA).

The structure of the committees, task forces, and other groups within the OMG reflect the structure of the OMA. Two committees oversee the technology adoption of a number of task forces (TFs) and special interest groups (SIGs).

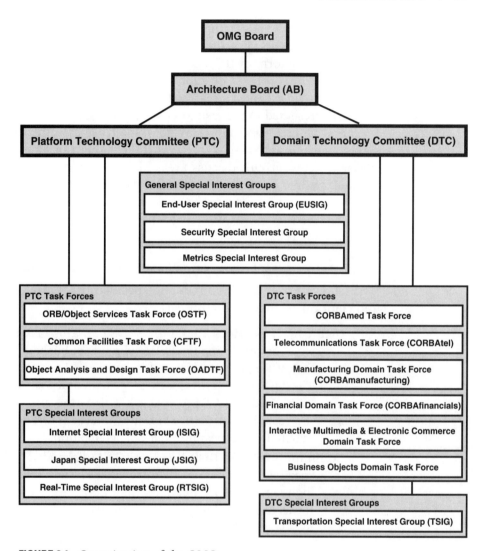

FIGURE 2.1 Organization of the OMG.

Platform Technology Committee (PTC). This committee is concerned with infrastructure issues: the Object Request Broker (ORB), Object Services, and the relationship of the OMA to object-oriented analysis and design.

Domain Technology Committee (DTC). This committee is concerned with technologies to support application development, in particular vertical markets such as manufacturing, electronic commerce, or health care.

Task forces may issue Requests for Proposals (RFPs). These are detailed statements of a problem that needs to be solved. Responses are solicited in the form of IDL specifications with object semantics explained in English. Two rounds of submissions are taken, usually three months apart, and then the most suitable specification is selected by a vote of members and presented to the task force's controlling committee.

Special interest groups may not issue RFPs directly or adopt technology specifications, but may do so with the support of a task force. Usually special interest groups discuss areas of common interest and report their findings to their controlling committee via documents and presentations. A number of special interest groups do not belong to either the PTC or the DTC. Instead they report directly to the Architecture Board.

1.2.1 PTC Task Forces and Special Interest Groups

The following are the task forces and special interest groups that report to the Platform Technical Committee:

ORB/Object Services Task Force (OSTF). This task force is responsible for specifying the ORB, which is published as the Common Object Request Broker Architecture and Specification (CORBA). The task force also specifies general purpose Object Services (published as CORBAservices). This is the area which supports the basic infrastructure of object interaction. This task force has adopted the largest number of specifications.

Common Facilities Task Force (CFTF) (disbanded). This task force specified technologies that provided services to applications at a high level. Its specifications were published as CORBAfacilities. It was disbanded in June 1997 because most of the work it undertook was undertaken by the Domain Task Forces. The distinction between the remaining "horizontal" facilities and Object Services has long seemed too subtle, and so future work will take place in other task forces.

Object Analysis and Design Task Force (OADTF). This task force is concerned with applying widely used object-oriented analysis and design methodologies to distributed object-oriented application development using CORBA. It is a new task force which has published some white papers but as yet no specifications.

Internet Special Interest Group (ISIG). The ISIG is concerned with the convergence between distributed objects and the Internet, both as a distribution mechanism and as a growing area of commercial activity.

Japan Special Interest Group (JSIG). The JSIG is a focus for Japanese developers of distributed objects and is particularly concerned with internationalization issues across the OMG.

Real Time Special Interest Group (RTSIG). The RTSIG is concerned with issues of guaranteed performance of requests to distributed objects, embedded systems, and fault tolerance.

1.2.2 DTC Task Forces and Special Interest Groups

The following are the task forces and special interest groups that report to the Domain Technical Committee.

CORBAmed Task Force (Healthcare). The CORBAmed task force is concerned with adopting specifications that meet the vertical domain requirements of the health care sector. It also promotes the use of object-oriented technology in the medical field.

Telecommunications Task Force (CORBAtel). CORBAtel is working toward adoption of specifications that meet the needs of telecommunications providers. It also promotes the OMG and liases with relevant telecommunications industry bodies.

Manufacturing Domain Task Force (CORBAmanufacturing). The MDTF promotes the use of CORBA technology in manufacturing industry computer systems and is adopting technology specifications tailored to that broad sector.

Financial Domain Task Force (CORBAfinancials). This task force promotes the use of financial services and accounting software based on OMG standards. They are adopting specifications for standard interfaces to this kind of software.

Interactive Multimedia and Electronic Commerce Domain Task Force. The IMCDTF is interested in on-line commerce, including rights and royalties, and electronic payment for media services.

Business Objects Domain Task Force (BODTF). The area covered by the BODTF is broad: it includes any standard objects used in business processes. This covers such areas as workflow, document processing, task scheduling, etc. The first RFP issued by the BODTF was controversial in that it did not solicit a single well-focused specification, but rather invited submitters to specify anything that they consider to be a Business Object. In the end a framework for business objects was adopted.

Transportation Special Interest Group (TSIG). The TSIG examines the requirements of the transportation industry in the development of Distributed Object Applications.

1.2.3 Architecture Board Special Interest Groups

The following special interest groups report directly to the AB.

End User Special Interest Group (EUSIG). The EUSIG is becoming increasingly important as the OMG membership shifts from representing mainly technology vendors to including a large number of users of the technology. The EUSIG seeks to emphasize the usability of the specifications adopted throughout the OMG from the point of view of application builders in business, the military, and government.

Security Special Interest Group. This SIG is similar to the EUSIG in that it feeds the security requirements of end users into the OMG-wide technology adoption process.

Metrics Special Interest Group. This SIG investigates the measurement of the performance of object technology and the processes by which the technology is developed.

Inactive SIGs. The following SIGs still exist, but are not meeting or currently developing documents:
  ♦ Database Special Interest Group
  ♦ Smalltalk Special Interest Group
  ♦ Parallel Object Systems Special Interest Group
  ♦ Class Libraries Special Interest Group

1.3 OMG Technology Adoption Process

The process, in brief, is as follows:

♦ A task force offers a Request for Information (RFI) on a particular technology area.
♦ RFI submissions are considered in the process of drawing up a Request for Proposals (RFP) which solicits submissions addressing its proposal from contributing members of the OMG.
♦ Any member company that wishes to respond to an RFP must submit a letter of intent (LOI) stating that they are willing to release a commercial implementation of their submitted specification within one year of its adoption, should it be chosen.
♦ A voting list is established from OMG members who express an interest in selecting from the submissions.
♦ A first submission takes place, usually about three months after the issue of the RFP. Typically there are three to six submissions.
♦ The task force session at one of the six annual OMG meetings will ask questions and provide feedback on the initial submissions.

♦ The submitters consider each other's specifications, and frequently some or all of them decide to produce a consensus merger of specifications which align fairly closely.

♦ Second (final) submissions are made, usually after another three months, and if there is more than one submission the choice of which to adopt is put to a vote.

♦ The adopted specification is presented to a Technical Committee plenary session and a yes/no vote to adopt the chosen submission is put to the entire OMG membership. This usually passes without problem.

♦ The Architecture Board then considers the broader implications of the new specification on the whole OMA. They may approve the specification unequivocally, suggest revisions, or simply reject the specification and issue a new RFP. Reissue of RFPs is not likely to occur.

♦ Once the AB is happy with the specification it is ratified by the OMG Board based on a further vote by members.

The form of submissions to the OMG's task forces and technical committees is usually a specification detailing the problem area that is being solved and proposing a number of interface definitions (in OMG IDL). The IDL is accompanied by English text describing the semantics of the objects and the roles and relationships to other objects in the specification and outside of it. The interfaces are described in terms of the actions of their operations and not in terms of a particular underlying implementation.

2   *The Object Management Architecture*

This section introduces the OMA and provides a summary of the technical parts of the third edition of the OMG publication *Object Management Architecture Guide,* which consists of two main parts: the Core Object Model (described in section 2.2) and the Reference Model (described in section 2.3).

2.1   Overview of the OMA

The OMA is the framework within which all OMG adopted technology fits. It provides two fundamental models on which CORBA and the other standard interfaces are based: the core object model and the reference model.

The Core Object Model defines the concepts that allow distributed application development to be facilitated by an Object Request Broker (ORB). The Core Object Model is restricted to abstract definitions which do not constrain the syntax of object interfaces or the implementations of objects or ORBs. It then defines a framework for refining the model to a more concrete form. The model provides the basis for CORBA, but is more relevant to ORB designers and implementers than to distributed object application developers.

The Reference Model places the ORB at the center of groupings of objects with standardized interfaces that provide support for application object developers. The groups identified are Object Services, which provide infrastructure; Domain Interfaces, which provide special support to applications from various industry domains; Common Facilities, which provide application-level services across domains; and Application Interfaces, which is the set of all other objects developed for specific applications. Since the disbanding of the Common Facilities Task Force (see section 1.2.1), the OMA Reference Model has not been redefined, and a number of specifications still populate this space in the OMA.

The Reference Model is directly relevant to CORBA programmers because it provides the big picture from which components and frameworks can be drawn to support developers of distributed applications. The Reference Model also provides the framework for the OMG's technology adoption process. It does this by identifying logical groupings of interface specifications that are provided by organizational groups (TFs and SIGs) which specify and adopt them.

2.2   Core Object Model

This section provides a detailed explanation of the theoretical underpinnings of CORBA. These specifics will not be of interest to everyone. We have tried to provide a readable summary of the contents of the OMG's *Object Management Architecture Guide*, but section 3 of this chapter on CORBA is written without assuming that the reader is familiar with the details of the Core Object Model. This section will mostly be of interest to readers with a background in object-oriented theory, but it starts from first principles and so is readable by anyone with a somewhat broader interest than simply using CORBA as an application development platform.

2.2.1   Scope of the Core Object Model

The main goals of the Core Object Model are portability and interoperability. The most important aspect of portability to consider is *design portability*. This means knowledge of an object's interface and the ability to create applications whose components do not rely on the existence or location of a particular object implementation. The core does not define the syntax of interface descriptions, but does describe the semantics of types and their relationships to one another.

Interoperability means being able to invoke operations on objects regardless of where they are located, which platform they execute on, or what programming language they are implemented in. This is achieved by the ORB, which relies on the semantics of objects and operations described in the Core Object Model. The ORB also requires some extensions to the core which provide specifications for specific communication protocols, an interface definition syntax, and basic services to object implementations. CORBA provides these extensions.

The Core Object Model is not a meta-model. This means that it cannot have many possible concrete instances of the basic concepts. It consists of an abstract set of concepts that allow understanding of objects and their interfaces. However, these concepts cannot be redefined or replaced, only extended and made more concrete. The Core Object Model is specialized using components and profiles to provide a concrete architecture for an ORB.

2.2.2 *Components and Profiles*

A *component* is an extension to the abstract Core Object Model that provides a more concrete specialization of the concepts defined in the core. The core together with one or more components produces what is called a *profile*. CORBA is a profile that extends the core with several components which provide specializations such as a syntax for object interfaces and a protocol for interoperation between objects implemented using different ORBs.

Figure 2.2 shows how components and profiles are used to add to the Core Object Model.

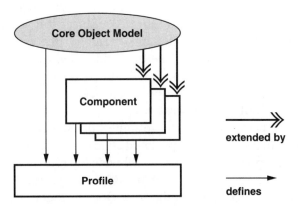

FIGURE 2.2 Components and profiles.

2.2.3 Concept Definitions

The Core Object Model is a classical object model. This means that actions in the system are performed by sending request messages to objects. The request will identify an operation and its parameters. The object will then interpret the message and perform some actions, and then possibly send a return message to the caller containing resulting values.

The concepts defined in the Core Object Model are

- Objects
- Operations, including their signatures, parameters, and return values
- Non-Object Types
- Interfaces
- Substitutability

Objects. Objects are defined simply as models of entities or concepts. For example, an object can model a document, a date, an employee, a subatomic particle, or a compiler. The important characteristic of an object is its identity, which is fixed for the life of the object and is independent of the object's properties or behavior. This identity is represented by an object reference.

Operations, signatures, parameters, and return values. An operation is an action offered by an object which is known to the outside world by its signature. The notion of sending a request to an object is equivalent to the notion of invoking an operation on an object.

An operation's signature has the following components: a name, a set of parameters, and a set of result types. Operation names are unique within a particular object. No syntax for describing operations and their types is provided.

When a request is sent to an object it nominates an operation and provides arguments matching the parameters in that operation's signature. The operation then performs some action on those arguments and will return zero or more results. It is important to note that object references may be returned as part of the result of an operation.

Operations may cause some side effects, usually manifested as changes in the encapsulated state of the object. When an object cannot process a request it will typically return an exception message, but exceptions are defined in a separate component that is part of CORBA, not in the Core Object Model.

The Core Object Model does not specify whether or not requests are accepted by an object in parallel or what the consequences of parallel execution would be if they were. An implementation of objects could choose to provide atomic operations or a sequence of operations for transaction management.

Non-Object Types. Unlike the object models of Smalltalk and Eiffel, there are types in the OMA core that are not objects. These are usually called data types. The set of objects and non-object types makes up the whole of the denotable values in the OMA.

While the Core Object Model does not specify a set of non-object types, another component of CORBA does. Even though the OMA core is designed to be extensible into several profiles via different sets of components, the likelihood of an alternative profile to CORBA being specified in the OMA is almost nonexistent. This design decision has been made so that new components can be added to CORBA in a consistent manner, and so that new versions of CORBA can be defined in terms of the makeup of its components and their versions.

2.2.4 *Interfaces and Substitutability*

An *interface* is a collection of operation signatures. Typically the interface to an object is the set of operations offered by that object, but this is left, once again, to CORBA to specify. Interfaces are related to one another by substitutability relationships. This means that an object offering an interface can be used in place of an object offering a "similar" interface. The Core Object Model simply defines substitutability as being able to use one interface in place of another without "interaction error." However, it is useful to examine a more concrete definition.

The simplest form of substitutability is when two interfaces offer exactly the same operations. Generally, if an interface A offers a superset of the operations offered by another interface B, then A is substitutable for B. Substitutability is not symmetrical, except in the simple case where A and B offer the same operations. However, it is transitive. That is, if A is substitutable for B and B is substitutable for a third interface C, then A is also substitutable for C.

2.2.5 *Inheritance*

Since interfaces may offer operations with the same signatures that have different purposes and semantics, it is useful to have an assertion of compatibility between them. In order to ensure a semantic relationship, the model introduces inheritance. If interface A inherits from interface B, then A offers all of the operations of B, and may also offer some additional operations. The set of operations of A is therefore a superset of the operations of

B, and hence A is substitutable for B. However, because the relationship between A and B is explicit we can be certain that the operations they have in common serve the same purpose, and A and B don't merely coincidentally share signatures. Figure 2.3 shows this example in a graphical form.

The Core Object Model defines *subtyping* as a form of substitutability dependent on inheritance of interfaces. That is, an interface A that inherits from an interface B is a subtype of B. We can also say that B is a supertype of A. In the Core Object Model, subtyping is the only acceptable form of substitutability.

The supertype of all objects in the Core Object Model is an abstract type *Object* that has an empty set of operations. The inheritance hierarchy places Object at the root and all other objects as its subtypes and is also called the type graph.

2.3 The Reference Model

The OMA Reference Model is an architectural framework for the standardization of interfaces to infrastructure and services that applications can use. The object-oriented paradigm emphasizes reusability of components that perform small, well-defined parts of an application's functionality. The

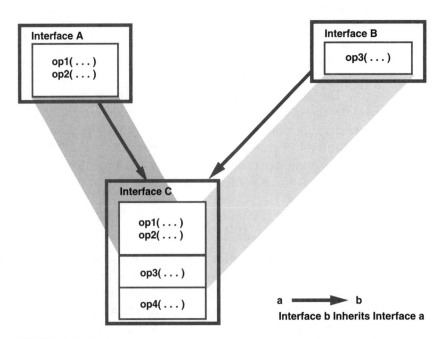

FIGURE 2.3 Inheritance.

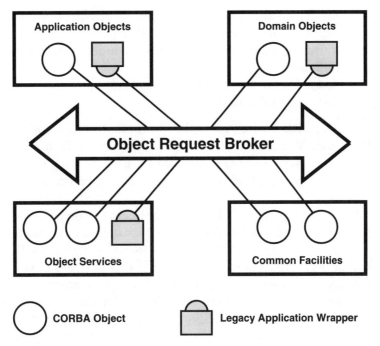

FIGURE 2.4 The OMA Reference Model.

Reference Model allows users of components to understand what support they can expect in what areas from ORB vendors and third-party component providers.

The Reference Model is shown in Figure 2.4, which identifies five main components of the OMA:

- ♦ Object Request Broker
- ♦ Object Services
- ♦ Common Facilities
- ♦ Domain Interfaces
- ♦ Application Interfaces

Only the last of these is not intended to have interfaces specified through OMG processes. Application objects are the project-specific part of an integrated application.

2.3.1 *Object Request Broker (ORB)*

The ORB is defined in the *Common Object Request Broker Architecture (CORBA) and Specification* document. CORBA builds on the OMA Core Object Model and provides

◆ An extended CORBA core including a syntax and semantics for an Interface Definition Language (IDL)

◆ A framework for interoperability, including two specific protocol definitions

◆ A set of language mappings from IDL to implementation languages (C, C++, Smalltalk, Ada'95)

The ORB is situated at the conceptual (and graphical) center of the Reference Model. It acts as a message bus between objects which may be located on any machine in a network, implemented in any programming language, and executed on any hardware or operating system platform. The caller only needs an Object Reference and well-formed arguments in the language mapping of choice to invoke an operation as if it were a local function and receive results. This is called location and access transparency.

At the heart of CORBA is the Interface Definition Language (IDL), which is covered in detail in section 3.4. It provides a way of defining the interfaces of objects independently of the programming language in which they are implemented. It is a strongly typed declarative language with a rich set of data types for describing complex parameters. An IDL interface acts as a contract between developers of objects and the eventual users of their interfaces. It also allows the user of CORBA objects to compile the interface definitions into hidden code for the transmission of invocation requests across networks and machine architectures without knowledge of the network protocol, the target machine architecture, or even the location of the object being invoked.

2.3.2   Object Services

This set of interface specifications provides fundamental services that application developers may need in order to find and manage their objects and data, and to coordinate the execution of complex operations. Object Services are the building blocks from which other components of the OMA can be constructed and which application objects may require. The OMG brand name for these services is *CORBAservices*. The published services include

◆ Naming
◆ Events
◆ Life Cycle
◆ Persistent Object (deprecated)
◆ Relationships
◆ Externalization
◆ Transactions

♦ Concurrency Control
♦ Licensing
♦ Query
♦ Properties
♦ Security (including IIOP over SSL)
♦ Time
♦ Collections
♦ Trading

Some of these are simply framework interfaces that will be inherited by application or other objects, for example, the Life Cycle Service. Others represent low-level components on which higher level application-oriented components can be built, for example, Transaction Service. Others provide basic services used at all levels of applications, such as the Naming and Trading Services. These last two services provide a means of locating objects by name or by type and properties for late binding in an application. See chapter 8 for a detailed description of these services.

2.3.3   Common Facilities

Common Facilities are those end-user-oriented interfaces that provide facilities across application domains. The first such specification adopted, published by the OMG as *CORBAfacilities*, is the Distributed Document Component Facility, based on OpenDoc. Work has been completed on Internationalization and Time Facilities, Data Interchange and Mobile Agent Facilities, as well as a Printing Facility. A Meta-Object Facility, which is a way of defining repositories for IDL and non-IDL types, and a Systems Management Facility have also recently been adopted.

2.3.4   Domain Interfaces

The OMG contains a large number of special interest groups and task forces which focus on particular application domains such as telecommunications, Internet, business objects, manufacturing, and health care. This area of standardization was separated from the Common Facilities in early 1996 where it was called Vertical Facilities. Several Requests for Information (RFI) and Requests for Proposals (RFP) are in progress in the Domain task forces. Some examples are the Common Business Object Facility, Product Data Management Enablers, and a Healthcare Patient Lexicon Service.

2.3.5   Specification Adoption in the OMG

Technology adoption in the OMG emphasizes the use of existing technologies and rapid market availability. To this end, submitters of specifications must vouch that an implementation of the specification exists and that, should their submission be adopted, they will make an implementation commercially available within a year of adoption. The adoption process is detailed in section 1.3.

3 Common Object Request Broker Architecture (CORBA)

This section provides a summary of the Common Object Request Broker: Architecture and Specification, version 2.0. The structure of the section is as follows:

- ♦ An overview of CORBA (section 3.1)
- ♦ The CORBA Object Model (section 3.2)
- ♦ The structure of the ORB (section 3.3)
- ♦ OMG Interface Definition Language (IDL) (section 3.4)
- ♦ The interfaces to the ORB and CORBA Object (section 3.5)
- ♦ The Basic Object Adapter (section 3.6)
- ♦ The Portable Object Adapter (section 3.7)
- ♦ A brief description of other language mappings (section 3.8)
- ♦ The Interoperability Architecture (section 3.9)
- ♦ TypeCodes, Any, and DynAny (section 3.10)
- ♦ The Dynamic Invocation and Dynamic Skeleton Interfaces (section 3.11)
- ♦ The Interface Repository (section 3.12)

3.1 Overview

CORBA is the specification of the functionality of the ORB, the crucial message bus that conveys operation invocation requests and their results to CORBA objects resident anywhere, however they are implemented. The CORBA specification provides certain interfaces to components of the ORB, but leaves the interfaces to other components up to the ORB implementer.

The notion of transparency is at the center of CORBA. *Location transparency* is the ability to access and invoke operations on a CORBA object without needing to know where the object resides. The idea is that it should be equally easy to invoke an operation on an object residing on a remote machine as it is to invoke a method on an object in the same address space.

Programming language transparency provides the freedom to implement the functionality encapsulated in an object using the most appropriate language, whether because of the skills of the programmers, the appropriateness of the language to the task, or the choice of a third-party developer who provides off-the-shelf component objects. The key to this freedom is an implementation-neutral interface definition language, OMG IDL, which provides separation of interface and implementation.

IDL interface definitions inform clients of an object offering an interface exactly what operations an object supports, the types of their parameters, and what return types to expect. A client programmer needs only the IDL to write client code that is ready to invoke operations on a remote object. The client uses the data types defined in IDL through a *language mapping.* This mapping defines the programming language constructs (data types, classes, etc.) that will be generated by the IDL compiler supplied by an ORB vendor.

The IDL compiler also generates *stub code* that the client links to, and this translates, or *marshals,* the programming language data types into a wire format for transmission as a request message to an object implementation. The implementation of the object has linked to it similar marshaling code, called a *skeleton,* that *unmarshals* the request into programming language data types. The skeleton can be generated by a different IDL compiler with a different language mapping. In this way the object's method implementation can be invoked and the results returned by the same means. Figure 2.5 illustrates the use of stub, skeleton, and ORB to make a remote invocation.

IDL and IDL compilers allow programs providing and using object interfaces to agree on the form of their exchanges, even though they may be developed completely independently, in different languages, and on different ORB technologies. This means that objects offering the same interfaces

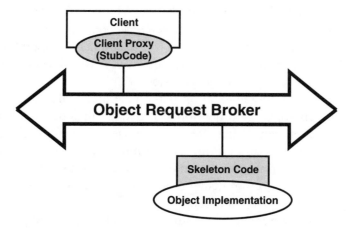

FIGURE 2.5 Stub, ORB, and skeleton.

are substitutable, and that clients can decide which object to use at run time with the assurance that there will be no interaction mismatches. Because the implementation of a particular object offering an interface is hidden, there may be quality of service differences, or even differences in the semantics of operations. The Trading Service allows clients to find the most appropriate object that matches their particular performance, location, cost, or other criteria.

The interfaces to components of the ORB are all specified in IDL. This provides a language-neutral representation of the computational interface of the ORB. However, certain parts of these definitions are designated as *pseudo-IDL (PIDL)*, which means that their implementations are not necessarily CORBA objects and data types. Any interface definition that is commented as pseudo-IDL may be implemented as a *pseudo-object*. This usually means that it is a library that is linked into the application using it. Although operations on pseudo-objects are invoked in the same way as operations on real CORBA objects, their references and pseudo-IDL data types cannot be passed as parameters to real CORBA objects.

3.2   Object Model

The OMA Core Object Model provides some fundamental definitions of concepts that are extended by the CORBA specification. CORBA uses the same concepts as the OMA core, but makes them more specific and concrete. The definitions here refer to the way in which these concepts are declared, but do not provide syntax for declarations. The syntax is provided by IDL (see section 3.4).

3.2.1   *Object Implementations and Object References*

It is necessary to distinguish between *object implementations* and *object references*. The former is the code that implements the operations defined by an IDL interface definition, while the latter is the object's identity, which is used by clients to invoke its operations.

An object implementation is the part of a CORBA object that is provided by an application developer. It usually includes some internal state, and will often cause side effects on things that are not objects, such as a database, screen display, or telecommunications network element. The methods of this implementation may be accessed by any mechanism, but in practice most object implementations will be invoked via the skeleton code generated by an IDL compiler.

Object references are handles to objects. A given object reference will always denote a single object, but several distinct object references may denote the same object. Object references can be passed to clients of objects, either as an operation's parameter or result, where the IDL for an operation nominates an interface type, or they can be passed as strings which can be turned into live object references that can have operations invoked on them.

Object references are opaque to their users. That is, they contain enough information for the ORB to send a request to the correct object implementation, but this information is inaccessible to their users. Object references contain information about the location and type of the object denoted, but do so in a sophisticated manner so that if the object has migrated or is not active at the time, the ORB can perform the necessary tasks to redirect the request to a new location or activate an object to receive the request.

Unless an object has been explicitly destroyed, or the underlying network and operating system infrastructure is malfunctioning, the ORB should be able to convey an operation invocation to its target and return results. The ORB also supports operations that interpret the object reference and provide the client with some of the information it contains.

3.2.2 Types

Types are defined using predicate logic in the CORBA specification. Object types are related in an inheritance hierarchy, with the type *Object* at the root. An object type derived from another can be substituted for it. Object types may be specified as parameters and return types for operations, and may be used as components in structured data types. A set of non-object types are defined with specific properties in CORBA. These are represented by constructs in OMG IDL. The usual kind of basic numeric, string, and boolean types are defined. A type called *Any* is also given as a basic type. It can store any legitimate value of a CORBA type in a self-describing manner. See Chapter 6 for detailed descriptions of Anys and Chapter 10 for examples using Anys.

The basic types can be used as components for a rich set of structured types, including structures, arrays, variable length sequences, and discriminated unions. The syntax and specification of CORBA types are given in the OMG IDL description.

3.2.3 Interfaces

An *interface* is a description of the operations that are offered by an object and can also contain structured type definitions used as parameters to those operations. Interfaces are specified in OMG IDL and are related in an inheritance hierarchy. In CORBA, interface types and object types have a one-to-one mapping. This is a restriction of the OMA Core Object Model, which implies that objects have single interfaces but does not state that this must be the case. The term *principal interface* is used to indicate the most specific (most derived) interface type that an object supports. The Multiple Interfaces RFP is currently soliciting submissions in the OMG, and a model for objects with multiple interfaces will probably be introduced in a revised CORBA specification.

3.2.4 Operation Semantics

There are two kinds of operation execution semantics defined for static (stub code) invocations:

At-Most-Once. An operation is a named action that a client can request an invocation of. The invocation of an operation results in the ORB conveying the arguments to the object implementation and returning the results (if any) to the requester, which is blocked and waiting for a successful termination or an exception. The semantics of the invocation are "at-most-once." That is, the operation will execute exactly once if a successful completion takes place, or if an exception is raised it will have executed no more than once.

Best-Effort. If an operation is declared using the oneway keyword then the requester does not wait for the operation to complete and the semantics is "best-effort." Both these kinds of requests can be made using the generated stubs or using the Dynamic Invocation Interface (DII), but the DII also offers a third type of execution semantics—*deferred-synchronous*. This allows the requester to send the request without blocking and at some later time to poll for the results.

3.2.5 Operation Signatures

Each operation has a signature, expressed in IDL, that contains the following mandatory components:

- ◆ An operation identifier (also called an operation name).
- ◆ The type of the value returned by the operation.
- ◆ A (possibly empty) list of parameters, each with a name, type, and direction indication. The direction will be one of in, out, or inout, stating that the parameter is being transmitted from the client to the object, is being returned as a result from the operation, or is client data to be modified by the operation, respectively.

An operation signature may also have the following optional components:

♦ A raises clause that lists user-defined exceptions that the operation may raise. Any operation may raise system exceptions.

♦ A oneway keyword that indicates "best-effort" semantics. The signature must have a void return type and may not contain any out or inout parameters or a raises clause.

♦ A context clause that lists the names of operating system, user, or client program environment values that must be transmitted with the request. Contexts are transmitted as sets of string pairs and are not type safe. Contexts are intended to play a similar role to environment variables known from various operating systems.

3.2.6 *Attributes*

An interface may contain *attributes*. These are declared as named types, with a possible readonly modifier. They are logically equivalent to a pair of operations. The first, an *accessor operation,* retrieves a value of the specified type. The second, a *modifier operation,* takes an argument of the specified type and sets that value. Readonly attributes will only have an accessor. Attributes cannot raise user-defined exceptions.

The execution semantics for attributes are the same as for operations. Attributes do not necessarily represent a state variable in an object, and executing the modifier operation with a particular argument does not guarantee that the same value will be returned by the next accessor execution. Section 3.4.6 contains a full syntax for operation and attribute declarations.

3.2.7 *Exceptions*

An *exception* is a specialized non-object type in OMG IDL. It is declared with the keyword exception and has a name and optional fields of named data values that provide further information about what caused the abnormal termination of an operation.

The standard IDL module, CORBA, contains declarations of 26 standard exceptions to address network, ORB, and operating system errors. These exceptions may be raised by any operation, either implicitly by the ORB or explicitly in the operation implementation. Each standard exception, also known as a system exception, has two pieces of data associated with it:

♦ A completion status, an enumerated type with three possible values— COMPLETED_YES, COMPLETED_NO, and COMPLETED_MAYBE—indicating that the operation implementation was either executed in full, not at all, or that this cannot be determined.

♦ A long integer minor code which can be set to some ORB-dependent value for more information.

Further user-defined exceptions may be declared in IDL and associated with operations in the raises clause of their signatures. An operation may only raise user exceptions that appear in its signature.

3.3 ORB Structure

As we have mentioned, OMG IDL provides the basis of agreement about what can be requested of an object implementation via the ORB. IDL, however, is not just a guide to clients of objects. IDL compilers use the interface definitions to create the means by which a client can invoke a local function and an invocation then happens, as if by magic, on an object on another machine. The code generated for the client to use is known as stub code, and the code generated for the object implementation is called skeleton code. Figure 2.6 shows the ORB core, stub and skeleton code, and the interfaces to the ORB.

These two pieces of generated code are linked into the respective client and object implementations, and they interface with the ORB run-time system to convey requests and results for static invocations. Static means that the IDL is statically defined at compile time, and only operations on known interface types can be invoked.

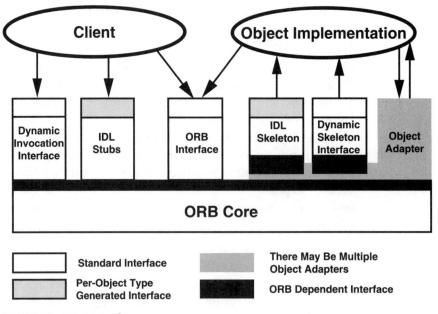

FIGURE 2.6 ORB interfaces.

The CORBA standard also defines an interface to allow requests to be built dynamically for any operation by a client. This is known as the *Dynamic Invocation Interface (DII)*. A symmetric interface is defined for responding to arbitrary requests, called the *Dynamic Skeleton Interface (DSI)*.

CORBA defines an interface for communicating with the ORB from either client or server. This interface deals mainly with ORB initialization and object reference manipulation.

Finally, object implementations need extra facilities for managing their interactions with the ORB. A component called an *Object Adapter* fills this role and is responsible for operating systems process management for implementations on behalf of the ORB and for informing the ORB when implementations are ready to receive requests.

3.3.1 Client Stubs

When a client wishes to invoke an IDL-defined operation on an object reference as if it were a local method or function call, it must link in stubs for the IDL interface which convey that invocation to the target object. In object-oriented implementation languages the stubs are instantiated as local proxy objects that delegate invocations on their methods to the remote implementation object. The stubs are generated from an IDL compiler for the language (and ORB environment) the client is using.

3.3.2 Dynamic Invocation Interface

A *Request* is a notional message that is sent to an object denoted by an object reference to request the invocation of a particular operation with particular arguments. The DII defines the form of such a message so that clients that know of an object by reference, and can determine its interface type, can build Requests without requiring an IDL compiler to generate stub code. A Request interface is defined in pseudo-IDL. It provides operations to set the target object for the invocation, name the operation to be invoked, and add arguments to send to it. It also provides operations to invoke the operation and retrieve any resulting values. As noted earlier, the implementation of pseudo-IDL is provided as a library and the operations map to local methods on a non-CORBA object.

The DII defines various types of execution semantics for operations invoked using Request pseudo-objects. The usual synchronous at-most-once semantics are available, as well as a deferred-synchronous option which sends the request and immediately returns to the client code to allow further processing while waiting for a response.

3.3.3 Implementation Skeleton

Once a Request reaches a server that supports one or more objects, there must be a way for it to invoke the right method on the right implementation object. The translation from a wire format to in-memory data structures (unmarshaling) uses the language mapping to the implementation language. This is achieved by the skeleton code generated by an IDL compiler.

3.3.4 Dynamic Skeleton Interface (DSI)

Implementation code may be written that deals with requests in a generic manner, looking at the requested operation and its arguments and interpreting the semantics dynamically. This is called the Dynamic Skeleton Interface and is realized by allowing the implementer access to the request in the form of a *ServerRequest* pseudo-object, which is the same as the DII Request, except for the invocation operations.

An example use of the DSI is a minimal wrapper around some legacy command processing code which accepts each request it receives with a single string argument. It then parses the string for a numeric value and sets this in a register before passing the operation name to an interpreter. It then checks the contents of the register, and unless an error bit is set, encodes the rest of the register as a numeric string and passes it back as the result. Clients can then write IDL that matches the expected pattern and use the generated stubs in a type-safe way to invoke the server which was implemented before the IDL was written.

3.3.5 Object Adapters

An Object Adapter is a component that an object implementation uses to make itself available through an ORB and which the ORB uses to manage the run-time environment of the object implementations. An adapter is used, rather than extending the interface to the ORB, so that different Object Adapters suitable for different implementations can be used for greater efficiency.

Currently CORBA defines two such interfaces, the Basic Object Adapter (BOA) and the Portable Object Adapter (POA). Their purpose is to generate and interpret object references, and to activate and deactivate object implementations. The interface to the BOA is described in detail in section 3.6, and the interface to the POA in section 3.7.

3.4 OMG Interface Definition Language (IDL)

OMG IDL is a declarative language for defining the interfaces of CORBA objects. It is a language-independent way in which implementers and users of objects can be assured of type-safe invocation of operations, even though the only other information that needs to pass between them is an object reference.

IDL is used by ORB-specific IDL compilers to generate stub and/or skeleton code that converts in-memory data structures in one programming language into network streams and then unpacks them on another machine into equivalent data structures in another (or the same) language, makes a method call, and then transmits the results in the opposite direction.

The syntax of IDL is drawn from C++, but it contains different and unambiguous keywords. There are no programming statements, as its only purpose is to define interface signatures. To do this a number of constructs are supported:

- ♦ Constants—to assist with type declarations
- ♦ Data type declarations—to use for parameter typing
- ♦ Attributes—which get and set a value of a particular type
- ♦ Operations—which take parameters and return values
- ♦ Interfaces—which group data type, attribute, and operation declarations
- ♦ Modules—for name space separation

All of the declarations made in IDL can be made available through the Interface Repository (IR). This is part of the CORBA specification and its interfaces are explained in section 3.12.

3.4.1 *Lexical Analysis*

OMG IDL uses the ISO Latin-1 character set.

Identifiers. Identifiers must start with a letter and may be followed by zero or more letters, numbers, and underscores. The only strange feature of the lexical analysis of IDL is that identifiers are case sensitive but cannot coexist with other identifiers that differ only in case. To put it another way, to identify the same entity the identifier must use the same case in each instance, but another identifier with the same spelling and different case may not coexist with it. For example, short DisplayTerminal and interface displayTerminal denote different entities, but may not both be declared in the same IDL. The reason for this is that language mappings to case-insensitive languages would not cope with both identifiers.

Preprocessing. The standard C++ preprocessing macros are the first thing to be dealt with in lexical analysis. They include #include, #define, #ifdef, and #pragma.

Keywords. Keywords are all in lowercase and other identifiers may not differ only in case.

Comments. Both styles of C++ comments are used in IDL. The "/*" characters open a comment, and "*/" closes it. These comments cannot be nested. The characters "//" indicate that the rest of a line is a comment.

Punctuation. The curly brace is used to enclose naming scopes, and closing braces are always followed by a semicolon. Declarations are always followed by a semicolon. Lists of parameters are surrounded by parentheses with the parameters separated by commas.

3.4.2 Modules and Interfaces

The purpose of IDL is to define interfaces and their operations. To avoid name clashes when using several IDL declarations together the *module* is used as a naming scope. Modules can contain any well-formed IDL, including nested modules. Interfaces also open a new naming scope and can contain constants, data type declarations, attributes, and operations.

```
// RoomBooking.idl
module RoomBooking {
  interface Room {};
};
```

Any interface name in the same scope can be used as a type name, and interfaces in other name scopes can be referred to by giving a scoped name that is separated in C++ style by double colons. For example, RoomBooking::Room is the name of the empty interface declared above. This name can also be written ::RoomBooking::Room to explicitly show that it is relative to the global scope.

Modules may be nested inside other modules and their contents may be named relative to the current naming scope. For example,

```
module outer {
  module inner { // nested module
    interface inside {};
  };

  interface outside { // can refer to inner as a local name
    inner::inside get_inside();
  };
};
```

The get_inside() operation returns an object reference of type ::outer::inner:inside, but may use the relative form of the name due to its position in the same scope as the inner module.

Interfaces may be mutually referential. That is, declarations in each interface may use the name of the other as an object type. To avoid compilation errors an interface type must be forward declared before it is used. That is,

```
interface A; // forward declaration

interface B { // B can use forward-declared interfaces as type names
  A get_an_A();
};

interface A {
  B get_a_B();
};
```

The preceding example declares the existence of an interface with name A before defining interface B, which has an operation returning an object reference to an A. It then defines A, which has an operation returning an object reference to a B. Forward declaration of interfaces is often used for formatting and readability rather than mutual recursion.

When a declaration in a module needs some mutual reference to a declaration in another module, this is achieved by closing the first module and reopening it after some other declarations. This is shown in the following declaration:

```
module X {
  // forward declaration of A
  interface A;
}; // close the module to allow interfaces A needs to be declared

module Y {
  interface B { // B can use X::A as a type name
    X::A get_an_A();
  };
}

module X { // re-open module to define A

  interface C { // C can use A unqualified as it is in the same scope
    A get_an_A();
  };

  interface A { // A can use Y::B as a type name
    Y::B get_a_B();
  };
};
```

Reopening modules is a recent addition to OMG IDL, and as yet many IDL compilers do not accept it as valid syntax. This is mainly due to the lack of such flexible name scoping mechanisms in programming language compilers. Java is one language that can support this correctly.

3.4.3 Inheritance

The set of operations offered by an interface can be extended by declaring a new interface which inherits from the existing one. The existing interface is called the *base interface* and the new interface is called the *derived interface*. Inheritance is declared by using a colon after the new interface name, followed by a base interface name, as the following example shows:

```
module InheritanceExample {

  interface A {
    typedef unsigned short ushort;
      ushort op1();
  };

  interface B : A {
    boolean op2(ushort num);
  };
};
```

In this example, interface B extends interface A and offers operations op1() and op2(). The data type declarations are also inherited, allowing the use of ushort as a parameter type in op2(). All interfaces implicitly inherit from CORBA::Object. This becomes clear when looking at the language mapping. In Java, for example, interface A will map to a Java interface A, which extends a Java interface called org.omg.CORBA.Object provided by the ORB. In the same manner interface B will map to a Java interface B which extends A.

CORBA IDL allows any non-object types declared in an interface to be redefined in a derived interface. We consider this to be an oversight, and it is not recommended that this feature ever be used. The beauty of inheritance is that it is a clean mechanism for determining subtyping and substitutability of interfaces. An object implementing interface B would be able to be used where an object of type A was required, as B is a subtype of A.

3.4.4 Multiple Inheritance

An interface may inherit from several other interfaces. The syntax is the same as single inheritance, and the base interfaces are separated by commas. For example,

```
interface C : A, B, VendorY::interfaceX {
  ...
};
```

The names of the operations in each of the inherited interfaces (including the operations they inherit from other interfaces) must be unique and may not be redeclared in the derived interface. The exception to this rule is when the operations are inherited into two or more classes from the same base class. This is known as *diamond inheritance* (the inheritance graph is the shape of a diamond). For example,

```
module DiamondInheritanceExample {

    interface Base {
        string BaseOp();
    };

    interface Left:Base {
        short LeftOp(in string LeftParam);
    };

    interface Right:Base {
        any RightOp(in long RightParam);
    };

    interface Derived:Left,Right {
        octet DerivedOp(in float DerivedInParam,
            out unsigned long DerivedOutParam);
    };
};
```

Figure 2.7 shows the IDL in graphical form. Both interfaces Left and Right contain the operation BaseOp(), but they can both be inherited by Derived because BaseOp() comes from the same base interface.

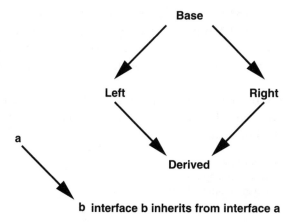

FIGURE 2.7 Diamond inheritance.

3.4.5 *Types and Constants*

The name of any interface declared in IDL becomes an object type name that may be used as the type of any operation parameter or return value or as a member in a structured type declaration, for example, to declare the length of an array. The basic types are rich enough to represent numerics, strings, characters, and booleans. The definitions of these are very precise to allow unambiguous marshaling. The structured types available in IDL are structures, discriminated unions, arrays, and sequences. Exceptions can be considered to be a special case of structures that are only used in raises clauses of operations.

The set of basic types provided by IDL and their required characteristics are as follows:

Type Keyword	*Description*
[unsigned] short	Signed [unsigned] 16-bit 2's complement integer
[unsigned] long	Signed [unsigned] 32-bit 2's complement integer
float	16-bit IEEE floating point number
double	32-bit IEEE floating point number
char	ISO Latin-1 character
boolean	Boolean type taking values TRUE and FALSE
string	Variable-length string of characters whose length is available at run time
octet	8-bit uninterpreted type
enum	Enumerated type with named integer values
any	Can represent a value from any possible IDL type, basic or constructed, object or non-object

The keyword typedef allows aliases to be created for any legal type declaration. In the case of template types (types that require a parameter to determine their length or contents) a typedef is required before the type can be used in an operation or attribute declaration. See the following string example.

Strings may be bounded or unbounded. Bounded strings are a template type. That is, their declaration contains a maximum length parameter in angle brackets. For example,

```
interface StringProcessor {
    typedef octstring string <8>;
    typedef centastring string <100>;

    //...
    octstring MiddleEight(in string str);
```

```
    centastring PadOctString(in octstring ostr, char pad_char);
};
```

Enumerated types are declared with a name, which can be used as a valid type thereafter, and a comma-separated list of identifiers. The identifiers used in an enum declaration must be unique within a name space. For example,

```
enum glass_color {gc_clear, gc_red, gc_blue, gc_green};
```

Any. The Any type has an API defined in pseudo-IDL which describes how values are inserted and extracted from it and how the type of its contained value may be discovered. This is addressed in Chapter 6.

Structures. Structures are declared with the keyword struct, which must be followed by a name. This name is usable as a valid type name thereafter. This is followed by a semicolon-separated list of named type fields, as in C and C++. For example,

```
interface HardwareStore {
  struct window_spec {
      glass_color color;
    height   float;
    width    float;
};
```

Discriminated unions. Discriminated unions are declared with the keyword union, which must be followed by a name. The name, once again, becomes a valid type name for use in subsequent declarations. The keyword switch follows the type name and it is parameterized by a scalar type (integer, char, boolean, or enum) which will act as the discriminator. The body of the union is enclosed in braces and contains a number of case statements followed by named type declarations. For example,

```
enum fitting_kind {door_k, window_k, shelf_k, cupboard_k};

union fitting switch (fitting_kind) {
   case door_k:    door_spec    door;
   case window_k:window_spec win;
   default:          float         width;
};
```

The default case is optional, but may not appear more than once. In each language mapping there is a means of accessing the discriminator value by name in order to determine which field of the union contains a value. The value of a union consists of the value of the discriminator, and the value of the element that it nominates. If the discriminator is set to a value not mentioned in a case label, and there is no default case, then that part of the union's value is undefined.

Sequences. Sequences are template types. That means that their declarations nominate other types which will be contained within the sequence. A sequence is an ordered collection of items that can grow at run time. Its elements are accessed by index. Sequences may be bounded or unbounded. All sequences have two characteristics at run time, a maximum and a current length. The maximum length of bounded sequences is set at compile time. The advantage of sequences is that only the current number of elements is transmitted to a remote object when a sequence argument is passed.

Sequence declarations must be given a typedef alias in order to be used as types in operation parameters or return types. Here are some example sequences of hardware fittings used to convey orders to a hardware store:

```
// union type "fitting" declared above.

typedef sequence <fitting> HardwareOrderSeq;
typedef sequence <fitting, 10> LimitedHWQrderSeq;

typedef sequence <sequence <fitting>, 3> ThreeStoreHWOrderSeq;
typedef sequence <sequence <fitting> > ManyStoreHWOrderSeq;
```

Sequence is the only unaliased complex type that may be used in angle brackets. All other types must be typedefed before sequences of them can be declared. Note that there is a space between the two closing angle brackets in the final declaration. If these were put side by side they would be parsed as the operator >>, which can be used when declaring integer constants. A better style would be to declare ThreeStoreHWOrderSeq as a sequence of HardwareOrderSeq.

Arrays. Arrays are also usually declared within a typedef, as they must be named before using them as operation parameter or return types. However, they may be declared as an element type of a union or member type of a struct.

Arrays at run time will have a fixed length. The entire array (regardless of useful content) will be marshaled and transmitted in a request if used in a parameter or return type. In contrast, sequences passed as arguments or returned as results will only be transmitted up to their length at the time of the invocation.

Arrays are declared by adding one or more square-bracketed dimensions containing an integer constant. For example,

```
typedef window[10] WindowVec10;
typedef fitting[3][10] FittingGrid;
```

```
struct bathroom {
    float      width;
    float      length;
    float      height;
    boolean    has_toilet;
    fitting[6] fittings;
};
```

Exceptions. Exceptions are declared in exactly the same manner as structures, using the keyword exception in place of struct. A set of standard exceptions, also known as system exceptions, is declared in the CORBA module. Here are some examples of user-defined exceptions:

```
exception OrderTooLarge {
    long max_items;
    long num_items_submitted;
};

exception ColorMismatch {
    sequence <color> other_window_colors;
    color          color_submitted;
};
```

It is good style to include values of arguments that are relevant to the cause of a failure in an exception. That way exception handling can be done by a generic handler that does not know what arguments were given that may have caused the exception. The handler can determine the context of the operation that raised the exception from the values in the exception.

Constants. Constant values can be declared at global scope or within modules and interfaces. The declaration begins with the keyword const, followed by a boolean, numeric, character, or string type name, an identifier, and then an equals sign and a value. Numeric values can be declared as expressions, with the full range of C++ bitwise, integer, and floating point mathematical operators available. For example,

```
const short max_storage_bays = 200;
const short windows_per_bay = 45;
const long max_windows = max_storage_bays * windows_per_bay;
const string initial_quote = "fox in socks on knox on blocks";
const HardwareStore::CashAmount balance = (max_storage_bays – 3) / 1.45
```

3.4.6   *Operations and Attributes*

Operation declarations are similar to C++ function prototypes. They contain an operation name, a return type (or void to indicate that no value is expected), and a parameter list, which may be empty. In addition an operation may have a raises clause, which specifies what user exceptions the operation may raise, and it may have a context clause, which gives a list of names of string properties from the caller's environment that need to be supplied to the operation implementation.

Lists of parameters to operations are surrounded by parentheses and the parameters are separated by commas. Each parameter must have a directional indicator so that it is clear which direction the data travels in. These are in, out, and inout, indicating client to object, return parameter, and client value modified by object and returned, respectively. These points are shown in the IDL that follows.

```
// interface HardwareStore cont..
    typedef float CashAmount;
    typedef sequence <window_spec> WindowSeq;

    CashAmount OrderFittings(in HardwareOrderSeq order)
      raises (OrderTooLarge);

    void OrderWindows(
        in WindowSeq      order,
        in CashAmount     willing_to_pay,
        out CashAmount total_price,
        out short         order_number)
      raises (OrderTooLarge, ColorMismatch)
      context ("LOCAL_CURRENCY");
```

Operations can be declared oneway if it is desirable for the caller to send some noncritical message to an object. Oneway operation invocations will use best-effort semantics. The caller will get an immediate return and cannot know for certain if the request has been invoked. For obvious reasons there can be no out or inout parameters declared on oneway operations. There must be no raises clause and the operation must have a void return type. The following declaration illustrates this.

```
// interface HardwareStore cont...

    oneway void requestAccountStatement(in short customer_id);
```

An attribute is logically equivalent to a pair of accessor functions, one to access the value, the other to modify it. Readonly attributes require only an accessor function.

Attributes are simpler to declare than operations. They consist of the keyword attribute followed by the type of the attribute(s) and then an attribute name list. The optional keyword readonly may precede the attribute declaration.

```
// interface HardwareStore cont...
```

```
readonly attribute CashAmount min_order, max_order;
readonly attribute FittingSeq new_fittings;
      attribute string quote_of_the_day;
```

The previous attributes could be replaced by the following IDL:

```
CashAmount min_order();
CashAmount max_order();
FittingSeq new_fittings();
string get_quote_of_the_day();
void set_quote_of_the_day(in string quote);
```

As declared, the operations and attributes are equivalent. The actual names chosen for the methods in the object implementation are determined by the language mapping. Attributes and operations can both raise standard exceptions. However, operations can be given raises clauses, allowing better handling of error conditions.

3.4.7 Contexts

Contexts provide a way of passing string-to-string mappings from the computing environment of the client to the object implementation. The specification does not define the way in which an ORB populates contexts to pass to objects. Some ORBs treat contexts as equivalent to UNIX or DOS environment variables. Others require users to build context objects explicitly. The string literals within a context clause must start with a letter and may end with "*", the wild card matching character. The matching character will cause the ORB to find all context items with the leading characters in common.

Contexts are a powerful concept but must be used with care. For example, the use of wild card pattern matching is especially dangerous, as the IDL author has no way at specification time of knowing what names will be defined in the context of all callers. A broad pattern match may cause many kilobytes of strings to be transmitted unnecessarily for an otherwise lightweight operation invocation. In general, contexts are a hole in an otherwise type-safe interface definition language.

3.5 ORB and Object Interfaces

The ORB interface is available directly to clients and object implementations for a few object management reasons. These include creating string representations of object references, and transforming them back again, copying and deleting object references, and comparing object references against the empty, or nil, object reference.

As already mentioned, there are a number of interfaces defined within the CORBA standard that use the IDL syntax for programming-language-neutral API definitions. They are interfaces to ORB components that are implemented as libraries or in whatever way ORB implementers see fit. The IDL is commented as pseudo-IDL.

3.5.1 Stringified Object References

As object references are opaque, the only way to correctly make an object reference persistent is to stringify it. A stringified object reference can be passed by means such as e-mail, web sites, or pen and paper, and when supplied as an argument to the string_to_object() operation it will produce a valid object reference that can be invoked. In order to use generated stubs to do this, the returned object reference must be passed to the narrow() method of the appropriate interface stub to cast the object reference into a reference to a more specific interface than Object.

```
module CORBA { //PIDL

  interface ORB {
    string object_to_string(in Object obj);
    Object string_to_object(in string obj);

    // several other operations are defined here but used in
    // other contexts, such as the ORB initialization and the DII
  };
};
```

The object_to_string() operation takes an object and produces a string. This string may be passed to the converse operation, string_to_object(), to generate a new object reference that can be invoked and will send its requests to the same object passed to object_to_string().

3.5.2 Managing Object References

This subsection addresses the pseudo-IDL for the CORBA::Object interface. This is the base interface for all CORBA objects and its operations can be invoked on any object reference. However, the functionality is implemented in the libraries provided by the ORB and results are not obtained by sending a request to the object implementation.

Object references, although opaque to their users, always contain certain information that can be extracted by using appropriate operations. The main components in an object reference are

◆ Abstract information about the name and location of the object implementation

- ♦ The interface type of the object
- ♦ Reference data, that is, a unique key that differentiates this object from other objects in the same implementation (server)

The get_implementation() and get_interface() operations provide access to the first two components, and the get_id() operation on the BOA interface provides access to the third. Many ORBs provide this information in other forms by additional operations not required by the standard.

```
module CORBA {

    interface Object { // PIDL
        implementationDef     get_implementation();
        interfaceDef          get_interface();
        boolean               is_nil();
        Object                duplicate();
        void                  release();
        boolean               is_a(in string logical_type_id);
        boolean               non_existent();
        boolean               is_equivalent(in Object other_object);
        unsigned long         hash(in unsigned long maximum);

        // the create_request operation used by the DII is defined here
    };
};
```

The get_implementation() operation returns an ORB-dependent interface called ImplementationDef, which the standard does not specify. This interface should provide information about how the object adapter launches implementations of objects. Usually the object adapter does this by starting a new process or task running from a particular executable file with certain arguments.

The get_interface() operation returns a standard interface from the Interface Repository. This allows a client to investigate the IDL definition of an interface via calls to objects that represent the IDL in the Interface Repository. This approach can be used to discover the operations available on an object reference when its type is unknown at compile time. The DII can then be used to invoke these operations.

The is_nil() operation returns TRUE if this object reference denotes no object. Object implementations that return object references as output parameters or return values may choose to return a nil object reference rather than raise an exception. Different language bindings implement object references differently and an invocation on a nil object reference may result in a fatal error.

The duplicate() and release() operations are very important in programming languages where programmers do explicit memory management (such as C and C++). Luckily in Java this is done for us automatically. These operations ensure correct management of copies of an object reference.

When an object reference is to be passed to another object, or thread of control, the opaque type which implements the object reference *must not* be copied by using features of the implementation language. The duplicate() operation must be used instead. The reason is that when a remote client uses an object reference, a proxy object is created locally for the client to invoke operations on directly. The proxy, in concert with the ORB, creates the request which ends up at the object implementation.

A proxy object keeps a counter of all object references that refer to it. This is called a reference count. If a copy of a reference to that proxy is created without the knowledge of the proxy, it cannot increase its reference count. When the counted references are released the proxy assumes that no other references to it exist and it will deallocate its resources and delete itself. Now the reference copied without using duplicate() refers to a deleted proxy and invocations made on it will incur a run-time error. This is illustrated in Figure 2.8.

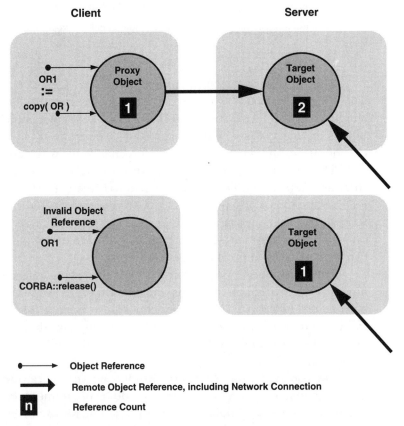

FIGURE 2.8 Invalid object reference copy.

When duplicate() is called to obtain a new copy of the object reference, the proxy will increase its reference count and wait for all references to call release() before cleaning up and going away. This makes the importance of using release() equally clear. If the last reference to a proxy is deleted without calling release() the proxy will continue to consume memory, and probably network resources, until the process or task in which it executes dies. Figure 2.9 illustrates this case.

Figure 2.10 shows the correct use of duplicate() and release() where the reference count in the proxy reflects the actual number of references to it.

Figure 2.11 shows what occurs when an object reference is duplicated for passing across machine boundaries. The figure does not show the temporary increase in the reference count on proxy object B before the skeleton code does a release() when passing the reference back to the client.

The is_a() operation returns TRUE if the Interface Repository identifier passed to it refers to a type of which this object is a subtype. It is mainly

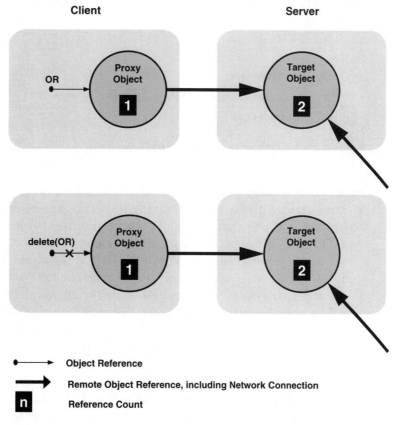

FIGURE 2.9 Invalid object reference deletion.

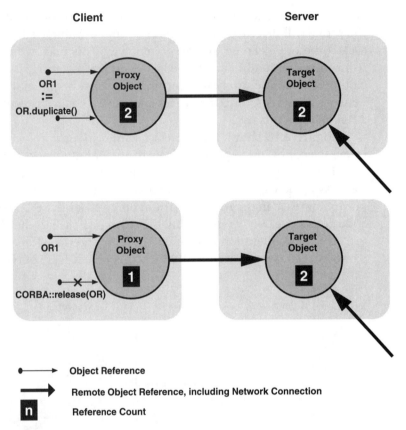

FIGURE 2.10 Correct use of duplicate() and release().

used in dynamically typed languages that cannot support a narrow() method. We recommend the use of narrow(), which can be attempted for various object types. It will return a valid object reference if it is of a compatible type. Otherwise it will return a nil object reference or raise an exception.

The non_existent() operation returns TRUE if the object implementation denoted by this reference has been destroyed. The ORB will return FALSE if the object exists or if it cannot determine the answer definitively.

The is_equivalent() operation is the *only* way within CORBA of determining whether two object references denote the same object. All references that are created by calling duplicate() on a single object reference will be equivalent to the original reference and with each other. Even so, it is possible that two references that actually denote the same object may return a FALSE result from this operation. That is, a TRUE result guarantees that the object denoted is the same, but a FALSE result does not guarantee that two references denote different objects. String representations obtained

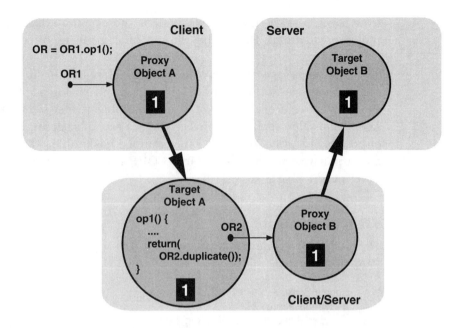

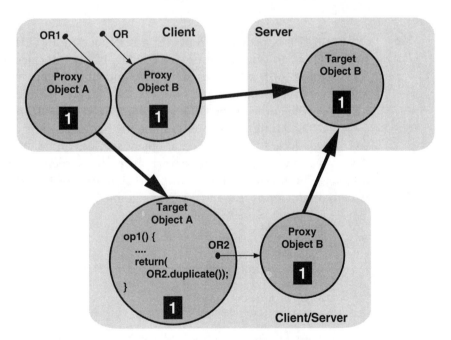

FIGURE 2.11 Proxy creation when passing object references.

from object_to_string() are ORB dependent and often are different every time they are generated. Hence they do not offer a means of comparing references.

The hash() operation provides a way of searching for an equivalent object reference that is more efficient than comparing a reference against every object reference in a list. The same object reference will return the same hash value each time. This provides a way of selecting a small number of possibly identical references in a chained hash table, which can be compared pairwise for a match. Most CORBA application programmers will never need to use is_equivalent() or hash().

3.5.3 Initialization

The CORBA module contains a pseudo-IDL operation ORB_init() for bootstrapping the ORB.

```
module CORBA { // PIDL
    typedef string ORBid;
    typedef sequence <string> arg_list;
    ORB ORB_init(inout arg_list argv, in ORBid orb_identifier);
};
```

ORB_init() is provided to obtain a reference to an ORB pseudo-object. Ordinarily operations must be associated with an interface, but ORB_init() is freestanding. ORB_init() takes the command line arguments from a UNIX shell-style process launch and removes any that are intended for the ORB. It also takes the name of the ORB to be initialized in the form of a string.

The ORB interface supports some further operations to allow any ORB user to get access to fundamental object services and/or facilities by name. The most important of these for object implementations is an object adapter. The following IDL shows the signature of BOA_init(), which is the way to obtain a reference to a BOA pseudo-object.

```
module CORBA {
  interface ORB { // PIDL
    typedef string OAid;
    typedef sequence <string> arg_list;

    BOA BOA_init(inout arg_list argv,
        in OAid boa_identifier);
```

As with the ORB initialization the argument list may be scanned for BOA-specific arguments and it will be returned with these removed. The object adapter identifier parameter, boa_identifier, must be passed a string specified by the particular ORB vendor.

The declarations following allow the ORB user to find out which basic services and facilities the ORB supports and obtain references to their objects. This mechanism is also used to obtain a POA reference. The list_initial_services() operation provides a list of the strings that identify the services and facilities, and the resolve_initial_references() operation takes these strings as an argument and returns an object reference.

```
// interface ORB cont ...
    typedef string ObjectId;
    typedef sequence <ObjectId> ObjectIdList;

    exception InvalidName {};

    ObjectIdList list_initial_services();

    Object resolve_initial_references (in ObjectId identifier)
        raises (InvalidName);

    }; // interface ORB
}; // module CORBA
```

The resolve_initial_references() operation is a bootstrap to get object references to the POA and CORBAservices, such as the Naming Service, Interface Repository, and Trading Service. The argument is a string specified in each CORBA service specification, for example, "NameService" for the Naming Service and "TradingService" for the Trader.

The type of interface expected as a return type is well known, and the object reference returned can be narrowed to the correct object type: CosNaming::NamingContext for the Naming Service and CosTrading::Lookup for the Trader. See Chapter 8 for a full explanation of how to obtain these references using the Java language binding and how to use them to obtain references to application objects.

3.6 Basic Object Adapter

For the object implementer, the BOA is the interface used to inform the ORB when objects come into existence and when running processes or tasks are ready to accept incoming requests on those objects. However, for the client the BOA is the component of the ORB that ensures that an invocation on an object reference always reaches a running object that can respond to it. That is, the BOA is capable of launching processes, waiting for them to initialize, and then dispatching requests to them. To do this it needs access to the Implementation Repository—a component proprietary to each ORB which stores information about where the executable code that implements objects resides and how to run it correctly.

The CORBA specification lists the creation, destruction, and lookup of information relating to object references as one of the BOA's primary functions. It provides PIDL descriptions of interfaces to do this. These will be described later for completeness. However, in effect, creation and destruction of object references is managed by code that is generated by IDL compilers as part of the implementation skeleton. When implementation objects are created their object references are usually created with them.

3.6.1 Registration, Activation, and Deactivation of Implementations

Let's look at what a program that implements some objects needs to do to allow the skeletons for those objects to be called and cause the methods of the objects to be invoked.

```
module CORBA { // PIDL

  interface BOA {
    void impl_is_ready (in ImplementationDef impl);
    void deactivate_impl (in ImplementationDef impl);
    void obj_is_ready (in Object obj, in ImplementationDef impl);
    void deactivate_obj (in Object obj);

    // continued ....
  };
};
```

The program implementing an object may have been started by some external means or by the BOA using the information in the Implementation Repository. The BOA should use policy information in the Implementation Repository to determine how to start the program (or *server process*) and what registration calls to expect. Four policies are explained in the CORBA specification:

Shared server activation policy. According to CORBA, each object should register itself with an obj_is_ready() operation if the process it runs in supports many objects. This is called the shared server activation policy. The obj_is_ready() operation is invoked to associate a running object implementation with an entity in the Implementation Repository. When an object can no longer respond to requests it should inform the BOA using the deactivate_obj() operation. Most ORBs provide automatic deregistration of objects in the destructor of the generated skeleton code.

Unshared server activation policy. In the unshared server activation policy the process encapsulates an application that supports only one object interface. In this case, when all the other initialization has been completed, the impl_is_ready() operation should be invoked. This associates the single object with an entity in the Implementation Repository. The deactivate_impl() operation informs the BOA that the server can no longer service requests.

Server-per-method activation policy. In the server-per-method policy a new process is started for each request received by the BOA. The standard says that no registration call is needed in this case, but ORBs that support this policy often require an impl_is_ready() call to notify the ORB that requests can be served.

Persistent server policy. A persistent server is a process that is started by some means other than BOA activation. Typically an operating system script or user command starts the server. In this case the impl_is_ready() operation should be used to register the server with the BOA.

Some ORBs' BOAs support only impl_is_ready() and don't allow objects to be activated individually, while others support both approaches, even in programs that use the shared activation policy. Some offer the above activation policies explicitly, but not necessarily using the registration operations specified. Others support orthogonal policies which consider the caller's identity. Most ORBs implement impl_is_ready() as a dispatch loop that doesn't return while the server is accepting requests and which calls deactivate_impl() if interrupted.

In short, BOA implementations vary a great deal, and object implementers should not only be aware of their responsibilities when initializing implementations, but should be aware of the peculiarities of their ORB. See Chapter 7 for details of what Java ORBs require.

3.6.2 BOA Implementation

The BOA is a logical component of the ORB, but its implementation is usually divided between the ORB daemon, the BOA pseudo-object and the generated code from the IDL compiler. As one would expect, the ORB daemon takes responsibility for launching processes. The BOA pseudo-object provides the interface that is invoked to register the objects.

Two common strategies are used by ORBs for object-oriented languages when incorporating the skeleton code into the object implementation. The first is to inherit the generated skeleton class into each implementation of an interface described in the IDL file. The base class is then responsible for supporting interactions between the ORB and the implementation methods. The second approach is to generate a proxy class that implements the same functionality as the skeleton class, but is not inherited by the class that implements the object's application semantics. When a logical CORBA object is instantiated the application implementer must actually instantiate two objects, the proxy object and an implementation object. The proxy object must then be given a reference to the implementation object so that it can delegate incoming requests there. This is called the *Tie* approach, as the application developer must "tie" the proxy and implementation objects together when they are created.

In the programming chapters of this book we use the inheritance approach, but Tie is covered in Chapter 10.

3.6.3   *Other Functions*

The BOA interface description provided in the CORBA module contains several additional operations which are seldom used by any ORB implementation. The generation of object reference is usually done implicitly when a programming language reference to an implementation object is passed as a parameter. The handling of authentication and access control is done by a higher level service. The reference data in an object reference may be used for many purposes, among them retrieval of persistent state. The following IDL supports object reference creation for non-object-oriented languages and retrieval of information from object references.

```
// interface CORBA::BOA PIDL cont ...

    interface Principal;
        typedef sequence <octet, 1024> ReferenceData;

    Object create(
        in ReferenceData        id,
        in InterfaceDefintf,
        in ImplementationDef impl);

    void dispose(in Object obj);
    ReferenceData get_id (in Object obj);

    void change_implementation (
        in Object       obj,
        in ImplementationDef impl);

    Principal get_principal (
        in Object       obj,
        in Environment ev);

    }; // interface BOA
}; // module CORBA
```

Generation of Object References. As explained in section 3.5.2, an object reference has three main components: a unique key within the server implementation, the object's interface type, and a way of locating its implementation, for example, an IP address and port number. Not surprisingly, these are the parameters that the create() operation needs to create a new object reference. It is unlikely that this operation will actually be offered in most ORB implementations, as object references are created implicitly from implementation objects by the ORB. The way to safely delete an object reference is by passing it to the dispose() operation.

The change_implementation() operation associates a new object implementation with a particular object reference. This must be done with care, making sure to deactivate the object before switching its implementation. There are security problems with providing access to a new object implementation using an existing object reference. Most objects will be associated with a single implementation for the duration of their lifespan.

Access Control. The get_principal() operation is used to determine the identity of a client that caused the activation of an object. It will generally be used by a higher level security service.

Persistence. The get_id() operation will return the reference data of an object reference which is guaranteed to be unique within the server that implements the object. This uniqueness means that it can be used as a key to a database table which contains a persistent state that survives between activations of a server.

3.7   The Portable Object Adapter

The semantics of the BOA specification were left intentionally vague because it was not clear which features would be required on various platforms or how implementations would be achieved. As a result, different vendors implemented different parts of the BOA with differences in their semantics. This implementation experience was used as the basis for the specification of the Portable Object Adapter (POA), which aims to eliminate these inconsistencies and standardize some of the proprietary features that have emerged to fill the gaps in the BOA specification.

3.7.1   POA Overview

The POA aims to provide a comprehensive set of interfaces for managing object references and their implementations, now called *servants*. The code written using the POA interfaces should now be portable across ORB implementations and have the same semantics in every ORB.

The POA defines standard interfaces to

♦ Map an object reference to the servant that implements that object
♦ Allow transparent activation of objects
♦ Associate policy information with objects
♦ Make a CORBA object persistent over several server process lifetimes

The use of pseudo-IDL has been deprecated in favor of an approach that uses ordinary IDL, which is mapped into programming languages using the standard language mappings, but which is *locality constrained*. This means that references to objects defined in POA may not be passed outside of a server's address space. One addition has been made to IDL: the native keyword. Parts of the specification tagged as native may be mapped to programming languages in a manner different from the standard language mappings.

The rest of this section will explain the architecture of the POA and provide an overview of the important interfaces it provides as well as the object activation policies that the interfaces may administer.

3.7.2   POA Architecture

First it is useful to provide definitions of some key concepts used in the POA specification:

Servant. An implementation object that provides the run-time semantics of one or more CORBA objects.

Object ID. An identifier, unique with respect to a POA, that the POA uses to associate a CORBA object identity with a servant.

Active Object Map. A table of associations between Object IDs and servants kept by a POA to allow it to dispatch incoming requests.

Incarnate. The action of providing a running servant to serve requests associated with a particular Object ID. A POA will keep this association in its active object map.

Etherealize. The action of destroying a servant associated with an Object ID, so that the Object ID no longer identifies a CORBA object with respect to a particular POA.

Default Servant. An object to which all incoming requests for Object IDs not in the Active Object Map are dispatched.

3.7.3   POA Policies

The policies used by POAs are divided into several interacting categories:

ID Uniqueness. Whether more than one Object ID may refer to the same servant object. The names of the policies are UNIQUE_ID and MULTIPLE_ID.

ID Assignment. Whether the POA or the programmer assigns Object IDs. The names of the policies are USER_ID and SYSTEM_ID.

Lifespan. Whether objects are transient or persistent. That is, whether the CORBA object is available to clients after the server process dies or whether it returns the OBJECT_NOT_EXIST exception when the server is reactivated. The names of the policies are TRANSIENT and PERSISTENT.

Servant Retention. Whether the POA keeps Object ID/servant associations in its Active Object Map or relies on default servants or servant locators to find servants for each request. The names of the policies are RETAIN and NON_RETAIN.

Request Processing. Whether the POA uses only the Active Object Map, only the default servant, only a servant locator, or some combination of these to locate the correct servant for incoming requests. The POA also relies on the value of the servant retention policy to determine its request processing behavior. The names of the policies are USE_ACTIVE_OBJECT_MAP_ONLY, USE_DEFAULT_SERVANT, and USE_SERVANT_MANAGER.

Servant Manager. A programmer-supplied object that manages servants. There are two subtypes of this abstract interface: activators and locators.

Servant Activator. An object that a POA uses to incarnate objects for continued use and then to etherealize them when their life cycle is complete.

Servant Locator. An object that a POA uses to obtain a servant to invoke a single operation on an object identified by an Object ID. A POA will not place this association in its Active Object Map.

The purpose of a POA is to dispatch incoming invocation requests to the correct servant object. It does so based on policies determined by the programmer of the CORBA server. This allows a range of behaviors from automatic generation of unique Object IDs, which are kept with servant references in the Active Object Map, to the use of programmer-supplied servant manager objects, which interpret Object IDs and return appropriate servants for invocations.

There can be more than one POA active in a particular server; however, there is always a root POA from which all of the other POAs are created. Each POA has a name relative to the POA in which it was created, and a find operation is defined to allow POAs to be located (and activated) by their parents. POAs themselves have manager objects which activate them and may change their processing state to allow them to suspend processing of requests or even to discard requests for some period (see Figure 2.12).

Thread Policy. To determine whether single or multiple threading is used so that safe deletion of servants may be achieved. The names of the policies are ORB_CTRL_MODEL and SINGLE_THREAD_MODEL.

Implicit Activation Policy. To determine whether the POA can implicitly activate a servant, or whether it needs to call a servant activator to do so. The names of the policies are IMPLICIT_ACTIVATION and NO_IMPLICIT_ACTIVATION.

Policies are specified as IDL interfaces in the PortableServer module. They all derive from a base interface called CORBA::Policy. The values that the

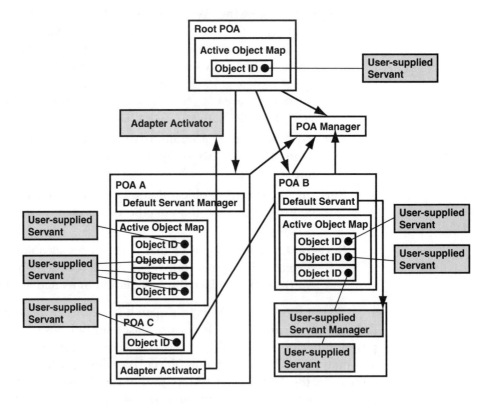

——— **Programming language Servant Pointer/Reference**

◄——— **CORBA Object Reference**

FIGURE 2.12 POA architecture.

policy objects represent are specified as read-only enum attributes. There are factory operations defined in the POA interface for creating these objects. For example, the LifespanPolicy object is specified as follows:

```
enum LifespanPolicy Value {
    TRANSIENT,
    PERSISTENT
};

interface LifespanPolicy {
    readonly attribute LifespanPolicyValue value;
};
```

with the following operation defined in the POA interface to create the object:

```
LifespanPolicy create_lifespan_policy(in LifespanPolicyValue value);
```

The way in which a new POA is created and initialized is by using the root POA (or one of its extant children) to create policy objects which are then passed in a sequence to the create_POA() operation.

Useful Policy Combinations for Child POAs

RETAIN and USE_ACTIVE_OBJECT_MAP_ONLY. This combination resembles the default situation of most ORBs implemented with the BOA. It relies on servers to explicitly activate new objects using the activate_object() or activate_object_with_id() operations.

RETAIN and USE_SERVANT_MANAGER. This is a portable way of allowing a server to implement a generic servant manager interface (namely ServantActivator). The POA uses the ServantActivator when an object is not found in the Active Object Map. Each ServantActivator supports the operation incarnate(), which takes an Object ID and returns the servant that implements the object identified.

RETAIN and USE_DEFAULT_SERVANT. This combination assumes that objects not found in the Active Object Map are to be implemented by a generic servant object (probably using the DSI), which is registered with the POA as its default servant. The POA will raise the OBJECT_ADAPTER system exception if no default servant has been registered.

NON_RETAIN and USE_DEFAULT_SERVANT. This is similar to the previous situation, except that no Active Object Map is kept, meaning that all requests are sent to the default servant.

NON_RETAIN and USE_SERVANT_MANAGER. The server will configure a POA to use this policy combination when it wishes to be in control of mapping each incoming invocation request to the appropriate servant. The servant manager used in this situation is a ServantLocator, which the POA calls using operations called preinvoke(), which obtains the servant which will service the request, and postinvoke(), which allows the server to clean up afterward.

3.7.4 POA Life Cycle

A reference to the root POA is always available from the ORB. Its name is RootPOA and is obtained using the ORB::resolve_initial_references() operation. It has a predetermined set of policies, which can be summarized by saying that all object references are transient, mapping a single servant to an Object ID which is set by the POA and retained in the Active Object Map. When a server is being initialized it is responsible for setting up any other (descendant) POAs that it requires to support its objects.

Creating POAs Manually. In order to create other POAs, the createPOA() operation must be invoked on the root POA. A hierarchy of POAs can be created by subsequently calling createPOA() on the resulting child. When a POA is no longer required its destroy() operation must be invoked. The other operation used in relation to children of a POA is find_POA(), which allows a relative name to be resolved, returning an existing or newly activated POA.

```
create_POA(in string adapter_name,
        in POAManager a_POAManager,
        in CORBA::PolicyList policies)
    raises (AdapterAlreadyExists, InvalidPolicy);
```

The create_POA() operation takes a name parameter and a POAManager parameter, which is usually a nil object reference, indicating that the ORB should assign a manager to the POA. It also requires a list of consistent policies, such as the combinations given previously.

```
find_POA (in string adapter_name, in boolean activate_it)
    raises (AdapterNonExistent);
```

The find_POA() operation may find child POAs that have been activated by create_POA() or they may be used to activate a POA using a preregistered adapter activator.

Adapter activators are associated with POAs at the time of their first creation and allow them to be made persistent when their objects are not being used and reactivated when required. The adapter activator for a POA is registered by setting the POA attribute called the_activator.

Adapter activators have a single operation:

```
boolean unknown_adapter(in POA parent, in string name);
```

This operation is called when find_POA() is invoked with the activate_it argument set to TRUE or when an invocation request is received nominating a POA that is not active. In this case the activators are called in succession from the one closest to the root to the furthest descendant. The parent parameter passes the reference of the parent POA to the activator. A typical activator implementation retrieves any stored information about the child, and uses the parent POA's policy operations to create the correct policies. It then uses its create_POA() operation to instantiate the child. If it can successfully create the child, the activator returns TRUE from the unknown_adapter() call. The ORB can then call unknown_adapter() on the adapter activator of the new child to activate the next POA in the chain. For example, if the currently instantiated POA hierarchy consists only of the root POA and its child A, an incoming request for an object controlled by a POA identified as "<root>/A/B/C" will result in the following calls (in pseudo-code):

```
if (A.the_activator.unknown_adapter (A, "B"))
    then B.the_activator.unknown_adapter(B, "C")
```

POA References to Other Objects. Certain POA policies require the assistance of other objects, such as managers, and the POA interface provides operations to set and get references to these objects. References to other objects are implicit in the POA's position in the hierarchy or are derived from the arguments provided to its parent at creation.

There are a number of attributes that POAs support:

```
readonly attribute string the_name;
readonly attribute POA the_parent;
readonly attribute POAManager the_manager;
attribute AdapterActivator the_activator;
```

The read-only attributes allow users of the POA (ORB and server implementers) to access the name of the POA with respect to its parent, the POA's parent, and its manager. The writable attribute the_activator must be set if this POA is not always created by the server initialization code.

If the USE_DEFAULT_SERVANT policy is set, a servant must be nominated as the default using:

```
void set_servant(in Servant p_servant) raises(WrongPolicy)
```

The default servant can be retrieved using:

```
Servant get_servant() raises (NoServant, WrongPolicy);
```

The WrongPolicy exception is raised by both operations if the USE_DEFAULT_ SERVANT policy is not set. NoServant is raised by get_servant() when set_servant() has not yet provided a default servant.

If the USE_SERVANT_MANAGER policy is set then the following operations are used in the same manner as set/get_servant() to initialize the ServantManager to be used by the POA:

```
void set_servant_manager(in ServantManager imgr)
    raises(WrongPolicy);
ServantManager get_servant_manager()
    raises(WrongPolicy);
```

3.7.5   *Using the POA to Create Object References*

The other operations of the POA interface are for mapping Object IDs to servants and for activating servants that already have Object IDs, thereby creating usable object references that can be handed to clients. If the USER_ID policy is set, servers can allocate their own Object IDs and map them to servants using the following operation:

```
void activate_object_with_id(
        in ObjectId id,
        in Servant p_servant)
    raises (ServantAlreadyActive, ObjectAlreadyActive, WrongPolicy);
```

The ServantAlreadyActive exception is raised if the servant is already mapped and the UNIQUE_ID policy is set. The ObjectAlreadyActive exception is raised when this Object ID is already in use.

When the SYSTEM_ID policy is set then activate_object_with_id() will raise the WrongPolicy exception and explicit server activation must be done using:

```
ObjectId activate_object(in Servant p_servant)
    raises (ServantAlreadyActive, WrongPolicy);
```

The return value is the POA's allocated Object ID for the new servant.

One more step is required (under the USER_ID policy) to make a usable object reference. The create_reference_with_id() operation is used to associate an object reference with an Object ID and hence with its active servant.

```
Object create_reference_with_id(
        in ObjectId oid,
        in CORBA::RepositoryId intf)
    raises(WrongPolicy);
```

The Object ID becomes associated with an object reference and conforms to the type specified in the Interface Repository using the RepositoryId provided as the intf argument.

The association between Object IDs and object references can be made by the POA when the policy is SYSTEM_ID:

```
Object create_reference(in CORBA::RepositoryId intf)
    raises(WrongPolicy);
```

Once the object is no longer required, its Object ID is deallocated and the mapping is removed from the Active Object Map using:

```
void deactivate_object(in ObjectId oid)
    raises(ObjectNotActive, WrongPolicy);
```

3.7.6   Discovering the Mappings in a POA

If the Active Object Map is being used (RETAIN policy is set) the following operations allow its mappings between Object ID, object reference, and servant to be interrogated:

```
ObjectId reference_to_id(in Object reference)
    raises (WrongAdapter, WrongPolicy);
Object id_to_reference(in ObjectId oid)
    raises (ObjectNotActive, WrongPolicy);
Servant reference_to_servant(in Object reference)
    raises (ObjectNotActive, WrongAdapter, WrongPolicy);
Servant id_to_servant(in ObjectId oid)
    raises (ObjectNotActive, WrongPolicy);
```

The mappings from servant to Object ID and reference can also be obtained if the UNIQUE_ID policy is set:

```
ObjectId servant_to_id(in Servant p_servant)
    raises(ServantNotActive, WrongPolicy);
Object servant_to_reference(in Servant p_servant)
    raises(ServantNotActive, WrongPolicy);
```

3.7.7   The Current Interface

When a servant implements methods for more than one Object ID it often needs to know which CORBA identity is associated with the request that has been dispatched to it. For this purpose an interface is defined that allows the servant to acquire information about its POA and its Object ID in that POA. The CORBA::Current interface is inherited by the PortableServer::Current interface, which adds the following operations:

```
POA get_POA() raises(NoContext);
```

This operation allows the servant to determine which POA processed the request, and to examine the policies of that POA.

ObjectId get_object_id() raises (NoContext);

This operation allows the Object ID relative to that POA to be discovered, and the servant can use this identity to access the correct state for the CORBA object it is serving for the current invocation.

3.8 Language Mappings

The OMG has standardized four language bindings and has RFPs issued to standardize several more. The current adopted specifications are: C, C++, Smalltalk, Ada '95, COBOL, and Java.

3.8.1 C

The C mapping was published along with the CORBA 1.1 specification. It provides an example of how to implement CORBA clients and servers in a non-object-oriented language. Operation and interface names are concatenated to provide function names and object references are passed explicitly as parameters.

3.8.2 C++

The C++ language mapping is the most widely supported language mapping at the moment. Its syntactic resemblance to IDL provides class definitions that very closely mirror IDL interface definitions. The generated stub code can be incorporated by inheritance into object implementation classes or delegate to them. The major drawback of this mapping is that implementers of clients and servers must pay very close attention to memory management responsibilities. The rules for allocation and deallocation of data memory are just as complex as old-style Remote Procedure Call (RPC) programming. Some helper classes are defined which can deallocate memory when they go out of scope, but these must be declared and used with care because they might deallocate memory that is still being used by another object.

3.8.3 Smalltalk

Smalltalk is a dynamically typed, single-inheritance object-oriented language in which all types are first-class objects. The data type mappings use existing Smalltalk classes and operations map to methods on classes. The way in which IDL interfaces map to Smalltalk objects is unconstrained. Explicit protocol mappings are made for some IDL types, such as unions and Anys, which provide a standard way of accessing their discriminators and TypeCodes, respectively. However, implicit mappings may be used by programmers.

3.8.4 COBOL

The IDL/COBOL mapping was adopted in 1997. As COBOL is not object oriented the mapping is not as natural as, for example, those for C++ or Java. In particular, IDL concepts such as name scopes, interfaces, and inheritance require complex mapping rules. The data type mapping is based on the optional COBOL typedef construct. However, older COBOL compilers may not provide typedefs, in which case the mapping has to use COBOL copy files as an alternative.

3.9 Interoperability

The CORBA 2.1 specification has a section called Interoperability. It specifies an architecture for interoperability, as well as an out-of-the-box interoperability protocol, running over TCP/IP, and a second, optional protocol which uses the DCE RPC transport.

The specification contains a lot of technical detail about the protocols specified and about bridging between proprietary protocols. Here we will give an overview of the framework within which the two specified protocols exist and of the mandatory Internet Inter-ORB Protocol (IIOP). The rest of the standard applies to ORB implementers and will not be covered.

3.9.1 The ORB Interoperability Architecture

The architecture contains definitions of ORB domains, bridges, and interoperable object references (IORs). It defines domains as islands within which objects are accessible because they use the same communication protocols, the same security, and the same way of identifying objects. In order to establish interoperability between domains, one of these elements must be replaced with a common element or a bridge must be set up to facilitate translation of the protocol, identity, authority, etc., between domains.

The approach of the architecture is to identify the things that can be used as common representations (canonical forms) between domains and then suggest ways in which ORB domains can create half-bridges that communicate using the common representation. The first step, a common object reference format, is defined as part of the architecture. An IOR contains the same information as a single domain object reference, but adds a list of protocol profiles indicating which communication protocols the domain of origin can accept requests in. The protocol interoperability problem is addressed in a separate component called the General Inter-ORB Protocol (GIOP). Allowance is also made for the introduction of third-party protocols called Environment-Specific Inter-ORB Protocols (ESIOPs) within this framework. Figure 2.13 illustrates the relationships between these protocols.

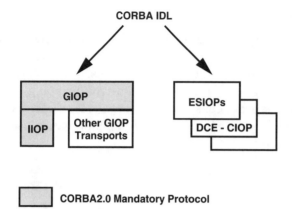

CORBA2.0 Mandatory Protocol

FIGURE 2.13 ORB protocols.

3.9.2   General Inter-ORB Protocol

The GIOP defines a linear format for the transmission of CORBA requests and replies without requiring a particular network transport protocol.

3.9.3   Internet Inter-ORB Protocol

The IIOP is a specialization of the GIOP which specifies the use of TCP/IP (the Internet Protocol). It defines some primitives to assist in the establishment of TCP connections. This protocol is required for compliance to CORBA 2.0 and is intended to provide a base-level interoperability between all ORB vendors' products, even though some vendors will continue to support proprietary protocols. Java ORBs are all implemented using IIOP.

3.9.4   Other Approaches

As can be seen in Figure 2.13, the interoperability architecture allows for the specification of ESIOPs which will provide "islands of interoperability," but which should be able to be bridged to other ORBs using IIOP. The first adopted ESIOP is the DCE Common Inter-ORB Protocol (DCE-CIOP), which was already used by a number of ORBs before the introduction of GIOP/IIOP.

An alternative implementation for GIOP can be expected for 1998. There are projects in progress to implement GIOP directly over ATM protocol layers. Most likely the implementation will choose AAL5.

Before the CORBA 2.0 specification was introduced, each ORB vendor had to choose or invent a protocol for the transmission of invocation requests and responses. Most vendors have a customer base with extant objects that use a certain protocol, and so it is in their interest to continue to support old protocols alongside IIOP. However, leading ORB products now support IIOP as their native protocol.

3.10 TypeCode, Any, and Dynamic Any

This section gives details about the interfaces to the generic container type Any and its supporting type, the TypeCode, which it uses to identify its contents. The ORB Portability Specification adopted by the OMG in 1997 extends the functionality available from Anys by adding a new interface called DynAny, which allows programmers to navigate the contents of Anys and access constituent parts without requiring compiled stub code with which to extract the entire contents of an Any.

3.10.1 Any

The Any type is a basic type in IDL. It designates a container that can contain a value of any IDL type and identifies the type of its contents for type-safe extraction of the value. The pseudo-IDL type TypeCode is used to identify the type of a value in an Any and can be used outside of the context of Anys to identify IDL types in general. TypeCodes are not IDL basic types, but they may be declared as parameters to operations and members of structured types.

As the keyword any in IDL is a basic type, and does not have a signature represented in PIDL, it is left to each language mapping to define the mechanism for inserting and extracting values from Anys and defining the TypeCodes that identify the values they contain.

3.10.2 Language Mapping for Any

The mapping for Anys in Java is given in Chapter 6 and provides methods on an Any class that allow the insertion and extraction of all basic types, as well as additional methods on Helper classes for IDL-defined types which produce Anys. To provide us with a very basic notion of what an Any is, let us have a look at the C mapping:

```
typedef struct CORBA_any {
     CORBA_TypeCode _type;
     void * _value;
} CORBA_any;
```

There are no helper functions defined in the mapping, and programmers are responsible (as is usual in C) for ensuring that the _value structure member is cast in a type-safe manner. To do this the programmer must compare the _type member against TypeCode constants that correspond to known IDL types and then cast the _value member to the mapped C type for that IDL.

3.10.3 TypeCode

The ORB specification defines a pseudo-IDL interface to a type called TypeCode, which is used to describe any IDL type. TypeCodes are one of only two PIDL types that can be used in IDL definitions as components of structured types or as parameter and return types of operations or attribute values. The other is Principal which is used for Security. The PIDL for TypeCodes is given in the Interface Repository section of the CORBA 2.1 document. However, they are implemented as a combination of library and IDL compiler-generated code and are available to CORBA programmers independent of the IR.

In concept a TypeCode consists of a *kind* field and a set of parameters that provide more information about that kind of TypeCode. For example, a TypeCode for a struct will give the name of the struct and the names and types (using recursive TypeCodes) of the members of that struct. The PIDL for TypeCode provides operations to allow the programmer access to the parameters, as well as an operation to compare TypeCodes for equality. All of the following PIDL is situated in the CORBA module.

TypeCode Kinds. The kinds of types in IDL are given as an enumeration. The kinds have been extended by the IDL Type Extensions Specification (OMG document ptc/97-01-01) to include wide characters and strings, fixed-point decimal numbers, and 64-bit integers and floating-point numbers. The extensions are given in italics below:

```
enum TCKind {
    tk_null, tk_void,
    tk_short, tk_long, tk_ushort, tk_ulong,
    tk_float, tk_double, tk_boolean, tk_char,
    tk_octet, tk_any, tk_TypeCode, tk_Principal, tk_objref,
    tk_struct, tk_union, tk_enum, tk_string,
    tk_sequence, tk_array, tk_alias, tk_except,
    tk_longlong, tk_ulonglong, tk_longdouble,
    tk_wchar, tk_wstring, tk_fixed
};
```

Internationalization is also supported implicitly by the character and string types, whose semantics now include the possible use of two byte characters.

TypeCode Operations. The TypeCode interface provides an equality operator whose semantics are not well defined.

```
interface TypeCode { // PIDL
    boolean      equal (in TypeCode tc);
```

Most ORB implementations perform a simple comparison that returns TRUE only when the types compared have the same Repository ID. That means that no structural comparisons are performed and no typedef aliasing is taken into account.

Making an analysis of a TypeCode begins with determining its kind with the kind() operation, so that other appropriate operations may then be chosen to find out more information about the type.

```
TCKind          kind();
```

Most types also have definitions stored in the IR, which can be used as an alternative source of type information. The id() operation returns the RepositoryId for any nonbasic type. Basic types are not stored in the IR, and if the TypeCode's kind is inappropriate, a BadKind exception is raised. This exception is raised whenever an operation inappropriate to a TypeCode's kind is invoked.

```
exception       BadKind {};
RepositoryId    id() raises (BadKind);
```

Object references and structured types except for sequences always have an interface or tag name. These are returned using the name() operation:

```
Identifier      name() raises (BadKind);
```

Structs, unions, enums, and exceptions contain named member fields. The number and names of these members are discovered using the following operations. The exception Bounds is raised by indexed operations when the index parameter exceeds the number of elements.

```
exception       Bounds {};
unsigned long   member_count () raises (BadKind);
Identifier      member_name (in unsigned long index)
                    raises (BadKind, Bounds);
```

The members of structs, unions, and exceptions (but not enums) each have a type as well. These are returned as nested TypeCodes, which can be interpereted in the same way as their parent TypeCode.

```
TypeCode        member_type(in unsigned long index)
                    raises (BadKind, Bounds);
```

Unions also have a discriminator type and label values of that type for each member, as well as an optional default case. The member_label() operation will return the value for each case. It returns an Any containing a zero octet for the default case, if it exists. The discriminator_type() operation returns the TypeCode of the ordinal type in the switch clause of the union, and the default_index() operation returns the index of the member which corresponds to the default case or zero if it does not exist.

```
any                member_label (in unsigned long index)
                        raises (BadKind, Bounds);
TypeCode           discriminator_type() raises (BadKind);
long               default_index () raises (BadKind);
```

Sequences and strings may be bounded to a certain length, and arrays are always of a fixed length. The return value from the length() operation is zero for unbounded sequences and strings.

```
unsigned long      length () raises (BadKind);
```

Arrays and sequences contain elements of a particular type, and typedef aliases also refer to a previously declared type. The content_type() operation returns a TypeCode which can be interrogated to find out what type they contain.

```
TypeCode           content_type () raises (BadKind);
```

Standard TypeCode Instances. The CORBA module defines TypeCode constants for all basic IDL types. For example, the constant_tc_long represents the TypeCode for longs.

IDL compilers usually generate TypeCode instances to correspond to all types in an IDL definition. They are named according to the language mapping. However, if no stubs are available for a particular type the ORB interface defines operations to create TypeCodes from relevant parameters and an Interface Repository Id to nominate the IDL in which the type belongs. These are seldom used, and we will only give an example here:

```
TypeCode create_union_tc (
    in RepositoryId id,
    in Identifier name,
    in UnionMemberSeq members
);
```

The UnionMemberSeq type is defined in the Interface Repository specification.

3.10.4 DynAny

The ability to access the contents of an arbitrary Any had not been specified in CORBA until the adoption of the ORB Portability specification, and very few ORB implementations provided the ability to do so without access to compiled stub code. The implementation of Object Services and other interfaces that use the type Any to pass arbitrary values for storage or transmission often requires some access to these values in order to perform their specified semantics. DynAny provides an interface to do this in a standard way. It is part of the CORBA module.

An Any must first be inserted into a DynAny before its values can be accessed. A DynAny cannot be used as an operation parameter directly, and so a conversion back to an Any is also required. This functionality is provided as follows:

```
Interface DynAny {
    exception Invalid {};
    void from_any (in any value) raises (Invalid);
    any to_any () raises (Invalid);
```

Assignment of one DynAny to another, production of a new copy of an existing DynAny, and the destruction of DynAnys are achieved using the following operations:

```
void assign (in DynAny dyn_any) raises (Invalid);
DynAny copy();
void destroy();
```

The DynAny interface also supports operations for the insertion and extraction of all the IDL basic types. These take the form of a pair of operations per basic type:

```
exception InvalidValue {};
exception TypeMismatch {};

void insert_basic_type (in basic_type) raises (InvalidValue);
basic_type get_basic_type() raises (TypeMismatch);
```

However, it is easy enough to insert and extract basic types from Anys, so DynAny extends this functionality by adding operations to traverse structured types. These return new DynAnys that refer to individual components of a structured type, which can be recursively traversed. The model is that of a cursor pointing to a current element.

```
DynAny current_component ();
boolean next ();
boolean seek (in long index);
void rewind ();
//...
};//interface DynAny
```

The boolean return values are set to TRUE if there is a component at the index that they move the cursor to. The components of structured types depend on the type. For example, the components of structures are their members and the components of arrays and sequences are their elements. The specification then defines a number of interfaces that inherit from DynAny to provide more specific access to the components of particular structured types. We will look at a number of significant examples.

Accessing Structs. The interface DynStruct provides a way of getting the names of structure members, and getting and setting their values:

```
typedef string FieldName;
struct NameValuePair {
    FieldName id;
    any value;
};
typedef sequence<NameValuePair> NameValuePairSeq;

interface DynStruct : DynAny {
    FieldName current_member_name ();
    TCKind current_member_kind ();
    NameValuePairSeq get_members ();
    Void set_members (in NameValuePairSeq value)
        Raises (InvalidSeq);
};
```

The operations inherited from DynAny are used to move the current cursor, and the new operations access the value at the cursor.

Accessing Enums. The type DynEnum provides attributes that allow access to and change of the value of an enum as either a string tag name or a long integer value:

```
interface DynEnum : DynAny {
    attribute string value_as_string;
    attribute unsigned long value_as_ulong;
};
```

3.11 Dynamic Invocation and Dynamic Skeleton Interfaces

This section describes the interfaces to the symmetrical pair of ORB components: the Dynamic Invocation Interface (DII) on the client side and the Dynamic Skeleton Interface (DSI) on the server side. The DII enables a client to invoke operations on an interface for which it has no compiled stub code. It also allows a client to invoke an operation in deferred synchronous mode. That is, it can send the request, do some further processing, and then check for a response. This is useful regardless of whether or not the interface type is known at compile time, as it is not available via a static, or stub-based, invocation.

The DSI is used to accept a request for any operation, regardless of whether it has been defined in IDL or not. The mechanism allows servers to implement a class of generic operations of which it knows the form but not the exact syntax. It helps in writing client code that uses compiled IDL stubs based on an abstract IDL template. The client can then invoke operations on a compiled proxy stub in a type-safe manner.

3.11.1 Requests (DII)

The heart of the DII is the Request interface. A Request has an object reference and a target operation name associated with it, as well as operations to add arguments. Once the Request has the correct arguments it is invoked using the invoke() operation, and this blocks in the same way as a stub invocation until the response (or an exception) is returned.

3.11.2 Deferred Synchronous Invocation

The send() operation provides the means for a deferred synchronous invocation. This returns to the caller immediately and allows the client to perform some processing while the request is being transmitted and executed. The get_response() operation, when called in this situation, will either block until the request has returned its response or, if a flag is set, it will return a status value indicating whether or not the request has completed. Operations are also provided, but not specified in PIDL, for sending the requests to multiple objects and getting the responses from these invocations.

The PIDL in the CORBA document does not specify the types of all the parameters and return values of the operations on a Request, and so we provide the details of these operations in Chapter 7, "ORB Run-Time System." The use of the DII in Java is demonstrated in Chapter 10.

3.11.3 ServerRequests (DSI)

In a particular object adapter implementation, an object reference is usually associated with an object implementation of the equivalent type in a particular language binding. However, an implementation that can deal with requests of several object types, called a Dynamic Implementation Routine (DIR), could be associated with an object reference instead. In this case, the object adapter does not look up a particular method and make an up-call by passing it the arguments in a request. Instead it creates a ServerRequest pseudo-object and passes this to the DIR. This is the definition of the ServerRequest interface:

```
module CORBA {

    pseudo interface ServerRequest {
        Identifier op_name();
        Context  ctx();
        void     params(inout NVList params);
        Any      result();
    };
};
```

The DIR can check the interface on which the request was made and look up its details using the Interface Repository. It could also be expecting requests of a known form and not require any IDL details. It can use the interface above to check the operation name, unpack the arguments, and find a location in which to place the result. The Java language mapping for the DSI is explained in Chapter 7.

3.11.4 Named Value Lists and Contexts

The PIDL for the Request and ServerRequest interfaces uses the PIDL type NVList to represent the values in an argument list. It is a type that is defined in each individual language mapping for the best implementation. However, it is logically equivalent to the following PIDL definition:

```
struct NamedValue {
    Identifier  name;
    any         argument;
    long        len; //length/count of argument value
    Flags       arg_modes; //in, out, or inout
};

typedef sequence <NamedValue> NVList;
```

The other type that is used in Requests is the Context. This is another construct that is more concretely defined in particular language bindings. Its PIDL may not be directly translated using the language mapping. The PIDL is not given here but is explained in full in Chapter 7.

3.12   Interface Repository

The IR is a fundamental service in CORBA that provides information about the interface types of objects supported in a particular ORB installation. It can be thought of as a set of objects that encapsulate the IDL definitions of all CORBA types available in a particular domain.

The Interface Repository specification defines a set of interfaces that correspond to each construct in IDL: module, interface, operation, sequence, constant, etc. It also uses the idea of a containment hierarchy to relate objects of these types to one another. The Container interface is inherited by all IDL construct description interfaces that contain other constructs, and the Contained interface is inherited by all the interfaces that describe IDL constructs contained in others. For example, an interface can be contained in a module and can contain an attribute.

The term *abstract interface* is used to indicate that an interface is only meant to be inherited into other interfaces. No objects of an abstract interface type will ever be instantiated. The term *concrete interface* is used to indicate that objects of this interface type will be instantiated.

All of the interfaces shown here are defined in the CORBA module. There are two mechanisms for finding out the properties of virtually all IDL constructs:

- ♦ The interfaces named *idl-construct*Def provide attributes and operations that explain the construct's properties and relationship to other IDL constructs. For example, SequenceDef is an interface definition with an attribute, bound, that gives the upper bound of a bounded sequence, or zero for an unbounded sequence. It has another attribute to return the type of the elements of the sequence it is describing.
- ♦ The Contained interface has a describe() operation that returns an enumerate value to identify the kind of IDL construct, and a value of type Any which contains a structure dependent on that kind. The CORBA module defines a structure corresponding to each IDL construct named *idl-construct*Description. The structure contains the name, the repository identifier, the container where this construct is defined, its version, and some other members depending on the kind. For example, InterfaceDescription contains a list of base interfaces of the interface it describes.

This design has received a good deal of criticism. Some of the problems that have been observed with the current specification are

- ♦ It contains a large amount of redundancy.
- ♦ Often operations return RepositoryIds, which then need to be resolved at the Repository interface rather than object references to the *idl-construct*Def objects denoted by the Ids.
- ♦ Values are returned in a generic manner by base interfaces (e.g., in an Any) and then need to be interpreted based on an enumerated type. This functionality should have been pushed down to well-typed operations in the derived interfaces.

We recommend that you use Figure 2.14 as a basis for understanding the relationships between interfaces, since the IR specification can get rather confusing.

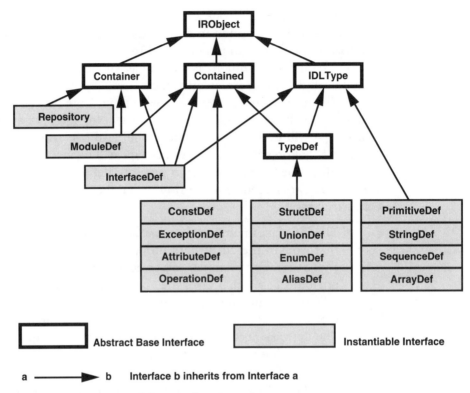

FIGURE 2.14 Structure of the Interface Repository.

3.12.1 The Abstract Base Interfaces

The interfaces to various syntactic constructs in IDL share common properties inherited from a number of abstract base interfaces which provide the common properties of these groups.

♦ The IRObject interface provides an attribute returning a value from an enumerated type that distinguishes between all IDL syntactic constructs. This attribute is available on all object references in the IR and allows the user to determine what kind of IDL construct description object they have a reference to.

♦ The Contained interface is inherited by all interfaces representing user-defined IDL constructs, and offers attributes to discover the name of the construct and to obtain a structure that describes it.

♦ The Container interface is inherited by the Repository, ModuleDef, and InterfaceDef interfaces of the IR and contains operations to look up and describe the contents of these containers. It also contains operations to create all the objects that inherit from Contained. These creation operations establish a containment relationship between the Container and the object that its operations create.

◆ The IDLType interface is inherited by all the interfaces that represent data types, including all the basic type interfaces and user-defined data type interfaces. It is also inherited by InterfaceDef because interface types can be used wherever data types are used in IDL. IDLType offers a single attribute that returns the TypeCode of the construct it describes.

◆ The TypedefDef interface is inherited by all the user-defined type interfaces that are given a type name: structs, unions, enums, and typedef aliases. It offers a single operation which describes the type.

3.12.2 Nondata-type Interfaces

There is an interface for each IDL construct that forms part of an interface:

◆ Repository. Top level naming scope. Can contain constants, typedefs, exceptions, interface definitions, and modules.

◆ ModuleDef. A logical grouping of interfaces. Can contain constants, typedefs, exceptions, interface definitions, and other modules.

◆ InterfaceDef. Can contain constants, typedefs, exceptions, operations, and attributes.

◆ AttributeDef.

◆ OperationDef. Consists of a list of parameters and raised exceptions.

◆ ExceptionDef.

3.12.3 Data Type Interfaces

The following objects are used to represent the data types that IDL offers:

◆ ConstantDef.

◆ StructDef.

◆ UnionDef.

◆ EnumDef.

◆ AliasDef. Typedefs that rename a defined type.

◆ PrimitiveDef. CORBA-defined types that cannot be changed by users.

◆ StringDef.

◆ SequenceDef.

◆ ArrayDef.

3.12.4 IDL Definitions of the IR Interfaces

The IDL for the IR separates the functionality of the operations and attributes into *read* and *write* sections. The implementations of the IR that we have seen only implement the read part of the specification. The repository is usually populated by the IDL compiler using proprietary means. The purpose of this section is to allow users to investigate the functionality of an interface at run time, so we will ignore the write interface.

The IRObject Interface. This base interface offers only a read-only attribute which indicates what kind of IDL object you have.

```
enum DefinitionKind {
   dk_none, dk_all,
   dk_Attribute, dk_Constant, dk_Exception, dk_interface,
   dk_Module, dk_Operation, dk_Typedef,
   dk_Alias, dk_Struct, dk_Union, dk_Enum,
   dk_Primitive, dk_String, dk_Sequence, dk_Array,
   dk_Repository
};

interface IRObject {
   readonly attribute DefinitionKind def_kind;
};
```

The Contained Interface.

```
typedef string VersionSpec;

interface Contained: IRObject {

   attribute RepositoryId id;
   attribute Identifier name;
   attribute VersionSpec version;
```

The read/write attributes are a global ID, a simple name, and a version (default set to 1.0).

```
readonly attribute Container defined_in;
readonly attribute ScopedName absolute_name;
readonly attribute Repository containing_repository;
```

The read-only attributes are the module, interface, or repository where the text of this construct is defined; the scoped name of this instance of the construct; and the repository object where this construct definition object is kept.

```
struct Description {
   DefinitionKind kind;
   any value;
};
Description describe ();
```

The describe() operation returns a Description structure containing a kind and a value. The value returned depends on the kind. We will see what values correspond to each kind when we reach the concrete interfaces. The type name for the value will be of the form *idl-construct*Description, for example InterfaceDescription for interfaces.

The Container Interface.

```
typedef sequence <Contained> ContainedSeq;

interface Container: IRObject {
    Contained lookup (in ScopedName search_name);
```

The lookup() operation finds an object with a scoped name relative to this container. If the scoped name begins with '::' then the name is found from the enclosing Repository.

```
ContainedSeq contents (
  in DefinitionKind limit_type
  in boolean exclude_inherited
);
```

The contents() operation returns a sequence of the objects in this container. The list may be limited to a certain type and may exclude inherited objects.

```
ContainedSeq lookup_name (
  in Identifier search_name
  in long levels_to_search
  in DefinitionKind limit_type
  in boolean exclude_inherited
);
```

The lookup_name() operation performs a recursive search down the containment hierarchy for a simple name. Restrictions can be placed on the number of levels to search, the types searched for, and whether or not to look at inherited objects.

The IDLType Interface.

```
interface IDLType:IRObject {
  readonly attribute TypeCode type;
};
```

This interface is inherited by built-in types like sequences and arrays, and offers only the TypeCode of the object.

The TypedefDef Interface.

```
interface TypedefDef: Contained, IDLType {};

struct TypeDescription {
  Identifier name;
```

```
        RepositoryId id;
        RepositoryId defined_in;
        VersionSpec version;
        TypeCode type;
    };
```

This interface combines the functions of the Contained and IDLType interfaces. As it is the base class for all user-defined data type description objects and a derived interface of Contained it has a description structure that is returned by the describe() operation which it inherits. The TypeDescription structure has a similar form to the other *idl-construct*Description structures. It serves for all interfaces derived from TypedefDef, as its type member can describe any CORBA type.

The Repository Interface. This interface is the outer shell of the containment hierarchy and it is where all the definitions for the base or primitive types are contained. It is also the starting point for browsing and allows users to find definitions using their repository Ids.

```
    enum PrimitiveKind {
        pk_null, pk_void, pk_short, pk_long, pk_ushort, pk_ulong,
        pk_float, pk_double, pk_boolean, pk_char, pk_octet,
        pk_any, pk_TypeCode, pk_Principal, pk_string, pk_objref
    };

    interface Repository: Container {
        Contained lookup_id (in RepositoryId search_id);
        PrimitiveDef get_primitive (in PrimitiveKind kind);
    };
```

The lookup_id() operation finds an object with a certain identifier in this repository. The get_primitive() operation returns a primitive definition object contained in this repository.

3.12.5 *The Multiply Derived Interfaces*

Figure 2.14 shows that ModuleDef and InterfaceDef are the only concrete interfaces in this specification that inherit directly from more than one abstract interface.

The ModuleDef Interface.

```
    interface ModuleDef: Container, Contained {};

    struct ModuleDescription {
        Identifier name;
        RepositoryId Id;
        RepositoryId defined_In;
        VersionSpec version;
    };
```

ModuleDef offers the operations from Container and Contained and a structure that allows them to be described in terms of name, Id, and version. This will be the value in the Any returned from Contained::describe() for modules.

The InterfaceDef Interface. The InterfaceDef interface inherits operations from all three of the second-level base interfaces.

```
interface InterfaceDef: Container, Contained, IDLType {
    attribute InterfaceDefSeq base_interfaces;
    boolean Is_a (in RepositoryId interface_id);
```

The base_interfaces attribute allows us to find all the interfaces that this interface directly inherits. Is_a() returns TRUE if this interface has the identifier passed as an argument and FALSE otherwise.

```
struct FullInterfaceDescription {
    Identifier name;
    RepositoryId Id;
    RepositoryId defined_in;
    VersionSpec version;
    OpDescriptionSeq operations;
    AttrDescriptionSeq attributes;
    RepositoryIdSeq base_interfaces;
    TypeCode type;
};

}; //InterfaceDef

FullInterfaceDescription describe_interface();

struct InterfaceDescription {
    Identifier name;
    RepositoryId Id;
    RepositoryId defined_in;
    VersionSpec version;
    RepositoryIdSeq base_interfaces;
};
```

The describe_interface() operation returns a FullInterfaceDescription structure which contains all the information about an interface's contents in a number of sequences that contain other *idl-construct*Description structures. A FullInterfaceDescription contains all the information needed to construct a Request to invoke an operation on an object of this interface type using the DII. See the DII section in Chapter 10 for an example of its use.

InterfaceDescription is the structure contained in the Any returned by the describe() operation inherited from Contained.

3.12.6   Interfaces Derived from TypedefDef

The TypedefDef abstract interface is derived from Contained and IDLType. TypedefDef adds a TypeCode attribute. All the interfaces derived from it are structured types that must be user defined.

StructDef.

```
struct StructMember {
   Identifier name;
   TypeCode type;
   IDLType type_def;
};

typedef sequence < StructMember > StructMemberSeq;

interface StructDef: TypedefDef {
   attribute StructMemberSeq members;
};
```

A StructDef describes its members by name and type, giving both a TypeCode and a reference to the object that describes that type.

UnionDef.

```
struct UnionMember {
    Identifier name;
   any label;
   TypeCode type;
   IDLType type_def;
};

typedef sequence < UnionMember > UnionMemberSeq;

interface UnionDef: TypedefDef {
   readonly attribute TypeCode discriminator_type;
   attribute IDLType discriminator_type_def;
   attribute UnionMemberSeq members;
};
```

A UnionDef describes its discriminator type with a TypeCode and by reference to the object describing that type with discriminator_type and discriminator_type_def, respectively. Its members are accessed in a similar manner to those of a structure, but contain a label value in addition to the name and type.

EnumDef.

```
typedef sequence < identifier > EnumMemberSeq;

interface EnumDef: TypedefDef {
   attribute EnumMemberSeq members;
};
```

The only information an enumerated type definition requires over that inherited from TypedefDef is the list of names used for its values.

AliasDef.

```
interface AliasDef: TypedefDef {
    attribute IDLType original_type_def;
};
```

Aliases are typedefs that simply provide a new name for an existing type. The AliasDef interface has an attribute that refers to the object that describes the original type.

3.12.7 Interfaces Derived from IDLType

These objects represent the primitives and system-defined types.

PrimitiveDef.

```
interface PrimitiveDef: IDLType {
    readonly attribute PrimitiveKind kind;
};
```

The kind attribute returns an enumerated value identifying the basic type that this object represents.

StringDef.

```
interface StringDef: IDLType {
    attribute unsigned long bound;
};
```

A bound value of 0 means that the string is unbounded.

SequenceDef.

```
interface SequenceDef: IDLType {
    attribute unsigned long bound;
    readonly attribute TypeCode element_type;
    attribute IDLType element_type_def;
};
```

A bound of 0 means that the sequence is unbounded. The other two attributes identify the type contained in the sequence by TypeCode and object reference.

ArrayDef.

```
interface ArrayDef: IDLType {
    attribute unsigned long length;
    readonly attribute TypeCode element_type;
    attribute IDLType element_type_def;
};
```

Multidimensional arrays are created by having another array as the element, described by element_type and identified by element_type_def.

3.12.8   Interfaces Derived Directly from Contained

ConstantDef.

```
interface ConstantDef: Contained {
   readonly attribute TypeCode type;
   attribute IDLType type_def;
   attribute any value;
};

struct ConstantDescription {
   Identifier name;
   RepositoryId id;
   RepositoryId defined_in;
   VersionSpec version;
   TypeCode type;
   any value;
};
```

A constant has a type described by type and referenced as another IR object in type_def. It also has a value. The ConstantDescription structure is returned as the value of the Any returned by the describe() operation inherited from Contained.

ExceptionDef.

```
interface ExceptionDef: Contained {
   readonly attribute TypeCode type;
   attribute StructMemberSeq members;
};

struct ExceptionDescription {
   Identifier name;
   RepositoryId id;
   RepositoryId defined_in;
   VersionSpec version;
   TypeCode type;
};
```

An exception, like a structure, has a list of members that return more specific information about the exception. The inherited describe() operation returns an ExceptionDescription structure in an Any.

AttributeDef.

```
enum AttributeMode {ATTR_NORMAL, ATTR_READONLY};
```

```
interface AttributeDef: Contained {
  readonly attribute TypeCode type;
  attribute IDLType type_def;
  attribute AttributeMode mode;
};

struct AttributeDescription {
  Identifier name;
  RepositoryId id;
  RepositoryId defined_in;
  VersionSpec version;
  TypeCode type;
  AttributeMode mode;
};
```

AttributeDef supplies information about an attribute's type, as well as a reference to the object in which that type is defined. The mode attribute indicates whether this is a read-only attribute or not. The inherited describe() operation returns an AttributeDescription structure in an Any.

OperationDef. Operations are perhaps the most complex entities that the IR describes. They contain parameters and return types and may also raise exceptions and carry context. Parameters are represented by structures, whereas definitions of exceptions are objects.

Here are the types required for the OperationDef interface and the OperationDescription structure:

```
enum OperationMode {OP_NORMAL, OP_ONEWAY};

enum ParameterMode {PARAM_IN, PARAM_OUT, PARAM_INOUT};

struct ParameterDescription {
  Identifier name;
  TypeCode type;
  IDLType type_def;
  ParameterMode mode;
};
typedef sequence < ParameterDescription > ParDescriptionSeq;

typedef Identifier ContextIdentifier;
typedef sequence < ContextIdentifier > ContextIdSeq;

typedef sequence < ExceptionDef > ExceptionDefSeq;
typedef sequence < ExceptionDescription > ExcDescriptionSeq;
```

This is the IDL for the interface which describes operations and the structure returned by the describe() operation inherited from Contained.

```
interface OperationDef: Contained {
  readonly attribute TypeCode result;
```

```
        attribute IDLType result_def;
        attribute ParDescriptionSeq params;
        attribute OperationMode mode;
        attribute ContextIdSeq contexts;
        attribute ExceptionDefSeq exceptions;
    };

    struct OperationDescription {
        Identifier name;
        RepositoryId id;
        RepositoryId defined_in;
        VersionSpec version;
        TypeCode result;
        OperationMode mode;
        ContextIdSeq contexts;
        ParDescriptionSeq parameters;
        ExcDescriptionSeq exceptions;
    };
```

The params attribute of OperationDef is a list of ParameterDescription structures. The contexts attribute gives a list of scoped names of context objects
that apply to the operation.

3.12.9   RepositoryIds

There are three forms of repository identifiers:

IDL format. The string starts with "IDL:" and then uses the scoped
name followed by a major and minor version number to globally
identify an object. Objects with the same major number are
assumed to be derived from one another. The identifier with the
larger minor number is assumed to be a subtype of the one with
the smaller minor number.

DCE UUID format. The string starts with "DCE:" and is followed by a
UUID, a colon, and then a minor version number.

LOCAL format. The string starts with "LOCAL:" and is followed by an
arbitrary string. This format is for use with a single repository
that does not communicate with ORBs outside its domain.

3

Java Overview

Java is an object-oriented programming language using similar principles to other object-oriented languages. This chapter discusses these principles as they apply to Java; correspondences to CORBA concepts are also noted. This is not a detailed Java tutorial. There are plenty of well-written books on Java. The topics we cover include interfaces, classes, and objects; inheritance; methods and exceptions; packages and name scoping; objects at run time; Java applets; and JavaBeans. We close the chapter with a Hello-World example. Although it is rather simple, it shows the principles of building Java applications and applets. In Chapter 5 we will distribute this example using CORBA.

1 Interface, Class, and Object

Java's three major object-oriented constructs are

Interface. The Java design concept. An interface only defines types, fields (data variables), and methods (actions); interfaces do not contain programming statements.

Class. The construct that implements the actions that objects perform. A class can either implement methods declared in an interface or it can declare and implement methods of its own.

Object. An instance of a class; a run-time entity. It encapsulates a state that is defined by the values of the fields of the object. The state of the object can be altered by directly modifying the value of public variables or by invoking methods on the object.

Figure 3.1 illustrates the relationship between Java interfaces, classes, and objects. Interfaces define the signature. A class implements the methods defined in the class or in an interface which it implements. Objects are runtime instances of a class executed on a virtual machine. Objects contain state.

The Java interface closely resembles CORBA IDL's interface. Java interfaces must be implemented by Java classes, while IDL interfaces can be implemented by constructs from various programming languages, including Java classes.

2 *Inheritance*

Java distinguishes between the inheritance of interfaces and the inheritance of implementations. Java allows multiple inheritance for interfaces, but only single inheritance for classes.

2.1 Classes

The inheritance relationship is declared with the keyword `extends`. For example, a class `Derived` inheriting from class `Base` is declared as

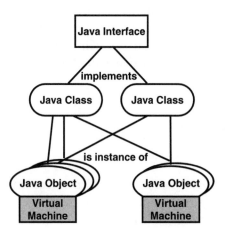

FIGURE 3.1 Relationship between interface, class, and object.

```
class Derived extends Base { ... }
```

The motivation to restrict the inheritance of classes is to avoid inconsistencies in the derived class. A typical example of such an inconsistency occurs in the case of diamond inheritance, as illustrated in Figure 3.2. If both classes Left and Right implement a method m(), then it is unclear if the method m() of the class Derived is Left.m() or Right.m(). If m() is also implemented in the Base class then the situation is even more complex. The restriction to single inheritance prevents such problems.

2.2 Interfaces

Since interfaces declare only signatures and not implementations, multiple inheritance is not so problematic. Naming conflicts when using multiple inheritance are handled by a set of clearly defined rules. Let's assume a diamond inheritance case, in which the interfaces Left and Right both declare a method m(). Then the following cases can occur:

◆ The two signatures differ in number, order, or type of arguments. Therefore the two methods are distinguishable. The methods need to be separately implemented in a class that implements the interface Derived.

◆ The two signatures have the same number and order of arguments and corresponding arguments are of the same type, but the methods have different result types. Therefore the two methods are not distinguishable when invoked. The interface Derived cannot be implemented.

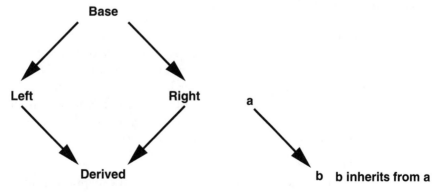

FIGURE 3.2 Diamond inheritance.

♦ The two signatures have the same number and order of arguments and corresponding arguments are of the same type. The methods have the same result type. There are two subcases:

The methods throw the same set of exceptions. The methods are identical and there is only one implementation of the two declarations.

The methods throw different sets of exceptions. There is one implementation of the method declaration that can only throw exceptions from the common subset, even if this is the empty set. A common implementation for both method declarations which throws exceptions only defined in one signature is not allowed.

2.3 Implementation of Interfaces

The relationship between interfaces and classes is declared with the keyword `implements`. A class can implement one or more interfaces. The implementation relationship has no influence on the inheritance relationship. For example, a class can extend a base class and implement two interfaces:

```
class Derived
    extends Base
    implements Interface1, Interface2 {
    // ....
}
```

OMG IDL defines multiple inheritance of IDL interfaces. IDL allows no operation overloading and so has an even simpler determination of the signature of derived interfaces. IDL interfaces correspond well to Java interfaces, and inheritance relationships can be mapped to Java naturally.

3 *Methods and Exceptions*

An object has methods that can be declared in an interface and are implemented by a class. Method declarations have parameters with a name and a type. The parameter passing semantics are *call-by-value*. This means that at run time an argument has a value when the method is invoked, which is passed to the implementation of the method. Once the method returns from the invocation the parameter still has the original value. Results of a method can be passed to the invoking object in two ways:

♦ As the method's result
♦ As values in fields (members) of an exception in the signature of the method

Exceptions are object instances of classes derived from the predefined class `java.lang.Exception`. Before an exception can be included in the signature of a method a corresponding exception class, and in particular its constructor, must be defined. For example, we can define

```
class mException extends Exception {
        // public member
        public int value;
        //constructor
        mException( int i ) {
                value = i;
        }
}
```

A method signature can contain multiple exceptions that are declared with the keyword `throws`.

```
int m( boolean flag ) throws mException {
        if( flag )
                throw new mException( 1 );
        else
                return 1;
}
```

For example, the method `m()` can return a value as a result or as a variable in an exception object.

OMG IDL defines operations which are an equivalent concept to Java methods. Operations can raise exceptions, which is equivalent to methods throwing exceptions. In CORBA there are system exceptions and user-defined exceptions. User-defined exceptions do not support inheritance as they do in Java.

4 Packages

Packages are Java's name-scoping mechanism. Name scopes achieve the following results:

- ◆ They group related classes and interfaces together.
- ◆ They allow the same names to be used inside different scopes and to be distinguished by qualifying them using the scope name.

Packages are declared by using the `package` keyword. There is a convention that the name of a package reflects the name of the directory in which the Java source code file is located. Package scopes can be nested within other scopes, and subpackages are usually kept in subdirectories. Names are constructed by using dot notation. Here is a package example:

```
// OuterPackage/myClass.java:
package OuterPackage;
public class myClass {
}
// OuterPackage/InnerPackage/myClass.java:
package OuterPackage.InnerPackage;
public class myClass {
     public OuterPackage.myClass my_object1;
     public myClass my_object2;
}
// OuterPackage/InnerPackage/myOtherClass.java:
package OuterPackage.InnerPackage;
public class myOtherClass {
     public myClass my_other_object1;
     public OuterPackage.InnerPackage.myClass my_other_object2;
}
```

In the previous example the types of my_object1 and my_object2 are different (the latter is a recursive declaration), and the types of my_other_object1 and my_other_object2 are the same. Java packages also provide access control to the interfaces and classes defined in the package by use of the public keyword.

Modules are OMG IDL's name-scoping construct. They provide grouping and qualified naming, but no usage restrictions. Qualified names in IDL are separated with a double colon—::—and names defined from the global scope can be preceded by a double colon.

5   Objects at Run Time

Objects are run-time instances of classes. An object is always associated with a Java Virtual Machine. The virtual machine allocates the memory for an object to keep its state and executes the Java byte code that represents the object's semantics.

A virtual machine can execute one or more objects. The machine can be implemented in hardware or run as an operating system process. Java does not handle invocations of methods across virtual machine boundaries. This has to be done through network APIs. Java's RMI API and Java ORBs provide high-level facilities to realize these invocations.

Within a Java virtual machine, an object can be represented simply by a piece of memory keeping its state and the byte code of the class representing its functionality. The program execution follows the method invocations and returns in a sequential, or single-threaded, manner (see Figure 3.3).

Alternatively, Java enables objects to have their own thread of execution. This is provided by the core package of the language, java.lang, in the

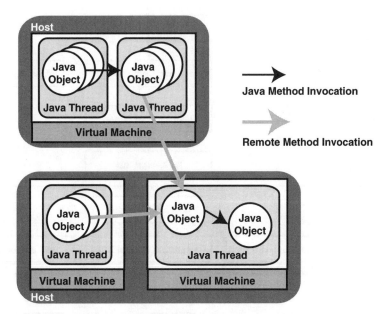

FIGURE 3.3 Java threading and remote invocation.

class `Thread`. This package also provides a predefined interface, `Runnable`, to objects whose behaviors are associated with a thread. The interface defines a single method:

```
public void run();
```

Classes can implement this method to define their particular run-time behavior, for example, the scheduling of the thread with respect to other threads, the synchronization between threads, or the interruption of other threads.

CORBA does not prescribe how to configure the run-time behavior of objects implementing IDL interfaces. Java ORBs are typically multi-threaded.

6   *Java Applets*

Applets are objects instantiated from the class `java.applet.Applet`. This class and other interfaces in the package `java.applet` allow applets to be executed in Web browsers and similar tools. Applets are anchored in documents that are usually marked up in HTML. Figure 3.4 illustrates the interfaces and classes of the package and their relationships to other interfaces and classes.

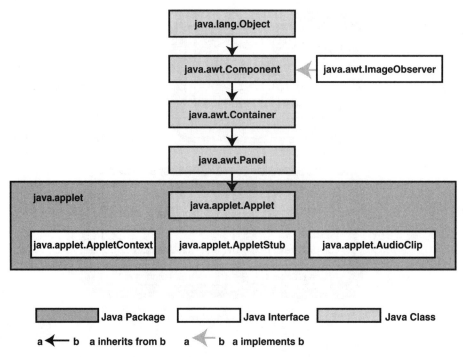

FIGURE 3.4 Package java.applet.

All applets extend the class `java.applet.Applet`. Due to the inheritance structure of the Applet class, an applet contains the basis for a GUI through the inherited class `java.awt.Panel`.

The interface `AppletContext` provides information about the applet's environment, for example, the document anchoring the applet. The interface `AppletStub` provides a communication mechanism between an applet and the browser in which it is executing. The stub, an object conforming to this interface, is attached to the applet using the applet's `setStub()` method. The interface `AudioClip` is a simple abstraction for playing an audio clip.

Applets are executed by the Java virtual machine in a Web browser or similar tool. These virtual machines enforce a number of security restrictions that the Java Virtual Machine does not. This is known as *applet sandboxing.*

First, applets are not allowed to access local resources, such as the file system, on the machine where the browser executes. They also cannot execute native code on that machine, without explicit permission from the user. The motivation for these restrictions is to prevent applets acting as viruses, for example, by executing commands to remove or alter local files. On the other hand, these restrictions disable a number of useful features, even some that would increase security. For example, it is not possible for an applet to access a smart card reader on a host machine to authenticate a user.

The second major restriction regards networking. Applets are only allowed to open socket connections to the host from which they were downloaded (the check is based on IP numbers). Enforcing this restriction has a major impact on distributed applications involving applets, in particular for CORBA-based applications. CORBA provides the concept of location transparency, that is, one can invoke an operation on an object regardless of its location. In Chapters 4 and 12 we explain approaches to achieving location transparency despite this restriction.

7   *Hello World Example*

In this section we introduce a simple Java example, a Hello World program. We show the optional definition of a Java interface and its implementation in a Java class. We then explain how to build both a Java application and an applet. In both cases an object of the implementation class is created and a method is invoked on the object. We return to the same example in Chapter 5 where we distribute the components using a Java ORB.

The Hello World example contains an object of a class GoodDay which provides a method hello(). This method returns a string containing the message "Hello World from *location*," where *location* is the name of a geographical location, for example, Brisbane.

7.1   Interface Specification

A Java interface defines the signature of an object, that is, its types, fields, and methods. Hence it allows various substitutable implementations. For our example we define the interface GoodDay, which has one method, hello().

```
package com.wiley.compbooks.vogel.chapter3.simple.HelloWorld;

interface GoodDay {
    // method
    public String hello();
}
```

7.2   Implementation

An interface is implemented by a class. For our example we have implemented the class GoodDayImpl. The keyword implements defines the relationship between the interface and its implementing class.

```
package com.wiley.compbooks.vogel.chapter3.simple.HelloWorld;

class GoodDayImpl implements GoodDay {

    private String location;

    // constructor
    GoodDayImpl( String location ) {
        this.location = location;
    }

    // method
    public String hello() {
        return "Hello World, from " + location;
    }
}
```

Java does not prescribe the use of interfaces. Classes can both define a signature and implement methods. If a programmer chooses not to define an interface, the class declaration above would change to

```
class GoodDayImpl {...}
```

The remainder of the class would be the same.

7.3 Application

The application that makes use of the class GoodDayImpl is also implemented as a class that we call Application. We only implement the main() method of this class.

```
package com.wiley.compbooks.vogel.chapter3.simple.HelloWorld;

import java.io.*;

public class Application {

    public static void main(String args[]) {

        // create object of class GoodDayImpl
        GoodDayImpl goodDay = new GoodDayImpl( "Brisbane" );

        // invoke method hello() and print result
        System.out.println( goodDay.hello() );
    }
}
```

Within the implementation of the method main() we create an object goodDay of the class GoodDayImpl. We invoke the method hello() on this object and print the result to standard output.

To run our application we have to compile the Java code

```
…/HelloWorld> java Application.java
```

We then start the Java run-time system with the application class. When we execute the application it prints the expected message

```
…> java com.wiley.compbooks.vogel.chapter3.simple.HelloWorld.Application
Hello World, from Brisbane.
```

7.4   Applet

An applet differs from an application in that it is only executable in the environment of a Web browser or similar tool. An applet needs to be anchored in an HTML document to be loaded by a browser. For our example we have written the following HTML file:

```
<html>
<header>
<! -- JavaHelloWorldApplet.html -->
<title>
Simple Hello World Example
</title>
<BODY BGCOLOR=15085A TEXT=FFD700 LINK==FFFFFF VLINK=FFFFFF ALINK=FFFFFF>
<center>
<pre>

</pre>
<h1>
Simple Hello World Example
</h1>
</center>
<pre>

</pre>
<center>
<applet
code=com/wiley/compbooks/vogel/chapter3/simple/HelloWorld/Applet.class
width=400 height=80>
</applet>
</center>

</body>
</html>
```

The HTML tag `<applet>` anchors the file containing our applet class, `Applet.class`.

An applet always extends the Java Applet class, `java.applet.Applet`. Our applet implementation uses JDK1.1's event model and hence implements the interface ActionListener. When implementing our applet we override the method init() of the Applet class. This method initializes the applet. Applets require a GUI, so we initialize such an interface within the init() method. We create two graphical elements, a button object hello_world_button of the class java.awt.Button and a text field object text_field of the class java.awt.TextField. The button object is used to cause the invocation of the hello() method. We register the button with the applet so that the button sends events to the applet. The results of the invocation are displayed in the text field. The two objects are displayed on the applet's panel using a simple layout manager, java.awt.GridLayout.

```java
package com.wiley.compbooks.vogel.chapter3.simple.HelloWorld;

import java.awt.*;
import java.awt.event.*;
import java.io.*;

public class Applet
      extends java.applet.Applet
      implements ActionListener {

   private GoodDay goodDay;
   private Button helloWorldButton;
private TextField textField;

public void init() {

   helloWorldButton = new Button("Invoke method");
   helloWorldButton.setFont(new Font("Helvetica",
      Font.BOLD, 20));
   helloWorldButton.setActionCommand("invoke");
   helloWorldButton.addActionListener( (ActionListener) this );

   textField = new TextField();
   textField.setEditable(false);
   textField.setFont(new Font("Helvetica", Font.BOLD, 14));

   setLayout( new GridLayout(2,1));
   add( helloWorldButton );
   add( textField );

   // create object
   goodDay = new GoodDayImpl("Brisbane");
}
```

To catch and process events we implement the method actionPerformed() of the interface EventListener. We check if the command which caused the event is "invoke," and if so we invoke the hello() method on the goodDay object.

We display the result of the invocation in the text field object using its method
`setText()`.

```java
public void actionPerformed( ActionEvent e ) {

        if( e.getActionCommand().equals("invoke") ) {

            // invoke the operation
            textField.setText( goodDay.hello() );
        }
    }
}
```

When the applet is loaded into a Web browser it appears as shown in
Figure 3.5. Figure 3.6 shows the applet after the button has been clicked, the
`hello()` method has been invoked, and its result displayed.

8 JavaBeans

Beans are Java's component model. The JavaBeans specification defines a
Java bean as a reusable software component that can be manipulated visu-

FIGURE 3.5   Applet in initial state.

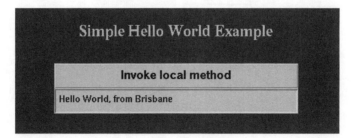

FIGURE 3.6   Applet after method invocation.

ally in a builder tool. There is no beans base class which all beans extend. Instead, a bean is a Java object that supports certain interfaces and follows certain conventions. Various beans can look quite different, but usually they support the following features which distinguish them from other Java objects. Figure 3.7 illustrates the features of JavaBeans.

Introspection. Introspection lets third-party objects, for example, builder tools, discover the interface of the Bean. There is a general low-level mechanism, called *reflection*, to discover the signature of an interface. The reflection API is available by default to all objects implemented with JDK1.1. Additionally the beans specification introduces naming conventions to aid in understanding the semantics of the methods in the signature. The most widely used conventions are for methods related to setting and getting properties and to sending and receiving events. A bean can also be explicitly described by a corresponding `BeanInfo` class.

Properties and Customization. The appearance and behavior of a bean can be modified directly by changing its properties. It can be modified indirectly by calling methods on a `Customizer` object that belongs to the bean. Properties allow a scripting language environment to control a bean.

Events. Beans Events allow communication between beans through the predefined Java event interfaces. The package `java.util` has been extend in Java 1.1 to add classes dealing with events. The details are explained in Chapter 11. There are also naming conventions for derived event classes and their methods.

Persistence. JavaBeans' persistence allows a customized bean to be stored for future use.

JavaBeans can be categorized as visible beans or invisible beans. Visible beans provide some kind of GUI, while invisible beans do not. The

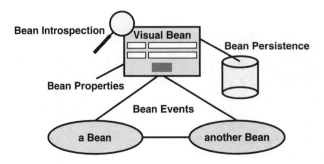

FIGURE 3.7 JavaBeans.

invisible beans implement non-GUI interfaces and provide some or all of the features described here.

In the context of CORBA, we see potential for Beans to be used in the following areas:

♦ Client side

> Visible CORBA client bean. A GUI client to a CORBA server can be made into a bean as shown in Figure 3.8. The GUI characteristics and the CORBA attributes are described as properties. The visible CORBA client bean can communicate with other local components via bean events. Such CORBA client components allow GUI programmers to put new interfaces together without having to know anything about CORBA and the CORBA-based server in the background. We have implemented an example of such a visible CORBA client bean for the authentication server which we introduce in Chapter 12.

> Invisible CORBA client bean. A simple client-side stub class (client-proxy) as generated by the IDL compiler can be extended to create a bean. Its introspection interface will allow a component to understand the proxy's interface and hence the target CORBA object's interface. The bean could also have properties which describe nonfunctional characteristics of the target object. Other beans can interact with these proxy beans via bean events as shown in Figure 3.9.

♦ Server Side

> Object implementation as a bean. A CORBA object implementation can be extended to become a bean. Besides providing introspection, the bean could have properties to describe related components or databases.

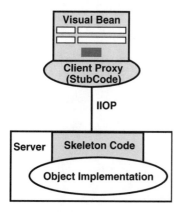

FIGURE 3.8 Visible CORBA client bean.

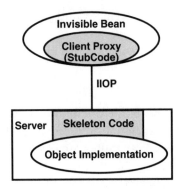

FIGURE 3.9 Invisible CORBA client bean.

Server as a bean. A server can be extended to become a bean. This bean's properties could describe characteristics of the ORB and object adapter initialization, such as naming domain or security domain. Other properties could describe the objects which are hosted by the server. Properties can also give policy information required for graceful shutdown, load balancing, or fault tolerance.

We expect to see the combination of beans and CORBA used mostly on the client side to provide benefits to application/GUI programmers. Details of the JavaBeans Event Model and its relationship to CORBA and the CORBA Event Service are given in Chapter 11. An example of a CORBA bean is shown in Chapter 12.

4

Overview
of Java ORBs

A Java ORB is an ORB that supports a Java language mapping for OMG IDL. This language mapping, or language binding, allows clients and objects to be implemented in Java. Typically Java ORBs are implemented in Java.

This chapter introduces the architecture of Java ORB applications. First we explain some necessary terminology. We then discuss the requirements for Java applications and applets to communicate with CORBA objects. Specifically we cover the following topics:

- ◆ Java applications as clients and servers
- ◆ Java applets as clients and servers
- ◆ Clients and servers implemented using other programming languages
- ◆ Standardization and productization of Java ORBs

1   *Terminology*

In this chapter and throughout the rest of the book we will use a number of terms that have specific technical meanings. Because both CORBA and Java are object-oriented and have similar object models at the interface level, some terms will apply to both. However, most of the time we will use different language to refer to concepts in each domain. Here is the way in which we differentiate:

Object. The term object refers to some program component that has a well-defined interface. We usually refer specifically to CORBA objects, whose interfaces are represented in OMG IDL, and Java objects, whose interfaces are represented by Java public variables and method declarations. CORBA objects have two parts:

- The part that allows the object's operations to be invoked from any location and using any programming language. The way this is implemented will become clear through the rest of this chapter.

- The part that implements the operations in the interface. This is referred to as an object implementation. In the ORBs that we are interested in, the object implementation will be a Java class.

Operation. An action that can be invoked on a CORBA object, as defined in IDL.

Method. An action that can be invoked on a Java object, as defined in that object's public class declaration. Java objects can implement CORBA interfaces. Methods on these objects correspond to operations in the CORBA interface.

Client. A role played by a program when it invokes a CORBA object operation.

Server. A role played by a program when it makes an object implementation available to a client. Many programs that are servers are also clients to other servers. We use the term CORBA server to refer to a program that performs specified interactions with an ORB to make known the existence of the CORBA objects that it hosts.

2 Clients and Servers as Java Applications

Figure 4.1 illustrates the simplest scenario involving Java ORBs: a client interacting with a server. Client and server are both implemented in Java. Figure 4.1 is an abstract representation of the client-server model in Java ORBs. We see five components in the figure. Two of these are Java virtual machines (JVMs) that allow the execution of the client and server programs. The other three are the client and server programs and the ORB. The client

FIGURE 4.1 Client-server model with Java ORBs: abstract view.

communicates with the ORB in order to convey a request for an operation invocation to the server, which then sends results via the ORB back to the client. The interfaces these components use are defined by the CORBA standard and by the application-specific IDL definitions that the object at the server supports.

Figure 4.2 shows a more concrete view of how the ORB performs the task of conveying an invocation from client to server. The lightly shaded objects in the diagram are all provided by the ORB (compare with Figure 2.5). The following subsections describe the functionality of each of these components.

2.1 Stub and Skeleton Code

The IDL compiler generates a number of Java classes known as stub classes for the client and skeleton classes for the server. The role of the stub class is to provide proxy objects that clients can invoke methods on. The proxy object method implementations invoke operations on the object implementation, which may be located remotely. If the object implementation is at a

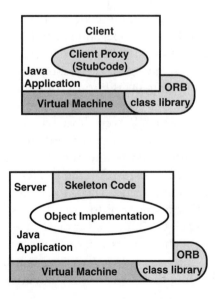

FIGURE 4.2 Client-server model with Java ORBs: concrete view.

remote location the proxy object marshals and transmits the invocation request. That is, it takes the operation name and the types and values of its arguments from language-dependent data structures and places them into a linear representation suitable for transmitting across a network. The code to marshal programmer-defined data types is an essential part of the stub code. The resulting marshaled form of the request is sent to the object implementation using the particular ORB's infrastructure. This infrastructure involves a network transport mechanism and additional mechanisms to locate the implementation object, and perhaps to activate the CORBA server program that provides the implementation.

The skeleton code provides the glue between an object implementation, a CORBA server, and the ORB, in particular the object adapter. The CORBA specification leaves many of the interfaces between the ORB core, object adapter, and server program partially or totally unspecified. For this reason different ORBs have different mechanisms for use by the object adapter to activate servers and for use by servers to inform the object adapter that their objects are ready to receive invocation requests.

The skeleton class implements the mechanisms by which invocation requests coming into a server can be unmarshaled and directed to the right method of the right implementation object. The implementation of those methods is the responsibility of the application programmer.

2.2   ORB and Object Adapter

The object adapter has a proprietary interface to the ORB that is not standardized in CORBA. This generally means that the object adapter functionality is implemented as part of the same code as the ORB, partially in libraries, partially in stub and skeleton code, and partially in a run-time daemon (for example, Visigenic's OSAgent). The marshaling routines in both stub and skeleton code exchange invocation requests and results via a network connection that is set up using ORB library code that must be linked into CORBA servers and clients. This code also communicates with the ORB run-time daemon that knows which servers host which objects and can locate and/or activate servers when requests are made to them.

The information about how objects and servers are associated with idle or running Java byte-code files is stored in the Implementation Repository and determined by activation policies. The Implementation Repository is a component of CORBA that is assumed to exist, but its interface is not specified and is different in each ORB. In the simplest case, objects are created by a server program and the objects exist as long as the server process/JVM does. In more sophisticated cases, objects can be activated on demand by, for example, loading their state from a database.

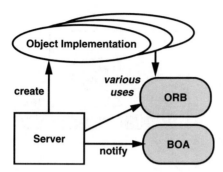

FIGURE 4.3 Java ORB server side.

Figure 4.3 illustrates the interactions between server programs, the objects they support, and the ORB run-time daemon. It shows a CORBA server that supports a number of CORBA objects. For example, a server's `main()` routine is used to create CORBA object instances and to notify the BOA of their availability to CORBA clients by using the operations `object_is_ready()` and `impl_is_ready()`, which are methods on a BOA pseudo-object. Remember that a pseudo-object is an implementation of a CORBA pseudo-IDL interface specification in an ORB-dependent manner (usually as a class library).

3 *Clients as Java Applets*

A Java applet can also be a CORBA client, as shown in Figure 4.4. For CORBA there is no difference between a Java application and an applet invoking CORBA objects. However, *applet sandboxing* introduces limitations. Applet sandboxing is a term used to describe a JVM in a Web browser with limited functionality to prevent damage to the local machine by untrusted applets. The limitations prevent access to local resources such as the file system, devices, and networking. Network calls are limited to using connections with the host from which the applet has been downloaded.

Java applet sandboxing is in conflict with CORBA location transparency. Location transparency means that clients can invoke operations in the same way on objects regardless of their physical location. An applet client is restricted to invoking operations on objects that are local or reside on its host of origin.

The problem is overcome by IIOP forwarders or gateways. The idea is that a client's stub code sends all its remote requests to an IIOP gateway which forwards them to the target object, wherever it may be. The target object sends the response back to the client via the IIOP gateway. This mechanism is illustrated in Figure 4.5.

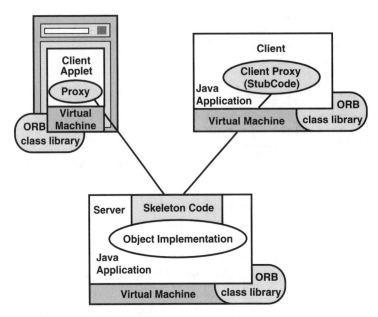

FIGURE 4.4 Client as Java applets.

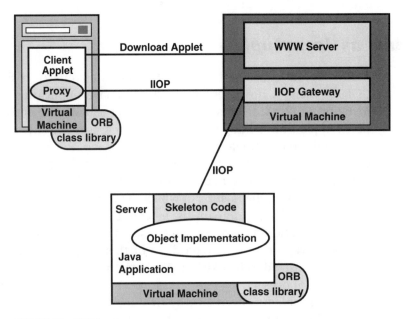

FIGURE 4.5 IIOP gateway.

Typically the IIOP gateway also acts as a safe portal through the firewall on the server side. It may also help the applet to bootstrap, that is, to obtain initial object references to services that it needs. We explain IIOP gateways in greater detail in Chapter 12.

4   Servers as Java Applets

A server can also be implemented as an applet. Again we face a restriction of CORBA functionality imposed by applet sandboxing. Since applets are not allowed to access resources on the host machine, object implementations cannot be made persistent nor can they make any data persistent. Typically objects which are hosted by applets have transient object references, which means that they are only valid for the lifetime of the applet. In all other respects applets initialize the ORB and an object adapter and create objects in the same way as normal servers do. Client to these objects have to communicate through an IIOP gateway unless they are located on the machine from which the applet was downloaded. Figure 4.6 shows a typical scenario.

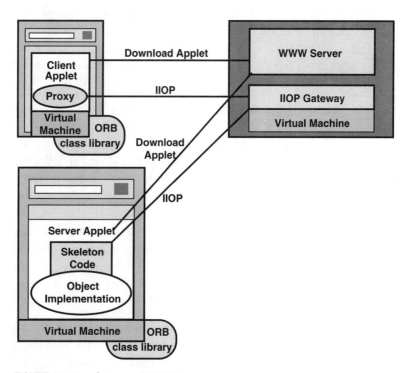

FIGURE 4.6   Applet as a CORBA server.

You will find that objects hosted by applets are mostly used for implementing various kinds of objects for servers to call back to. However, another example of applet servers is explained in Chapter 10 in which objects communicate from applet to applet. In Chapter 13 we provide various design patterns involving callback mechanisms which are also applicable to applets.

Applets acting as servers need to handle two event loops: one to deal with incoming CORBA requests and the other to deal with applet events such as those caused at the GUI. This is a non-trivial issue in C and C++ ORBs, but Java threads handle this problem elegantly.

Signed applets have the same capabilities as Java applications as long as the browser user applies the necessary settings. Hence signed applets can potentially open IIOP connections to servers on arbitrary hosts and have access to local resources.

5   Clients and Servers Implemented with Non-Java ORBs

Since CORBA provides multiple programming language mappings for OMG IDL, clients and servers can be implemented in a wide variety of languages. There are many motivations to use other languages, for example, to integrate legacy code or to exploit specific skills of a software engineering team. Other programming languages are made available by ORB vendors in these ways:

> **Within the same ORB or ORB family.** This requires an IDL compiler that generates the stub and skeleton code in the required programming language. The implementation of the ORB and BOA pseudo-objects must be accessible via an API wrapper in this programming language or they must be reimplemented in this language. The ORB run-time system, including daemons and configuration files, can be shared.

> **With different ORBs using CORBA 2.0 interoperability.** Implementations in different languages using the development and run-time environments of different ORBs can communicate using IORs and IIOP. This is often referred to as communication across ORB domain boundaries.

In Figure 4.7 any of the clients can access any of the servers. The IIOP channel between the Java ORB and the other ORB is symbolic of a bridging of ORB domains. However, when actual communication occurs between a

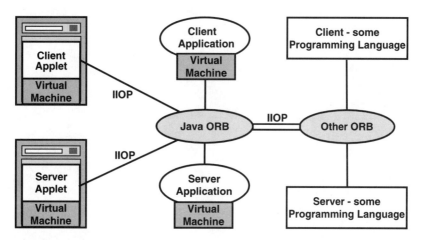

FIGURE 4.7 Interoperability.

client and a server in different ORB domains, the client's stub code simply uses the information in an IOR to communicate with the foreign ORB daemon on the correct host in order to establish a direct connection to the skeleton code of the remote server. Once this connection is established, the ORB daemon plays no further part in the interaction.

6 Standards and Products

OMG's Platform Technical Committee voted in favor of the final and unified IDL to Java mapping specification in April 1997. The specification was officially adopted a few months later by approval from the Architecture Board and the OMG Board.

The adopted specification is not complete. The chapter on server side mapping has been intentionally left open to allow for completion and subsequent inclusion of the Portable Object Adapter specification. The Portable Object Adapter is explained from an IDL point of view in Chapter 2. Details of the IDL/Java mapping are explained in Chapters 6 and 7.

Java ORBs are implemented and distributed by a large number of organizations. There are industrial-strength implementations available, including services such as Security, Transactions, Naming, and Events. Lightweight Java ORBs are included as part of JDK1.2 and the Netscape browser. Java ORBs are also available in Java development environments such as Borland's JBuilder and as research prototypes which include source code. There are too many implementations to list them in this book.

A First Java ORB Application

In this chapter we will use two Hello World examples to introduce the principles of building distributed applications with Java ORBs. Those examples expand the Hello World example introduced in Chapter 3. We will implement a client which is a Java application, a client which is a Java applet, and a server hosting an object implementation. Figure 5.1 illustrates the components of our examples.

All code is available in electronic form from www.wiley.com/comp-books/vogel. We used Visibroker for Java version 3.0 to develop and run our examples. As long as standard CORBA features are used the ORB you choose does not matter. Various ORB products which conform to the CORBA specification differentiate themselves with implementation details that have an impact on performance and scalability. Most also have extensions to the CORBA core.

This chapter starts with a summary of the development process for CORBA applications in Java (section 1). We give detailed explanations of the development of a simple example application (sections 2–8) and then extend this to include more features, including the use of the BOA (section 9). In Chapter 9 we will return to application development with a substantial

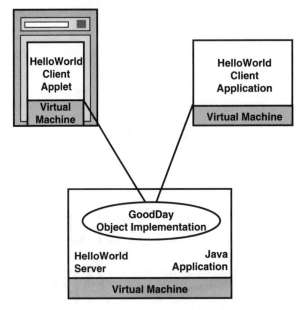

FIGURE 5.1 Hello World application.

example. Chapter 13 introduces a number of design patterns for scalability and performance.

1 Summary of the CORBA Development Process

The examples presented in this chapter will follow roughly the same steps:

- ♦ Write some IDL that describes the interfaces to the object or objects that will be used or implemented.
- ♦ Compile the IDL file. This produces the stub and skeleton code that implements location transparency. That is, it will convert an object reference into a network connection to a remote server and then marshal the arguments we provide to an operation on the object reference, convey them to the correct method in the object denoted by our object reference, execute the method, and return the results.
- ♦ Identify the IDL compiler-generated interfaces and classes that we need to use or specialize in order to invoke or implement operations.
- ♦ Write code to initialize the ORB and inform it of any CORBA objects that we have created.

◆ Compile all the generated code and our application code with a Java compiler.

◆ Run the distributed application.

Figure 5.2 shows the use of IDL and the IDL compiler when building the application.

When you execute the IDL compiler for the Java ORB you have installed, it will generate two sets of Java code files: stub code to create proxy objects which a client can use for making invocations on object references of the interface types defined in the IDL file, and skeleton code for access to objects that support those interfaces.

2 Environment Setup

Before we can start with the examples we have to set up a working environment. We implemented the examples with Visibroker for Java and Sun MicroSystem's Java Development Kit (JDK) version 1.1. For setups in dif-

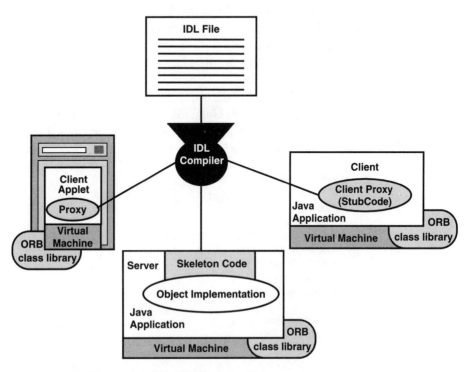

FIGURE 5.2 Building the Hello World application.

ferent environments, the reader is referred to the installation manuals for the particular products and platforms.

We use JDK 1.1, assuming that the path is set appropriately and that the Java compiler *javac* and the Java run-time system *java* are installed. We also use Visigenic Software's Visibroker for Java version 3.0, assuming that the path and classpath are set appropriately. Visibroker's IDL compiler is called *idl2java*. To enable persistent CORBA objects we run Visibroker's directory agent:

```
unix> osagent &
dos> osagent-C
```

and to overcome applet sandbox and firewall restrictions we run the gate-keeper, Visibroker's IIOP gateway and HTTP tunneling mechanisms:

```
prompt> gatekeeper &
```

3   *Interface Specification*

Our first example provides the same functionality as the one introduced in Chapter 3. However, a client invokes an operation `hello()` on the interface of a potentially remote object of type GoodDay. The result of the invocation is a message that is printed by the client.

For any CORBA application we must write an IDL specification that defines data types and interfaces, including attributes and operations. For our example, we defined an IDL interface called HelloWorld which resembles the Java interface of the Hello World example from Chapter 3. We place the IDL file HelloWorld.idl, containing this definition, in a directory which repre-sents its location in the book: com/wiley/compbooks/vogel/chapter5/simple.

```
//HelloWorld.idl

module com {
module wiley {
module compbooks {
module vogel {
module chapter 5 {
module simple {
module HelloWorld {

  interface GoodDay {
    string hello();
  };

};};};};};};};
```

The file contains the specification of a hierarchy of modules. It is good specification style to use modules to create a separate name space for an application or its major components, and to follow the same naming conventions that have been introduced for Java packages.

Within the module HelloWorld we define one interface: GoodDay. The interface is not in any inheritance relationship. It provides one operation hello(). This operation does not have any parameters and returns a result of type string.

As we will see in the implementation, the object returns a string describing its locality as part of the result of the operation hello(). The operation returns a message saying: "Hello World, from location."

4 Compiling the IDL

The next step in the application development is to compile the IDL to generate the stub and skeleton code. The compile command in Visibroker for Java that creates portable code which complies with the IDL/Java mapping specification is

```
classes> idl2java -portable
         com/wiley/compbooks/vogel/chapter5/simple/HelloWorld.idl
```

The IDL compiler maps each module to a Java package and uses Java conventions for putting packages in directories. Both directory and package are named after the IDL module. The Java package contains Java interfaces and classes implementing stub, skeleton, and other code to support your distributed application. To distinguish between generated code and handwritten code, we create another package called com.wiley.compbooks .vogel.chapter5.simple.HelloWorldImpl, which contains the client, the applet, the object implementation, and the server classes.

The following files are generated by the IDL compiler:

```
GoodDay.java
GoodDayHolder.java            GoodDayHelper.java
_portable_st_GoodDay.java     _GoodDayImplBase.java
GoodDayOperations.java        _tie_GoodDay.java
```

The IDL interface GoodDay is mapped to a Java interface of the same name in the file GoodDay.java. The class GoodDayHolder provides support to handle IDL inout and out parameters, as you will see toward the end of this chapter. The class GoodDayHelper contains miscellaneous methods, most importantly the narrow() method. In Chapter 6 we explain the complete mapping from OMG IDL to Java and also the meaning of the generated Java classes and interfaces.

The remaining files that are generated by Visibroker's IDL compiler contain classes which have general functionality, but have ORB-specific names. The Java ORB Portability Interfaces, which we explain in Chapter 6, will ensure the portability of code from one ORB to another. The class `_portable_st_GoodDay` contains the stub code which forms a client-side proxy for the object implementation. The class `_GoodDayImplBase` contains the skeleton code which can be used without an explicit object adapter.

The interface `GoodDayOperations` and the class `_tie_GoodDay` are used for the Tie mechanism on the server side. This is explained in Chapter 6 and demonstrated by an example in Chapter 10.

5   A Client as a Java Application

When implementing a client as a Java application, we don't have to worry about the restrictions which exist for applets, and so we can explain CORBA programming in its usual form. A client implementation follows these steps:

- ♦ Initialize the CORBA environment; that is, obtain a reference to the ORB.
- ♦ Obtain an object reference for the object on which to invoke operations.
- ♦ Invoke operations and process the results.

5.1   Generated Java Interface

The Java interface which corresponds to the interface defined in IDL extends a base class for CORBA Object and defines a Java method `hello()` which returns a Java string.

```
// generated Java - GoodDay.java

package com.wiley.compbooks.vogel.chapter5.simple.HelloWorld;

public interface GoodDay extends org.omg.CORBA.Object {
    public java.lang.String hello();
};
```

5.2   Initializing the ORB

We define a Java class `Client` in our implementation package and define the `main()` method for this class. Initializing an ORB means obtaining a reference to an ORB pseudo-object. The ORB is called a pseudo-object because its methods will be provided by a library in communication with the runtime system, and its pseudo-object reference cannot be passed as a parameter to CORBA interface operations. Excluding that restriction, however, a reference to an ORB looks like any other object reference.

```
package
com.wiley.compbooks.vogel.chapter5.simple.HelloWorldImpl;

import java.io.*;
import org.omg.CORBA.*;
import com.wiley.compbooks.vogel.chapter5.simple.HelloWorld.*;

public class Client {

    public static void main(String args[]) {

        try {
            // initialize the ORB
            ORB orb = ORB.init (args, null);
```

After we have declared the package to which our client class belongs, imported the appropriate classes, and declared the class and the main method, we initialize the ORB. The static method init() on the class org.omg.CORBA.ORB returns an instance of an ORB.

5.3   Obtaining an Object Reference

References to objects can be obtained by various means, as explained in Chapter 8. Here we use a rather unsophisticated method. Object references are opaque data structures. However, an object reference can be made persistent by converting it into a string (as we show when explaining the server). This is known as *stringifying* an object reference. The resulting string is called a *stringified object reference*. Stringified object references are reconvertible into "live" object references. This is done using the two corresponding operations object_to_string() and string_to_object() defined on the CORBA::ORB interface. Stringified interoperable object references can be converted into working object references by any CORBA 2.0-compliant ORB.

```
// get object reference from command-line argument
org.omg.CORBA.Object obj = orb.string_to_object( args[0] );
```

For this example client we assume that a stringified object reference is provided as the first argument to the client program. It is then provided as the argument to the method string_to_object(), which is invoked on the

ORB pseudo-object. The method returns an object reference of type CORBA::Object, the base type of all CORBA objects, which is mapped to the interface org.omg.CORBA.Object. You have to use the fully qualified name to avoid confusion with java.lang.Object. To make use of the object it needs to be narrowed to the appropriate type. Narrowing is equivalent to down-casting in some object-oriented programming languages. The narrow operation is type safe because it returns a null object reference if the object reference passed to it is not of a correct type. If it successfully returns a non-null reference then we can be sure that the reference is valid, and of the correct type. It can also raise the exception CORBA::BAD_PARAM.

The narrow method is defined in the class GoodDayHelper.

```
GoodDay goodDay = GoodDayHelper.narrow( obj );
if( goodDay == null ) {
   System.err.println(
      "stringified object reference is of wrong type");
   System.exit( -1 );
}
```

Note that you should always use a narrow() operation when you have to down-cast a CORBA object and never the Java casting mechanism.

5.4   Invoking the Operation

Once the ORB is initialized and an object reference is obtained, CORBA programming looks very much like standard object-oriented programming. One invokes methods on objects and it looks exactly the same for remote and local objects.

```
System.out.println( goodDay.hello() );
```

Our simple client invokes the method hello() on the object good_day and the result is printed to standard output.

The last thing to consider is handling exceptions which might occur. Since there are no user exceptions raised by the hello() operation, we only have to catch and process CORBA system exceptions, which can be thrown by any CORBA-related method including the initialization of the ORB, the narrow call, and the hello() method.

```
      catch(SystemException ex) {
         System.err.println(ex);
      }
   }
}
```

Note that the SystemException class is defined in the package org.omg.CORBA.

5.5 Compiling and Executing the Client

To make the client program executable by a Java virtual machine it needs to be compiled. This is done by calling the Java compiler.

```
HelloWorldImpl> javac Client.java
```

We execute the client by calling the Java run-time system with two arguments: the name of the client class and a stringified object reference. You will see how to generate this string when we consider the server implementation.

```
… > java
com.wiley.compbooks.vogel.chapter5.HelloWorldImpl.Client
IOR:000000000000002149444c3a53696d706c6548656c6c6f576f726c642f4
76f6f644461793a312e30000000000000000001000000000000004c0001000000
00000e3133302e3130322e3137362e3900fc7d0000003000504d43000000010
000001a53696d706c6548656c6c6f576f726c643a3a476f6f64446179000000
00000002febddb22
```

The client then prints the expected message.

```
Hello World, from Brisbane
```

6 A Client as an Applet

When writing a client as an applet you have to follow the same steps as for the application client. You also have to make the following additions and alterations:

- ◆ Anchor the applet in an HTML page to make it addressable and loadable.
- ◆ Provide a GUI to enable interaction through a Web browser.
- ◆ Extend the Java applet class and override some of its methods.
- ◆ Use a different ORB initialization.

6.1 Anchoring the Applet into HTML

To make an applet accessible over the Web it needs to be anchored into an HTML page. When a browser downloads such a document, the Java byte code representing the anchored applet will also be received and executed by the browser. Here is an example HTML file:

```
<html><header><title>
Hello World Example
</title>
```

```
<center><h1>
Hello World Example
</h1></center>

<center>
<applet
code=com/wiley/compbooks/vogel/chapter5/simple/HelloWorldImpl/Applet.class
   width=400 height=80>
</applet>
</center>

</body></html>
```

For our simple applet we have an HTML file `HelloWorldApplet.html` which contains only a header and a reference to our applet class `com.wiley.compbooks.vogel.chapter5.HelloWorldImpl.Applet`.

There may be a need for parameter tags in the applet tag. These are very ORB and browser dependent and you should look up details in the relevant reference manuals.

6.2   Initializing the Applet

We define our applet as a class `Applet` which extends the Java applet class `java.applet.Applet`. Within the class we declare a number of private variables:

- `goodDay`—to hold the object reference of the remote object
- `helloWorldButton`—a button to enable users to invoke the method
- `textField`—a text field to display the result of the method

Then we override the method `init()` inherited from the applet base class. First, we initialize the GUI components, that is, we create a Button and a TextField object and set some properties of these objects. Then we define the layout of the user interface using the Java layout manager `GridLayout` and add the two GUI components to the layout. We also register the applet as an event listener at our hello world button according to the JDK 1.1 event model and set the action command to "invoke."

```
package
   com.wiley.compbooks.vogel.chapter5.simple.HelloWorldImpl;

import java.awt.*;
import java.awt.event.*;
import java.io.*;
import org.omg.CORBA.*;
import com.wiley.compbooks.vogel.chapter5.simple.HelloWorld.*;
```

```
public class Applet
        extends java.applet.Applet
        implements ActionListener {

    private ORB orb;
    private GoodDay goodDay;
    private Button helloWorldButton;
    private TextField textField;

    public void init() {

        helloWorldButton = new Button("Invoke remote method");
        helloWorldButton.setFont(new Font("Helvetica",
            Font.BOLD, 20));
        helloWorldButton.setActionCommand("invoke");
        helloWorldButton.addActionListener( (ActionListener) this );

        textField = new TextField();
        textField.setEditable(false);
        textField.setFont(new Font("Helvetica", Font.BOLD, 14));

        setLayout( new GridLayout(2,1));
        add( helloWorldButton );
        add( textField );
```

6.3   Locating Objects

In the next step we locate an object implementation. In the application client we did this using a stringified object reference. Since the stringified IOR are rather inconvenient for applets, we use Visibroker's proprietary object location mechanisms provided by the OSAgent. Details on how to locate an object are provided in Chapter 8.

To initialize the Visibroker ORB we again call the method init(), this time with one argument, the applet object itself (using the Java keyword this to do so). This initialization changes the behavior of the stub. As part of its bootstrap code the stub will establish a connection to an instance of Visibroker's Gatekeeper, which it expects to be running on the machine where the applet has been downloaded from. The Gatekeeper is a CORBA object as well as an HTTP server. Besides the initial bootstrapping for a CORBA-enabled applet the GateKeeper performs the following tasks:

♦ It reenables CORBA location transparency and callbacks to objects hosted by applets which are otherwise impossible due to applet sand-boxing.

♦ It provides an HTTP tunneling mechanism to overcome client-side firewalls.

Details of these problems and their solutions are discussed in Chapter 12.

To obtain a reference to the remote object we use Visibroker's OSAgent. The agent provides a proprietary directory service. The interface to this service is a method called `bind()`, which is generated for each IDL interface type and is located in its Helper class, for example, GoodDayHelper. The `bind()` method returns a reference to an object of the specified interface type, if one is available. If there are multiple objects of that interface type available, object references are returned in a round-robin fashion. Applet initialization is finished with the catching and processing of exceptions.

```
try {
    // initialize the ORB (using this applet)
    orb = ORB.init( this );

    // bind to object
    goodDay = GoodDayHelper.bind( orb );
}
catch(SystemException ex) {
    System.err.println("ORB is not initialized");
    System.err.println(ex);
}
}
```

Other Java ORBs provide `bind()` operations of different flavors or use the CORBA Naming Service (but then there is still the bootstrap problem). In Chapter 8 we explore the details of object discovery.

6.4 Handling Applet Events

To handle events from the graphical user interface, in our case from the Hello World button, we implement the method `actionPerformed()` of the interface `java.applet.awt.event.ActionListener`. This method handles GUI events of type `ActionEvent`. In this case we have only to deal with one event, which is fired when the hello world button is pressed. This event is associated with the command "invoke."

```
public void actionPerformed( ActionEvent e ) {

    if( e.getActionCommand().equals("invoke") ) {

    // invoke the operation
    try {
        textField.setText( goodDay.hello() );
    }

    // catch CORBA system exceptions
    catch(SystemException ex) {
```

```
                    System.err.println(ex);
                }
            }
        }
    }
```

We check if the action command of the event was "invoke." If not, we do nothing. Otherwise we invoke the method `hello()` on the object `goodDay`. We display the result of the invocation in the text field. Again we watch for possible CORBA system exceptions and print them if they occur.

6.5 Compiling and Executing the Applet

To make the applet executable it needs to be compiled. This is done by calling the Java compiler.

```
HelloWorldImpl> javac Applet.java
```

To execute the applet we have to point a Java-enabled Web browser to the URL of the HTML document which anchors our applet. Figure 5.3 shows the initial state of the applet's execution in the browser.

Once the button has been clicked, the result of the operation invocation is displayed in the text field as shown in Figure 5.4.

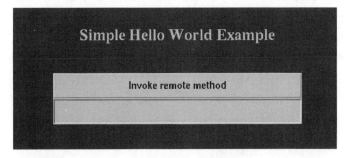

FIGURE 5.3   Hello World applet—initial state.

FIGURE 5.4   Hello World applet—invoked method.

7 *An Object Implementation*

Now we turn to the implementation of the object whose interface has been specified in IDL. This implementation is also known as the *servant class*. The IDL/Java mapping specification defines a *servant base class* which is named after the IDL interface: *_InterfaceNameImplBase*. This base class is a skeleton. There are alternatives to this implementation style. We explain one of them later in the chapter. The two main ways of associating object implementation classes with a skeleton class are by *inheritance* or *delegation*.

The inheritance approach involves a Java implementation class extending the servant base class. The servant base class is an abstract implementation of the Java interface which corresponds to the IDL interface. The object implementation is an extension of the base class and implements the methods.

The delegation approach is also known as the Tie method. This is done by providing the skeleton with a reference to an implementation object. This is explained in detail in Chapter 10.

In our example we have an implementation class GoodDayImpl which extends the servant base class _GoodDayImplBase. As in the implementation of the GoodDayImpl class shown in Chapter 3, we declare a private variable, location, which will hold a string identifying the location of the service. Here we mean the geographical location, as shown in the previous client examples.

We also have to implement the constructor of the class. The constructor has one parameter which it assigns to the private variable location.

```
package
com.wiley.compbooks.vogel.chapter5.simple.HelloWorldImpl;

import org.omg.CORBA.*;
import com.wiley.compbooks.vogel.chapter5.simple.HelloWorld.*;

public class GoodDayImpl extends _GoodDayImplBase {

    private String location;

    // constructor
    GoodDayImpl( String location ) {

        // initialize location
        this.location = location;
    }

    // method
    public String hello() {

        return "Hello World, from " + location;
    }
}
```

We implement the method `hello()`, which returns a string composed of the message "Hello World, from" and the value of the variable `location`.

Again we have to compile the Java source into byte code:

```
HelloWorldImpl> javac GoodDayImpl.java
```

8   A Server

Now we have to implement a server class. This class initializes the environment, creates the implementation object, makes it available to clients, and listens for events.

The server class for our example is called `Server`. We only implement the `main()` method in this class. We check for the right number of arguments, one of which indicates the location of the server. A server is responsible for initializing the ORB, creating the object, and making the object accessible.

We initialize the ORB in the same way we did on the client side calling `ORB.init()`, which returns a reference to the ORB pseudo-object. We then create an instance of the servant class `goodDayImpl` by calling Java's `new` operator and supply one argument to the constructor which we copy from the command-line argument.

```
package com.wiley.compbooks.vogel.chapter5.simple.HelloWorldImpl;

import java.io.*;
import org.omg.CORBA.*;
import com.wiley.compbooks.vogel.chapter5.simple.HelloWorld.*;

public class Server {

   public static void main(String[] args) {

      if( args.length != 1 ) {
         System.out.println(
            "Usage: java
com.wiley.compbooks.vogel.chapter5.simple.HelloWorldImp
            <location> ");
         System.exit( 1 );
      }

      try {
         //init ORB
         ORB orb = ORB.init (args, null);

         // create a GoodDay object
         GoodDayImpl goodDayImpl = new GoodDayImpl( args[0] );
```

At this stage we only have a Java object. To make it into a CORBA object we must enable the object to receive CORBA operation invocations. There are various ways to achieve this. Typically this is done via an object adapter. The IDL/Java mapping specification, however, allows another, simpler way to do so. The ORB class provides a method, connect(), which converts the Java object into a CORBA object by making it invokable by CORBA clients. Note that the servant becomes a transient CORBA object. The object reference of a transient object is only valid for the lifetime of a particular instance of the servant. We explain and compare transient and persistent object references in detail in Chapter 6. Objects can be deactivated by calling disconnect() on the ORB.

```
// export the object reference
orb.connect( goodDayImpl );

// print stringified object reference
System.out.println( orb.object_to_string( goodDayImpl ) );

// wait for requests
java.lang.Object sync = new java.lang.Object();
synchronized (sync) {
    sync.wait();
}
    }
    catch(Exception e) {
        System.err.println(e);
    }
  }
}
```

Once we connect our object implementation, goodDayImpl, we print its stringified object reference to the standard output. Finally, the server waits for incoming requests. Again we catch possible exceptions.

8.1 Compiling and Starting the Server

We have to compile the Java source into byte code:

```
HelloWorldImpl> javac Server.java
```

We now start the server:

```
> java com.wiley.compbooks.vogel.chapter5.simple.HelloWorldImpl.Server
Brisbane
```

This prints out a stringified IOR which looks like this:

IOR:000000000000002149444c3a53696d706c6548656c6c6f576f726c642f476f6f644
461793a312e3000000000000000001000000000000004c000100000000000e3133302e31
30322e3137362e3900fc7d0000003000504d43000000010000001a53696d706c6548656
c6c6f576f726c643a3a476f6f64446179000000000000002febddb22

It's probably a good idea to redirect standard output to a file. In our example we call this file `shw.ior`:

```
simple> java com.wiley.compbooks.vogel.chapter5.simple.
HelloWorldImpl.Server Brisbane > shw.ior
```

Now we can really run our clients as we have shown earlier. A client can be conveniently started using the IOR file:

```
simple> java com.wiley.compbooks.vogel.chapter5.simple.
HelloWorldImpl.Client 'cat shw.ior'
```

9 *Extending the Hello World Example*

In this section we will modify the simple Hello World example to introduce another feature. In this example the server will not only return a message but also the current time at the server's location. We will look at some new aspects of application development and revisit some of the issues discussed in the earlier version of this example application. Specifically we deal with

♦ Further aspects of the specification of interfaces
♦ Parameter mapping and the semantics of parameter passing
♦ The development of a client
♦ Applet implementations
♦ The implementation of an object
♦ Using a Basic Object Adapter

9.1 Interface Specification

We again specify an interface GoodDay with an operation hello(). The module is again called HelloWorld. But to avoid name clashes with the previous example, all code will be developed in the package `com.wiley.compbooks.vogel.chapter5.extended`.

The signature of the operation is different. Its result is still a string, but this time the operation has parameters and it returns the description of the server's location. The parameters are tagged as out, meaning that their values will be supplied by the invoked object. They are both of type short and their intended meaning is that they hold the current time at the server's location: hour holds the hour and minute the minute.

```
module com {
module wiley {
...
module extended {
module HelloWorld {

  interface GoodDay {
    string hello(
      out short hour,
      out short minute );
  };

};...};
```

9.2   Parameter Mapping

An out parameter in an IDL operation has pass-by-result semantics. This means that a value for this parameter will be supplied by the invoked object. The value will be available to the client after the invocation is completed.

The parameters in Java operations have pass-by-value semantics, meaning that a value is passed from the caller to the invoked object. There is a mismatch in the semantics of parameter passing between IDL and Java for IDL's out and inout parameters. The solution is provided by *Holder objects*. Instead of passing an argument itself, an object is used as an argument to the Java method. The Holder object contains a variable value of the type of the IDL parameter. This way the Java object's reference passed need not change, but contents may change as a result of the invocation (see Figure 5.5).

Holder classes for predefined IDL types are provided in the package org.omg.CORBA, as listed in Chapter 6. The IDL compiler generates Holder

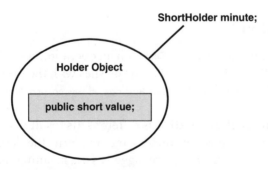

FIGURE 5.5 Holder objects.

classes *TypeNameHolder* for user-defined types. In our examples we use the predefined Holder class `org.omg.CORBA.ShortHolder`.

9.3 A Client

The main difference to the previous example is that we create two objects, `minute` and `hour`, of the class `org.omg.CORBA.ShortHolder` for the out parameters of the `hello()` operation.

```
package com.wiley.compbooks.vogel.chapter5.extended.HelloWorldImpl;

import java.io.*;
import org.omg.CORBA.*;
import com.wiley.compbooks.vogel.chapter5.extended.HelloWorld.*;

public class Client {

    public static void main(String args[]) {

        // create Holder objects for out parameters
        ShortHolder minute = new ShortHolder();
        ShortHolder hour = new ShortHolder();

        try {
            // initialize the ORB
            ORB orb = ORB.init(args, null);

            // get object reference from command-line argument
            org.omg.CORBA.Object obj = orb.string_to_object( args[0] );

            // and narrowed it to GoodDay
            GoodDay goodDay = GoodDayHelper.narrow( obj );

            if( goodDay == null ) {
                System.err.println(
                    "stringified object reference is of wrong type");
                System.exit( -1 );
            }
```

9.3.1 Invoking the Operation

After we initialize the ORB and obtain a narrowed object reference, we invoke the operation. We assign the result of the operation to a string `location`. After the successful return of the invocation, the variables named `value` in the two holder objects will carry values set by the invoked object.

```
            // invoke the operation
            String location = goodDay.hello( hour, minute );
```

```
        // print results to stdout
        System.out.println("Hello World!");
        if( minute.value < 10 )
            System.out.println("The local time in " + location +
                " is " + hour.value + ":0" + minute.value + "." );
        else
            System.out.println("The local time in " + location +
                " is " + hour.value + ":" + minute.value + "." );
    }

    // catch exceptions
    catch(SystemException ex) {
        System.err.println(ex);
    }
  }
 }
}
```

When we print out the results we obtain the time at the remote location from the variable `value` of the holder objects `hour.value` and `minute.value`. We compile the client as before and execute the client. The stringified object reference must refer to an object that provides the extended Hello World interface. The following is a typical result:

```
> java com.wiley.compbooks.vogel.chapter5.extended.HelloWorldImpl.Client
IOR:000000000000001b49444c3a48656c6c6f576f726c642f476f6f644461793
a312e30000000000001000000000000004c000100000000000e3133302e31303
2e3137362e39008384000003000504d43000000000000001448656c6c6f576f72
6c643a3a476f6f644461790000000000c476f6f644461794964d706c00

Hello World!
The local time in Brisbane is 16:42.
```

9.4   An Applet

The applet implementation does not add much new. We have the same structure as in the simple example and we make additions and modifications as in the aforementioned client. We add two private variable declarations to the class and create the corresponding objects within the method `init()`.

```
import java.awt.*;
import java.awt.event.*;
import org.omg.CORBA.*;
import com.wiley.compbooks.vogel.chapter5.extended.HelloWorld.*;

public class Applet
    extends java.applet.Applet
    implements ActionListener {

    private ShortHolder minute;
    private ShortHolder hour;
```

```
private GoodDay goodDay;
private String text;
private String locality;
private Button helloWorldButton;
private TextField textField;

public void init() {

    minute = new ShortHolder();
    hour = new ShortHolder();

    helloWorldButton = new Button("Invoke remote method");
    helloWorldButton.setFont(new Font("Helvetica",
        Font.BOLD, 20));
    helloWorldButton.setActionCommand("invoke");
    helloWorldButton.addActionListener( (ActionListener) this );

    textField = new TextField();
    textField.setEditable(false);
    textField.setFont(new Font("Helvetica", Font.BOLD, 14));

    setLayout( new GridLayout(2,1);
    add( helloWorldButton );
```

9.4.1 Invoke the Operation

In the method `actionPerformed()`, we invoke the operation and display the result in the text field.

```
public void actionPerformed( ActionEvent e ) {

        if( e.getActionCommand().equals("invoke") ) {

        // invoke the operation
        try {
           locality = new String( goodDay.hello( hour, minute ) );
        }
        // catch exceptions
        catch(SystemException ex) {
           System.err.println(ex);
        }
        if( minute.value < 10 )
           text = new String("The local time in " + locality +
               " is " + hour.value + ":0" + minute.value + "." );
        else
           text = new String("The local time in " + locality +
               " is " + hour.value + ":" + minute.value + "." );
        textField.setText( text );
    }
  }
}
```

When the applet is compiled and loaded into a browser via an HTML page, we see a user interface as shown in Figure 5.3. When the button is clicked and the operation invoked we see the following text in the display.

```
Hello World! The local time in Brisbane is 16:44.
```

9.5 Object Implementation

The variable declarations and the constructor are as in the class `GoodDayImpl` of the first example, but the signature of the method `hello()` has changed. There are now two `short` holder objects as parameters.

We create an object `date` which holds the time information of the system. The corresponding class is defined in `java.util.Date`. We retrieve the hour and the minute by invoking the methods `getHours()` and `getMinutes()` on the object. We assign the values to the corresponding `value` variables of the container objects. We return the locality as in the earlier example.

This time, however, we use the Visibroker skeleton class, which is generated by the IDL compiler in the class `_sk_GoodDay`, and the BOA. The BOA is defined in the CORBA specification, but is not complete. ORB vendors have filled in the gaps in different ways. As a consequence, BOA-based object implementations and servers are not portable. Given that the BOA was the only standard way to implement CORBA servers, until the recent introduction of the POA, it became quite popular. As the POA is not yet implemented, BOA implementations are the only way to get more sophisticated features on the server side other than the connect operations provided by the ORB. A more detailed overview of object adapters is given in Chapter 2.

```java
package com.wiley.compbooks.vogel.chapter5.extended.HelloWorldImpl;

import java.util.Date;
import org.omg.CORBA.*;
import com.wiley.compbooks.vogel.chapter5.extended.HelloWorld.*;

public class GoodDayImpl extends _sk_GoodDay {

    private String location;

    // constructor
    GoodDayImpl( String location ) {
        super( location );
        this.location = location;
    }

    // method
    public String hello(
        ShortHolder hour,
```

```
    ShortHolder minute
  ) {

  // get local time of the server
  Date date = new Date();
  hour.value = (short) date.getHours();
  minute.value = (short) date.getMinutes();

  return location;
  }
}
```

The server implementation in the class `Server` now uses the BOA. Once the ORB is initialized, we obtain a reference to an instance of the BOA by calling `BOA_init()` on the ORB object. We then create an instance of the servant as before. To make it a CORBA object, this time we call the method `obj_is_ready()` on the BOA. This call makes the servant accessible by CORBA clients. Again we print out the stringified object reference. Finally we call `impl_is_ready()` on the BOA which puts the server in an infinite loop waiting for incoming calls.

```java
package com.wiley.compbooks.vogel.chapter5.extended.HelloWorldImpl;

import org.omg.CORBA.*;
import com.wiley.compbooks.vogel.chapter5.extended.HelloWorld.*;

public class Server {

  public static void main(String[] args) {
    try {
      //init orb
      ORB orb = ORB.init (args, null);

      //init basic object adapter
      BOA boa = orb.BOA_init();

      // create a GoodDay object
      GoodDayImpl goodDayImpl = new GoodDayImpl( args[0] );

      // export the object reference
      boa.obj_is_ready( goodDayImpl );
      System.out.println( orb.object_to_string( goodDayImpl ) );

      // wait for requests
      boa.impl_is_ready();
    }
    catch(SystemException e) {
      System.err.println(e);
    }
  }
}
```

6

OMG IDL
to Java Mapping

This chapter explains the mapping from OMG IDL to Java as defined by the OMG IDL/Java Mapping standard (document orbos/97-02-01). The chapter should be seen mainly as a reference.

The mapping begins with the basic IDL data types, then the structured data types are presented. Later sections detail the mappings for operations and attributes, interfaces and their inheritance relationships, and finally modules.

1   Reserved Names

A number of names and name patterns are reserved by the mapping and should not be used by programmers. For each user-defined IDL type called *IDLType* and each primitive Java type *JavaType* the following names are reserved: *IDLType*Helper, *IDLType*Holder, *JavaType*Helper, and *JavaType*-Holder.

For each IDL interface *IDLInterface*, the name *IDLInterface*Package is also reserved. All keywords of the Java language are also reserved. If a programmer uses one of the Java keywords in IDL, it will be mapped to the name with a leading '_', for example, class in IDL will be mapped to _class in Java.

2   Basic Data Types

The mapping for basic data types is straightforward due to the similarity between the IDL basic types and Java primitive types. (See Table 6.1.)

2.1   Boolean

The IDL type boolean is mapped to the Java type boolean. The IDL constants TRUE and FALSE are mapped to the Java constants true and false.

2.2   Char and Wide Char

The IDL type char is mapped to the Java type char. The IDL char is an 8-bit type using the ISO 8859.1 character set and the Java char is a 16-bit type using the UNICODE character set. When a value of type char is outside the range defined for the IDL type char, the exception CORBA::DATA_CONVERSION is raised. The IDL type wchar, which has been recently added to OMG IDL, is a 16-bit type which corresponds exactly to the Java char.

2.3   Octet

The IDL type octet is mapped to the Java type byte.

2.4   Integer Types

There is a difference between OMG IDL and Java with respect to the various IDL integer types. OMG IDL defines short and unsigned short (16 bit), long and

TABLE 6.1   Basic Data Type Mappings

IDL Type	Java
boolean	boolean
char	char
wchar	char
octet	byte
short/unsigned short	short
long/unsigned long	int
long long/unsigned long long	long
float	float
double	double

unsigned long (32 bit), and as a recent extension, long long and unsigned long long (64 bit). Java has the types short (16 bit), int (32 bit), and long (64 bit), which are all signed.

Obviously there is a mismatch between unsigned integer types in IDL and the signed integer types in Java. For example, the int type in Java is capable of representing all the values for the signed IDL type long, but not all of the values of the IDL type unsigned long, since values from $2^{31} - 1$ to $2^{32} - 1$ cannot be represented. Nonetheless, both signed and unsigned short in IDL map to short in Java, the IDL signed and unsigned long types both map to Java int, and the IDL signed and unsigned long long types both map to Java long.

2.5   Floating-Point Types

The IDL floating-point types, float and double, are mapped to the corresponding Java floating point types float and double. Both languages have adopted the IEEE Standard for Binary Floating-Point Arithmetic (ANSI/IEEE Std. 754-1985).

3   *Holder Classes*

To accommodate the passing of inout and out parameters in Java, which can only pass arguments by value, there are holder classes for IDL predefined and user-defined types. Holder classes for user-defined types are generated by the IDL compiler. Holder classes for IDL predefined types are provided as part of the CORBA class library.

3.1   Holder Classes for Basic Data Types

Holder classes for the basic IDL data types are defined in the package org.omg.CORBA:

```
package org.omg.CORBA;

final public class IntHolder {
    public int value();
    public IntHolder() {}
    public IntHolder( int initial ) {
        value = initial;
    }
}

final public class LongHolder {
    public long value();
    public LongHolder() {}
```

```
        public LongHolder( long initial ) {
            value = initial;
        }
    }

final public class ByteHolder {
    public byte value();
    public ByteHolder() {}
    public ByteHolder( byte initial ) {
        value = initial;
    }
}

final public class FloatHolder {
    public float value();
    public FloatHolder() {}
    public FloatHolder( float initial ) {
        value = initial;
    }
}

final public class DoubleHolder {
    public double value();
    public DoubleHolder() {}
    public DoubleHolder( double initial ) {
        value = initial;
    }
}

final public class CharHolder {
    public char value();
    public CharHolder() {}
    public CharHolder( char initial ) {
        value = initial;
    }
}

final public class BooleanHolder {
    public boolean value();
    public BooleanHolder() {}
    public BooleanHolder( boolean initial ) {
        value = initial;
    }
}
```

Other predefined holder classes will be shown in the relevant sections.

3.2   Holder Classes for User-defined Types

A holder class for a user-defined type *Type* is generated by the IDL compiler according to the following pattern:

```
final public class TypeHolder {
     public Type value;
     public TypeHolder() {}
     public TypeHolder( Type initial ) {}
     public void _read(org.omg.CORBA.portable.InputStream i )
{ … }
     public void _write(org.omg.CORBA.portable.OuputStream o )
{ … }
     public org.omg.CORBA.TypeCode _type() { … }
}
```

The value field allows a value to be inserted into and extracted from the holder. There are constructors to create empty and initialized holders. The _read() and _write() methods are used by marshaling code. The _type() method provides an easy way to access the TypeCode of a user-defined type.

4   String Types

OMG IDL defines strings and wide strings which can be either bounded or unbounded. All IDL strings and wide strings are mapped to a Java object of the class java.lang.String.

Since the upper bound of a bounded string or wide string is not mapped, an application programmer has to be aware of this bound when creating the corresponding Java String object. However, the stub code generated from the IDL checks the correctness of the string bound at run time and raises the exception CORBA::MARSHAL if it is exceeded. If the range in a character of the string is violated, the exception CORBA::DATA_CONVERSION is raised.

The holder class for strings and wide strings is defined in the package org.omg.CORBA as follows:

```
final public class StringHolder {
     public java.lang.String value();
     public StringHolder() {}
     public StringHolder( java.lang.String initial ) {
          value = initial;
     }
}
```

5   Enums

An IDL enum type is mapped to a generated Java final class with the same name as the enum. This class defines a pair of static data members for each enum member, one of type `final int` and the other of the type of the generated class. The `int` version is used as an index type, for example, to access an array member, and the class constructor version is used for strongly typed parameter passing. There's also a public method `value()` and a constructor for the enum class. The mapping follows the template:

```
// Java
public final public class enum_name {
      // static data members for each enum member
            public static final int_enum_member = <value>;
            public static final enum_name = new enum_name(
_enum_member );

      public int static value() { … }

      //constructor
      private enum_name( int ) { … }
}
```

Here is an example enum in IDL:

enum Slot { am9, am10, am11, pm };

which is mapped to the following Java class:

```
final public class Slot {

  final public static int _am9 = 0;
  final public static int _am10 = 1;
  final public static int _am11 = 2;
  final public static int _pm = 3;
  final public static Slot am9 = new Slot (_am9);
  final public static Slot am10 = new Slot(_am10);
  final public static Slot am11 = new Slot(_am11);
  final public static Slot pm = new Slot(_pm);

  private int __value;

  private Slot(int value) {
    this.__value = value;
  }
  public int value() {
    return __value;
  }

  public static Slot from_int(int $value) {
      switch($value) {
          case _am9:    return am9;
          case _am10:   return am10;
          case _am11:   return am11;
```

```
        case _pm:      return pm;
        default:       throw new org.omg.CORBA.BAD_PARAM("Enum out of range:
                       + (4 - 1) + "]: " + $value);
    }
}
```

A holder class is also generated for each enum type. The class is named after the IDL enum with the suffix `Holder`. The holder class follows the pattern we just explained. The following holder class is generated for the previous example:

```
final public class SlotHolder

  implements org.omg.CORBA.portable.Streamable {

  public Slot value;

  public SlotHolder() {}

  public SlotHolder(Slot value) {
    this.value = value;
  }

  public void _read(org.omg.CORBA.portable.InputStream input) {
    value = SlotHelper.read(input);
  }

  public void _write(org.omg.CORBA.portable.OutputStream
output) {
    SlotHelper.write(output, value);
  }

  public org.omg.CORBA.TypeCode _type() {
    return SlotHelper.type();
  }
}
```

6   Struct

An IDL struct is mapped to a Java final class that provides fields for the members of the struct and some constructors. The class is named after the struct. There is a constructor which has a parameter for each member of the struct and initializes the object properly. A second constructor, the null constructor, only creates the object; the values of the structure members have to be filled in later.

Here is an example IDL struct:

```
struct TestStruct{
        short a_short;
        long a_long;
    };
```

which is mapped to the Java class:

```
final public class TestStruct {

  public short a_short;
  public int a_long;

  public TestStruct() {}

  public TestStruct( short a_short, int a_long ) {
    this.a_short = a_short;
    this.a_long = a_long;
  }
```

A holder class is also generated:

```
final public class TestStructHolder implements
org.omg.CORBA.portable.Streamable {

  public TestStruct value;

  public TestStructHolder() {}

  public TestStructHolder(TestStruct value) {
    this.value = value; }

  public void _read(org.omg.CORBA.portable.InputStream input) {
    value = TestStructHelper.read(input);
  }

  public void _write(org.omg.CORBA.portable.OutputStream
output) {
    TestStructHelper.write(output, value);
  }

  public org.omg.CORBA.TypeCode _type() {
    return TestStructHelper.type();
  }
}
```

7   *Unions*

An IDL union is mapped to a Java final class that provides a constructor, an accessor method for the discriminator, accessor methods for each of the branches, and various modifier methods. The constructor is a null constructor, which means that values for the discriminator and the corresponding branch must be set explicitly by using a modifier method.

The accessor method for the discriminator `discriminator()` returns a value of the type defined in the IDL switch expression. The accessor method for a branch is named after the branch. The accessor has no parameters and returns a value of the type corresponding to the branch.

There are modifier methods for each of the cases including the default case. If there is more than one case label per branch, the modifier sets the discriminant to the value of the first case label of that branch. There are additional modifier methods generated which take an explicit discriminator parameter.

Note that it is illegal to specify a default case when the explicitly defined cases already cover the whole range of the discriminator type. The IDL compiler should detect this error.

Here is an example union for which Java code is generated:

```
enum Slot { am9, am10, am11, pm };

union TestUnion switch( Slot ){
    case am9: boolean boolean_flag;
    case am10:
    case am11: char char_flag;
    default: short short_flag;
};
```

```
// Java
final public class TestUnion {

  private java.lang.Object _object;
  private Slot _disc;

  public TestUnion() {}

  public Slot discriminator() {
    return _disc;
  }
  public boolean boolean_flag() {
    if( _disc != (Slot) Slot.am9 && true ) {
      throw new org.omg.CORBA.BAD_OPERATION("boolean_flag");
    }
    return ((java.lang.Boolean) _object).booleanValue();
  }

  public char char_flag() {
    if( _disc != (Slot) Slot.am10 && _disc != (Slot) Slot.am11
&& true ) {
```

```
        throw new org.omg.CORBA.BAD_OPERATION("char_flag");
    }
    return ((java.lang.Character) _object).charValue();
}

public short short_flag() {
    if( _disc == (Slot) Slot.am9 || _disc == (Slot) Slot.am10
||
        _disc == (Slot) Slot.am11 || false ) {
        throw new org.omg.CORBA.BAD_OPERATION("short_flag");
    }
    return (short) ((java.lang.Integer) _object).intValue();
}

public void boolean_flag(boolean value) {
    _disc = (Slot) Slot.am9;
    _object = new java.lang.Boolean(value);
}

public void char_flag(char value) {
    _disc = (Slot) Slot.am10;
    _object = new java.lang.Character(value);
}

public void char_flag(Slot disc, char value) {
    _disc = disc;
    _object = new java.lang.Character(value);
}

public void short_flag(Slot disc, short value) {
    _disc = disc;
    _object = new java.lang.Integer(value);
}
```

The holder class for the example is

```
final public class TestUnionHolder
    implements org.omg.CORBA.portable.Streamable {

    public TestUnion value;
    public TestUnionHolder() {
    }

    public TestUnionHolder(TestUnion value) {
        this.value = value;
    }

    public void _read(org.omg.CORBA.portable.InputStream input) {
        value = TestUnionHelper.read(input);
    }
```

```
    public void _write(org.omg.CORBA.portable.OutputStream
output) {
       TestUnionHelper.write(output, value);
    }

    public org.omg.CORBA.TypeCode _type() {
       return TestUnionHelper.type();
    }
}
```

8   *Typedef*

Java has no aliasing for types, unlike IDL which uses the typedef for aliases. Consequently, IDL typedefs are ignored. This means that the base type has to be used where the typedef name is expected in the Java implementation. An exception to this rule is that new types are generated for IDL array and sequence typedefs. These mappings are shown in the corresponding sections. There are also helper and holder classes generated for each typedef.

9   *Exception Type*

The mapping for exception type definitions is explained in this section. However, the raises clause for IDL operations, which makes use of exceptions, is explained with the mapping for operations. The mapping for exceptions is similar to that for structs. A user-defined IDL exception is mapped to a generated Java class that provides instance variables for the fields of the exception and some constructors. The class is named after the exception. There are also CORBA system exceptions provided by the ORB library.

9.1   **User-defined Exceptions**

User-defined exceptions are part of an exception hierarchy, as shown in Figure 6.1. The generated classes are declared final and extend the class `org.omg.CORBA.UserException`. A generated class has a data member for each of the exception declaration's members. Additionally it has two constructors, one of which has a parameter for each field of the class and initializes the object properly. The other constructor is the null constructor, which only creates the object, leaving the values of the fields to be filled in later.

Here is an example exception declaration in IDL:

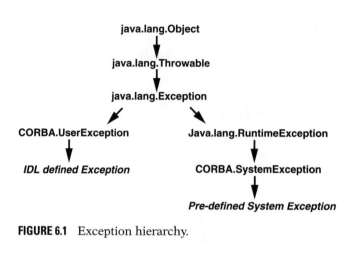

FIGURE 6.1 Exception hierarchy.

```
exception SomethingWrong {
    string reason;
    long id;
};
```

The generated Java code is

```
final public class SomethingWrong extends
org.omg.CORBA.UserException {

  public java.lang.String reason;
  public int id;

  public SomethingWrong() {}
  public SomethingWrong( java.lang.String reason, int id ) {
    this.reason = reason;
    this.id = id;
  }
}
```

The generated holder class is

```
final public class SomethingWrongHolder
  implements org.omg.CORBA.portable.Streamable {

  public SomethingWrong value;

  public SomethingWrongHolder() {}
  public SomethingWrongHolder(SomethingWrong value) {
    this.value = value;
  }
```

```
public void _read(org.omg.CORBA.portable.InputStream input) {
  value = SomethingWrongHelper.read(input);
}
public void _write(org.omg.CORBA.portable.OutputStream
output) {
  SomethingWrongHelper.write(output, value);
}
public org.omg.CORBA.TypeCode _type() {
  return SomethingWrongHelper.type();
}
}
```

9.2 CORBA System Exceptions

Table 6.2 lists all CORBA system exceptions and their mapping to Java exceptions.

TABLE 6.2 CORBA System Exceptions in Java

CORBA Exceptions	*CORBA Exceptions in Java*
CORBA::BAD_CONTEXT	org.omg.CORBA.BAD_CONTEXT
CORBA::BAD_INV_ORDER	org.omg.CORBA.BAD_INV_ORDER
CORBA::BAD_OPERATION	org.omg.CORBA.BAD_OPERATION
CORBA::BAD_PARAM	org.omg.CORBA.BAD_PARAM
CORBA::BAD_TYPECODE	org.omg.CORBA.BAD_TYPECODE
CORBA::COMM_FAILURE	org.omg.CORBA.COMM_FAILURE
CORBA::CTX_RESTRICT_SCOPE	org.omg.CORBA.CTX_RESTRICT_SCOPE
CORBA::DATA_CONVERSION	org.omg.CORBA.DATA_CONVERSION
CORBA::FREE_MEM	org.omg.CORBA.FREE_MEM
CORBA::IMP_LIMIT	org.omg.CORBA.IMP_LIMIT
CORBA::INITIALIZE	org.omg.CORBA.INITIALIZE
CORBA::INTERNAL	org.omg.CORBA.INTERNAL
CORBA::INTF_REPOS	org.omg.CORBA.INTF_REPOS
CORBA::INV_FLAG	org.omg.CORBA.INV_FLAG
CORBA::INV_IDENT	org.omg.CORBA.INV_IDENT
CORBA::INV_OBJREF	org.omg.CORBA.INV_OBJREF
CORBA::MARSHAL	org.omg.CORBA.MARSHAL
CORBA::NO_IMPLEMENT	org.omg.CORBA.NO_IMPLEMENT
CORBA::NO_MEMORY	org.omg.CORBA.NO_MEMORY
CORBA::NO_PERMISSION	org.omg.CORBA.NO_PERMISSION
CORBA::NO_RESOURCES	org.omg.CORBA.NO_RESOURCES
CORBA::NO_RESPONSE	org.omg.CORBA.NO_RESPONSE
CORBA::OBJECT_NOT_EXIST	org.omg.CORBA.OBJECT_NOT_EXIST
CORBA::PERSIST_STORE	org.omg.CORBA.PERSIST_STORE
CORBA::TRANSIENT	org.omg.CORBA.TRANSIENT
CORBA::UNKNOWN	org.omg.CORBA.UNKNOWN

10 Arrays

IDL arrays are mapped to Java arrays. That means there is no particular Java data type or class generated. An application programmer just defines a Java array of the mapped base type of the IDL array. For example, to create an instance of the following IDL array in a Java application:

```
typedef long long_array[10][5];
```

a programmer has to declare and allocate the array in the Java application code:

```
int[] [] a_long_array;
a_long_array = new int[10] [5];
```

The IDL compiler generates a holder class for the array typedef.

```
final public class long_arrayHolder
  implements org.omg.CORBA.portable.Streamable {

  public int[] [] value;

  public long_arrayHolder() {}
  public long_arrayHolder(int[] [] value) {
    this.value = value;
  }

  public void _read(org.omg.CORBA.portable.InputStream input) {
    value = long_arrayHelper.read(input);
  }
  public void _write(org.omg.CORBA.portable.OutputStream
output) {
    long_arrayHelper.write(output, value);
  }

  public org.omg.CORBA.TypeCode _type() {
    return long_arrayHelper.type();
  }
}
```

11 Sequences

Sequences are similarly mapped to arrays. That is, no data type or class is generated. The bound of bounded sequences is checked at run time and the exception BAD_PARAM is raised if it is violated.

Here are some example sequences in IDL:

```
typedef sequence< long, 10 > bounded_10_seq;
typedef sequence< long > unbounded_seq;
```

As with arrays, it is the application programmer's responsibility to declare and create a Java array of the corresponding member type. For our example we would declare

```
//Java
int[] a_bounded_sequence;
int[] an_unbounded_sequence;
a_bounded_sequence = new int[10];
an_unbounded_sequence = new int[20];
```

The corresponding helper classes are

```
final public class bounded_10_seqHolder
  implements org.omg.CORBA.portable.Streamable {

  public int[] value;

  public bounded_10_seqHolder() {}
  public bounded_10_seqHolder(int[] value) {
    this.value = value;
  }

  public void _read(org.omg.CORBA.portable.InputStream input) {
    value = bounded_10_seqHelper.read(input);
  }
  public void _write(org.omg.CORBA.portable.OutputStream
output) {
    bounded_10_seqHelper.write(output, value);
  }
  public org.omg.CORBA.TypeCode _type() {
    return bounded_10_seqHelper.type();
  }
}
final public class unbounded_seqHolder
  implements org.omg.CORBA.portable.Streamable {

  public int[] value;

  public unbounded_seqHolder() {}
  public unbounded_seqHolder(int[] value) {
    this.value = value;
  }
  public void _read(org.omg.CORBA.portable.InputStream input) {
    value = unbounded_seqHelper.read(input);
  }
  public void _write(org.omg.CORBA.portable.OutputStream
output) {
    unbounded_seqHelper.write(output, value);
  }
```

```
public org.omg.CORBA.TypeCode _type() {
  return unbounded_seqHelper.type();
}
}
```

12   *The Any Type*

The IDL Any type is a predefined, self-describing type which can hold values of an arbitrary IDL type (including another Any). It describes the type information about the contained value using a TypeCode, which is explained in Chapter 7.

The IDL Any is mapped to the predefined class `org.omg.CORBA.Any`. This class provides methods to store values in and retrieve values from an Any object. These methods deal only with predefined IDL types. The Helper classes which are generated for user-defined types contain methods to insert values into and extract values from Anys. An instance of the Any class can be obtained from the ORB, by calling its method `create_any()`, as explained in Chapter 7.

12.1   General Methods on the Class Any

The type of an Any object can be obtained and modified with the methods

```
org.omg.CORBA.TypeCode type();
void type(org.omg.CORBA.TypeCode );
```

If you change the type of an Any that is already initialized with a value, the value is discarded. If you try to extract the value of an Any where only the type has been set, but no value was supplied, the exception CORBA:: BAD_OPERATION is raised. You should not use the type modifier method unless you intend to use this Any as an out parameter. Additionally there are methods to supply the value of an Any in the form of a CORBA input stream and to extract the value as an CORBA output stream:

```
abstract public void read_value(
        org.omg.CORBA.portable.InputStream,
        org.omg.CORBA.TypeCode )
    throws org.omg.CORBA.MARSHAL;

abstract public void write_value(
org.omg.CORBA.portable.OutputStream )
```

The read method throws an exception if the value of the input stream does not match the supplied type code. You can use these two methods if you want to create Any objects dynamically (as shown in Chapter 10). They are also used for inserting and extracting arbitary values for user-defined types. However, the main motivation for a stream interface is to create a portability API for use by the IDL compiler when generating marshaling code. If the API is used, then stubs and skeletons generated by an IDL compiler can use the CORBA class libraries of any compliant ORB.

12.2 IDL Predefined Types

There is a pair of methods for inserting and extracting each predefined IDL type *type*. These methods following the pattern

```
abstract public void insert_type( type )
    throws org.omg.CORBA.BAD_OPERATION;
abstract public type extract_type()
    throws org.omg.CORBA.BAD_OPERATION;
```

Table 6.3 lists the complete set of insert and extract methods.

12.3 User-defined Types

The specification cannot prescribe any specific methods for inserting user-defined values into the Any class, but Anys have generic methods to insert input streams and extract output streams. This means that methods can be generated in helper classes by the IDL compiler which use these ORB implementation constructs.

A user-defined IDL type, *usertype*, will have the following methods in its helper class *usertypeHelper*:

```
public static void insert(Any a, usertype t) {...}
public static usertype extract(Any a) {...}
```

The `insert()` method is implemented by creating a stream that is inserted into the Any. The `extract()` method uses the output stream from an Any to get its value and create a user-defined type.

In Chapter 10 we explain how to use the Any type and illustrate this with several examples.

13   *Interfaces*

IDL interfaces are mapped to public Java interfaces of the same name. These Java interfaces are implemented on the client side by the generated

TABLE 6.3 Insert and Extract Methods

```
public class org.omg.CORBA.Any {
{
    public abstract org.omg.CORBA.TypeCode type();
    public abstract void type(org.omg.CORBA.TypeCode);

    public abstract void read_value(
        org.omg.CORBA.portable.InputStream,
        org.omg.CORBA.TypeCode);
    public abstract void write_value(
        org.omg.CORBA.portable.OutputStream);
    public abstract org.omg.CORBA.portable.OutputStream
        create_output_stream();
    public abstract org.omg.CORBA.portable.InputStream
        create_input_stream();

    public abstract boolean equal(org.omg.CORBA.Any);

    public abstract short extract_short();
    public abstract void insert_short(short);

    public abstract int extract_long();
    public abstract void insert_long(int);

    public abstract long extract_longlong();
    public abstract void insert_longlong(long);

    public abstract short extract_ushort();
    public abstract void insert_ushort(short);

    public abstract int extract_ulong();
    public abstract void insert_ulong(int);

    public abstract long extract_ulonglong();
    public abstract void insert_ulonglong(long);

    public abstract float extract_float();
    public abstract void insert_float(float);

    public abstract double extract_double();
    public abstract void insert_double(double);

    public abstract boolean extract_boolean();
    public abstract void insert_boolean(boolean);

    public abstract char extract_char();
    public abstract void insert_char(char);

     public abstract char extract_wchar();
    public abstract void insert_wchar(char);
```

TABLE 6.3 *(Continued)*

```
    public abstract byte extract_octet();
    public abstract void insert_octet(byte);

    public abstract org.omg.CORBA.Any extract_any();
    public abstract void insert_any(org.omg.CORBA.Any);

    public abstract org.omg.CORBA.TypeCode extract_TypeCode();
    public abstract void
insert_TypeCode(org.omg.CORBA.TypeCode);

    public abstract org.omg.CORBA.Object extract_Object();
    public abstract void insert_Object(org.omg.CORBA.Object);
    public abstract void insert_Object(org.omg.CORBA.Object,
        org.omg.CORBA.TypeCode);

    public abstract java.lang.String extract_string();
    public abstract void insert_string(java.lang.String);

    public abstract java.lang.String extract_wstring();
    public abstract void insert_wstring(java.lang.String);

    public abstract org.omg.CORBA.Principal
extract_Principal();
    public abstract void insert_Principal(
        org.omg.CORBA.Principal);
    // public abstract void insert_Streamable(
    //     org.omg.CORBA.portable.Streamable);
    // public org.omg.CORBA.Any();
}
```

stub code. On the server side, interfaces are implemented by the generated skeleton code and the programmer-provided servant class. There are also helper classes and holder classes for each IDL interface type.

Let's assume we have defined an IDL interface called *InterfaceName*. The following Java interface and helper and holder classes are generated by the IDL compiler. Additional interfaces and classes are generated for the client and server side, which we explain in separate sections.

```
InterfaceName
```

The Java interface *InterfaceName* extends the CORBA object base class, org.omg.CORBA.Object:

```
public interface InterfaceName extends org.omg.CORBA.Object {
... }
```

This interface contains the mappings of IDL type and exception definitions within the IDL interface, as explained in the previous sections. It also contains mappings of IDL constants, attributes, and operations defined within the IDL interface, which are explained in the following sections.

Clients obtain references to objects which implement this interface.

*InterfaceName*Helper

The class *InterfaceName*Helper contains the same methods for use with Anys as all other user-defined types (see section 12.3) as well as a static narrow() method:

```
abstract public class InterfaceNameHelper {
  public static InterfaceName narrow (org.omg.CORBA.Object
object) {
     ...
  }
  ...
}
```

This method allows objects of type org.omg.CORBA.Object to be narrowed to the more specific interface type *InterfaceName*.

ORB implementers can choose to provide additional methods in this class. For example, Visibroker for Java provides bind() methods of various flavors to automatically obtain object references of this interface type from the OSAgent.

*InterfaceName*Holder

The class *InterfaceName*Holder is the usual holder class for inout and out parameters. It also provides methods to deal with input and output streams, and the method _type() to obtain the TypeCode of the interface.

```
final public class TesterHolder
  implements org.omg.CORBA.portable.Streamable {

  public Tester value;

  public TesterHolder() { ... }
  public TesterHolder(Tester value) { ... }

  public void _read(org.omg.CORBA.portable.InputStream input) {
... }
  public void _write(org.omg.CORBA.portable.OutputStream
output) { ... }

  public org.omg.CORBA.TypeCode _type() { ... }
}
```

13.1   Portability Issues

Possibly the most important characteristic of Java is the portability of Java programs in byte-code format. As a consequence, Java applets can be executed in Web browsers on almost any platform. The IDL/Java mapping aims to provide a similar level of portability with the ORB.

The CORBA 2.0 specification, and conformant ORB implementations, provide interoperability between applications developed with products from different vendors. The portability of CORBA applications from one ORB to another, however, remains an unsolved problem. Restricting applications to use only standard CORBA features, and the decoupling of CORBA-specific parts from application-specific parts, can ease the porting process but does not automate it. This does not match the expectations of the Java community. For example, it is expected that you should be able to develop a CORBA-enabled applet with one vendor's ORB and run the applet with another vendor's ORB in the same way as you can run an applet on any vendor's JVM.

The problem is that the CORBA specification does not address issues below the interface specification level, and so does not ensure portability. There are two separate problems, one on the client side, the other at the server involving both the object implementation and the object adapter.

Client operation invocations on object references are well defined in the various IDL/programming language mappings, including the one for Java. This means that the application is portable from one ORB to another. The problem is that there is no OMG specification for the stub code, which means that the IDL must be recompiled and the new stubs linked into the client. That seems to be reasonable for porting applications in a traditional computing environment. However, for a Java and browser-based environment, it is hardly acceptable. When a Java class is loaded into a remote browser that provides a Java ORB run-time environment, it should just function. Providing many sets of stub code to match different ORB environments is not acceptable.

At the server side there are two portability problems. One is similar to what we have just discussed for the client side. To run objects in a browser, a single skeleton class must function regardless of the browser's ORB run-time environment.

These problems have been addressed in the IDL/Java mapping specification by the introduction of Portability Interfaces which we explain in detail in the next section.

The other server-side problem is caused by the fact that CORBA is underspecified—in particular the Basic Object Adapter. To make their ORBs work, the various ORB implementers have made their own interpretations of the specification and have had to make extensions to what is defined in the CORBA specification. The OMG reacted to this situation by issuing an RFP called "ORB Portability Enhancement." The core of the resulting specification (OMG document orbos/97-04-14) is the definition of a Portable Object Adapter (POA). We introduced the POA in Chapter 2. The POA mapping for Java was not included in the first version of the IDL/Java mapping, and work to add it is not complete at the time of writing.

13.2 Java ORB Portability Interfaces

Note that this section describes portable stubs and skeletons as background information for the interested reader only. You don't have to know how these things are implemented when writing a Java/CORBA application.

The Java ORB Portability Interfaces address the portability of stub and skeleton classes generated by IDL-to-Java compilers. The basic idea is that stubs and skeletons use the Dynamic Invocation Interface (DII) and the Dynamic Skeleton Interface (DSI), respectively. The DII and the DSI are fully specified in the CORBA specification and hence provide a portability layer consisting of common interfaces across CORBA-compliant ORB implementations (see Figure 6.2). In addition, a vendor-independent implementation of the interface `org.omg.CORBA.Object` has been defined.

The Java ORB Portability Interfaces consist of the following interfaces and classes defined in the Portability Package `org.omg.CORBA.portable`:

- The class `org.omg.CORBA.portable.ObjectImpl` which implements the interface `org.omg.CORBA.Object` in a standard way (using the interface `org.omg.CORBA.portable.Delegate` to hide the ORB-specific implementation).
- The interfaces and classes which deal with streaming, that is, the transformation of IDL type instances into streams and vice versa. Streams are used for marshaling operation parameters and results, and for the insertion of complex data types into and their extraction from Any objects.

Details of these classes and interfaces are explained in the following sections.

13.2.1 A Portable CORBA Object Implementation

The class `org.omg.CORBA.portable.ObjectImpl` is a proxy implementation of the interface `org.omg.CORBA.Object` since it delegates all method invocations to an

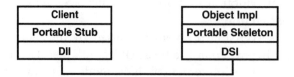

FIGURE 6.2 ORB portability architecture.

implementation of the interface `org.omg.CORBA.portable.Delegate`. **ORB** vendors can choose to implement this interface in any way they choose.

Table 6.4 shows the class `org.omg.CORBA.portable.ObjectImpl`. Most noticeable is the declaration of a delegate `_delegate` and the methods to set and get the delegate. The remainder is a straightforward implementation of the interface `org.omg.CORBA.Object` which calls the delegate.

Table 6.5 shows the declaration of the interface `rg.omg.CORBA.portable.Delegate`. It is very similar to the interface `org.omg.CORBA.Object`. The only difference is the extra parameter in each of the operations which refers to the object on which the operation was originally invoked.

13.2.2 Portable Streams

Portable streams are used for marshaling of operation parameters and results and for the insertion into and extraction of values from Any objects. There are

TABLE 6.4 Portable CORBA Object Implementation

```
package org.omg.CORBA.portable;

abstract public class ObjectImpl
    implements org.omg.CORBA.Object {

    Delegate _delegate;

    public Delegate _get_delegate() {

        if( _delegate == null ) {
            throw new org.omg.CORBA.BAD_OPERATION();
        }
         return _delegate;
    }

    public void _set_delegate( Delegate delegate ) {

        _delegate = delegate;

    }

    public org.omg.CORBA.ImplementationDef
_get_implementation() {

        return _get_delegate().get_implementation( this );
    }

    // and so on for all other operations defined in the
    // interface org.omg.CORBA.Object
```

TABLE 6.5   Portable Delegate Interface

```
package org.omg.CORBA.portable;

public interface Delegate {

    org.omg.CORBA.ImplementationDef get_implementation(
        org.omg.CORBA.Object self);

    org.omg.CORBA.InterfaceDef get_interface(

        org.omg.CORBA.Object self);

    org.omg.CORBA.Object self duplicate(
        org.omg.CORBA.Object self);

    void release (org.omg.CORBA.Object self);

    boolean is_a(
        org.omg.CORBA.Object self,
        java.lang.String repository_id );

    boolean non_existent (org.omg.CORBA.Object self);

    boolean is_equivalent(
        org.omg.CORBA.Object self,
        org.omg.CORBA.Object rhs);

    int hash(org.omg.CORBA.Object self, int max );

    org.omg.CORBA.Request request(
        org.omg.CORBA.Object self,
        java.lang.String operation);

    org.omg.CORBA.Request create_request(
        org.omg.CORBA.Object self,
        org.omg.CORBA.Context ctx,
        java.lang.String operation,
        org.omg.CORBA.NVList arg_list,
        org.omg.CORBA.NamedValue result);

    org.omg.CORBA.Request create_request(
        org.omg.CORBA.Object self,
        org.omg.CORBA.Context ctx,
        java.lang.String operation,
        org.omg.CORBA.NVList arg_list,
        org.omg.CORBA.NamedValue result,
        org.omg.CORBA.TypeCode [] excepts,
        String contexts);
}
```

two kinds of streams, input and output, which are defined in the classes
`org.omg.CORBA.portable.InputStream` and `org.omg.CORBA.portable.OutputStream`,
which are shown in Tables 6.6 and 6.7, respectively.

Input streams provide methods to read values from a linear representation and output streams provide methods to write values to this form. These methods can only be provided for predefined IDL types. Methods for user-defined types will be generated by the IDL compiler and placed in

TABLE 6.6 Input Stream

```
package org.omg.CORBA.portable;

public abstract class InputStream {

    boolean read_boolean();
    char read_char();
    char read_wchar();
    byte read_octet();
    short read_short();
    short read_ushort();
    int read_long();
    int read_ulong();
    long read_longlong();
    long read_ulonglong();
    float read_float();
    double read_double();
    java.lang.String read_string();
    java.lang.String read_wstring();

    void read_boolean_array(boolean[], int, int);
    void read_char_array(char[], int, int);
    void read_wchar_array(char[], int, int);
    void read_octet_array(byte[], int, int);
    void read_short_array(short[], int, int);
    void read_ushort_array(short[], int, int);
    void read_long_array(int[], int, int);
    void read_ulong_array(int[], int, int);
    void read_longlong_array(long[], int, int);
    void read_ulonglong_array(long[], int, int);
    void read_float_array(float[], int, int);
    void read_double_array(double[], int, int);

    org.omg.CORBA.Object read_Object();
    org.omg.CORBA.TypeCode read_TypeCode();
    org.omg.CORBA.Any read_any();
    org.omg.CORBA.Principal read_Principal();
}
```

TABLE 6.7 Output Stream

```
package org.omg.CORBA.portable;

public abstract class OutputStream {

    public abstract org.omg.CORBA.portable.InputStream
        create_input_stream();

    public abstract void write_boolean(boolean);
    public abstract void write_char(char);
    public abstract void write_wchar(char);
    public abstract void write_octet(byte);
    public abstract void write_short(short);
    public abstract void write_ushort(short);
    public abstract void write_long(int);
    public abstract void write_ulong(int);
    public abstract void write_longlong(long);
    public abstract void write_ulonglong(long);
    public abstract void write_float(float);
    public abstract void write_double(double);
    public abstract void write_string(java.lang.String);
    public abstract void write_wstring(java.lang.String);

    public abstract void write_boolean_array(
        boolean[], int, int);
    public abstract void write_char_array(char[], int, int);
    public abstract void write_wchar_array(char[], int, int);
    public abstract void write_octet_array(byte[], int, int);
    public abstract void write_short_array(short[], int, int);
    public abstract void write_ushort_array(short[], int, int);
    public abstract void write_long_array(int[], int, int);
    public abstract void write_ulong_array(int[], int, int);
    public abstract void write_longlong_array(long[], int,
int);
    public abstract void write_ulonglong_array(long[], int,
int);
    public abstract void write_float_array(float[], int, int);
    public abstract void write_double_array(double[], int,
int);
    public abstract void write_Object(org.omg.CORBA.Object);
    public abstract void
write_TypeCode(org.omg.CORBA.TypeCode);
    public abstract void write_any(org.omg.CORBA.Any);
    public abstract void write_Principal(
        org.omg.CORBA.Principal);
}
```

Helper classes. The signatures for the Helper class methods are defined in the interface `org.omg.CORBA.portable.Streamable`:

```
public interface Streamable {
    void _read(org.omg.CORBA.portable.InputStream istream);
    void _write(org.omg.CORBA.portable.InputStream ostream);
    org.omg.CORBA.TypeCode _type();
}
```

The ORB serves as a factory for output streams by providing the method `create_output_stream()`. Input streams are created from output streams by their method `create_input_stream()` (see Table 6.7).

13.3 Client-side Mapping

After all this background information on the Java ORB Portability Interfaces, we return to the mapping of an IDL interface to Java, and how it is used on the client side. A client obtains an object reference in the usual way, for example, via `string_to_object()`, from a Naming or Trading Service, or from a third-party object. Regardless of the mechanism used to obtain an object reference, a client-side proxy object is created. The client-side proxy is an instantiation of the stub class, which is an implementation of the Java interface corresponding to the IDL interface.

The stub class is an ORB-specific layer that sits between the defined Java interface and the portability layer we discussed in the previous section. The IDL/Java mapping only prescribes that the stub class must be implemented by using the DII. Figure 6.3 illustrates how the various layers, interfaces, and classes fit together.

As an example of stub class generation we use Visibroker for Java. It creates a portable stub class called `_portable_st_InterfaceName`. When we look at the mapping of operations we see how the DII can be used as a portability layer.

In a client program, you need only declare an object reference of the Java interface type, such as

```
Tester myTester;
```

and assign a value to the variable, for example,

```
CORBA.Object obj = orb.string_to_object( iorString );
myTester = TesterHelper.narrow( obj );
```

The client program can now invoke methods on this object in the usual Java manner. The difference is in the execution of the method. The proxy object forwards the call to the implementation object by calling the DII,

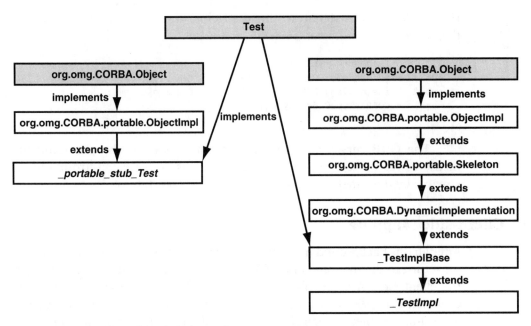

FIGURE 6.3 Portable stub and skeleton classes.

which in turn calls the portable ORB library to send the call to the remote object via the CORBA transport protocol, IIOP.

13.4 Server-side Mapping

An object implementation has to implement the Java interface that has been generated from the IDL interface. There is a class called the *servant base class* which implements the Java interface and provides the skeleton code for a portable transient object implementation. The servant base class is generated by the IDL compiler and follows this naming scheme:

```
public class _InterfaceNameImplBase implements InterfaceName {
    ...
}
```

You would then implement the interface by providing the application semantics of the operations. Your implementation class (conventionally called *InterfaceName*Impl) is attached to the skeleton by extending the implementation base class:

```
public class InterfaceNameImpl extends _InterfaceNameImplBase {
    ...
}
```

On the server side, the object adapter, which defines how the object is accessed when a client makes an operation invocation, is a gray area. You have the following choices to make your object implementation accessible via the ORB:

◆ No object adapter, using the ORB's connect operation
◆ Basic Object Adapter, using the Inheritance approach
◆ Basic Object Adapter, using the Tie approach
◆ Portable Object Adapter

CORBA object references can be transient or persistent. A transient object reference is only valid for the lifetime of a particular object implementation. A persistent object reference can survive several server lifetimes. Its implementation can also be activated and deactivated in a server. For example, you may not create an instance of the implementation when starting the server, but it will be created when a client uses its reference. The instance may move to a different JVM or host. If the original instance disappears a replica may be used instead. Obviously the ORB and the object adapter have to provide far more sophisticated functionality for persistent objects than for transient ones.

Another thing that is controlled by an object adapter is the threading model. There are many variations of threading models, but the most common ones are

◆ Single-threaded servers. All incoming invocations are sequential, and queued if necessary.
◆ Multithreaded—one thread per client. For each client, which typically means each connection to the server, a thread will be provided.
◆ Multithreaded—one thread per request. Each incoming request gets its own thread (up to a maximum number of threads in the pool). When the request is completed the thread is returned to the pool.

So far, threading policies have not been addressed by the OMG prior to specifying the POA, and ORB implementers provide control of the threading models in different ways. Even the POA only acknowledges that threads exist and are controlled by the ORB, it does not specify complex threads policies.

13.4.1 *No Object Adapter*

An object implementation can be made available to potential clients without an object adapter. This functionality is provided by the ORB, which has a method called `connect()` that allows requests to be delivered to a transient CORBA servant object. A servant can be disconnected by calling the method `disconnect()` on the ORB. The full signatures of the methods are

```
public class ORB {
    void connect( org.omg.CORBA.Object obj );
    void disconnect( org.omg.CORBA.Object obj );
    ...
}
```

When a client invokes a method on a disconnected object, the ORB raises the exception CORBA::OBJECT_NOT_EXIST. Connecting or disconnecting an object multiple times has no additional effect.

13.4.2 *Basic Object Adapter*

The BOA is defined in the CORBA specification as a pseudo-object. Although the IDL/Java mapping does not explicitly specify the BOA interface, it is part of the CORBA specification and is implemented by various Java ORB products, including OrbixWeb and Visibroker for Java. A reference to a BOA pseudo-object can be obtained from the ORB using the method:

```
public class ORB {
    ...
    org.omg.CORBA.BOA BOA_init();
    ...
}
```

Java ORBs which implement the BOA have their IDL compilers generate skeleton classes suitable for connecting to the BOA. Visibroker for Java's IDL compiler generates a skeleton class for each IDL interface *InterfaceName* which is called _sk_*InterfaceName*.

A servant can be connected to the skeleton class by inheritance:

```
public class InterfaceNameImpl extends sk_InterfaceName {
    ...
}
```

Alternatively, the servant can be connected to the skeleton by delegation or aggregation, which is also known as the Tie approach. To support the Tie approach, Visibroker for Java generates an interface called *InterfaceName*-Operations and a class _tie_*InterfaceName*. The Tie class extends the skeleton and privately declares a delegate of type *InterfaceName*Operations. The two constructors set the delegate to point at the servant class that implements the operations. The methods corresponding to the IDL operations are implemented by calling the same methods on the delegate and returning the values produced by the delegate.

```
public class _tie_InterfaceName extends sk_InterfaceName {

  private InterfaceNameOperations _delegate;
```

```
   public _tie_InterfaceName( InterfaceNameOperations
delegate,
      java.lang.String name) {
      super(name);
      this._delegate = delegate;
   }
   public _tie_InterfaceName( InterfaceNameOperations
delegate) {
      this._delegate = delegate;
   }

  // implementing operations by delegation
  ...
}
```

The interface `InterfaceNameOperations` is quite similar to the Java interface `InterfaceName`, but it does not inherit the CORBA Object interface:

```
public interface InterfaceNameOperations {
   // declaring methods for IDL attributes and operations
}
```

The programmer's servant class implements the interface `InterfaceName-Operations`:

```
public class InterfaceNameImpl
   implements InterfaceNameOperations {
   // implementing methods
}
```

The major advantage of the Tie approach is that it allows the servant to extend an application-specific base class. The Tie mechanism is used in Chapter 10.

14 *Constants*

Following the Java conventions for constants, IDL constants are generally mapped to a static final variable that has the value of the constant. The attributes of the variable ensure the semantics of an IDL constant: `static` ensures that instances of that class have the same value, and `final` ensures that the value cannot be overridden. However, IDL constants are mapped differently depending on where they are defined in the IDL specification. The two cases which are distinguished are constant declarations within and outside of an interface.

14.1   Constants within Interfaces

A constant that is defined within an interface is mapped to a final public static field of the Java interface which is generated for the IDL interface containing the constant. The field is named after the IDL constant. The type of the field corresponds to the mapped IDL type of the constant. The field is initialized as defined in the IDL definition. The following example illustrates the mapping. The IDL constant MaxSlots

```
interface Tester{
    const short MaxSlots = 8;
};
```

is mapped to the field MaxSlots in the Java class Tester:

```
public interface Tester extends org.omg.CORBA.Object {
  final public static short MaxSlots = (short) 8;
  . . .
}
```

14.2   Constants Outside Interfaces

IDL constants that are defined outside interfaces are mapped to a public interface named after the IDL constant. This interface contains a public final static variable that is always called value. This variable is initialized to the value of the constant.

Declaring the same IDL constant as above, but outside an interface

```
const short MaxSlots = 8;
```

leads to the following Java mapping:

```
public interface MaxSlots {
  final public static short value = (short) 8;
}
```

15   *Attributes*

IDL attributes are mapped to Java methods: an accessor method, and, if the attribute is not declared readonly, a modifier method. Both methods have the same name as the IDL attribute but they differ in their signatures. The accessor method does not have parameters and it returns a value of the attribute type (mapped to Java). The modifier method return type is void and has one parameter of the attribute type.

Here are two example attributes in an IDL interface:

```
interface Tester {
        attribute string name;
        readonly attribute long id;
}
```

which map to the following Java methods, defined in the Java interface `Tester`:

```
public interface Tester extends org.omg.CORBA.Object {

    public void name(java.lang.String name);

    public java.lang.String name();

    public int id();
}
```

16   *Operations*

IDL operations are mapped to methods in the Java interface that correspond to the IDL interface. The type of the operation result is mapped to
Java according to the mapping for data types previously described. The
mapping of the parameter types depends on their direction tag.

16.1   Parameter Semantics

IDL defines three different parameter passing modes, indicated by the tags
in, inout, and out. The tag in defines pass-by-value semantics: a client supplies
a value which is left unchanged during the time of the invocation. The tag
out defines pass-by-result semantics: the server supplies a value which will
be available to the client after the invocation returns. The tag inout defines
pass-by-reference semantics: the client supplies a value which is subject to
change by the server. The modified value is available to the client after the
invocation returns.

Java only defines pass-by-value semantics for method parameters. This
matches the semantics for in parameters only. To map inout and out parameters, additional mechanisms are needed.

When a Java client invokes a method and supplies a Java object reference as an argument, the invoked object can modify the state of the object
that was referenced by the parameter. After the invocation, the client still
has the same reference to the object, but the object itself has been modified.

This mechanism is used to handle inout and out parameters in Java. Java
objects called holder objects are used as containers for these parameters.

References to the holder objects are passed instead of the parameters themselves. This mechanism is illustrated in Figure 6.4.

As we have already seen in the mappings of the various data types, holder classes follow the same pattern: they have a public instance variable called `value` which holds the actual value of the parameter. These classes also provide a couple of constructors. One is a null constructor (intended for `out` parameters); the other is a constructor which has a parameter of the contained type (intended for `inout` parameters).

16.2 Mapping from Operations to Methods

IDL operations are mapped to Java methods of the same name. An operation's result type is mapped according to mapping for data types. The IDL void return type is mapped to Java `void`. IDL in parameters are also mapped according the mapping for IDL types. However, IDL inout and out parameters are mapped to the Holder classes which are generated for their IDL type.

IDL operations can explicitly raise one or more user-defined exceptions and can also implicitly raise system exceptions. Java methods which map IDL operations may always throw CORBA system exceptions which extend `java.lang.RuntimeException`. We have already seen that IDL exceptions map naturally to Java exceptions and that all mappings of user exception types are extensions of the Java class `org.omg.CORBA.UserException` which itself extends `java.lang.Exception`. The raises clause of an IDL operation is mapped to a throw clause on the equivalent Java method. As an example, we use an operation that has parameters with all the different tags and raises a user-defined exception.

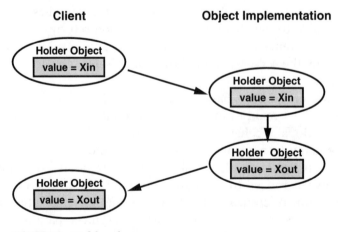

FIGURE 6.4 Holder classes.

```
exception SomethingWrong {
    string reason;
    long id;
};

interface Tester {

    boolean test( in string name, inout boolean flag, out long
id )
        raises( SomethingWrong );
};
```

The operation is mapped to a method whose out and inout parameters are Holder objects.

```
public interface Tester extends org.omg.CORBA.Object {

  public boolean test(
    java.lang.String name,
    org.omg.CORBA.BooleanHolder flag,
    org.omg.CORBA.IntHolder id
  ) throws SomethingWrong;
}
```

16.3   Portable Stub Implementation

In this section we want to examine how Visibroker for Java implements the stub class with the Java ORB Portability Interfaces. As we explained earlier, the stub code uses the DII to invoke operations. This section once again provides extra information for the interested reader, but it is not needed to write Java ORB applications. We will use the IDL from the previous section as an example.

The class _portable_st_Tester extends the portability layer represented by the class org.omg.CORBA.portable.ObjectImpl and implements the Java interface Tester. The body of the class implements the method test(). For our example, the following portable stub class is generated:

```
public class _portable_stub_Tester
    extends org.omg.CORBA.portable.ObjectImpl
    implements Tester {
  . . .
  public boolean test(
    java.lang.String name,
    org.omg.CORBA.BooleanHolder flag,
    org.omg.CORBA.IntHolder id
  ) throws SomethingWrong {

    // create a DII request
```

```
      org.omg.CORBA.Request _request = this._request("test");

      // set the return type

_request.set_return_type(_orb().get_primitive_tc(org.omg.CORBA.
TCKind.tk_boolean));

      // fill request and arguments
      org.omg.CORBA.Any $name = _request.add_in_arg();
      $name.insert_string(name);

      org.omg.CORBA.Any $flag = _request.add_inout_arg();
      $flag.insert_boolean(flag.value);

      org.omg.CORBA.Any $id = _request.add_out_arg();

$id.type(_orb().get_primitive_tc(org.omg.CORBA.TCKind.tk_long))
;

      // add the exception to the request
      _request.exceptions().add(SomethingWrongHelper.type());

      // invoke the request
      _request.invoke();
```

After the Request has been invoked, it is checked to see if an exception has occurred, and if so a corresponding Java exception is created and thrown.

```
      // check for exceptions
      java.lang.Exception _exception =
_request.env().exception();

      if(_exception != null) {

        if(_exception instanceof
org.omg.CORBA.UnknownUserException) {
            org.omg.CORBA.UnknownUserException _userException =
              (org.omg.CORBA.UnknownUserException) _exception;

if(_userException.except.type().equals(SomethingWrongHelper.typ
e())) {
            throw
SomethingWrongHelper.extract(_userException.except);
          }
        }
        throw (org.omg.CORBA.SystemException) _exception;
      }
```

If there is no exception, the result and the values of the inout and out parameters are extracted from the Request object and assigned to the value fields of the holder arguments to the method. Finally, the result is returned.

```
        // assign result and values of inout and out parameters

        boolean _result;

        _result = _request.return_value().extract_boolean();

        flag.value = $flag.extract_boolean();

        id.value = $id.extract_long();

        return _result;

    }

}
```

16.4   Portable Skeleton Implementation

A portable skeleton class is generated by the Visibroker for Java IDL compiler. This class is implemented using the DSI. For our example the class
`_TesterImplBase` is generated.

```
abstract public class _TesterImplBase
    extends org.omg.CORBA.DynamicImplementation
    implements Tester {
...
```

All DSI-based object implementations must implement the interface
`org.omg.CORBA.DynamicImplementation`. Its single method `invoke()` has one parameter which is a Server Request object. The ServerRequest interface is explained
in detail in Chapter 7.

```
public void invoke (org.omg.CORBA.ServerRequest _request) {
    Tester _self = this;
    java.lang.Object _method =
_methods.get(_request.op_name());
    if(_method == null) {
      throw new
org.omg.CORBA.BAD_OPERATION(_request.op_name());
    }
    int _method_id = ((java.lang.Integer) _method).intValue();
    switch(_method_id) {
    case 0: {
```

If the `test()` method is selected, its invocation follows these steps.
First, a parameter list containing Named Value objects for each of the
parameters we expect from test() is created. The Named Values are given
only a TypeCode and a flag and are added to the parameter list. Then the

parameter list is given to the Server Request, which places the incoming argument values into it.

```
try {
    org.omg.CORBA.NVList _params = _orb().create_list(0);

    org.omg.CORBA.Any $name = _orb().create_any();

$name.type(_orb().get_primitive_tc(org.omg.CORBA.TCKind.tk_stri
ng));
        _params.add_value("name", $name,
org.omg.CORBA.ARG_IN.value);

        org.omg.CORBA.Any $flag = _orb().create_any();
$flag.type(_orb().get_primitive_tc(org.omg.CORBA.TCKind.tk_bool
ean));
        _params.add_value("flag", $flag,
org.omg.CORBA.ARG_INOUT.value);

        org.omg.CORBA.Any $id = _orb().create_any();

$id.type(_orb().get_primitive_tc(org.omg.CORBA.TCKind.tk_long))
;
        _params.add_value("id", $id,
org.omg.CORBA.ARG_OUT.value);

        _request.params(_params);
```

Now variables are declared for each parameter to the method implementation and initialized from the _params NVList object that the Server Request has now populated. The method on the implementation object (_this) is invoked.

```
        java.lang.String name;
        name = $name.extract_string();

        org.omg.CORBA.BooleanHolder flag = new
org.omg.CORBA.BooleanHolder();
        flag.value = $flag.extract_boolean();

        org.omg.CORBA.IntHolder id = new
org.omg.CORBA.IntHolder();
        boolean _result = _self.test(name,flag,id);
```

The values of the inout and out parameters are then inserted into the Any objects owned by the Server Request's parameter list _param, so that they can be returned to the caller. There is also an Any object created for the result in which the method's return value is inserted. Now the Server Request object contains all the values produced by the implementation ready to be sent back to the client.

```
org.omg.CORBA.Any _resultAny = _orb().create_any();
_resultAny.insert_boolean(_result);

_request.result(_resultAny);

$flag.insert_boolean(flag.value);
$id.insert_long(id.value);
}
```

If the method implementation raised an exception, it must be placed into the Any object set in the except() method on the Server Request.

```
catch(SomethingWrong _exception) {
  org.omg.CORBA.Any _exceptionAny = _orb().create_any();
  SomethingWrongHelper.insert(_exceptionAny, _exception);
  _request.except(_exceptionAny);
      }
      return;
    }
    }
    throw new org.omg.CORBA.MARSHAL();
  }
}
```

16.5   Parameter Management

Table 6.8 summarizes the responsibilities of the invoking client and the object implementation for the declaration, creation, and initialization of parameters and operation result.

TABLE 6.8   Parameter Management Responsibilities

	Invoking Client	*Object Implementation*
Operation result	Declares variable of return type and assigns result.	Declares variable, creates and initializes instance, and returns instance.
in parameters	Declares variable, creates and initializes instance, and passes to invocation.	Declares parameter and uses value passed.
inout parameters	Declares variable, creates Holder object, initializes with a value, and passes to invocation.	Declares Holder parameter, modifies value field of Holder parameter.
out parameters	Declares variable, creates Holder object, and passes to invocation.	Declares Holder parameter, initializes value field of Holder parameter.

17 *Inheritance*

OMG IDL allows multiple inheritance for interfaces, that is, an IDL interface can inherit from any number of interfaces. Java allows only single inheritance for classes, that is, a class can extend only one superclass (see Chapter 3). The Java language designers deliberately made this decision to avoid semantic problems caused by the inheritance of implementations. Java interfaces consist only of signatures. This means that multiple inheritance for interfaces does not imply implementation inheritance, and so is allowed in Java.

Since IDL interfaces are mapped to Java interfaces, the mapping of inheritance is straightforward. A Java interface representing a derived IDL interface, D, extends all the Java interfaces representing the base interfaces of D. The following example illustrates inheritance by using a diamond inheritance structure (see Figure 6.5).

```
interface Base {
        void baseOp();
};

interface Left:Base {
        void leftOp();
};

interface Right:Base {
        void rightOp();
};

interface Derived:Left, Right { };
```

When we look at the generated code we see the same pattern mirrored by the Java interfaces:

```
public interface Base extends org.omg.CORBA.Object { ... }
public interface Left extends Base { ... }
```

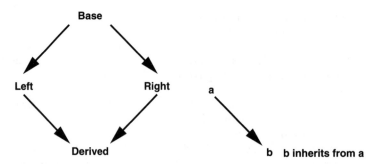

FIGURE 6.5 Diamond inheritance.

```
public interface Right extends Base { ... }
public interface Derived extends Left, Right { ... }
```

It is interesting to examine the generated stub and skeleton classes, since Java classes do not support multiple inheritance. As can be seen, there is no problem with the skeleton classes because they extend only the class `org.omg.CORBA.portable.Skeleton` and implement the corresponding Java interface.

```
abstract public class _sk_Base extends
org.omg.CORBA.portable.Skeleton
    implements Base { … }
abstract public class _sk_Left extends
org.omg.CORBA.portable.Skeleton
    implements Left { … }
abstract public class _sk_Right extends
org.omg.CORBA.portable.Skeleton
    implements Right { … }
abstract public class _sk_Derived extends
org.omg.CORBA.portable.Skeleton
    implements Derived { … }
```

However, the situation is different for the stub classes. They extend the base stub class corresponding to a base IDL interface. But when there is more than one base interface, as with our interface Derived, the class has to choose which base type to extend.

```
public class _st_Base extends org.omg.CORBA.portable.ObjectImpl
        implements Base {
public class _st_Left extends _st_Base implements Left {
public class _st_Right extends _st_Base implements Right {
public class _st_Derived extends _st_Left implements Derived {
```

A look into the full implementation of the stub class _sk_Derived reveals the solution to this problem.

```
public class _st_Derived extends _st_Left implements Derived {
…
private Right _Right;
…
  public void rightOp() {
    this._Right.rightOp( );
  }
}
```

The stub class privately declares an instance of a proxy class for the interface Right and explicitly implements the method rightOp() which calls the object _Right.

A related problem is how to deal with the inheritance structure in implementation classes. This problem is addressed in the same way by the Tie, or delegation, approach and is explained by an example in Chapter 10.

18   Modules and Name-Scoping Rules

Modules provide a name scope for identifiers in IDL specifications to prevent clashes with identifiers used in other specifications. Java provides packages for scoping identifiers. IDL modules are mapped to Java packages of the same name, where each package corresponds to a directory in the file system. The IDL compiler creates a subdirectory named after the IDL module. All generated files containing mapped interfaces and classes for the contents of a module are put into this directory. The files created contain a corresponding package declaration.

Modules can be nested, that is, one can define modules within modules. Nested module definitions result in a corresponding nesting of subpackages and subdirectories.

Additional packages are created for data-type definitions within the scope of an interface. These packages are named after the interface with a suffix Package. They are nested in the package corresponding to the module in which the interface is defined. Figure 6.6 illustrates these mapping rules.

The following IDL provides an example of the scoping rules discussed previously. It also illustrates a little-known IDL feature, namely, that mod-

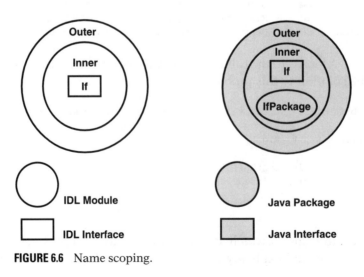

FIGURE 6.6   Name scoping.

ules can be reopened, which allows for complex cross-module dependencies. You should be aware that this feature is generally not implemented by C and C++ ORBs due to the lack of appropriate support in the programming language. Although C++ has namespaces to provide name scoping, they are rarely implemented by C++ compiler and run-time systems. So if you plan to use C or C++ to implement part of your system you should avoid using this feature.

```
module A{

    exception ModuleException{};
};

module B{

    interface B1 {};

    module C{
        interface C1{};
    };
};

module A{

    interface A1: B::B1, B::C::C1{

        attribute string name;
        exception InterfaceException{};
        boolean test( in string name, inout boolean flag, out long id)
            raises( ModuleException, InterfaceException );
    };
};

module B{
    interface B2: A::A1 {};
};
```

When the IDL is compiled, the following package structure is created:

◆ Package A

> Exception ModuleException and its helper and holder classes
>
> Interface A1, its skeleton and stub classes and interfaces, and helper and holder classes
>
> Package A1Package
>
> Exception InterfaceException and its helper and holder classes

♦ Package B

Interface B1, its skeleton and stub classes and interfaces, and helper and holder classes

♦ Package C

Interface C1, its skeleton and stub classes and interfaces, and helper and holder classes

Interface B2, its skeleton and stub classes and interfaces, and helper and holder classes

7

ORB Run-time System

The CORBA 2.0 specification defines the ORB run-time system in the form
of the pseudo-objects ORB, BOA, and Object. Other pseudo-objects assist in
dynamic invocations, dynamic server responses, TypeCode creation, and
name/value pair manipulation. They are called pseudo-objects because they
provide interfaces like normal CORBA objects, but the operations on those
interfaces are implemented in libraries and do not usually result in a remote
invocation. Until recently interfaces of pseudo-objects were specified in
OMG IDL which was commented as pseudo-IDL or PIDL. Now an additional keyword in IDL, pseudo, allows interfaces to be declared explicitly as
pseudo-interfaces. In this chapter we explain the language mapping of
pseudo-objects for Java as specified in the IDL/Java Language Mapping
standard. There are a few omissions from the standard, notably missing
raises clauses in some operation declarations. Where these are actually
required, we have included them in the pseudo-IDL and the corresponding
throws clause of the mapped method. We expect the next revision of the
IDL/Java mapping standard to reflect these changes.

According to the OMA, pseudo-IDL may be mapped in a manner different to other IDL, if this is necessary for the clean implementation of

ORBs in a particular language. In Java the mapping of pseudo-IDL follows the mapping for all other IDL very closely, with a few exceptions. One of these is the BOA interface, which is not well enough specified to allow its operations to be mapped in a standard way. The Java Language Mapping does not map BOA at all, but it does provide a few extensions to the ORB interface to replace it until the Portable Object Adapter (POA) specification becomes widely adopted. When this occurs the Java Mapping will be extended to map the POA interfaces. In this chapter we will show the mappings for the BOA as implemented in the Visiboker for Java and OrbixWeb products. This chapter contains mappings for the following interfaces:

- Object (section 1)
- ORB (section 2)
- BOA (section 3)
- TypeCode (section 4)
- Types used for dynamic invocations (section 5)
- Dynamic Invocation Interface (section 6)
- Dynamic Skeleton Interface (section 7)

1 Object Interface

All CORBA objects, that is, objects which have been specified in OMG IDL and implemented in a CORBA environment, are extensions of the interface CORBA::Object. This interface defines operations that are applicable to any object. These operations are implemented by the ORB local to the client that has a reference to the object instead of being passed to the (possibly remote) object implementation.

In this section we will discuss the mapping of the IDL operations into Java. The mapping of the interface type itself is

IDL Interface	`pseudo interface CORBA::Object;`
Java interface	`package org.omg.CORBA;`
	`public interface Object {...};`

The following sections each explain an operation in the Object interface.

1.1 get_implementation()

The Implementation Repository contains information that allows the ORB to locate and activate object implementations. This information is accessible from an object with an IDL interface CORBA::ImplementationDef. Note that the specification of CORBA::ImplementationDef is left to particular ORB implementations since it deals with operating system-specific information. The operation returns an object which can then be queried about details of the object implementation.

IDL operation	ImplementationDef get_implementation();
Java method	`ImplementationDef _get_implementation();`

1.2   get_interface()

The Interface Repository contains type information about IDL-defined types. Although the Interface Repository can be modified directly through an IDL-defined interface (see Chapter 2), the type information is usually created and stored by the IDL compiler, with the appropriate options switched on. The type information for a CORBA object's interface type is represented by objects with the IDL interface CORBA::InterfaceDef. Operations on this interface allow clients to query the Interface Repository about the details of the data types, operations, and attributes supported by the object. The operation get_interface() returns an InterfaceDef object reference that represents the interface type of the object it was called on.

IDL operation	InterfaceDef get_interface();
Visibroker method	`InterfaceDef _get_interface();`

The use of this method is demonstrated in Chapter 10.

1.3   is_nil()

An object reference can be tested to see if it is nil (denotes no object) by the operation is_nil(). However, Java uses the null type as a nil object reference. Therefore a test like `if( obj == null )` is used in place of is_nil().

1.4   duplicate() and release()

There is no need to map the operations duplicate() and release() because Java provides memory management for object references as it does for any other object or data type. However, the mapping does provide these operations for completeness.

IDL operation	Object duplicate();
Java method	`org.omg.CORBA.Object _duplicate();`
IDL operation	void release();
Java method	`void _release();`

1.5 is_a()

The operation is_a() tests if an object is of the interface type supplied as an argument. The string argument is interpreted as a Repository Id. Chapter 2 explains the format of these identifiers.

IDL operation   boolean is_a(in string logical_type_id);

Visibroker method   `boolean _is_a(String Identifier);`

The `_is_a()` method returns true if the object is of the type identified. This means either that the object's type and the identified type are the same, or that the identified type is a base type of the object's type. A false return value does not necessarily mean that the object is not substitutable.

1.6 non_existent()

The operation non_existent() can be used to test if an object has been destroyed. It returns true if the ORB can authoritatively determine that the referenced object does not exist. Otherwise it returns false. Note that a false return value may not mean that the object still exists.

IDL operation   boolean non_existent();

Java method   `boolean _non_existent();`

1.7 is_equivalent()

The operation is_equivalent() determines if two object references are equivalent, that is, are identical or refer to the same object. The operation returns true if the object reference on which the operation was called and the reference other_object are known to be equivalent, otherwise it returns FALSE. Note that a FALSE return value does not mean that the object could not possibly be the same.

IDL operation   boolean is_equivalent(in Object other_object);

Java method   `boolean _is_equivalent(Object that);`

1.8 hash()

The operation hash() is used to effectively manage large numbers of object references. It generates a hash value for the object reference on which the operation is called. The hash value relates to an ORB-internal identifier. As usual with hash functions, different object references can result in the same hash value and further operations such as is_equivalent() need to be called.

IDL operation	unsigned long hash(in unsigned long maximum);
Java method	`int _hash(int maximum);`

2 ORB Interface

The ORB interface provides operations to bootstrap a CORBA application. This includes the conversion of object references into strings and vice versa, and the resolution of initial references. Also, because the decision not to map the BOA was made, a number of additional operations were added to the ORB interface to allow objects to be made available for invocations. We will introduce these in section 2.3. BOA pseudo-objects are still available in ORB implementations, but their mappings are necessarily implementation dependent. We will show the BOA interfaces for Visibroker for Java and OrbixWeb in section 3.

Other operations are defined on the ORB pseudo-interface that are concerned with TypeCodes (see section 4), Contexts (section 5), the Dynamic Invocation Interface (section 6), and the Dynamic Skeleton Interface (section 7). The mappings for those operations are explained in the appropriate sections.

The ORB interface is mapped as follows:

IDL Interface	pseudo interface ORB;
Java class	`package org.omg.CORBA;`
	`abstract class ORB {...}`

2.1 ORB Initialization

Before an application can use the operations on the ORB interface it needs a reference to an ORB pseudo-object. ORBs in Java applets require different initializations to Java applications to overcome applet security restrictions. This initialization is performed by calling static methods in the ORB class.

Initialization for Java Applications

IDL operation	ORB ORB_init(inout arg_list argv, in ORBid orb_iden-tifier);
Java default method	`public static ORB init();`
Java method for applications	`public static ORB init (String[] args,` `Properties props);`
Java method for applets	`public static ORB init (Applet app,` `Properties props);`

Visibroker method   `public static ORB init(Applet app);`
for applets

The default `init()` method returns a reference to a "singleton" ORB which acts only as an Any and Typecode factory (see section 4). All other operations called from an applet on this ORB object will raise a system exception.

The other two standard methods are designed specifically for use by Java applications and applets, respectively. The application version of `init()` can take arguments that were given to the application at start-up, as well as a list of Java properties. The applet version must be passed a pointer to the applet, and may also take a list of properties. There are two standard properties that the ORB will know how to interpret. However, particular ORB products may recognize other proprietary properties.

The standard properties are

♦ `org.omg.CORBA.ORBClass`—which contains the name of an ORB implementation class

♦ `org.omg.CORBA.ORBSingletonClass`—which contains the name of the "singleton" ORB implementation that acts only as a TypeCode factory

Additionally Visibroker provides an `init()` method for applets which only has one parameter of type Applet. However, it initializes the ORB with parameters set in the applet tag in the HTML file, for example:

```
<applet ...>
<param name= org.omg.CORBA.ORBClass value=com.visigenic.vbroker.CORBA.ORB>
</applet>
```

Similarly Visibroker's parameterless `init()` method understands `-D` Java flags, for example, `-ORBservices=CosNaming`.

2.2 Converting Object References into Strings and Vice Versa

Object references can be externalized by converting them into strings. A stringified object reference can be conveniently stored in a file or passed around by means other than CORBA, for example, by e-mail. A stringified object reference can be reconvertible into a real object reference, which refers to the same object as the original one.

There are two operations at the ORB interface which stringify and destringify object references. The object_to_string() operation converts an IOR into a string.

IDL operation	string object_to_string(in Object obj);
Java method	`String object_to_string(Object obj);`

The operation string_to_object() converts a stringified object reference back into an IOR.

IDL operation	Object string_to_object(in string obj);
Java method	`Object string_to_object(String str);`

It is guaranteed that a stringified IOR produced by object_to_string() is reconvertible by string_to_object() regardless of which ORB the operations are invoked on. Note that the result of string_to_object() is of type CORBA::Object and must be narrowed to the object type expected.

2.3   Connecting Objects to the ORB

Since the BOA is not mapped in the IDL/Java mapping, another mechanism for making the ORB aware of new CORBA objects that can receive requests is provided. This is done by extending the ORB interface to add new operations.

IDL operation	void connect(Object obj);
Java method	`public abstract void connect(Object obj);`

IDL operation	void disconnect(Object obj);
Java method	`public abstract void disconnect(Object obj);`

When a server (or client creating a callback) wishes to make an object implementation usable by clients, it should call connect(), passing the reference to the object instance. When the object should no longer accept requests the disconnect() method should be called. After connecting an object to the ORB, further calls to connect() have no additional effect. The same applies when passing a disconnected object's reference to disconnect(). It is important that when an object is no longer needed that you call disconnect() so that it can be garbage collected. The ORB, or the implicit object adapter, holds a reference to the object which needs to be released by calling disconnect() on the object.

The connect() operation only establishes a transient object reference, which will no longer be valid when the program stops running. Therefore most Java ORBs still provide their own mappings for the BOA in order to establish persistent object references and to provide other features such as control of the threading model or enabling of Secure Socket communication. These mappings are necessarily ORB specific, as the standard is underspecified. Section 3 shows two examples of ORB products' BOA mappings.

2.4 BOA Initialization

Besides initializing an ORB, if a server needs persistent object references, it needs to initialize an object adapter (OA). Until mid-1997 the only OA that was standardized by the OMG was the Basic Object Adapter (BOA). Now the Portable Object Adapter (POA) has been specified, and POA implementations are expected to replace the BOA during 1998. The concept of the BOA was introduced in Chapter 2. The interface to the BOA will be discussed in section 3.

The ORB pseudo-interface provides the operation BOA_init() which is mapped to Java differently in Visibroker and OrbixWeb:

IDL operation	BOA BOA_init(inout arg_list argv, in OAid boa_identifier);
Visibroker methods	`BOA BOA_init()`
	`BOA BOA_init(java.lang.String threadingPolicy,`
	`java.util.Properties properties);`
OrbixWeb object	static `Orbix` object provides BOA—needs no initialization

The second version of Visibroker's BOA initialization allows you to specify the threading model and to pass properties, for example, to specify a thread pool or to determine the port on which the object adapter will accept connections for the server. To set the port on which a server listens is important for firewall configurations and the creation of permanent (stringified) IORs to be used for bootstrapping.

3   Basic Object Adapter Interface

In section 2 we introduced the operation BOA_init(), which initializes a BOA and provides a server with a pseudo-object reference to a BOA. In this section we will introduce the operations specified in BOA pseudo-interface and their mapping to Java. Since the BOA is underspecified, each ORB implements it differently, so we will provide separate mappings for Visibroker and OrbixWeb. The BOA's IDL pseudo-interface CORBA::BOA is mapped to the Java interface CORBA.BOA.

3.1   Activation and Deactivation

The operation object_is_ready() makes the specified object available to CORBA clients. In OrbixWeb this applies only to servers that support "unshared activation mode," that is, they have only one object per server. All other OrbixWeb servers make all their objects available at once using impl_is_ready().

IDL operation	void object_is_ready(in Object obj,
	in ImplementationDef impl);
Visibroker method	`void obj_is_ready(Object object)`
OrbixWeb methods	`void obj_is_ready(Object oref,`
	`String impl,`
	`int timeOut)`
	`throws SystemException;`
	`void obj_is_ready(Object oref,`
	`String impl)`
	`throws SystemException;`

The OrbixWeb arguments are `oref`, the reference to the implementation object; `impl`, which is the server name; and `time_out`, which is the object's lifetime in milliseconds.

In Visibroker an object reference can be passed to clients, for example, via a Naming or Trading Service, or externalized with object_to_string() as soon as an object is created, but the operations that object supports can only be invoked after `obj_is_ready()` has been called for that object. If you don't call `obj_is_ready()` for an object, the ORB run-time system throws an exception which is caught in the skeleton which then calls `obj_is_ready()`.

The operation deactivate_object() deactivates the specified object. Once an object has been deactivated it is no longer accessible to clients. An attempt to invoke a method on a deactivated object will raise the exception `CORBA.NO_IMPLEMENT`. In OrbixWeb this operation is only applicable to servers using the "unshared activation mode."

IDL operation	void deactivate_object(in Object obj);
Visibroker method	`void deactivate_obj(Object object);`
OrbixWeb method	`voiddeactivate_obj(Object object)`
	`thows SystemException;`

It is important to call `deactivate_obj()`, even if you didn't call `obj_is_ready()`, to make sure that an object can be garbage collected.

The operation impl_is_ready() activates objects on a per-server basis, that is, all objects that have been created by a particular server are made accessible to clients. In OrbixWeb this method is used instead of `obj_is_ready()`.

IDL operation	void impl_is_ready(in ImplementationDef impl);
Visibroker method	`void impl_is_ready()`
OrbixWeb method	`void impl_is_ready()`

Visibroker, however, implements the method with slightly different semantics. Visibroker requires a call to `obj_is_ready()` for each object. The method `impl_is_ready()` makes a program listen for requests to the objects it has created. Calling this method in Visibroker is optional. It can be omitted if there is another thread running, for example, an event loop controlling a graphical user interface.

4 *TypeCode Interface*

TypeCodes can represent type information about any IDL type. Many IDL data types are structured and contain other types within them. These are represented as nested TypeCodes. In this section we will look at how TypeCodes are identified and compared (section 4.1), navigated to discover their component parts (section 4.2), and created without use of IDL stub code (section 4.3). The `TypeCode` pseudo-interface is mapped to an abstract Java class in the package `org.omg.CORBA`.

IDL interface   pseudo interface CORBA::TypeCode;

Java interface   `public abstract class TypeCode {...}`

The following sections explain the mapping of the operations in the TypeCode interface to Java methods in the corresponding class. The use of TypeCode is illustrated by an example in Chapter 10 in the context of the type Any and by the example Trader code in Chapter 8.

4.1 Types Used by TypeCodes

The CORBA module defines a pseudo-IDL definition of an enum, TCKind. This enum defines constants to distinguish between various "kinds" of TypeCodes. Different operations are allowed on different kinds of TypeCodes.

IDL type   enum TCKind{ tk_null, tk_void, tk_short, tk_long,....}

Java class

```
public final class TCKind {
    public static final int _tk_null = 0;
    Public static final
        TCKind tk_null = new TCKind(_tk_null);
    ...
}
```

This is the same as the mapping for any other IDL enumeration, except that no holder and helper classes are defined, as this type will never be used in making remote invocations. The complete definition of the TCKind class follows:

```
public final class org.omg.CORBA.TCKind extends java.lang.Object {
    public static final org.omg.CORBA.TCKind tk_null;
    public static final org.omg.CORBA.TCKind tk_void;
    public static final org.omg.CORBA.TCKind tk_short;
    public static final org.omg.CORBA.TCKind tk_long;
    public static final org.omg.CORBA.TCKind tk_ushort;
    public static final org.omg.CORBA.TCKind tk_ulong;
    public static final org.omg.CORBA.TCKind tk_float;
    public static final org.omg.CORBA.TCKind tk_double;
    public static final org.omg.CORBA.TCKind tk_boolean;
    public static final org.omg.CORBA.TCKind tk_char;
    public static final org.omg.CORBA.TCKind tk_octet;
    public static final org.omg.CORBA.TCKind tk_any;
    public static final org.omg.CORBA.TCKind tk_TypeCode;
    public static final org.omg.CORBA.TCKind tk_Principal;
    public static final org.omg.CORBA.TCKind tk_objref;
    public static final org.omg.CORBA.TCKind tk_struct;
    public static final org.omg.CORBA.TCKind tk_union;
    public static final org.omg.CORBA.TCKind tk_enum;
    public static final org.omg.CORBA.TCKind tk_string;
    public static final org.omg.CORBA.TCKind tk_sequence;
    public static final org.omg.CORBA.TCKind tk_array;
    public static final org.omg.CORBA.TCKind tk_alias;
    public static final org.omg.CORBA.TCKind tk_except;
    public static final org.omg.CORBA.TCKind tk_longlong;
    public static final org.omg.CORBA.TCKind tk_ulonglong;
    public static final org.omg.CORBA.TCKind tk_longdouble;
    public static final org.omg.CORBA.TCKind tk_wchar;
    public static final org.omg.CORBA.TCKind tk_wstring;
    public static final org.omg.CORBA.TCKind tk_fixed;
    public static final org.omg.CORBA.TCKind tk_estruct;
}
```

There are two exceptions defined in the CORBA specification that are raised when a query on a TypeCode is invalid. These are exception Bounds {}; and exception BadKind {};. Bounds is usually raised when an indexed query parameter exceeds the length of the list being queried, for example, when asking for the fourth member of a struct with only two members. BadKind is raised when an inappropriate query is made for the kind of TypeCode, for example, asking for the discriminator type of a string. They are mapped in the usual way to exceptions in the package org.omg.CORBA.TypeCodePackage.

4.2   Identifying and Comparing TypeCodes

The operation equal() returns true if the TypeCode is structurally equivalent to its argument tc, and false otherwise.

IDL operation	`boolean equal( in TypeCode tc);`
Java method	`public abstract boolean equal(TypeCode tc);`

The operation kind() returns an enum of type TCKind indicating the kind of TypeCode. For example, tk_union when it defines a union type or tk_alias when it defines a typedef.

IDL operation	TCKind kind();
Java method	public abstract TCKind kind();

The operation id() returns a Repository Id (which is a string) for a type in the Interface Repository (see Chapter 2).

IDL operation	RepositoryId id() raises (BadKind);
Java method	public abstract String id() throws TypeCodePackage.BadKind;

The operation name() returns the unscoped name of the type as specified in IDL. This is only valid for tk_objref, tk_struct, tk_union, tk_enum, tk_alias, and tk_except.

IDL operation	Identifier name() raises (BadKind);
Java method	public abstract String name() throws TypeCodePackage.BadKind;

4.3 Navigating TypeCodes

Once the TCKind of a TypeCode is identified, we can determine what other sorts of information a TypeCode will contain. For example, if the kind is tk_struct, we can expect it to have a list of named members, each of which will have a name and a TypeCode of its own. Whereas if the kind is tk_string, we can only expect to find out what its bound is, or if it is an unbounded string.

4.3.1 Methods for Structured Types

The operation member_count() returns the number of members in the type description. It is only valid for the following TypeCode kinds: tk_struct, tk_union, tk_enum, and tk_except.

IDL operation	unsigned long member_count() raises (BadKind);
Java method	public abstract int member_count() throws TypeCodePackage.BadKind;

The operation member_name() returns the name of the indexed member. It is only valid for the following TypeCode kinds: tk_struct, tk_union, tk_enum, and tk_except.

IDL operation	Identifier member_name(in unsigned long index) raises (BadKind, Bounds);

Java method	`public abstract String member_name(int index)`
	`throws TypeCodePackage.BadKind,`
	`TypeCodePackage.Bounds;`

The operation member_type() returns the type of the indexed member. It is only valid for the following TypeCode kinds: `tk_struct`, `tk_union`, and `tk_except`.

IDL operation	TypeCode member_type(in unsigned long index)
	raises (BadKind, Bounds);
Java method	`public abstract TypeCode member_type(int index)`
	`throws TypeCodePackage.BadKind,`
	`TypeCodePackage.Bounds;`

4.3.2 Methods for Unions

The following three operations are for discovering more information about union definitions. They will raise the BadKind exception if called on a TypeCode that is not of kind `tk_union`.

The operation member_label() returns the label value of a case statement for the member at the index provided.

IDL operation	any member_label(in unsigned long index)
	raises (BadKind, Bounds);
Java method	`public abstract Any member_label(int index)`
	`throws TypeCodePackage.BadKind,`
	`TypeCodePackage.Bounds;`

The operation discriminator_type() returns the type of the union discriminator.

IDL operation	TypeCode discriminator_type() raises (BadKind);
Java method	`public abstract TypeCode discriminator_type()`
	`throws TypeCodePackage.BadKind;`

The operation default_index() returns the member index of the default case of the union, if one is declared.

IDL operation	long default_index() raises (BadKind);
Java method	`public abstract int default_index()`
	`throws TypeCodePackage.BadKind`

4.3.3 Methods for Template Types

The operation length() returns the number of elements contained by the type. It returns zero for unbounded strings and sequences. It is only valid for the following TypeCode kinds: `tk_string`, `tk_sequence`, and `tk_array`.

IDL operation	unsigned long length() raises (BadKind);
Java method	`public abstract int length()`
	`throws TypeCodePackage.BadKind`

The operation `content_type()` returns the base type of the template types (`tk_sequence`, `tk_array`) or the aliased type (`tk_alias`).

IDL operation	TypeCode content_type() raises (BadKind);
Java method	`public abstract TypeCode content_type ()`
	`throws TypeCodePackage.BadKind`

4.4 Creating TypeCodes

TypeCodes are created using operations in the CORBA::ORB interface. All the TypeCode creation methods follow a similar pattern. The result of each method is the newly created TypeCode object. These methods must be recursively applied for TypeCodes of nested types.

4.4.1 Structured and Flat Types

The methods to create TypeCodes for structured and flat types, that is, structs, unions, enums, aliases, exceptions, and interfaces, have the same first two parameters:

- ♦ The first parameter is a Repository Id specifying the unique identifier used in the Interface Repository to identify the type in its IDL context. These are usually of the form "`IDL:modulename/interfacename/type-name:1.0`"; see Chapter 2 for details about Repository Ids.
- ♦ The second parameter is the unscoped type name of the type, which corresponds to the last component of an IDL Repository Id before the version number.

Further parameters provide specific type information depending on the kind of TypeCode.

The method `create_struct_tc()` creates a TypeCode describing an IDL struct. The parameter `members` provides a sequence of name/type pairs defining the members of the struct.

```
public final class org.omg.CORBA.StructMember extends java.lang.Object {
    public java.lang.String name;
    public org.omg.CORBA.TypeCode type;
    public org.omg.CORBA.IDLType type_def;
}

public abstract TypeCode create_struct_tc(
    String id,
```

```
   String name,
   StructMember members[]);
```

The method `create_union_tc()` creates a TypeCode describing an IDL union. The parameter `discriminator_type` gives the type of the discriminator, that is, the type used in the switch statement. The parameter `members` provides a sequence of value/name/type triples defining the members of the union.

```
public final class org.omg.CORBA.UnionMember extends java.lang.Object {
   public java.lang.String name;
   public org.omg.CORBA.Any label;
   public org.omg.CORBA.TypeCode type;
   public org.omg.CORBA.IDLType type_def;
}

public abstract TypeCode create_union_tc(
   String id,
   String name,
   TypeCode discriminator_type,
   UnionMember members[]);
```

The method `create_enum_tc()` creates a TypeCode describing an IDL enum. The parameter `members` provides an array of strings defining the members of the enum.

```
public abstract TypeCode create_enum_tc(
   String id,
   String name,
   String members[]);
```

The method `create_alias_tc()` creates a TypeCode describing an IDL typedef alias. The parameter `original_type` is the TypeCode for the aliased type.

```
public abstract TypeCode create_alias_tc(
   String id,
   String name,
   TypeCode original_type);
```

The method `create_exception_tc()` creates a TypeCode describing an IDL exception. The parameter `members` provides a sequence of name/type pairs defining the members of the exception. Note that exceptions are created using the same parameters as structs, but they have a different TCKind.

```
public abstract TypeCode create_exception_tc(
   String id,
   String name,
   StructMember[] members]);
```

The method `create_interface_tc()` creates a TypeCode describing an IDL interface.

```
public abstract TypeCode create_interface_tc(
    String id,
    String name);
```

4.4.2 Template Types

The methods to create `TypeCodes` for template types, that is, strings, sequences, and arrays, have the same first parameter, `length`. This parameter specifies the length of bounded types. A zero value specifies an unbounded type.

The method `create_string_tc()` creates a TypeCode describing an IDL string.

```
public abstract TypeCode create_string_tc(int length);
```

The method `create_wstring_tc()` creates a TypeCode describing an IDL wstring.

```
public abstract TypeCode create_wstring_tc(int length);
```

The method `create_sequence_tc()` creates a TypeCode describing an IDL sequence. The parameter `element_type` is the type of the elements contained by the sequence.

```
public abstract TypeCode create_sequence_tc(
                        int length,
                        TypeCode element_type);
```

The method `create_recursive_sequence_tc()` creates a TypeCode describing a recursive IDL sequence within a structured type. For example,

```
struct binary_tree {
    element short;
    branch sequence <binary_tree, 2>;
};
```

which defines a binary tree of short values.

```
public abstract TypeCode create_recursive_sequence_tc(
                                int length,
                                int offset);
```

The parameter `offset` determines how many levels up in the type hierarchy the TypeCode's definition can be found. In our example the offset would be

1, as the type referred to as the sequence element type is the immediately enclosing TypeCode.

The method `create_array_tc()` creates a TypeCode describing an IDL array. The parameter `element_type` determines the type of the elements contained in the array.

```
public abstract TypeCode create_array_tc(
    int length,
    TypeCode element_type);
```

5 *Types Used for Dynamic Invocations*

There are a number of common types that are used to represent parameters and return values in the DII and DSI. In this section we introduce

+ Flags—which indicate the direction of operation parameters (section 5.1)
+ Named Values—used to describe parameters and results of operations (section 5.2)
+ Named Value Lists—used to describe the parameter list of an operation (section 5.3)
+ Environment—which is used to check whether an invocation returned successfully or raised an exception (section 5.4)

5.1 Flags

When constructing lists of arguments for operation invocations the programmer must specify whether the argument will be in, out, or inout. Pseudo-IDL constants are defined for this purpose:

```
typedef unsigned long Flags;
const Flags ARG_IN = 1;
const Flags ARG_OUT = 2;
const Flags ARG_INOUT = 3;
```

These are mapped in the same way as ordinary IDL constants, and become interfaces in the package `org.omg.CORBA`.

```
public interface ARG_IN {
    public static final int value = 1;
}
public interface ARG_OUT {
    public static final int value = 2;
}
```

```
public interface ARG_INOUT {
   public static final int value = 3;
}
```

5.2   Named Values

A Named Value was originally specified in CORBA 2.0 as a struct, but its definition has changed to a more appropriate pseudo-interface:

```
typedef string identifier;
pseudo interface NamedValue {
    readonly attribute identifier name;
    readonly attribute any value;
    readonly attribute Flags flags;
};
```

The attribute name determines the name of a parameter. The attribute value carries the type and value of a parameter, encapsulated in an Any. The flags attribute determines if a parameter is in, inout, or out.

The type NamedValue is mapped as follows:

```
public abstract class NamedValue {
   public abstract String name();
   public abstract Any value();
   public abstract int flags();
}
```

As you can see, this class only allows access to the contents of a Named Value that is already initialized. Named Values must be created using the following method on the ORB object:

```
NamedValue create_named_value (String name,
                               Any    value,
                               int    flags);
```

The value part of the NamedValue can be modified by using the value() method to obtain a reference to its Any component, which supports methods for updating its contents. In the same way the name part of the Named Value can be modified using the String object returned by the name() method.

5.3   Named Value Lists

The interface NVList represents a list of Named Values. It was defined in pseudo-IDL in the CORBA 2.0 specification, but its definition has also been updated to a pseudo-interface for the Java mapping:

```
pseudo interface NVList{
    readonly attribute unsigned long count;
    NamedValue add(in Flags flags);
    NamedValue add_item(in identifier item_name, in Flags flags);
    NamedValue add_value(in identifier item_name,
                    in any val,
                    in Flags flags);
    NamedValue item(in unsigned long index) raises (CORBA::Bounds);
    void remove(in unsigned long index) raises (CORBA::Bounds);
};
```

This interface is mapped to the Java class `public abstract class NVList {...}`.

These operations and their mappings to methods in the `NVList` class are explained in the following section.

5.3.1 *Adding Elements to NVLists*

There are three operations that add new Named Values to the NVList. Each of them initializes an additional part of the Named Value.

The add() operation creates a new Named Value which contains only a flag, and adds it to the list.

IDL operation	NamedValue add(in Flags flags);
Java method	`public abstract void add(int flags);`

The name and value of the `NamedValue` created can be added later by obtaining a reference to the `NamedValue` object using the `item()` method.

The operation add_item() is used to create a new Named Value which has a name and a flag, and add it to the list. This is most suitable for adding out parameters, which have the flag CORBA::ARG_OUT, and a parameter name, but no initial value. However, a value can be added as explained in section 5.2.

IDL operation	NamedValue add_item(in identifier item_name, in Flags flags);

Java method	`public abstract void add_item(`
	`    String item_name,`
	`    int flags`
	`);`

The operation add_value() creates a fully initialized Named Value and adds it to the list. This is usually used to add in or inout parameters, which have the flag CORBA::ARG_IN or CORBA::ARG_INOUT, as well as a name for the parameter and a value for the argument being supplied by the caller.

IDL operation	NamedValue add_value(in identifier item_name,
	            in any val,
	            in Flags flags);

Java method
```
public abstract void add_value(
    String item_name,
    Any val,
    int flags
);
```

5.3.2   List Management

The NVList pseudo-interface provides the operation count() which returns the total number of items in the list. This is mapped to an accessor method of the same name in Java.

IDL attribute
```
readonly attribute unsigned long count;
```

Java method
```
public abstract int count();
```

The item() operation returns the indexed element from the list. It will raise a Bounds exception if the index is larger than the list length. In Java the Bounds exception is defined in the CORBA package as well as in TypeCodePackage.

IDL operation
```
NamedValue item(in unsigned long index)
    raises (CORBA::Bounds);
```

Java method
```
public abstract NamedValue item(int index)
    throws org.omg.CORBA.Bounds;
```

The Named Value returned from the `item()` method is owned by the NVList, and modifications to its name or value will update the list.

The remove() operation removes the indexed element from the list. It also raises Bounds if the index is greater than the list length.

IDL operation
```
void remove(in unsigned long index)
    raises (CORBA::Bounds);
```

Java method
```
public abstract void remove(int index)
    throws org.omg.CORBA.Bounds;
```

5.4   Environment

The Environment pseudo-object stores the exceptions that may be raised during an invocation. It is not represented in IDL because exceptions cannot be used as attributes or operation parameters. The CORBA 2.0 specification defines C and C++ programming language APIs to the Environment, and the IDL/Java Mapping specification defines the following mapping:

```
package org.omg.CORBA;

public abstract class Environment {
    void exception(java.lang.Exception except);
    java.lang.Exception exception();
```

```
        void clear();
}
```

The set method `exception()` allows an exception to be raised by a server. The caller provides an argument of a derived type of `java.lang.Exception`, which is the base class of all CORBA exceptions in Java. The accessor method of the same name allows this exception to be retrieved by the client once the call is completed. We will see how this class is used in sections 6 and 7.

5.5 Context Interface

A context object contains a list of properties which are pairs of names and values. CORBA restricts values to type `string`. The intended role of context objects is similar to that of environment variables in various operating systems, which can determine a user's or an application's preferences. They could be defined for a system, for a user, or for an application. Context objects can be manipulated by concatenating their property lists or by arranging them into context trees.

Operations can be declared with a context by adding a context clause after the raises expression. A context is made available to the server by an additional argument to the stub and skeleton interfaces. When an operation with a context is invoked through either the stub or the DII, the ORB will insert the values of the properties of the specified context.

5.5.1   Creating a Context Object

Contexts are organized into trees. Each context has an internal reference to its parent context. The root context is the global default context. The pseudo-interface `Context` is mapped to a Java abstract class in the package `org.omg.CORBA`.

IDL interface	pseudo interface Context;
Java class	`public abstract class Context {...}`

The ORB pseudo-interface provides the operation get_default_context() to obtain the root context. The equivalent method is provided by the Java class `CORBA.ORB`.

IDL operation	Context get_default_context();
Java method	`public abstract Context get_default_context();`

5.5.2   Manipulating a Context Object

The pseudo-interface Context provides operations to add values to a context object. The operation set_one_value() sets the value of a named property.

IDL operation	void set_one_value(in Identifier propname, in any propvalue);
| Java method | ```
public abstract void set_one_value (
                    String propname,
                    Any propvalue
              );
``` |

The value is supplied as an Any rather than a string, although the value contained must be a string. This is for compatibility with Named Values which have values of type Any.

The operation set_values() sets the values of those properties named in the values parameter.

IDL operation	void set_values(in NVList values);
| Visibroker method | ```
public abstract void set_values(
                    NVList values);
``` |

Note that the flags of the items of the NVList must be 0 and that the TypeCode field of the values of the items must represent a string. Values can be read with the operation get_values().

IDL operation	NVList get_values(in Identifier start_scope, in Flags op_flags, in Identifier pattern);
| Visibroker method | ```
NVList get_values (
        String start_scope,
        int op_flags,
        String pattern
    );
``` |

The pattern parameter specifies the name of the returned properties. A string can specify multiple property names by using a naming convention with a wildcard "*" similar to the notations used in various operating system shells. The parameter start_scope determines the scope of this query within the context hierarchy. The naming of scopes is implementation dependent. The op_flags parameter can have the value CORBA::CTX_RESTRICT_SCOPE, which limits the scope to the specified start_scope. A zero flag uses the whole context tree.

The operation delete_values() deletes the named property from the context object. If propname contains a wildcard then multiple properties may be deleted.
```

IDL operation	void delete_values(in Identifier propname);
Java method	`public abstract void delete_values (`
	`                              String propname );`

There is a read-only attribute that allows the name of the current Context to be discovered. The attribute is mapped to an accessor method in Java.

IDL attribute	readonly attribute Identifier context_name;
Java method	`public abstract String context_name()`

The name of a context is determined when it is created, as we will see in the following section.

5.5.3 *Manipulating the Context Object Tree*

There are additional operations on the context object to manipulate the context tree. The operation create_child() creates a new context object that is a child of the object on which the operation is invoked.

IDL operation	Context create_child(
	in Identifier child_ctx_name
	);
Java method	`public abstract Context create_child(`
	`                      String child_ctx_name`
	`                  );`

The tree may be navigated to its root using the attribute parent.

IDL attribute	readonly attribute Context parent;
Java method	`public abstract Context parent();`

The `parent()` method returns `null` if the context is the global default context.

6 Dynamic Invocation Interface

The Dynamic Invocation Interface (DII) enables clients to invoke operations on objects without compile-time knowledge of their IDL type, that is, without the stub code generated by the IDL compiler. A client creates a *Request*, which is the dynamic equivalent to an operation. A Request contains an object reference, an operation name, and type information and values of the arguments which are supplied by the client. Once initialized with all these parameters a Request can be invoked, which has the same semantics as invoking the operation using stub code.

Request is a pseudo-IDL interface that provides the operations to initialize an operation invocation request and then dynamically invoke an operation on an object. Requests are created by the ORB.

6.1 Creating a Request

In Java a Request object is created by calling methods on object references (Java objects of type org.omg.CORBA.Object). However, the IDL pseudo-operation shown below is found in the ORB interface.

IDL operation in ORB	Status create_request(
	in Context ctx,
	in Identifier operation,
	in NVList arg_list,
	inout NamedValue result,
	out Request request,
	in Flags req_flags);
Java methods on	Request _create_request(
CORBA.Object	Context ctx,
	String operation,
	NVList arg_list,
	NamedValue result
	);
	Request _create_request(
	Context ctx,
	String operation,
	NVList arg_list,
	NamedValue result,
	ExceptionList exclist,
	ContextList ctxlist
	);

The two methods are identical, except that the second version adds some extra type information, as explained by the following parameter descriptions. The flags parameter to the IDL operation is used for memory management for some programming languages, and is not mapped in Java.

- ctx—specifies the execution context of the Request (see section 5.5)
- operation—determines the name of the operation to be invoked
- arg_list—provides the arguments to that operation
- result—a Named Value with its value initialized to contain only the type expected as the result from the operation

♦ exclist—a list of TypeCodes that indicates the user exceptions that are declared in the operation's raises clause
♦ ctxlist—a list of strings that corresponds to the names in the context clause of an operation declaration

The newly created Request object is returned as the result of the Java method.

There is an additional operation to create partially initialized Request objects:

```
Request _request (String operation)
    throws SystemException
```

All the parameters provided to _create_request() must be set using the resulting object's interface as described later.

6.2   Request Interface

The pseudo-IDL for Request was originally defined in the CORBA 2.0 specification. It has also been redefined in the IDL/Java Mapping. The first part of the interface definition, which defines read-only attributes (and one read/write attribute) to access the contents of the Request, is as follows:

```
pseudo interface Request {
    readonly attribute Object target;
    readonly attribute Identifier operation;
    readonly attribute NVList arguments;
    readonly attribute NamedValue result;
    readonly attribute Environment env;
    readonly attribute ExceptionList exceptions;
    readonly attribute ContextList contexts;
    attribute Context ctx;
    // operations follow
    . . .
};
```

The target attribute is the object reference from which the Request was obtained. The operation, result, arguments, and ctx attributes are the same as the arguments supplied to the first version of the _create_request() method defined previously. The exceptions and contexts attributes are the same as the additional arguments supplied to the second version of the _create_request() method. These additional attributes can be used to check that the operation is of the type expected, since the exceptions and context strings will be the same as in the Interface Repository.

The Request pseudo-interface is mapped to the Java abstract class org.omg.CORBA.Request. The attributes map according to the standard language mapping, into equivalent accessor methods (and a set method for ctx):

```
public abstract Object target();
public abstract String operation();
public abstract NVList arguments();
public abstract NamedValue result();
public abstract Environment env();
public abstract ExceptionList exceptions();
public abstract ContextList contexts();
public abstract Context ctx();
public abstract void ctx(Context c);
```

6.2.1 Initializing a Request

Operations are defined for adding arguments when a Request has not been initialized with an argument list, for example, when it was created with the _request() method. The following operations each create a new Named Value in the Request's arguments NVList. Each operation sets the appropriate flag in the Named Value, and some also set the name.

```
any add_in_arg();
any add_named_in_arg(in string name);
any add_inout_arg();
any add_named_inout_arg(in string name);
any add_out_arg();
any add_named_out_arg(in string name);
```

In Java these operations are mapped to equivalent methods:

```
public abstract Any add_in_arg();
public abstract Any add_named_in_arg(String name);
public abstract Any add_inout_arg();
public abstract Any add_named_inout_arg(String name);
public abstract Any add_out_arg();
public abstract Any add_named_out_arg(String name);
```

If a value is required in an argument, as in the case of in and inout parameters you can then set the value using the interface to the returned Any. This Any is owned by the Named Value created by the operation.

Unless the Request was fully initialized by creating it with create_request(), one further initialization is required to set up a Request for invocation. The return type must be set. This is done with the following operation/method:

IDL operation	void set_return_type(in TypeCode tc);
Java method	public abstract void set_return_type(TypeCode tc);

6.2.2   Invoking a Request Synchronously

When the Request is correctly initialized it can be invoked by calling several different operations. The simplest of these is the invoke() operation/method:

IDL operation   void invoke();

Java method   `public abstract void invoke();`

The `invoke()` method is a blocking synchronous call, and when it returns the invocation has completed. The Environment attribute env must then be checked for its status because the operation may have raised an exception. If an exception has been raised it can be accessed by calling the `exception()` accessor method on the Environment returned from the `env()` method of the Request. If the result is null, then the operation has completed successfully.

If the operation has returned successfully, its result is set in the result attribute of the Request and the inout and out parameters have been modified in the Request's arguments attribute by the object implementation. These are accessed via the `result()` and `arguments()` methods, respectively.

6.2.3   Invoking a Request Asynchronously

The operation send_deferred() allows an asynchronous invocation to be made. The semantics are that the operation returns without waiting for the target object to complete the invocation.

IDL operation   void send_deferred();

Visibroker methods   `public abstract void send_deferred();`

It is paired with the operations get_response() and poll_response() which allow the caller to check for results at a later time.

IDL operation   void get_response();

Java methods   `public abstract void get_response();`

The operation result and any inout or out parameters won't be valid until `get_response()` has been called and has returned. The method `get_response()` blocks until the result as well as inout and out parameters from an operation invocation initiated by the `send_deferred()` method are returned.

The operation poll_response() has a boolean return value. It will return true if the invocation is complete and the result and the inout and out parameters are ready for inspection. If it returns false then the invocation is not complete and the attributes which contain the results will have undefined values. Once a true result is returned, the get_response() method must be called.

IDL operation   boolean poll_response();

Java methods   `public abstract boolean poll_response();`

6.2.4 Invoking a Oneway Operation Request

The operation send_oneway() is for sending oneway operation invocation requests. These invocations have no return values, and so no further calls to the Request are required.

IDL operation	void send_oneway();
Java method	`void send_oneway();`

6.2.5 Invoking Multiple Requests

The CORBA specification provides operations for making multiple Requests. These operations are defined on the ORB pseudo-interface:

```
void send_multiple_requests_oneway(in RequestSeq req);
void send_multiple_requests_deferred(in RequestSeq req);
boolean poll_next_response();
Request get_next_response();
```

These are mapped in the standard way to methods in the ORB class:

```
public abstract void send_multiple_requests_oneway(Request[] req);
public abstract void send_multiple_requests_deferred(Request[] req);
boolean poll_next_response();
Request get_next_response();
```

The method send_multiple_requests_oneway() takes a list of initialized Request objects and sends them all. No further action is needed because one-way operations do not return.

The method send_multiple_requests_deferred() takes a list of initialized Requests and invokes them asynchronously. When they return, the completed Requests are given back to the user one at a time using the get_next_response() method. The get_next_response() method will block if there are no completed Request invocations, until one returns. It returns null if all outstanding responses have been returned. The caller may use the poll_next_response() method to check if any Requests have completed before calling get_next_response(). A return value of true indicates that a Request has completed, and false indicates that none is yet ready.

7 Dynamic Skeleton Interface

The DII provides a mechanism to invoke operations from a client without compile-time knowledge about the interface. The Dynamic Skeleton Interface (DSI) provides a similar mechanism for the other side. It allows the ORB to invoke an object implementation without compile time knowledge about the interface, that is, without a skeleton class. For an object implementation, calls via a compiler-generated skeleton and the DSI are not distinguishable.

The idea behind the DSI is to invoke all object implementations via the same, general operation. This is specified in an abstract class DynamicImplementation that contains an operation, called by the ORB, to convey the original request to the server. This class presents a pseudo-object of type ServerRequest to the server to allow it access to information about the operation being invoked and its arguments. It also uses references to the contents of this object to return the results of the invocation.

7.1   ServerRequest Interface

The pseudo-IDL specification of ServerRequest in the CORBA 2.0 specification provides operations that are rewritten in a pseudo-interface shown in the Java Mapping Specification. However, the Java Mapping provides one additional operation that allows the setting of exceptions. As with the Request pseudo-object, ServerRequest is mapped to a public abstract class in the org.omg.CORBA package.

IDL interface	pseudo interface Server Request;
Java class	`public abstract class ServerRequest {...}`

The operation op_name() returns the name of the operation that was invoked.

IDL operation	Identifier op_name();
Java method	`public abstract String op_name();`

The operation ctx() provides the invocation Context of the operation.

IDL operation	Context ctx();
Java method	`public abstract Context ctx();`

The params() operation takes an NVList as an argument. This list must contain the names and parameter direction flags of the arguments expected by the server for the operation given by op_name(). When the params() operation returns the ORB will have inserted the values of incoming arguments into the NVList for use by the server. This NVList will also be used to return the new values for inout and out parameters once the server has finished processing.

IDL operation	void params(in NVList parms);
Java method	`public abstract void params(NVList params);`

The result() operation has an Any parameter for the result of the invocation.

IDL operation   void result(in any res);

Java method   `public abstract void result (Any a);`

The Java Mapping specification provides the additional operation exception(). This operation allows the invocation to return an exception instead of a result.

IDL operation   void exception(in any ex);

Java method   `public abstract void exception(Any a);`

7.2　DynamicImplementation Class

Servers that wish to use the DSI must implement the abstract class DynamicImplementation, which extends the base class used for all object implementations:

```
package org.omg.CORBA;

public abstract class DynamicImplementation
        extends org.omg.CORBA.portable.ObjectImpl {
    public abstract void invoke(org.omg.CORBA.ServerRequesr request);
}
```

Servers then use the ServerRequest argument of the invoke() method in the manner just described to access the operation name and its arguments and to set the results of executing this operation.

8

Discovering Services

This chapter provides an overview of mechanisms for discovering CORBA objects. We explain the two most important CORBA Services for locating objects: the Naming Service (section 2), which finds objects by name, and the Trading Service (section 3), which finds objects by type and properties. However, there is still the question of how to find initial references to instances of those services. In section 1, we explain the operations on the ORB pseudo-interface which can be used for bootstrapping.

In section 4, Naming and Trading domains are introduced. This section discusses which object instance is returned by the bootstrapping operations.

Finally, section 5 explains how ORBs name and locate servers and objects by using proprietary mechanisms. Although these mechanisms are not standardized, and hence not portable or interoperable, they are quite popular due to their simplicity.

1 Bootstrapping

CORBA solves the bootstrapping problem by providing a pair of operations on the ORB pseudo-interface:

- list_initial_services()—list the names of initial services which are available from the ORB.
- resolve_initial_references()—returns an initial object reference to a named service. For example, a naming context is returned when a Naming Service reference is requested.

We introduced these operations in Chapter 2 and explained their Java mapping in Chapter 7. We show how to use these operations in the Naming Service example in the following section.

These two operations only provide a bootstrapping mechanism for the services offered by a particular ORB implementation because the mechanism for registering services with the ORB is not defined by CORBA. However, the standard interface to the ORB ensures the portability of application code.

Furthermore, these two operations do not provide full bootstrap support. The problem is that it is not clear which object instance will be returned when several are available. We discuss this problem in more detail in section 4 where we introduce the concept of domains as a solution.

An alternative way to bootstrap applications is to use proprietary mechanisms provided by various ORB implementations. We have a closer look at some of the options in section 5.

2   The CORBA Naming Service

The Naming Service allows object implementations to be identified by name and is thus a fundamental service for distributed object systems. This section is organized as follows:

- We give an overview and explain how to use the Naming Service (section 2.1).
- We explain the interface specification in detail (section 2.2).
- We provide an example (section 2.3).

2.1   Overview of the Naming Service

The Naming Service provides a mapping between a name and an object reference. Storing such a mapping in the Naming Service is known as *binding an object* and removing this entry is called *unbinding*. Obtaining an object reference which is bound to a name is known as *resolving the name*.

Names can be hierarchically structured by using contexts. Contexts are similar to directories in file systems and they can contain name bindings as well as subcontexts.

The use of object references alone to identify objects has two problems for human users, first, because object references are opaque data types, and second, their string form is a long sequence of numbers. When a service is restarted, its objects typically have new object references. However, in most cases clients want to use the service repeatedly without needing to be aware that the service has been restarted.

The Naming Service solves these problems by providing an extra layer of abstraction for the identification of objects. It provides readable object identifiers for the human user; users can assign names that look like structured file names, a persistent identification mechanism, and objects that bind themselves under the same name regardless of their object reference.

The typical use of the Naming Service involves object implementations binding to the Naming Service when they come into existence and unbinding before they terminate. Clients resolve names to objects, on which they subsequently invoke operations. Figure 8.1 illustrates this typical usage scenario.

2.2   Interface Specification

The central interface is called NamingContext and it contains operations to bind names to object references and to create subcontexts. Names are sequences of NameComponents. NamingContexts can resolve a name with a single component and return an object reference. They resolve names with more than one component by resolving the first component to a subcontext and passing the remainder of a name to that subcontext for resolution.

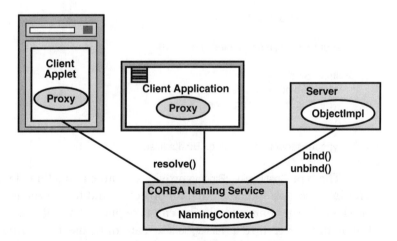

FIGURE 8.1   Typical use of the CORBA Naming Service.

2.2.1   The Name Type

The CosNaming module provides type definitions used to identify objects by names:

```
module CosNaming {

  typedef string Istring;

  struct NameComponent {
    Istring id;
    Istring kind;
  };

  typedef sequence <NameComponent> Name;
```

The type Istring is used to define the Name type for future compatibility with internationalized strings. At the time of writing, this type is defined to be string. A NameComponent has two fields: id contains the string that will actually be matched when a name is resolved; kind is available for application-specific purposes and may or may not be interpreted by the Naming Service. We recommend that the kind field always be initialized to the empty string.

The Name type is a sequence of component, or atomic, names and no syntax is given for the textual representation of names. This allows application programs to use separators such as the UNIX file system "/" character to separate components when printing names for users.

2.2.2   Bindings

The Binding type provides information about the bindings in a context:

```
// module CosNaming

enum BindingType {nobject, ncontext};

struct Binding {
  Name binding_name;
  BindingType binding_type;
};

typedef sequence <Binding> BindingList;
```

The type CosNaming::Binding provides a name and a flag of type BindingType. The value ncontext indicates that an object bound to a name is a NamingContext at which further name resolution can take place. The value nobject means that the binding, even if to a NamingContext, cannot be used for further resolution.

2.2.3 *Adding Names to a Context*

There are two operations for binding an object to a name in a context, and two for binding another context to a name.

```
// module CosNaming

interface NamingContext {

// we elide the exceptions declared here

void bind(in Name n, in Object obj)
    raises(NotFound, CannotProceed, InvalidName, AlreadyBound);
void rebind(in Name n, in Object obj)
    raises(NotFound, CannotProceed, InvalidName);

void bind_context(in Name n, in NamingContext nc)
    raises(NotFound, CannotProceed, InvalidName, AlreadyBound);
void rebind_context(in Name n, in NamingContext nc)
    raises(NotFound, CannotProceed, InvalidName);
```

The bind() and bind_context() operations associate a new name with an object. In the case of bind_context() the object must be of type NamingContext. We will see how to create new contexts in the following section. If the name used has more than one component, the NamingContext will expect that all but the last component refers to an existing nested context, and it will make the binding in the context resolved by the first part of the name. For example, consider Figure 8.2.

We use the "/" character as a separator for NameComponents. In our example we invoke the bind() operation on the NamingContext object we have called "Context1" with the parameters "Context2/Context5/MyName" and some object reference. This results in a new atomic name, "MyName," being bound to the object in the "Context5" context (see Figure 8.3). The BindingType of the resulting binding will be nobject.

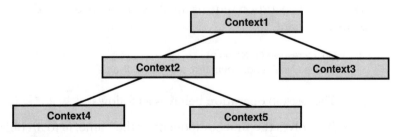

FIGURE 8.2 Naming context structure—before binding.

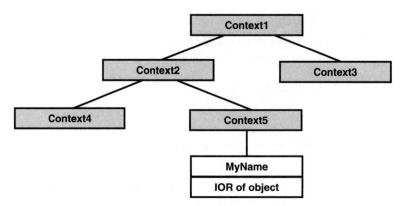

FIGURE 8.3 Naming context structure—after binding.

If we invoked bind_context with the same parameters (although the object reference must be to a NamingContext) then the same situation would result. However, the BindingType will be ncontext, and the "Context5" context would then be able to resolve names like "MyName/x/y/z" by passing the remainder, "x/y/z," to the new "MyName" context.

The rebind() and rebind_context() operations work the same as bind() and bind_context(), but rather than raising an exception if the name already exists, they simply replace the existing object reference.

2.2.4   Removing Names from a Context

The operation unbind() will remove a name and its associated object reference from a context or one of its subcontexts.

```
void unbind(in Name n)
    raises(NotFound, CannotProceed, InvalidName);
```

2.2.5   Name Resolution

The resolve() operation returns an object reference bound to a name supplied as its argument.

```
Object resolve (in Name n)
    raises(NotFound, CannotProceed, InvalidName);
```

The resolve() operation behaves as follows:

◆ It resolves the first component of the name, n, to an object reference.
◆ If there are no remaining components, it returns this object reference to the caller.

◆ Otherwise it narrows the object reference to a NamingContext and passes the remainder of the name to its resolve() operation.

Implementations of the Naming Service will probably optimize this process so that the narrow() and resolve() operations are not called repeatedly. However, the result will logically be the same as that produced by the previous algorithm.

2.2.6 Exceptions

Here are the exceptions omitted above:

```
// interface NamingContext

enum NotFoundReason {missing_node, not_context, not_object};

exception NotFound {
  NotFoundReason why;
  Name rest_of_name;
};

exception CannotProceed {
  NamingContext cxt;
  Name rest_of_name;
};

exception InvalidName{};
exception AlreadyBound {};
exception NotEmpty{};
```

The NotFound exception indicates that the name does not identify a binding. It may be raised by any operation that takes a name as an argument. The Naming Service specification does not explain the meaning of the why member of this exception, but we make the following interpretation: At some stage of tracing the leading name components down to the context in which the final component is bound to a (possibly noncontext) object reference one of these situations occurs:

◆ A NameComponent does not exist in the context expected (missing_node).
◆ A leading NameComponent is bound to an object with a binding type of nobject rather than ncontext, or an ncontext binding is bound to an object of a type other than NamingContext (not_context).
◆ The object reference bound to a NameComponent denotes a destroyed object (not_object).

If this happens, the rest_of_name member returns the rest of the sequence from the unresolvable name onward. This is not explicitly specified in the Naming Service.

The CannotProceed exception returns a NamingContext object reference and a part of the original name. It indicates that the resolve() operation has given up, for example, for security or efficiency reasons. However, the client may be able to continue at the returned context. The rest_of_name member returns the part of the name that should be passed to the returned context ctx for resolution.

The InvalidName exception indicates that the name is syntactically invalid. For example, it might contain a zero-length NameComponent. The names acceptable to different Naming Services may vary.

The AlreadyBound exception may be raised by bind operations. It informs the caller that a name is already used and cannot be overridden without using a rebind operation.

NotEmpty is an exception raised by the destroy() operation defined later. Contexts that still contain bindings cannot be destroyed.

2.2.7 Context Creation

There are operations to create new contexts defined in the NamingContext interface.

```
// interface NamingContext

NamingContext new_context();
NamingContext bind_new_context(in Name n)
    raises(NotFound, AlreadyBound, CannotProceed, InvalidName);
```

New NamingContexts may be created and later used alone or bound into other contexts using bind_context(). They can also be created with a particular name and bound in a single operation. new_context() produces an empty NamingContext that can be used anywhere. bind_new_context() also creates a new context, but binds it as a subcontext of the context on which the operation is invoked. It can raise the usual exceptions for an operation that takes a name as an argument.

2.2.8 Context Destruction

When a context is no longer used, and all the bindings it contained have been unbound, it can be destroyed.

```
// interface NamingContext

void destroy()
    raises(NotEmpty);
```

The destroy() operation will delete a context as long as it contains no bindings. Be sure at the same time to remove any bindings that may refer to this context.

2.2.9 Browsing Contexts

A NamingContext supports browsing of its contents by use of the list() operation.

```
// interface BindingIterator; has been forward declared

// interface NamingContext

void list ( in unsigned long how_many,
      out BindingList bl, out BindingIterator bi);

}; // end of interface NamingContext
```

The parameters of the list() operation allow the caller to specify how many bindings to return in a BindingList sequence. The rest will be returned through an iterator object (which are explained here) referred to by the bi parameter, which will be a nil object reference if there are no further bindings.

2.2.10 Binding Iterators

A BindingIterator object will be returned if the number of bindings in a context exceeds the how_many argument value of the list() operation invoked on the context.

```
// module CosNaming

interface BindingIterator {
  boolean next_one(out Binding b);
  boolean next_n(in unsigned long how_many,
                out BindingList bl);
  void destroy();
};
}; //end of module CosNaming
```

If there are remaining bindings, the next_one() operation returns TRUE and places a Binding in its out parameter. The Naming Service specification is ambiguous about whether it should return FALSE when this is the last binding in the iterator or on the next call.

The next_n() operation returns a sequence of at most how_many bindings in the out parameter bl. It also returns FALSE if there are no further bindings to be iterated over. It is not specified whether the FALSE value should be returned with the last binding or on the next call.

The destroy() operation allows the iterator to deallocate its resources and it will render the object reference invalid. Iterators may sometimes be implemented so that they time out or are deleted on demand for resource recovery.

2.2.11   The Names Library

The Naming Service also defines some pseudo-IDL for a Names Library. This is a set of operations intended to ease the creation and manipulation of names. To our knowledge it has not been implemented in any Naming Service product, and so we will omit details of this part of the specification.

Users typically type in strings to nominate objects. In our examples we use a Java class library, introduced in section 2.3, which allows the use of strings in a convenient syntax to access the Naming Service.

2.3   Using the Naming Service from a Java Client

This subsection contains some of the methods for an EasyNaming class that will be used in subsequent chapters. This class allows applications to obtain a stringified object reference to a NamingContext and then use string arguments with the "/" character as a name separator to identify objects relative to that context.

First let's look at the declaration of the class, its private fields, and constructors. There are two constructors, one of which obtains a root context via the ORB, the other which uses a stringified object reference for bootstrapping.

```
package com.wiley.compbooks.vogel.chapter8.naming;

import org.omg.CosNaming.*;
import org.omg.CosNaming.NamingContextPackage.*;

public class EasyNaming {

    private NamingContext root_context;

    public EasyNaming( org.omg.CORBA.ORB orb ) {

        // initialize Naming Service via ORB
        try {
            System.out.println("Initial services: " );
            String[] services = orb.list_initial_services();
            if( services.length == 0 )
                System.out.println("No services available");
```

```
        for( int i = 0; i < services.length; i++ )
            System.out.println( services[i] );
        org.omg.CORBA.Object obj = orb.resolve_initial_references(
            "NameService");
        root_context = NamingContextHelper.narrow( obj );
        if( root_context == null ) {
            System.err.println("Returned IOR is not a Naming Context");
                System.out.println("Giving up ...");
                System.exit( 11 );
        }
    }
    catch( org.omg.CORBA.ORBPackage.InvalidName inex ) {
        System.err.println( inex );
    }
    catch(org.omg.CORBA.SystemException corba_exception) {
        System.err.println(corba_exception);
    }
}
```

We first list all available initial services by calling `list_initial_services()`. This is not needed to initialize the object, but we use the opportunity to demonstrate the use of the ORB bootstrap operation. We then try to obtain a reference to a root context of the Naming Service by calling `resolve_initial_references()` on the ORB. We obtain an object reference of the type CORBA::Object which we narrow to a NamingContext. If the `root_context` is `null`, the obtained object is of the wrong type and we give up.

Alternatively, there is a constructor that initializes the EasyNaming object with a stringified object reference for a root context. This constructor can be used for cross-ORB bootstrapping.

```
EasyNaming( org.omg.CORBA.ORB orb, String ior_string ) {

        // initialize Naming Service via stringified IOR
        try {
            org.omg.CORBA.Object obj = orb.string_to_object( ior_string );
            root_context = NamingContextHelper.narrow( obj );
            if( root_context == null ) {
                System.err.println("Returned IOR is not a Naming Context");
                    System.out.println("Giving up ...");
                    System.exit( 11 );
            }
        }
        catch(org.omg.CORBA.SystemException corba_exception) {
            System.err.println(corba_exception);
        }
}
```

Both constructors will create an object with a properly initialized `root_context` private field. We can now look at the methods provided by the EasyNaming class.

A method called `str2name()` takes a UNIX file name string format (always starting with a "/" character, as all names are relative to our root context) and produces a CosNaming::Name, which is mapped to a Java array of CosNaming.NameComponent. The method's signature is defined, and the implementation of the class EasyNaming can be found on the website.

```
public NameComponent[] str2name( String str )
        throws InvalidName {
    ...
}
```

The EasyNaming class provides methods equivalent to the operations on naming contexts, but accepts string arguments. The `bind_from_string()` and `rebind_from_string()` methods also allow the use of names that refer to nonexistent contexts and create subcontexts as necessary. This allows us to exercise the bind() or rebind() operations, as well as resolve(), to check the existence of a subcontext, and bind_new_context() to create the subcontexts that don't already exist. This is how we implement `bind_from_string()`:

```
    throws InvalidName, AlreadyBound, CannotProceed, NotFound,
        SystemException {

    NameComponent[] name = str2name( str );
    NamingContext context = root_context;
    NameComponent[] _name = new NameComponent[1];

    try {
        root_context.bind( name, obj );
    }
    catch( NotFound not_found ) {
        // bind step by step

        // create and bind all non-existent contexts in the path
        for( int i = 0; i < name.length - 1; i++ ) {
            _name[0] = name[i];
            try {
                // see if the context exists
                context = NamingContextHelper.narrow(
                    context.resolve( _name ) );
                System.out.println("Resolved " + _name[0].id);
            }
            catch( NotFound nf ) {
                System.out.println("Creating " + _name[0].id);
                // if not then create a new context
                context = context.bind_new_context( _name );
            }
            // let other exceptions propagate to caller
        }
        // bind last component to the obj argument
```

```
        _name[0] = name[ name.length - 1 ];
        context.bind( _name, obj );
    }
    // let other exceptions propagate to caller
}
```

First the `str` argument is converted to a Naming Service name and an attempt is made to bind the `obj` argument using the bind() operation. If one of the contexts in the name path is not found, the method `bind_from_string()` descends the context hierarchy, one `NameComponent` at a time. If a component resolves correctly to a context then that context is used to test the name of the next component. If the resolve() operation fails then the name component is used to create a new subcontext. This continues until the final component, which is then bound in the final subcontext to the object reference passed as an argument.

Similarly we have implemented a more convenient method for resolving names. Following we show the implementation of the method `resolve_from_str()`, which directly calls the resolve operation on the root context after having converted the string name into a Naming Service name.

```
public org.omg.CORBA.Object resolve_from_string( String str )
    throws InvalidName, NotFound, CannotProceed, InvalidName,
        SystemException {

    return root_context.resolve( str2name( str ) );
}
```

We have implemented other methods, matching the operations on naming contexts, which use string names instead of Naming Service names. The complete implementation of `EasyNaming` is shown in the Appendix on the companion website.

3   *Trading Service*

The Trading Service has its basis in the ISO Open Distributed Processing (ODP) standards. The trader work in this group had reached a Draft International Standard (DIS) level within ISO when responses were due for OMG's Object Services RFP 5. The submitters to the RFP were mostly people who had been working on the ODP standard, which enabled the convergence of the Trading standards from both groups. Even though ODP uses OMG IDL as an interface specification language, implementations of ODP standards may use any technology. However, the common underlying semantics of the two efforts greatly enhances the prospects for future cross-platform interworking.

3.1 Overview of Trading

Traders are repositories of object references that are described by an interface type and a set of property values. Such a description of an interface is known as a *service offer*. Each service offer has a *service type,* which is a combination of the interface type of the object being advertised and a list of properties that a service offer of this service type should provide values for.

An *exporter* is a service or some third party acting as an agent for the service which places a service offer into a trader. That service offer can then be matched by the trader to some client's criteria.

A client that queries a trader to discover a service is called an *importer.* An importer provides the trader with a specification of a service type and a constraint expression over the properties of offers of that type. The constraint expression describes the importer's requirements.

A long-standing example of a trading scenario is that of printing services. Currently system administrators configure new printers in a network by providing a unique name for a new device and then notify potential users by e-mail, news, or notice board. Then each user must remember the printer's name and type it into a dialog box in an application. A better way to discover new printers is to allow applications or users to provide their requirements to the application, which then sends the print job to the most appropriate printer. This is achieved as follows:

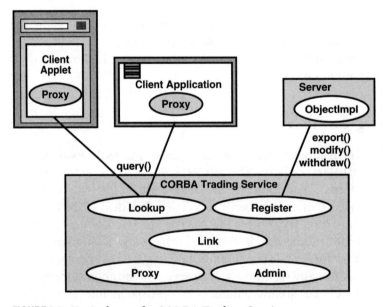

FIGURE 8.4 Typical use of a CORBA Trading Service.

♦ We assume that new printers are provided with an implementation of a standard printing interface, specified in IDL. For example,

```
module com {
...
module chapter8 {
module Printing{
  interface Printer {
    typedef string filename;

    exception PrinterOffLine {};

    void print_file(in filename fn)
      raises(PrinterOffLine);

    short queue_length()
  raises(PrinterOffLine);
  };
};
};};};};
```

♦ Then we define a service type that nominates the Printer interface and a number of property names and types; for example, the printer's location, its language (ASCII, PostScript, HP Laser Jet, etc.), its resolution in DPI, its color properties, its print queue length, and its name.

♦ Each printer is then advertised by exporting a service offer to the trader. For convenience we will refer to the following example printers by their "name" property:

Property	*Value*
building	"A Block"
floor	2
language	postscript
resolution	150
color	black
queue_len	——> [PrinterObjectRef]->queue_length()
name	"12ps"

Property	*Value*
building	"A Block"
floor	3
language	postscript
resolution	300
color	black

queue_len	——>[PrinterObjectRef]->queue_length()
name	"monster"

Property	Value
building	"A Block"
floor	7
language	postscript
resolution	150
color	256color
queue_len	——>[PrinterObjectRef]->queue_length()
name	"rib"

♦ Applications configure print requests based on user preferences, either from a user's environment, a dialog box, or a text query. This results in a constraint expression that can be passed to the trader in an import query. For example,

```
building == "A Block" && floor <= 5 && language == "postscript"
```

♦ This query would result in matching two printers ("12ps" and "monster"). The query can ask for the resulting service offers to be ordered according to a *preference expression.* This provides the matched service offers in order based on some minimal, maximal, or boolean expression. For example, a preference to give us the highest resolution printers first would be expressed as

```
max resolution
```

The `queue_len` property is a *dynamic property,* which means that its value is not stored but looked up each time a query is made. So we would probably have a default preference criterion of `min queue_len`. This would sort the printers that are returned so that we print to the one that matches the constraint expression *and* has the shortest queue.

Let's imagine that a new color printer is installed in Block A and that it is higher in resolution than the "rib" printer. All users who want high resolution will have this maximized in their preferences, and when they next require a color printer the new printer is automatically selected when their application does an import. If, on the other hand a new printer is installed on floor 1 of the building, then people who used to walk upstairs to collect printouts will have their ordinary black-and-white postscript print jobs directed to the new printer on their floor, without having to change their environment or even knowing the name of the printer. In this way they will be informed of a new device as soon as they trade for a printer and the new one meets their requirements.

Of course it is hard to set requirements and preferences when you don't know what is available. Some applications that regularly use the Printer interface will have browsers built in to allow users to see all available printers and their properties by querying the trader with a simple constraint such as:

```
building == "A Block".
```

3.1.1   Service Types and Service Offers

Service types are templates from which service offers are created. They ensure that groups of services that offer the same interface and have the same nonfunctional considerations are grouped together. This allows efficient searching and matching of service offers in the trader. Most importantly, it allows exporters and importers to use the same terminology (property names) to describe a common set of features so that expressions written in terms of those properties will always be evaluated correctly.

3.1.2   Export and Lookup of Service Offers

Any program may export a service offer to a trader if it has an object reference to some application object and knowledge of the implementation behind the reference so that it can describe the properties of that object. Often services will advertise themselves by exporting a service offer.

Any client that is compiled using a set of IDL stubs for a particular interface may assign any valid object reference to a variable at run time and execute operations on that object. As new implementations of servers become available, a client may wish to select objects based on some proximity, quality of service, or other characteristics. To do this it formulates a constraint expression in terms of the property names of a service type. This expression determines which service offers of that type match the client's requirements.

A client may also ask a trader to sort the matching service offers based on some preference expression that emphasizes the values of particular properties. The trader will return a sorted list of matching service offers and the client will then use the object reference extracted from one of these.

3.1.3   Trader Federation

Each trader contains a database of service offers it searches when it receives an import request. It may also store a number of *links* to other traders to which it can pass on queries to reach a larger set of service offers. Links are named within a trader and consist of an object reference to the Lookup interface of another trader, as well as some rules to determine when to use the link to satisfy an importer's request. Traders that are linked in this manner are said to be interworking, or *federated*.

Federated queries are import requests passed from one trader via its links to other traders, and perhaps by them to other traders and so forth. These queries can be constrained by policies passed in by the initial importer, by the policies of each trader, and by the rules stored in the links themselves.

3.2 Overview of the Trading Service Interfaces

In this section we give an overview about the specification of the CORBA Trading Service. The specification includes the following interface definitions:

♦ Service Type Repository
♦ Trader Components
♦ Lookup
♦ Iterators
♦ Register
♦ Link
♦ Admin
♦ Proxy
♦ Dynamic properties

We will look at each of these in separate subsections next.

3.2.1 Service Type Repository

We have seen the importance of service types in the scenario presented in section 3.1. If a service offer does not provide an object reference of a known type then it is impossible for an importer to invoke operations on the object references it gets back. In the same way, service types are important for writing constraint expressions. If a service offer's property names and types vary then the constraint and preference expressions that express the requirements of an importer will fail to match relevant service offers. For example, if one service offer for a Printer described its floor via the property ("Floor", "ground"), and another as the property ("level", 4), then it would be impossible to compare them for proximity.

Service types are stored in the Service Type Repository. A service type consists of a name, an interface type, and a set of property specifications. A property specification gives the name and TypeCode of properties that will occur in service offers of this type. Properties are also given modes which allow them to be specified as read-only and/or mandatory. Read-only properties may not be modified after export. Mandatory properties must be included in a service offer to be accepted as an instance of this service type.

The data types and operations for the Service Type Repository are contained in the CosTradingRepos::ServiceTypeRepository interface. Most traders will implement a compiler for a service type language (for which there is no standard syntax) and browsing tools to enable importers to compose queries to a trader without needing to write clients to the Service Type Repository. The only type needed when importing via a trader is ServiceTypeName, which is a string.

```
typedef sequence <CosTrading::ServiceTypeName> ServiceTypeNameSeq;

enum PropertyMode {
  PROP_NORMAL, PROP_READONLY,
  PROP_MANDATORY, PROP_MANDATORY_READONLY
};

struct PropStruct {
  CosTrading::PropertyName name;
  CORBA::TypeCode value_type;
  PropertyMode mode;
};

typedef sequence <PropStuct> PropStructSeq;

typedef CosTrading::Istring Identifier; // IR::Identifier

struct IncarnationNumber {
  unsigned long high;
  unsigned long low;
};

struct TypeStruct {
  Identifier if_name;
  PropStructSeq props;
  ServiceTypeNameSeq super_types;
  boolean masked;
  IncarnationNumber incarnation;
};
```

Substitutability of Service Types. Service types, like IDL interfaces are substitutable via an inheritance relationship. For IDL interfaces this simply means that all the attributes and operations defined in the base interface become part of the derived interface. However, in service types there are three aspects to substitutability:

- ♦ The interface type of a derived service type may be a subtype of the interface type in the base service type.
- ♦ The property set may be extended in a derived service type with new property names (and their associated type and mode specifications).

♦ Inherited properties may be strengthened. That is, nonmandatory properties may be made mandatory, and modifiable properties may be made read-only. However, the data type of an inherited property must remain the same.

When an importer queries the trader it may receive service offers of a subtype of the requested service type, in the same way that object references to subtypes of a required interface type may be passed where a base type is required.

The masked member of the TypeStruct allows service types to be declared as abstract base service types. The incarnation member is assigned an increasing index so that queries on service type definitions can be restricted to those that were defined after some other service type which has a lower incarnation number.

Creating and Deleting Service Types. Exporters and trader administrators will often want to write code to define a new service type. This is done by populating a PropStructSeq and then calling the add type() operation.

```
IncarnationNumber add type (
    in CosTrading::ServiceTypeName name,
    in Identifier if name,
    in PropStructSeq props,
    in ServiceTypeNameSeq super type,
) raises (
    CosTrading::IllegalServiceType,
    ServiceTypeExists,
    InterfaceTypeMismatch,
    CosTrading::IllegalPropertyName,
    CosTrading::DuplicatePropertyName,
    ValueTypeRedefinition,
    CosTrading::UnknownServiceType,
    DuplicateServiceTypeName
);
```

The name parameter is the name of the service type, which is used by importers to nominate the types of service offers they wish to search over. The if_name parameter is a Repository Id which identifies the type of the object to be advertised by service offers of this type. The properties expected in service offers of this type are given in the props parameter. The final parameter specifies a list of existing service types which are being subtyped by the new service type. The rules for inheritance of service types are explained above. The exceptions are mostly self-explanatory, and many of them relate to conditions in which the properties added or modified in a subtype do not follow the compatibility rules.

Service types should not be removed from a repository unless no service offers of this type are currently exported to the trader. Even in this case it is probably better to mask service types (see below) than delete them, as this avoids the reuse of old service type names, which can lead to confusion. On the rare occasions when a service type should be deleted, the operation remove_type() performs this action.

```
void remove type (
    in CosTrading::ServiceTypeName name
) raises (
    CosTrading::IllegalServiceType,
    CosTrading::UnknownServiceType,
    HasSubTypes
);
```

A known service type cannot be removed if it has sub types, and the exception HasSubTypes is raised in these circumstances.

Obtaining Service Type Information. The repository has operations to list the service types it holds. It can also describe them, either in terms of their supertypes and additional or modified properties, or in terms of the properties that must go into a service offer to conform to this type.

The operation list_types() returns all the service type names in the repository:

```
ServiceTypeNameSeq list_types (
    in SpecifiedServiceTypes which_types
);
```

The operation describe_type() returns a TypeStruct that contains the service type's definition as it was added to the repository. It does not include any properties inherited from its supertypes.

```
TypeStruct describe_type (
    in CosTrading::ServiceTypeName name
) raises (
    CosTrading::IllegalServiceType,
    CosTrading::UnknownServiceType
);
```

The fully_describe_type() operation, on the other hand, gives a full list of properties derived from all of a type's supertypes. This operation would usually be called by importers and exporters who want to know what properties to expect in a service offer of this type.

```
TypeStruct fully_describe_type (
    in CosTrading::ServiceTypeName name
) raises (
    CosTrading::IllegalServiceType,
    CosTrading::UnknownServiceType
);
```

Masking Types. Masking a service type is used to either deprecate an existing service type, for which there are already offers in the trader, or to declare an abstract base service type which must be subtyped before service offer instances will be accepted by the trader. As a service type becomes widely used, people think of additional properties of a service that they wish to describe. So rather than simply adding nonstandard extra properties to their service offers they create a new service type that subtypes the existing type. If the new properties become important, or widely accepted, then the old type can be masked to prevent new service offers being created without the extra properties.

The operation mask_type() indicates that this type is no longer used, at least in its base form:

```
void mask_type (
    in CosTrading::ServiceTypeName name
) raises (
    CosTrading::IllegalServiceType,
    CosTrading::UnknownServiceType,
    AlreadyMasked
);
```

The unmask_type() operation reverses this masking, and the trader will once again accept offers of this type. The Trading Service authors think that this operation will seldom be used.

```
void unmask type (
    in CosTrading::ServiceTypeName name
) raises (
    CosTrading::IllegalServiceType,
    CosTrading::UnknownServiceType,
    NotMasked
);
```

3.2.2   TraderComponents—Finding the Right Interface

The trader defines five separate interfaces:

- ♦ Lookup, where importers make queries
- ♦ Register, where exporters advertise new service offers
- ♦ Link, where links to federated traders are administered
- ♦ Admin, where policies of the trader are administered
- ♦ Proxy, where legacy mechanisms for advertising services are added so that they look like service offers

A single interface, TraderComponents, is inherited by all the interfaces listed here. This allows users to locate the other interfaces supported by a particular trader implementation.

```
interface TraderComponents {

    readonly attribute Lookup lookup_if;
    readonly attribute Register register_if;
    readonly attribute Link link_if;
    readonly attribute Proxy proxy_if;
    readonly attribute Admin admin_if;
};
```

3.2.3   Lookup

The Lookup interface is used by importers to find service offers that meet their needs. It offers a single operation, query(), that requires a specification of the service type and matching constraint expression and returns a list of service offers. The signature for query() is significantly more complex than this simple explanation would indicate:

```
void query (
    in ServiceTypeName type,
    in Constraint constr,
    in Preference pref,
    in PolicySeq policies,
    in SpecifiedProps desired_props,
    in unsigned long how_many,
    out OfferSeq offers,
    out OfferIterator offer_itr,
    out PolicyNameSeq limits_applied
) raises (
    IllegalServiceType,
    UnknownServiceType,
    IllegalConstraint,
    IllegalPreference,
    IllegalPolicyName,
    PolicyTypeMismatch,
    InvalidPolicyValue,
    IllegalPropertyName,
    DuplicatePropertyName,
    DuplicatePolicyName
);
```

The third parameter, pref, is a minimizing, maximizing, or boolean sorting expression that tells the trader which matched offers to return first. The policies parameter allows the importer to influence the way in which the trader searches its service offers and the way in which it propagates the query to other traders. Often query invocations will be given an empty PolicySeq since the trader administrator will configure the trader to allow a trade-off between search space and resource usage that will deliver appropriate services to users.

A desired_props argument must be provided so that the trader knows whether to return properties of the service offers that matched or simply the object references to the services. The SpecifiedProps type is defined as follows:

```
enum HowManyProps { none, some, all};

union SpecifiedProps switch ( HowManyProps ) {
  case some: PropertyNameSeq prop_names;
};
```

Sometimes a service type will contain many properties that do not interest a particular importer. In this case the importer will need to specify in the prop_names field of the desired_props which property values to return. In many cases the choice to ignore the property values or to require all the values is sufficient.

The how_many parameter specifies that the importer wishes to receive a certain number of offers back in the form of a sequence (in the offers out parameter). The rest of the offers will be obtained through an iterator, whose object reference is returned in the offer_itr out parameter (see section 3.2.4). Typically, importers are interested in

- Getting back a small number of offers so that they can ensure that one service is actually available at the time
- Examining a large number of service offers for direct comparison outside the trader

In the first case an importer may save the trader the time and resources of creating an iterator by specifying a policy called return_card. This policy instructs the trader to return only the number of matching service offers specified by the policy. Making its value the same as the how_many argument will prevent the creation of an iterator. The creation of policies is dealt with in section 3.2.4.

3.2.4 *Iterators*

An iterator is an object that controls a logical list of objects or data items and can return them to a client a few at a time. We use the term logical list because the object supporting the iterator may produce new items for the list as they are required. This is a common style used in many OMG specifications. In the trader two iterators are specified:

- OfferIterator is used when a large number of service offers are returned from the Lookup::query operation.
- OfferIdIterator is used to return all of the OfferIds held in a particular trader from the Admin::list_offers operation.

They have essentially the same interface, so we will look at only one of them here.

```
interface OfferIterator {
    unsigned long max_left (
    ) raises (
        UnknownMaxLeft
    );

    boolean next_n (
        in unsigned long n,
        out OfferSeq offers
    );

    void destroy ();
};
```

The max_left() operation provides an upper bound on the number of offers that the iterator contains. If the offers are being constructed a few at a time, then the upper bound may not be easily calculated, so the UnknownMaxLeft exception will be raised. The next_n() operation will return up to *n* offers in the offers out parameter, and a return value of FALSE indicates that no other offers are contained in the iterator.

Although the trader may clean up iterators from time to time to re-claim resources, responsible clients will call destroy() on iterators as soon as they have extracted enough offers.

3.2.5 *Register*

The Register interface provides operations for advertisers of services. The most important operations are

- ◆ export()—advertises a service offer in the trader and returns an identifier for it
- ◆ withdraw()—removes an identified service offer from the trader
- ◆ describe()—returns the properties of an identified service offer
- ◆ modify()—allows an exporter to change the values of non-read-only properties of a service offer

Other operations allow exporters to withdraw all service offers matching a particular query, and to obtain the Register interface of a linked trader by name.

```
OfferId export (
    in Object reference,
    in ServiceTypeName type,
    in PropertySeq properties
) raises (
```

```
    InvalidObjectRef,
    IllegalServiceType,
    UnknownServiceType,
    InterfaceTypeMismatch,
    IllegalPropertyName, // e.g. prop_name = "<foo-bar"
    PropertyTypeMismatch,
    ReadonlyDynamicProperty,
    MissingMandatoryProperty,
    DuplicatePropertyName
);
```

The export() operation takes three parameters that describe a service and places that service offer in the trader's database for return as a result of an importer's query. The reference parameter must contain an object reference of the type specified in the service offer named by the second parameter, type. The properties parameter must contain a value for each mandatory property in the service type and may contain values for other properties. All values provided for property names specified in the service type must be of the property type specified, and additional properties of any other name and type may also be included. Any non-read-only property value may be replaced by a structure of the following type:

```
struct DynamicProp {
    DynamicPropEval eval_if;
    TypeCode returned_type;
    any extra_info;
};
```

This will cause the property's value to be determined at import time, which means that the constraint will be evaluated on up-to-date information. The printer example above has a property that reflects the length of the current print queue. The eval_if member is an object reference to a standard interface that has a single operation which returns an Any. The returned_type member is the type of the value expected in that Any, and must match the type specified for this property in the service type.

The exceptions that may be returned are mostly self-explanatory. The ReadonlyDynamicProperty exception indicates that it is illegal for a read-only property to change after export.

The withdraw() operation passes the trader an OfferId returned from a previous export(), and the trader will remove the corresponding service offer from its database.

```
void withdraw (
    in OfferId id
) raises (
    IllegalOfferId,
```

```
    UnknownOfferId,
    ProxyOfferId
);
```

The other withdraw operation, withdraw_using_constraint(), will remove all service offers that match a particular constraint expression. This should generally only be used by the administrator.

The describe() operation returns an OfferInfo structure corresponding to the id parameter. OfferInfo contains exactly the same information as the three parameters to export(): an object reference, a service type, and a sequence of properties.

```
struct OfferInfo {
  Object reference;
  ServiceTypeName type;
  PropertySeq properties;
};

OfferInfo describe (
  in OfferId id
) raises (
  IllegalOfferId,
  UnknownOfferId,
  ProxyOfferId
);
```

The modify() operation allows exporters to change the properties contained in a particular service offer. Some traders do not allow the modification of service offers and will raise the NotImplemented exception. Traders that implement this operation must succeed on all modifications, or fail on all. Properties listed in the del_list parameter will be deleted if possible, and property values in modify_list will replace current values in the identified service offer, if this is allowed. The reasons the operation may fail are reflected in its long raises clause. In short, the two list parameters may be inconsistent, or the caller may be trying to modify something read-only or delete something mandatory.

```
void modify (
  in OfferId id,
  in PropertyNameSeq del_list,
  in PropertySeq modify_list
) raises (
  NotImplemented,
  IllegalOfferId,
  UnknownOfferId,
  ProxyOfferId,
  IllegalPropertyName,
  UnknownPropertyName,
```

```
    PropertyTypeMismatch,
    ReadonlyDynamicProperty,
    MandatoryProperty,
    ReadonlyProperty,
    DuplicatePropertyName
);
```

The resolve() operation is for obtaining a reference to the Register interface of another trader, to which this trader has a named link. This is how one exports service offers to and withdraws them from federated traders.

```
Register resolve (
    in TraderName name
) raises (
    IllegalTraderName,
    UnknownTraderName,
    RegisterNotSupported
);
```

3.2.6 Link

Links can be considered a specialization of service offers. They advertise other traders that can be used to perform federated queries. The Link interface therefore looks much the same as the Register interface, with operations to add and remove, as well as describe and modify links. Each link has four associated pieces of information: its name, its object reference (to a Lookup interface) and two policies on link following. Most users of traders do not need to know what links a trader has or how they are followed. The trader administrator sets up link policies and trader defaults.

3.2.7 Admin

The Admin interface contains a large number of operations to set the policies of a trader and operations to list the OfferIds of service offers contained in the trader. Ordinary trader users can query the attributes of the other interfaces to determine the current policies of a trader, but will never need to use the Admin interface. Some traders will not even offer this interface because all policy will be determined by the implementation.

3.2.8 Proxies and Dynamic Properties

Proxies are objects that sit alongside service offers, but hide some legacy mechanism of service creation or discovery. Most traders will not support the Proxy interface. Traders that do, return identical results from a proxy as from a normal service offer.

Dynamic properties are a mechanism to allow a service to provide a property value at import time that reflects the current state of the service. We have seen in the explanation of the export operation that the value of a non-read-only property may be replaced by a DynamicProp structure. This will cause the trader to call back to an interface supported by the service (or some associated server) to obtain the property value when the constraint expression of a query is being evaluated. The object reference provided in that structure must be of the following interface type:

```
interface DynamicPropEval {
  any evalDP (
    in CosTrading::PropertyName name,
    in TypeCode returned_type,
    in any extra_info
  ) raises (
    DPEvalFailure
  );
};
```

When evaluating a dynamic property, the trader invokes the evalDP() operation of the eval_if member of the DynamicProp, passing the property name and the returned_type and extra_info members of the structure. It receives an appropriate value in return.

The evaluation of a query that involves calling back to several services to determine the dynamic value of a property can be very costly, and some traders will not support dynamic properties, as indicated by the SupportAttributes::supports_dynamic_properties boolean attribute. However, for some services the information is invaluable for determining their suitability for a purpose. For example, a printer that is one floor up from me and has a zero-length queue is much more useful than one in the same room that has thirty jobs queued or is out of toner.

3.3   Exporting a Service Offer

In this section we will provide an example implementation of the Printer interface introduced in section 3.1. The server that supports objects of this type will export service offers describing the printer objects to the trader. In this way, printer clients can choose printers using an expression of their requirements, rather than the usual method of choosing the name of a printer they know.

The Printer interface is very simple, and emulates the kind of command-line interface provided by UNIX print commands such as lpr. The purpose of this implementation is to show how a minimal wrapper of this kind of service, which describes printer attributes in service offers, can allow users more flexibility. They can not only choose a printer based on some capability that it has, such as high resolution, but they can also choose it based on its current state, such as the length of its print queue. In addition, users can discover new printers that they were previously unaware of.

The environment in which we implemented this server is one in which many different operating systems run on different machines. Although they all have access to the same file systems via NFS, it is too complex to integrate all the different printing services, and printing is only available on some machines. One way of extending printer availability is to install this server on one of the printing machines, using a CORBA client on the other machines which passes the name of the file to be printed.

The implementation of the Printer Server has the usual steps. The first of these, specifying the interface of a CORBA object, has already been done in section 3.1, although we will extend this IDL to facilitate the evaluation of dynamic properties. The second is to compile the IDL, and following that we need to implement the Trading Printer interface, and write a server that creates instances of the implementation class. Our server will also create service offers for the printers it creates and export these to the trader.

3.3.1 Implementing the Printer Interface

We intend to allow the trader to use its dynamic property evaluation to get the printer queue length at query time, so that clients of the trader can sort their returned printer service offers according to the length of the queue. In order to do this we need to implement the interface CosTradingDynamic::DynamicPropEval so that the trader can call its evalDP() operation to get the queue_len property of each printer service offer. The best way to do this is to create a new interface that multiply inherits from the printer and the dynamic property evaluation interfaces. We reopen the Printing module and define a new interface as follows:

```
module com {
...
module chapter8 {
module Printing {
  interface TradingPrinter : Printer,
       CosTradingDynamic::DynamicPropEval {};
};
};};};};
```

The IDL compiler generates the following classes and interfaces:

```
Printer.java      example Printer.java

PrinterHelper.java example TradingPrinter.java
```

```
PrinterHolder.java portable stub Printer.java

PrinterOperations.java      portable stub TradingPrinter.java

TradingPrinter.java         sk Printer.java

TradingPrinterHelper.java   sk TradingPrinter.java

TradingPrinterHolder.java   st Printer.java

TradingPrinterOperations.java      st TradingPrinter.java

PrinterImplBase.java        tie Printer.java

TradingPrinterImplBase.java      tie TradingPrinter.java
```

Our implementation of the TradingPrinter interface is done in the class PrinterImpl, which extends the default skeleton class TradingPrinterImplBase. We define the package, which corresponds to the module structure, and import the classes in the org.omg.CORBA package, as well as those for our generated IDL and the generated classes for the CosDynamicTrading IDL module.

```
package com.wiley.compbooks.vogel.chapter8.PrinterImpl;

import org.omg.CORBA.*;
import com.wiley.compbooks.vogel.chapter8.Printing.*;

import com.wiley.compbooks.vogel.chapter8.Printing.PrinterPackage.*;

import CosTradingDynamic.*;

class PrinterImpl extends TradingPrinterImplBase {
```

Because the printer interface is so simple, we only need PrinterImpl to know the command we will use to find the queue length, the command to print files, and the name of the printer to which it will send them. Therefore we define three private string members to store the commands and the name, and a constructor which accepts three corresponding string arguments. The additional member ret_type is for the dynamic property evaluation return type.

```
private String print command;
private String queue command;
private String printer name;
private TypeCode ret_type;
    // constructor
    PrinterImpl (String p command,
                String q command,
                String name.
                TypeCode dp_eval_ret_type) {

        print_command = new String[3];
        print_command[0] = p_command;
```

```
                     print_command[1] = "-P" + name;
                     print_command[2] = "";
                     queue_command = new String[2];
                     queue_command[0] = q_command;
                     queue_command[1] = "-P" + name;
                     printer_name = name;
                     ret_type = dp_eval_ret_type;
          }
```

We could have chosen to initialize printer objects with all the characteristics we will export in their service offers, but because we don't define any attributes or operations to retrieve these properties, there is no point in doing so. Instead we make the server aware of these characteristics and it exports service offers with corresponding property values on the objects' behalf.

The remainder of the implementation consists of the methods mapped from the IDL operations. The first of these is print_file():

```
    public void print file (String fn)
          throws PrinterOffLine
{
    try {
        Process p;
        Runtime run = Runtime.getRuntime();
        print_command[2] = fn;
        p = run.exec(print_command);
    }
    catch (java.io.IOException ioe) {
        System.err.println(ioe);
        throw new PrinterOffLine();
    }
}
```

The method is implemented very simply by concatenating the print command, the printer name, and the file name and executing it via the Runtime object's exec() method. The queue_len() method is also implemented by making a call to a UNIX executable, which makes the crude assumption that the output of the queue command lists two lines of header information of 80 characters, followed by a line of 80 characters for each queued job.

```
public short queue length()
      throws PrinterOffLine
{
      short len = 0;
         try {
         Process p;
         Runtime run = Runtime.getRuntime();
         queue_command[2] = fn;
```

```
            p = run.exec(print_command);

            len = (short) (p.getInputStream().available()/80 - 2); return len;
        }
        catch (java.io.IOException ioe) {
            System.err.println(ioe);
            throw new PrinterOffLine();
        }

    }
```

The other method that must be implemented is for the dynamic property evaluation operation evalDP(). Its parameters are extracted from the value of any dynamic property in a service offer. This value will always be of type

```
struct DynamicProp {
    DynamicPropEval eval if;
    TypeCode returned type;
    any extra info;
};
```

The eval_if member of this struct will be a reference to our PrinterImpl object, and the other two parameters will be passed to the evalDP() operation on that interface. This is what we implement here:

```
public Any evalDP (
            String name,
            TypeCode returned type,
            Any extra info)
    throws DPEvalFailure {

    if ( name != "queue len" ) {
        throw new DPEvalFailure();
    }

if (!returned type.equal (ret_type) {
        throw new DPEvalFailure();
    }

    Any ret val = orb().create any();
    try {
        ret val.insert short(this.queue length());
    }
    catch (PrinterOffLine pol) {
        throw new DPEvalFailure();
    }

    return ret val;
    }
}
```

The name argument to the evalDP() method is the name of the property in the service offer being evaluated. We are expecting only one such name, queue_len, and if we receive any other, we will throw the DPEvalFailure exception. The result of the evaluation must be an Any with the TypeCode passed in the returned type argument. If the TypeCode expected is not the typecode passed by the server to our constructor then we also raise an exception. We are not expecting any extra information (such as arguments to supply to a method call), so we then create an Any object and place the result of the call to queue_length() into it and return the Any. The last failure condition may occur when the printer is off-line and cannot return a queue length value. In this case we also throw the DPEvalFailure exception.

3.3.2 Implementing the Printer Server

Now that we have an implementation of a PrinterImpl class that satisfies the requirements of printer clients and the trader, we will implement a server that creates printer objects and service offers that represent their characteristics and then exports them to the trader. We have used the DSTC Trader implementation for testing. Since it was not incorporated into Java ORB products at the time of writing, the ORB bootstrap resolve_initial_reference() could not be used to obtain a reference to a trader by passing it the string "TradingService." Instead, the application uses a helper class called IORFile that reads an interoperable object reference from a file and produces a string that we can pass to the ORB::string_to_object() operation. The implementation of the IORFile class can be found on the website.

Our server will take the following command-line arguments:

♦ A file name where the trader's object reference is kept
♦ A command to send a file to the printer that takes the printer name and a file name
♦ A command to check the printer queue length that takes a printer name
♦ The characteristics of one or more printers including each printer's name, resolution in DPI, building location, and floor number.

The PrinterServer class is in the same package as the PrinterImpl class, and it needs to import the CORBA classes, the printer IDL classes, and the trader IDL classes:

```
package com.wiley.compbooks.vogel.chapter8.PrinterImpl;

import org.omg.CORBA.*;
import com.wiley.compbooks.vogel.chapter8.IORFile.*;
import com.wiley.compbooks.vogel.chapter8.Printing.*;
import com.wiley.compbooks.vogel.chapter8.Printing.PrinterPackage.*;
```

```
import CosTrading.*;
import CosTrading.Register.*;
import CosTrading.RegisterPackage.*;
import CosTradingRepos.*;
import CosTradingRepos.ServiceTypeRepositoryPackage.*;
import CosTradingDynamic.*;

public class PrinterServer {
```

The server contains a single method, main():

```
   public static void main (String[] args) {

      int num printers;
      PrinterImpl[] printers;
      String printer name;
   if( args.length < 7 || args.length % 4 != 3) {
            System.out.println("Usage: vbj
com.wiley.compbooks.vogel.chapter8.Printing.PrintServer TraderIORFile
print_command queue_len_command name
resolution
building floor [ name res build floor ... ]");
            System.exit (1);
      }
```

An array is declared for storing references to the printers. Various ORB and trader variables are declared, and then the usual ORB initialization is carried out.

```
// allocate an array to store Printer Implementation Objects

num_printers = (args.length-3) / 4;
printers = new PrinterImpl[num printers];
int i;

try {
   ORB orb;
   BOA boa;

   //initialize the ORB and BOA
   orb = ORB.init (args,null);
   boa = orb.BOA init();

   // Trader object reference declarations
   Lookup lookup;
   Register register;
   ServiceTypeRepository st repos;

   // get the trader reference from the command line
   // and initialize the ServiceTypeRepository and Register
   // interface references from the initial Lookup interface
```

```
IORFile trader_ref = new IORFile(args[args.length - 1]);
org.omg.CORBA.Object obj =
        orb.string to object(trader ref.get ior string());
lookup = LookupHelper.narrow(obj);
if (lookup == null) {
  System.err.println("Lookup narrowed incorrectly");
  System.exit(1);
}

register = lookup.register if();
        obj = register.type repos();
st repos = ServiceTypeRepositoryHelper.narrow(obj);
if (st_repos == null) {
  System.err.println("ServiceTypeRepository narrowed incorrectly");
  System.exit(1);
}
```

The trader's reference is obtained from the file supplied on the command line using an instance of the IORFile class. The first reference for a trader is to a Lookup interface, from which we obtain references to its Register interface, and the service type repository. The service type repository reference returned from the attribute type_repos is specified as type Object in the standard, in anticipation of the interface ServiceTypeRepository being replaced by a repository specified by the Meta Object Facility, which was adopted by the OMG in September 1997. This is why the returned reference must be narrowed.

The next thing we need to do is to check if the service type that we want to use is already defined in the service type repository. We do this by checking the result of a call to the describe_type() operation, which will raise the UnknownServiceType exception if it is not yet created.

```
// check for Service Type existence
// and create a new Service Type if it does not exist

boolean type_exists = false;
String repos_id =
"IDL:com/wiley/compbooks/vogel/chapter8/Printing/Printer:1.0";
String serv_type_name = repos_id;
IncarnationNumber incarn_num;
TypeStruct type desc;
try {
    type_desc = st_repos.describe_type(serv_type_name);
    System.out.println("called describe type - returned type-
desc");
    type_exists = true;
}
catch (UnknownServiceType ust) {
    System.out.println("called describe_type - raised
```

```
UnknownServiceType");
            type_exists = false;
        }
        catch (IllegalServiceType ist) {
            System.err.println(ist);
            System.exit (1);
        }
        catch (SystemException se) {
            System.err.println(se);
            System.exit (1);
        }
```

If the service type is not present then we must create it. We will use the same properties as shown when we introduced the printing example in section 3.1. We make all the properties mandatory so that we can be sure that a query using any property name in the service type will be evaluated on all service offers of this type.

```
if (! type_exists) {
    System.out.println("service type does not exist");
    // we will create a new service type

    // create a prop stuct list with the property names
    // for a printer service type

    PropStruct[] st props = new PropStruct[7];
    st props[0] = new PropStruct( "name",
                        orb.create string tc(0),
                        PropertyMode.PROP MANDATORY);

    st props[1] = new PropStruct( "building",
                        orb.create_string_tc(0),
                        PropertyMode.PROP MANDATORY);

    st props[2] =
            new PropStruct ("floor",
                        orb.get_primitive_tc(TCKind.tk_short),
                        PropertyMode.PROP_MANDATORY);

    st props[3] =
            new PropStruct ("resolution",
                        orb.get_primitive_tc(TCKind.tk_short),
                        PropertyMode.PROP_MANDATORY);
    st_props[4] = new PropStruct( "queue_len",
                        DynamicPropHelper.type(),
                        PropertyMode.PROP_MANDATORY);

    st props[5] =
            new PropStruct ("color",
                        orb.get_primitive_tc(TCKind.tk short),
```

```
PropertyMode.PROP_MANDATORY);
            st props[6] = new PropStruct ( "language",
                                 orb.create_string tc(0),
                                 PropertyMode.PROP_MANDATORY);
```

The other arguments required by the repository's **add_type()** operation are a service type name, an interface's Repository Id, and a list of supertypes. We are using the interface's Repository Id as the service type name, and will not use any supertypes.

```
            // create an empty super type list
            String[] super_types = new String[0];
            // add the new Service Type
            // we use the Interface Type string as the service
            // type name
            System.out.println("about to add type");
            incarn_num = st_repos.add_type( serv type name,
                                 repos_id,
                                 st props,
                                 super_types);
            System.out.println("Created Service Type:" +
                                 serv type name);
            System.out.println("Incarnation Number: high=" +
                                     incarn_num.high);
            System.out.println("                   low=" +
                                 incarn num.low);
        }
```

Now we are ready to create a template service offer, which we can reuse for all the printers that we will export. This server is only going to support printers that are black and white and use postscript, so we can set the values for the color and language properties now. The other property that will share a value for all service offers is queue len, which will contain a DynamicProp. It will be initialized with the type expected from the dynamic evaluation, but the actual object reference will be added once the printer object is created.

```
            // create Service Offer Property Seq to use for export
            Property[] so props = new Property[7];

            // create a Dynamic Property for queue length evaluation
            DynamicProp queue prop =
                    new DynamicProp(null,
                                 orb.get primitive tc(TCKind.tk short),
                                 orb.create any());

            // The first 5 properties will be different for each
            // printer, so we initialize them in the loop below

            so props[0] = new Property( "name", orb.create any());
            so props[1] = new Property( "building", orb.create any());
```

```
so props[2] = new Property( "floor", orb.create any());
so props[3] = new Property( "resolution", orb.create any());
so props[4] = new Property( "queue len", orb.create any());

// the last two properties' values are assumed by this server
// so we initialize them for all printers

so props[5] = new Property( "color", orb.create any());
so props[5].value.insert string("black");
so props[6] = new Property( "language", orb.create any());
so props[6].value.insert string("postscript");
```

The next step is to process the command line arguments and create printers with the corresponding characteristics. We do this in a loop, creating the `PrinterImpl` objects, making them available to the ORB, and then updating the template service offer to advertise them.

```
for (i = 0; i < num_printers; i++) {

        // create a Printer object and register it with the BOA
        printers[i] = new PrinterImpl(
                                args[1],
                                args[2],
                                args[i*4 + 3],
                        orb.get_primitive_tc(TCKind.tk_short)
                           );
        boa.obj_is_ready(printers[i]);

        System.out.println("Created printer: " + args[i*4 + 3]);
        // initialize the properties we get from the command line

        // name
        so_props[0].value.insert_string(args[i*4 + 3]);
        // resolution
        so_props[1].value.insert_short(
                        Short.parseShort(args[i*4 + 4]));
        // building
        so_props[2].value.insert_string(args[i*4 + 5]);
        // floor
        so_props[3].value.insert_short(
                        Short.parseShort(args[i*4 + 6]));
        // update the dynamic prop struct and insert into
        // the queue_len property of the service offer
        queue_prop.eval_if = printers[i];
        DynamicPropHelper.insert (so_props[4].value,
                                queue_prop);
        // export the service offer
        register.export (printers[i],
                        serv_type_name,
                        so_props);
```

```
        System.out.println("Exported printer: " +
                           args[i*4 + 3]);
    } // end for loop
```

Once the printers are all created and their offers exported, we call `impl_is_ready()` to allow the server to accept incoming requests. We also have to catch the various CORBA user and system exceptions that can be raised, as well as the `NumberFormatException` that can be thrown when parsing `short` arguments.

```
        // let the BOA take requests for our printers
        boa.impl is ready();
    }
    catch (NumberFormatException ne) {
        System.err.println("Badly formatted numeric argument");
        System.err.println(ne);
        System.exit (1);
    }
    catch (UserException ue) {
        System.err.println("User exception caught");
        System.err.println(ue);
        System.exit (1);
    }
    catch (SystemException se) {
        System.err.println("System exception caught");
        System.err.println(se);
        System.exit (1);
    }
  }
}
```

3.4 Finding an Object Using a Trader

In this section we use Visibroker for Java to implement a simple Java application client that trades for a suitable `Printer` object to send its print job to. The application is implemented as a class `PrintClient`, in which we implement a single method, `main()`. The application expects two mandatory and two optional arguments:

- ♦ A name of the file where the IOR to a CosTrading::Lookup object is stored
- ♦ The name of the file we wish to print
- ♦ A constraint expression to select suitable printers
- ♦ A preference expression to order the printer service offers returned

The structure of the application is as follows:

- ♦ The class usage is checked for the appropriate number of arguments.
- ♦ We obtain a reference to a `Lookup` object.

♦ The command-line arguments to the application are processed.
♦ Some basic policies for a trader query are established.
♦ The query is made.
♦ The returned Printer objects are tried in order until one successfully prints the file.

Let's look at the code starting with the package declaration, the imported classes, the PrintClient class definition, and the command-line argument check:

```
package com.wiley.compbooks.vogel.chapter8.PrintClient;

import org.omg.CORBA.*;
import com.wiley.compbooks.vogel.chapter8.naming.IORFile.*;
import com.wiley.compbooks.vogel.chapter8.Printing.*;
import com.wiley.compbooks.vogel.chapter8.Printing.PrinterPackage.*;

import CosTrading.*;
import CosTrading.Lookup.*;
import CosTrading.LookupPackage.*;
import CosTrading.Register.*;
import CosTrading.RegisterPackage.*;
import CosTradingRepos.*;
import CosTradingRepos.ServiceTypeRepositoryPackage.*;
import CosTradingDynamic.*;

public class PrintClient {
{

    public static void main(String args[]) {

        if( args.length < 2 || args.length > 4 ) {
            System.out.println(
"usage: PrintClient trader_ior_file
printfile [constraint [preference]]");
            System.exit( 1 );
        }
```

The application exits if it has not been run with the two mandatory arguments.

The next piece of code declares some variables and then initializes the ORB and obtains a reference to the trader's Lookup interface.

```
try {
        ORB orb;
        BOA boa;

        //initialize the ORB and BOA
        orb = ORB.init (args, null);
        boa = orb.BOA init();
```

```
            // some general purpose variables
            Any policy any = orb.create any();
            org.omg.CORBA.Object obj;

            // get reference to trader lookup interface
        Lookup lookup;
            IORFile ior_file = new IORFile( args[0] );
            obj = orb.string to object( ior_file.get_i);
        lookup = LookupHelper.narrow( obj );

            if( lookup == null ) {
                System.err.println("Lookup IOR of wrong type, exiting ...");
                System.exit( 1 );
            }
```

The IORFile class opens and reads the file given as a command-line argument and produces a string for use with the ORB's string_to_object() method. We then narrow the reference obtained.

The next step is to prepare the query for a printer. We use any constraint and preference strings received from the command line and provide suitable defaults when they are not provided.

```
// determine the constraint
String constr;
if( args.length > 2 )
   constr = args[2];
else
   constr = "";

// determine the prefs
String prefs;

if (args.length > 3 )
   prefs = args[3];
else
   // if no preference, compare the offers for shortest queue
   prefs = "min queue_len";
```

An empty constraint string will match all service offers of the right type. If the user does not supply a preference, then we use a default that orders the returned printers by shortest queue length. Now we set parameter values and policies to ensure that we get a reasonable result.

```
            // set some basic policies
        CosTrading.Policy[] query_pols = new CosTrading.Policy[2];

            //declare variables needed in the query()
```

```
        short num_offers = 3;
    String serv type name =

"IDL:com/wiley/compbooks/vogel/chapter8/Printing/Printer:1.0";
        SpecifiedProps desired props;
        OfferSeqHolder return offers = new OfferSeqHolder();
        OfferIteratorHolder iter = new OfferIteratorHolder();
        PolicyNameSeqHolder limits = new PolicyNameSeqHolder();
```

We will ask for at most three offers back, as this provides a reasonable likelihood of one printer being operational. We initialize a short variable `num offers` to the value 3. This is used in the policy `return_card` which specifies the maximum number of service offers to return from a query. If we then pass the same value to the `query()` operation's `how_many` parameter, we can ensure that all of the results will come back in the offers `out` parameter, and we will not have to process an iterator.

```
        // we want at most 3 offers back
    policy any.insert short( num_offers );
query pols[0] = new CosTrading.Policy("return_card", policy any);
```

The other policy we will pass to the trader is `use_dynamic_properties`, which tells the trader to evaluate the `queue_len` property dynamically so that the value used is up to date.

```
        // we want to use dynamic props to find printer queue length
    policy any.insert boolean(true);
        query pols[1] = new CosTrading.Policy("use_dynamic_properties",

policy any);
```

The `desired_props` parameter to `query()` lists the property names whose values we want returned with the query result. For easy processing, in this example we will ask for only the printer name, which assumes that users of our application know their printers by name so that they can go and pick up a printout from the right location. Remember that by using the trader we can discover new printers that only the system administrator knows about. A more advanced printing application would probably ask for all the properties and provide the user with information on the location of printers, which would enable newly discovered printers to be found by location.

```
        // we want back only the name property
        String[] desired_prop_names = new
String[1];
        desired_prop_names[0] = "name";
        desired_props = new
```

```
SpecifiedProps();

desired props.prop names(desired prop names);
```

The SpecifiedProps type is a union, so we must initialize its value and discriminator. Java mapping specifies that a method corresponding to a union branch name will set the discriminator for us. We use the method prop_names() to set the value of the only branch.

Having created objects or variables for each of the parameters to the query() method, we can now invoke it:

```
    // make a query
    try {
        my_lookup.query(
serv type name,
        constr,
        prefs,
        query_pols,
        desired_props,
        num_offers,
        return_offers,
        iter,
        limits);
}
```

Since we have set the value in policy return_card to the value of num_offers (the size of the sequence we are prepared to accept back into our return_offers object) we can ignore the iterator. We also ignore the feedback from the trader about what policy restrictions it applied to our query, which are returned in the limits object. This time we must catch the user exceptions as well as any system exceptions. Rather than catching each of the ten possible user exceptions that the query() operation could raise, we will catch the base class of all of these, CORBA.UserException.

```
        // catch exceptions
catch (UserException ue) {
        System.err.println("Query failed - User Exception: " + ue);
        System.exit(1);
    }
catch (SystemException se) {
        System.err.println("Query failed: " + se);
        System.exit(1);
    }
```

Having received a response from the trader we will now attempt to use the service offers to print the file. We do this by entering a loop which exits once the print_file() operation has been invoked successfully on one of the objects returned in a service offer. First we declare and initialize some variables, including a string and an Any to extract the printer's name from the single returned property in each service offer.

```
// send job to printer
int i = 0;
boolean printed = false;
String pname = "";
Any return any = orb.cre
```

Then we enter the loop.

```
        // we'll try all the returned printers until one works
        while (i < return_offers.value.length - 1 && !printed) {
            try {
    return any =
                return offers.value[i].properties[0].value;
                pname = return any.extract string();
                Printer printer =
                    PrinterHelper.narrow(return offers.value[i].refer-
ence);
                if (printer == null) {
                    system.out.println ("Printer" + pname + "not
found.");

                    i++;
                    continue;
                }
                printer.print_file( args[1] );
                printed = true;
                System.out.println("File " + args[1] +
                    " sent to printer " + pname);
            }
```

If the string extraction from `return_any` and the narrow of the reference work, then we attempt to print the file named in the second command-line argument. If the `print_file()` call works, the termination variable is set to true, a message is printed, and the loop will exit. Other possibilities are that the printer is off-line or that the invocation fails for some other reason.

```
            catch (PrinterOffLine pol) {
                System.out.println("Printer " + pname + " offline!");
            }
        catch (SystemException se
        System.out.println("Printer " + pname +
" raised: " + se);
            }
            i++;
        }
```

Finally, we catch any system exceptions that are raised during ORB initialization.

```
        }
        catch (SystemException se) {
            System.out.println(se);
        }
    }
}
```

Any failures to print are notified to the user, and the next printer is tried.

This is an example of how we might run the application:

```
.../Print> java com.wiley.compbooks.vogel.chapter8.PrintClient.PrintClient
trader.io
/home/dud/myfile.ps \
    'language == "postscript" && floor < 4'
```

Our constraint expression expresses our need for a postscript printer somewhere on the lower floors of our building. We do not specify a preference, as the default preference for the shortest print queue length is suitable. The execution may result in the following output:

```
Printer 12ps offline!
File /home/dud/myfile.ps sent to printer monster
```

3.4.1 *Possible Enhancements to the PrintClient*

The example exercises the query() operation, demonstrates how to pass policies and how to specify the properties we want back, and shows how to extract the returned property values. However, it does not deal with the situation where no service offers match the constraint expression.

A more sophisticated printer query might look up the user's default printer constraint expression and preferences from a file if none were supplied on the command line. It could also check that at least one working printer offer is returned, and if not, it could make a less specific query with an empty constraint string to match all available offers of the service type.

In the case where the first attempt fails, it could query for all printers and ask for all of their properties to be returned, then display a list and allow the user to select an appropriate printer. This would require that the return_card policy not be set, and that an iterator be used, since the number of offers returned would be unpredictable. When making a query that might match a large number of offers, it is often best to set the how_many argument to zero and have a single loop process the iterator. This avoids having to have two loops, one for the returned sequence of offers and the other to invoke the next_n() operation on the returned iterator reference.

4   *Domains*

As we saw in section 1, the operation resolve_initial_references() returns an object of type CORBA::Object, but this object is expected to be of a specific type depending on the service name specified as a parameter. For the Naming Service, you narrow the object to a NamingContext and for the Trading Service to a Lookup object. The question we want to discuss in this section is which object instance the method `resolve_initial_reference()` returns for a given service name.

It might appear that the answer is the root context of the Naming Service and the Lookup interface to the root trader in a Trader federation. However, there are a number of problems with this answer.

First of all, what is *the* Naming or Trading Service. CORBA does not define an association between the ORB and services, and there is also no such thing as *the* ORB. When you obtain an ORB pseudo-object by calling `org.omg.ORB.init()`, a local instance of the class `org.omg.ORB` is created which implements the operations defined in the pseudo-interface CORBA::ORB. Furthermore, novice users sometimes assume that an ORB is associated with an IP subnet—this is not the case! Whenever your ORB is initialized locally and obtains a reference to an object, you can invoke operations on that object.

As you see, the ORB does not solve our problem. What we want is something which allows us to share the same instances of initial services among a set of objects and clients. We call this a *domain*. There are multiple kinds of domains. In this context we have a naming domain and a trading domain, that is, a set of objects and clients that share the same Naming Service or Trading Service, respectively.

In the case of the Naming Service we face an additional problem. The Naming Service specification does not define a structure for the relationships between naming context objects. Even though you organize your naming contexts as a tree, the Naming Service does not know this. Hence any context may to be returned by resolve_initial_references().

So a domain is specific to a specific service and identifies which initial object instance provided by such a service is returned. All members of a domain will obtain the same initial object. For the Naming Service, this means that all clients and objects that belong to the same naming domain obtain the same context object when calling orb.resolve_initial_ reference("NameService").

CORBA only provides a minimal interface for choosing domains. The only hook available is the parameters that can be used to initialize the ORB object. The Java language binding defines the following alternatives of the ORB's init() operation:

```
ORB init();
ORB init( Applet applet, Properties props );
ORB init( String[] args, Properties pros );
```

Using these parameters, we can pass command-line arguments to initialize the local ORB object so that it belongs to a certain naming and/or trading domain. Alternatively, Java properties can be used for this purpose.

Visibroker's Naming service can be started as shown here. It creates a context factory which in turns creates an initial context object. The context has an object name with is specified by the first parameter, in our case "ROOT".

```
vbj -DORBServices=CosNaming
com.visigenic.vbroker.services.CosNaming.ExtFactory ROOT /tmp/ns_log
```

Now you can start clients (to the Naming service) which define their naming domain by specifying an initial context. This can be done by two mechanisms. First, by specifying the name of a context, in our example "ROOT", by setting the property DSVCnameroot:

```
vbj -DORBServices=CosNaming -DSVCnameroot=ROOT <your class>
```

Second, by specifying the stringified IOR of an initial context:

```
vbj -DORBservices=CosNaming -DSVCnameIOR="IOR:000.." <your class>
```

The latter is particularly useful for ORB interoperability. The same mechanisms can be applied to the Trader Service.

5   *Proprietary Object Location*

A number of ORB implementations provide proprietary mechanisms to locate objects. Examples of such mechanisms are the bind() methods provided by Visibroker and OrbixWeb. Although the similarity of the names and signatures suggests interoperability, this is not the case. The bind methods use quite different mechanisms.

Although these bind mechanisms are neither interoperable nor portable between different ORB implementations, they are quite popular among application programmers. In fact these mechanisms ease the bootstrapping of applications and provide additional features. For example, Visibroker provides load balancing, fault tolerance through replicas, and automatic object activation.

We introduce the binding mechanisms of Visibroker for Java and OrbixWeb. The mechanisms introduced here are uniform across the product suites of the vendors that implement them. Java ORB access to CORBA objects implemented in other languages will rely on using the equivalent mechanism in another ORB in the same family. We do not provide any details on how this is achieved, and the reader is referred to the product documentation.

Finally, we explain the Web Naming mechanism as provided by Visigenic and Netscape. A client, in particular an applet client, can use a Web Server to obtain initial object references.

5.1   Visibroker

Visibroker's mechanism for binding objects requires the object implementer to assign names to objects when instantiating them. The name is then used to automatically register the object implementation with a Visibroker Smart Agent. Clients of the object can then use their knowledge of these names to *bind* to the objects.

The Visibroker-generated skeleton classes all have a constructor that accepts a string, which is the implementation name for a particular object, assigned by the object implementer. This name is then used by clients to obtain a reference to an object of a particular type by using the `bind()` methods generated in the Helper class for that interface type. Let's have a look at an example constructor for an implementation of an interface X:

```
class Ximpl extends _sk_X {

  // constructor

  Ximpl( String bind_name ) {

    super( bind_name );
  }
```

The object created using this constructor will now be accessible to any client that uses the `XHelper` class. The client has to pass the same name to `bind()` method on that class. There are four variants of the `bind()` method:

```
public static X bind( org.omg.CORBA.ORB orb )
   throws CORBA.SystemException
```

The first version takes the **ORB** pseudo-object as its only argument, and will select an object of the correct type at random.

```
public static X bind(org.omg.CORBA.ORB orb, String name)
    throws CORBA.SystemException
```

The second version finds an object of type x which registered itself under the name name.

```
public static X bind(org.omg.CORBA.ORB orb, String name, String host)
        throws CORBA.SystemException
```

This bind() method works the same as the second version, but is restricted to finding implementations on the machine host.

```
public static X bind(org.omg.CORBA.ORB orb,
                        String name,
                        String host,
                        CORBA.BindOptions options)
    throws CORBA.SystemException
```

The final version allows the client to specify options by creating an object of class CORBA.BindOptions and updating its boolean fields:

- defer_bind—do not make a connection to the target object until the first invocation
- enable_rebind—reconnect to the target object if the connection is lost

Object implementations with the same name are treated as replicas. That is, if a client holds an IOR to an object and this object isn't accessible anymore, the invocation will be automatically rerouted by the Smart Agent. The address information in the run-time representation of the IOR, that is, the client side proxy, will be automatically updated. When multiple object instances match a bind request, the Smart Agent returns object references in a round-robin fashion—a simple but in many cases adequate load balancing mechanism. Finally, as long as an object implementation is registered with the Object Activation Daemon, the Smart Agent creates an object instance if there are none of the requested specifications available.

5.2 OrbixWeb

OrbixWeb also has a bind mechanism, which is a way of allowing clients access to servers by names assigned to them in the Implementation Repository. Servers can also name their objects by assigning *markers* to them. These become a part of their object references.

The Orbix Implementation Repository is maintained by the *Orbix daemon*, which is responsible for launching servers as their objects are required. The daemon supports an IDL interface, IT_daemon, which allows servers' names to be associated with executable code. Iona supplies utility programs which invoke its operations. The most important of these utilities is called `putit`. An example C++ server registration for a server which creates objects of type X with markers listed on the command line is as follows:

```
putit Xserver "/local/orbix_servers/bin/Xserver myObject"
```

OrbixWeb also supplies a utility called `jrunit` which allows Java servers to be launched. It takes a class name, a class path, and class arguments from its command line and runs the class on a Java virtual machine. Here is an example of how to register a similar Java server for X objects.

```
putit JXserver "/OrbixWeb/bin/jrunit X \
        /local/orbix_servers/classes/local/classes myObject"
```

Orbix servers create object references by storing the following components into the *reference data* (or *object key*) section of an IOR or an Orbix native object reference:

♦ The server name (as registered with the Implementation Repository)
♦ A unique identifier, or *marker,* for the individual object to which the reference refers

The combination of a server name and marker uniquely identify each object that an Orbix daemon is responsible for activating. The machine name and port number through which the daemon is contacted is also stored in an IOR.

Orbix then makes servers and objects available to clients by generating an extra static method on each object reference (`interface-name`) class. This method is called `_bind()`, and has three signatures. For example, for interface X the following methods are generated in class x.

```
public static final X _bind()
```

The simplest version of `_bind()` will use the local Orbix configuration to find a server of the same name as the interface type on which the method is called. Its use is not recommended.

```
public static final X _bind(String markerServer)
```

The second version, which has a single parameter named `markerServer`, expects a string with a colon separating the name of an object's marker and the name of a server in the Implementation Repository.

```
public static final X _bind(String markerServer, String host)
```

The final version of _bind() is the same as the second, except that it may contact the Orbix daemon on a remote machine.

There are a number of ways of using the markerServer parameter. If the marker is left empty this allows any object of the correct type to be selected. Here are some example markerServer arguments and the objects they denote:

markerServer argument	*Description*
":Xserver"	Any object of the correct type that runs in "Xserver"
"myObject:JXserver"	The object with the marker "myObject" in the same server
"Xserver"	An error

The Orbix Naming Service is available via the CORBA::ORB::resolve_initial_references() operation, but there is also a distinguished marker/server name, "root:NS", for a starting context for use with the CosNaming.NamingContext._bind() method.

5.3 Web Naming Service

The Web Naming Service is used to associate an IOR with a URL. This service is provided by Visibroker for Java and is often used in the Netscape release of the product. The service is defined in IDL as shown here.

```
module WebNaming
  exception InvalidURL{};
  exception CommFailure{};
  exception ReqFailure{};
  exception AlreadyExists{};

  interface Resolver {

    Object locate( in string url )
      raises( InvalidURL, CommFailure, ReqFailure );

    void force_register( in string url, in Object obj )
      raises( InvalidURL, CommFailure, ReqFailure );

    void register( in string url, in Object obj )
      raises( InvalidURL, CommFailure, ReqFailure, AlreadyExists );
  };
};
```

The operation locate() resolves a URL string to an object reference of type CORBA::Object. The operations force_register() and register() register an object under a certain URL. The operation force_register() overwrites existing entries, whereas register() raises the exception AlreadyExists when there is an object already bound to this URL. Instead of calling locate() on a Resolver object, a client can use a different flavor of the bind() method, which takes the URL string as the second argument and returns an IOR of the expected type.

Behind the scenes the Resolver object creates a file containing the stringified object reference of the registered object. The Resolver object contacts the identified web server via HTTP to put or get this file.

An initial reference to the Web Naming Service is obtained from the resolve_initial_references() on the ORB. The key string for this service is "WebNamingResolver".

9

Building Applications

In this chapter we will explain how to build applications using Java ORBs. We have selected a simple room booking system as an example. Because we want to demonstrate CORBA features rather than prove that we can implement a sophisticated booking system, we have kept the application-specific semantics simple. But, as will be seen in the IDL specification, we have chosen a very fine-grain object model that allows the creation of many CORBA objects and the demonstration of invocations between them. We will also demonstrate the use of the CORBA Naming Service. We discuss various design approaches and patterns in Chapter 13, where we revisit the room booking application. This chapter covers the development of an entire application including interface specification (section 1), implementing objects (section 2), implementing a server (section 3), implementing a factory (section 4), starting servers (section 5), and clients as applications and applets (section 6).

1   *Application Specification*

The room booking system allows the booking of rooms and the cancellation of such bookings. It operates over one-hour time slots from 9 A.M. to 4 P.M. To keep things simple we do not consider time notions other than these slots, so there are no days or weeks. The rooms available to the booking system are not fixed; the number and the names of rooms can change. When booking a room, a purpose and the name of the person making the booking should be given. We do not consider security issues and anyone can cancel any booking.

The following key design decisions were made:

♦ Rooms and meetings are CORBA objects.
♦ A Meeting object defines a purpose and the person responsible for the meeting.
♦ A Meeting Factory creates meeting objects.
♦ A Room stores Meetings indexed by time slots.
♦ Rooms have a name and register themselves under this name with the Naming Service.

Figure 9.1 illustrates a typical configuration of the room booking system. There are three Room servers which all have one Room object implementation. There is also a Meeting Factory server which has created a Meeting Factory object. The Meeting Factory has created several Meeting objects which are in the same process space, which corresponds to a JVM in the Java case. There is also a Naming Service which has various Naming Context objects forming a context tree. The Room and the Meeting Factory object implementations are registered with the Naming Service.

1.1   IDL Specification

The IDL specification of the Room Booking system is contained in a hierarchy of modules as motivated in Chapter 5. It contains a number of interface specifications: Meeting, MeetingFactory, and Room.

The interface Meeting has two attributes: purpose and participants, which are both of type string and both readonly. The attributes describe the semantics of a meeting. It also has a oneway operation destroy() to complete its life cycle.

Meeting objects are created at run time by a Meeting Factory which is specified in the interface MeetingFactory. It provides a single operation CreateMeeting() which has parameters corresponding to the attributes of the Meeting object and returns an object reference to the newly created Meeting object.

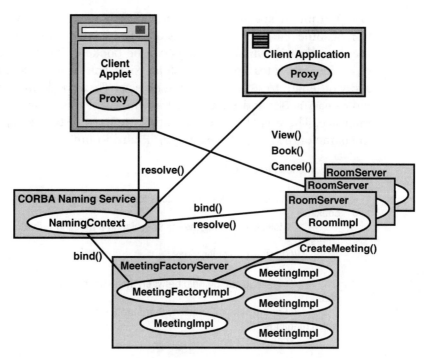

FIGURE 9.1 Room booking system—a typical configuration.

```
module com {
module wiley {
 . . .
module chapter9 {
module RoomBooking {
    interface Meeting {

        // A meeting has two read-only attributes which describe
        // the purpose and the participants of that meeting.

        readonly attribute string purpose;
        readonly attribute string participants;
        oneway void destroy ();
    };

    interface MeetingFactory {
    // A meeting factory creates meeting objects.
    Meeting CreateMeeting( in string purpose, in string participants);
    };
```

Within the specification of the interface Room, we start with the definition of some data types and a constant. There is the enum Slot which defines the time slots in which meetings can be booked. The constant MaxSlots, of type short, indicates how many slots exist. The typedef Meetings defines an array of length MaxSlots of Meeting objects. Then we define two exceptions, NoMeetingInThisSlot and SlotAlreadyTaken which are raised by operations in the interface. There is also a readonly attribute name of type string which carries the name of the room, for example, "Board Room".

```
interface Room {

        // A Room provides operations to view, make and cancel
bookings.
        // Making a booking means associating a meeting with a
time-slot
        // (for this particular room).

        // Meetings can be held between the usual business
hours.
        // For the sake of simplicity there are 8 slots at
which meetings
        // can take place.

        enum Slot { am9, am10, am11, pm12, pm1, pm2, pm3, pm4
};

        // since IDL does not provide means to determine the
cardinality
        // of an enum, a corresponding constant MaxSlots is
defined.
        const short MaxSlots = 8;

        // Meetings associates all meetings of a day with time
slots
        // for a room.

        typedef Meeting Meetings[ MaxSlots ];

        exception NoMeetingInThisSlot {};
        exception SlotAlreadyTaken {};

        // The attribute "name" names a room.

        readonly attribute string name;

        // View returns the bookings of a room.
        // For simplicity, the implementation handles only
bookings
        // for one day.
```

```
        Meetings View();

        void Book( in Slot a_slot, in Meeting a_meeting )
            raises(SlotAlreadyTaken);

        void Cancel( in Slot a_slot )
            raises(NoMeetingInThisSlot);
    };
};...};
```

There are three operations defined in the interface Room. The operation View() returns Meetings, the previously defined array of Meeting objects. The meaning is that a Meeting object reference indicates that this Meeting is booked into the indexed slot. A null object reference means that the indexed slot is free.

The operation Book() books the meeting a_meeting in the slot a_slot of the Room object on which the operation is invoked. The operation raises the SlotAlreadyTaken exception if there is already a meeting booked into the specified slot.

The operation Cancel() removes the meeting at the slot a_slot. It raises the NoMeetingInThisSlot exception if there is no meeting in the slot.

1.2   Compiling the IDL specification

When we compile the IDL specification with Visibroker's compiler, idl2java, the compiler generates different Java interfaces and classes depending on the compiler flags chosen. Here we show the files we use in our implementation, which is based on the following assumptions:

- ♦ Clients use portable stubs.
- ♦ Lightweight objects have transient IORs and are connected without an explicit object adapter.
- ♦ Heavyweight objects have persistent IORs and are connected via the BOA using the inheritance approach.

There is a Java interface for each of the IDL interfaces:

```
MeetingFactory.java Meeting.java Room.java
```

The holder classes are used when the objects are our or inout parameters:

```
MeetingFactoryHolder.java MeetingHolder.java RoomHolder.java
```

Among other methods, the helper classes contain the `narrow()` methods for each interface:

```
MeetingFactoryHelper.java MeetingHelper.java RoomHelper.java
```

Implementation base classes and skeleton classes are generated for each interface. In our example we use the following classes:

```
_MeetingImplBase.java
_sk_MeetingFactory.java _sk_Room.java
```

Our clients always use portable stubs:

```
_portable_stub_MeetingFactory.java
_portable_stub_Meeting.java _portable_stub_Room.java
```

Additionally, there are classes for constants, data types, and exceptions defined within the IDL interface Room which are in the Java package RoomPackage:

MaxSlots.java	Slot.java
MeetingsHelper.java	SlotAlreadyTaken.java
MeetingsHolder.java	SlotAlreadyTakenHelper.java
NoMeetingInThisSlot.java	SlotAlreadyTakenHolder.java
NoMeetingInThisSlotHelper.java	SlotHelper.java
NoMeetingInThisSlotHolder.java	SlotHolder.java

2   Implementing Objects

The classes we have to implement are for the IDL interfaces Meeting and Room. We make the Meeting object implementation portable by extending the implementation base class. For the Room object implementation, we use the BOA inheritance approach, that is, an object implementation class extends the skeleton class generated by the compiler, which allows Rooms to have persistent object references.

2.1   Implementing the Meeting Object

We implement the Meeting object in a class MeetingImpl which extends the implementation base class _MeetingImplBase. We define two private variables purpose and participants which correspond to the attributes with the same names. The constructor has two parameters which are used to initialize the two private variables.

```
package com.wiley.compbooks.vogel.chapter9.RoomBookingImpl;

import org.omg.CORBA.*;
import com.wiley.compbooks.vogel.chapter9.RoomBooking.*;
```

```
class MeetingImpl extends _MeetingImplBase {

    private String purpose;
    private String participants;
// constructor
MeetingImpl( String purpose, String participants) {

    this.purpose = purpose;
    this.participants = participants;
}
```

IDL attributes are mapped to Java methods. These consist of an accessor method, and a modifier method if the attribute is not readonly. Since the attributes of the interface Meeting are readonly we only have to implement the accessors. Their implementation is straightforward; they just return the value of the corresponding private variable.

```
// attributes
public String purpose() {
    return purpose;
}

public String participants() {
    return participants;
}
```

We also implement the destroy() method by disconnecting the object from the ORB, so that it can be garbage-collected once all other references to it are released.

```
    public void destroy() {
        _orb.().disconnect(this);
    }
}
```

The method _orb() is a Visibroker shortcut that calls ORB.init(). The init() method only initializes the ORB the first time it is called, otherwise it returns the reference to the ORB singleton.

2.2   Implementing the Room Object

The Room object is implemented in the class RoomImpl, extending the corresponding skeleton class, _sk_Room. We declare two private variables: name to hold the name of the Room object and meetings to hold the array of booked meetings. Within the constructor we assign the only argument, determining the name of the room to be created, to our private variable room.

```
// RoomImpl.java
package com.wiley.compbooks.vogel.chapter9.RoomBookingImpl;
```

```
import org.omg.CORBA.*;
import com.wiley.compbooks.vogel.chapter9.RoomBooking.*;
import
com.wiley.compbooks.vogel.chapter9.RoomBooking.RoomPackage.*;

class RoomImpl extends _sk_Room {

    private String name;
    private Meeting[] meetings;
    // constructor
    RoomImpl( String name ) {
        this.name = name;
        meetings = new Meeting[ MaxSlots ];
    }
```

As introduced in Chapter 6, IDL bounded arrays are mapped to Java arrays. However, it is the application programmer's responsibility to initialize the array to the length declared in the IDL. The ORB only provides a runtime check to ensure that the specified boundaries hold. Our variable meetings is such a bounded array. We use the constructor to initialize it appropriately. The length of the array is defined in the specification of the interface Room as a constant MaxSlots. This constant is mapped by a generated class variable MaxSlots in the interface Room.

```
package com.wiley.compbooks.vogel.chapter9.RoomBooking;

public interface Room extends org.omg.CORBA.Object {

    final public static short MaxSlots = (short) 8;
        ...
}
```

The attribute name is read-only and hence only the accessor method needs to be implemented. It returns the value of the corresponding private variable.

```
public String name() {
    return name;
}
```

The operations of IDL interfaces are mapped to Java methods. The implementation of the method View() is rather straightforward. It returns the array meetings which holds the object references to the currently booked meetings.

```
public Meeting[] View() {
    return meetings;
}
```

The method Book() has two parameters: one determines the slot in which a meeting should be booked and the second identifies the meeting object. We check if the slot is empty, that is, if the object reference indexed by the slot is nil. Although CORBA defines Object_NIL, and the pseudo-interface CORBA::Object provides a corresponding operation is_nil(), the IDL/Java mapping shortcuts this by defining a nil CORBA object reference as a Java null. Hence we check if the indexed slot is null. If the slot is empty we assign the meeting to the slot, otherwise we raise the exception SlotAlreadyTaken. The class for the exception is defined in the package RoomPackage since the corresponding IDL exception was defined in the interface Room.

```
public void Book( Slot slot, Meeting meeting )
    throws SlotAlreadyTaken {

    if( meetings[slot.value()] == null ) {
            meetings[slot.value()] = meeting;
    }
    else {
        throw new SlotAlreadyTaken();
    }
    return;
}
```

The method Cancel() is implemented similarly. We check if the slot is occupied, and if so we assign a null object to the slot. To allow the object to be garbage-collected we must also remove the last remaining reference to it, which is held by the ORB, in fact by an implicitly defined object adapter. This is done by calling the method destroy() on the Meeting object. In the case where there is no meeting object in the indexed slot, we throw the exception NoMeetingInThisSlot.

```
    public void Cancel( Slot slot )
        throws NoMeetingInThisSlot {
        if( meetings[slot.value()] != null ) {
            meetings[slot.value()].destroy();
            meetings[slot.value()] = null;

        }
        else {
            throw new NoMeetingInThisSlot();
        }
    }
}
```

3 Building Servers

To instantiate the object implementations and to make them available to clients we have to implement a server. This is code that at run time executes as an operating system process or task. In the Java case it is a Java virtual machine in which object instances run. There can be one server per object or a server can handle multiple objects. A server has four fundamental tasks:

◆ Initialize the environment, that is, get references to the pseudo-objects for the ORB and the BOA
◆ Create objects
◆ Make objects accessible to the outside world
◆ Execute a dispatch loop to wait for invocations

Additional server tasks can include the registration of the objects with the Naming Service or the Trading Service.

The server RoomServer does the four fundamental tasks and registers the newly created room with the Naming Service. This is achieved by defining a class RoomServer and implementing its method main(). We define two strings that are used when registering the Room object with the Naming Service. Then we check that the number of arguments is correct and exit the program if it is not. We expect one argument determining the name of the Room object.

To use the Naming Service successfully, objects that want to share information via the Naming Service have to agree on a naming convention. For this example we use the following convention, which is illustrated in Figure 9.2: Under a root context we have a context "Building Applications" that contains two contexts called "Rooms" and "MeetingFactories", respectively. We bind Room objects into the context "Rooms" and the Meeting Factory object into the context "MeetingFactories". Following this convention will ensure that clients can locate the appropriate objects. Note that the Trading Service provides a more formal approach to categorization based on service types (see Chapter 8).

According to this naming convention we initialize the variable context_name with a corresponding string version of the Room context name.

```
package com.wiley.compbooks.vogel.chapter9.RoomBookingImpl;

import org.omg.CORBA.*;
import org.omg.CosNaming.NamingContextPackage.*;
import com.wiley.compbooks.vogel.chapter8.naming.*;
import com.wiley.compbooks.vogel.chapter9.RoomBooking.*;

public class RoomServer {

    public static void main(String[] args) {

        String context_name, str_name;

        if( args.length != 1 ) {
            System.out.println("Usage: vbj
```

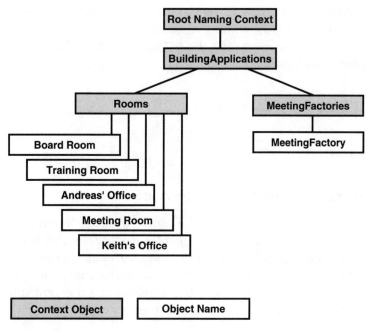

FIGURE 9.2 Naming convention.

```
com.wiley.compbooks.vogel.chapter9.RoomBookingImpl.RoomServer
room_name");
            System.exit( 1 );
        }

        context_name = new
String("/BuildingApplications/Rooms/");
```

3.1 Initializing the ORB

The first task is to initialize the ORB and the BOA. To get a reference to the ORB we call the class method `init()` on the class `CORBA.ORB`. We call `BOA_init()` on the ORB pseudo-object `orb`. This returns a reference to a BOA object.

```
try {
    //init
    ORB orb = ORB.init(args,null);
    BOA boa = orb.BOA_init();
```

3.2 Creating an Object and Notifying the BOA

The second task is to create the Room object. We create an instance of the class `RoomImpl` and provide the name as a parameter to the constructor (see section 2.2 for the definition of that class). Then we perform the third task: we notify the BOA about the existence of the Room object. We invoke the method `obj_is_ready()` on the BOA and provide the reference to the Room object as a parameter.

```
// create the Room object
RoomImpl room = new RoomImpl( args[0] );

// export the object reference
boa.obj_is_ready(room);
```

3.3   Registering with the Naming Service

The next step is to register the object with the Naming Service. The class `EasyNaming` provides a convenient interface to the Naming Service, as explained in detail in Chapter 8. Its constructor obtains an initial context of a Naming Service via the ORB's bootstrap mechanisms. The class `EasyNaming` handles simple names including contexts in a notation similar to the notation of file names in various operating systems:

```
/<context1>/<context2>/.../<contextn>/<name>
```

It parses strings in this format and creates Naming Service names of type CosNaming::Name, which maps to `CosNaming.NameComponent[]` in Java.

We initialize such a string in the variable `str_name`, for example, with a value "/BuildingApplications/Rooms/Board Room". We then bind the Room object to the name corresponding to this string by calling `bind_from_string()` on the object `easy_naming`.

```
// register with naming service
EasyNaming easy_naming = new EasyNaming( orb );

str_name = context_name + args[0];

easy_naming.bind_from_string( str_name, room );
```

3.4   Entering the Dispatch Loop

The fourth task of the server is to enter a dispatch loop by calling `impl_is_ready()` on the BOA to wait for incoming invocations.

Finally, we catch exceptions. If an exception of type `AlreadyBound` is raised, we realize that a room with our room's name is already registered with the Naming Service. We handle any exception that is raised by printing the exception's string representation and exiting.

```
// wait for requests
        boa.impl_is_ready();
    }
    catch( AlreadyBound already_bound ) {
        System.err.println("Room " + context_name + args[0]
            " already bound.");
        System.err.println("exiting ...");
    }
    catch(UserException ue) {
        System.err.println(ue);
        System.err.println("Room " + context_name + args[0]
            " already bound.");
    }
    catch(SystemException se) {
        System.err.println(se);
    }
}
}
```

4   *Building Factories*

A factory is an object implementation with a particular design pattern. The difference from ordinary objects is that factories provide methods to dynamically create new objects. They perform the same initialization of new objects as a server's `main()` method; that is, they create objects and make them invokable. The process of building factories contains the same steps as building any other server: implementing the object and implementing the server.

4.1   Meeting Factory Object Implementation

The Meeting Factory implementation, the class `MeetingFactoryImpl`, is an extension of the corresponding skeleton class `_sk_MeetingFactory`. We declare a private variable for the ORB reference. The constructor initializes the ORB.

```
package com.wiley.compbooks.vogel.chapter9.RoomBookingImpl;

import org.omg.CORBA.*;
import com.wiley.compbooks.vogel.chapter9.RoomBooking.*;

class MeetingFactoryImpl extends _sk_MeetingFactory {

    private ORB orb;

    // constructor
    MeetingFactoryImpl() {
```

```
        try {
            orb = ORB.init();
        }
        catch(SystemException e) {
            System.out.println(e); }
    }
```

The only method of the Meeting Factory, CreateMeeting(), is shown below. Its parameters correspond to those of the Meeting object constructor, MeetingImpl(). We pass the parameters to the MeetingImpl constructor which creates a new instance of a Meeting object. We store the reference to this object in the variable newMeeting. Once the object is created we connect the object to the ORB, which makes the object invokable via the reference, which we then return to the caller.

```
public Meeting CreateMeeting(
        String purpose, String participants ){

        MeetingImpl newMeeting =
            new MeetingImpl(purpose, participants);

        try {
            orb.connect( newMeeting );
        }
        catch(SystemException e) {
            System.out.println(e); }

        return newMeeting;
    }
}
```

4.2   Meeting Factory Server

The Meeting Factory server follows the same pattern as the Room server. We initialize the ORB and the BOA, create the Meeting Factory object, and notify the BOA.

```
package com.wiley.compbooks.vogel.chapter9.RoomBookingImpl;

import java.io.*;
import org.omg.CORBA.*;
import com.wiley.compbooks.vogel.chapter8.naming.*;
import com.wiley.compbooks.vogel.chapter9.RoomBooking.*;

public class MeetingFactoryServer {

    public static void main(String[] args) {

        String str_name;
```

```
      if( args.length != 0 ) {
      System.out.println("Usage: java MeetingFactoryServer");
      System.exit( 1 );
      }

      str_name = new String(

"/BuildingApplications/MeetingFactories/MeetingFactory");

      try {
          //initialise ORB
          ORB orb = ORB.init();

          // initialise BOA
          BOA boa = orb.BOA_init();

          // create the MeetingFactory object
          MeetingFactoryImpl meeting_factory =
              new MeetingFactoryImpl();

          // export the object reference
          boa.obj_is_ready(meeting_factory);
```

In the Meeting Factory server we use the Naming Service differently from the way we use it in the Room server. Instead of binding a name to the object reference we rebind it. This means that when there is already an object bound to the name we have chosen, we override the old binding. We use the method `rebind_from_string()` of the class `EasyNaming` which calls `rebind()` on the Naming Context.

Note that we use rebind only to demonstrate another feature of the Naming Service; the rebind semantics are not implied by the Meeting Factory.

```
// register with naming service
          EasyNaming easy_naming =
              new EasyNaming( orb );

          // register with the CORBA Naming Service
          easy_naming.rebind_from_string( str_name,
meeting_factory );
```

We finish by calling `impl_is_ready()` to wait for incoming invocations and then catch exceptions.

```
      // enter event loop
      boa.impl_is_ready();
  }
  catch(Exception e) {
```

```
                    System.err.println(e);
            }
        }
    }
}
```

5 Starting Servers

Starting the servers requires the following steps. As explained in Chapter 8, we have defined a naming domain to which all components of our application belong. We do this by setting the root context to a naming context called "ROOT".

Start Naming Service

```
> vbj -DORBservices=CosNaming
  com.visigenic.vbroker.services.CosNaming.ExtFactory
  ROOT /tmp/ns_log
```

Start Meeting Factory server

```
> vbj -DORBservices=CosNaming -DSVCnameroot=ROOT
  com.wiley.compbooks.vogel.chapter9.RoomBookingImpl.
  MeetingFactoryServer &
```

Start Room servers

```
> vbj -DORBservices=CosNaming -DSVCnameroot=ROOT
  com.wiley.compbooks.vogel.chapter9.RoomBookingImpl.
  RoomServer "Board Room" &

> vbj -DORBservices=CosNaming -DSVCnameroot=ROOT
  com.wiley.compbooks.vogel.chapter9.RoomBookingImpl.
  RoomServer "Training Room" &

> vbj -DORBservices=CosNaming -DSVCnameroot=ROOT
  com.wiley.compbooks.vogel.chapter9.RoomBookingImpl.
  RoomServer "Meeting Room" &

> vbj -DORBservices=CosNaming -DSVCnameroot=ROOT
  com.wiley.compbooks.vogel.chapter9.RoomBookingImpl.
  RoomServer "Andreas' Office" &

> vbj -DORBservices=CosNaming -DSVCnameroot=ROOT
  com.wiley.compbooks.vogel.chapter9.RoomBookingImpl.
  RoomServer "Keith's Office" &
```

6 Building Clients

Clients can be implemented as Java applications or applets. The differences between the two kinds of client are

Different initialization of graphical user interface. When using Java's AWT classes to build a GUI, the class `java.awt.Component` is the base class from which any GUI class is derived. The Applet class `java.applet.Applet` is an extension of the Component class and can be used directly to create a user interface. The GUI for an application is based on the class `java.awt.Frame`, which is also an extension of the Component class.

Different initialization of the ORB. The main difference here is applet sandboxing, which we discussed in Chapter 4. This constrains the establishment of network connections to the host where the applet was loaded from. Another issue is client-side firewalls, which also stop network connections to arbitrary ports. These factors make applets quite different from ordinary Java applications. Java ORBs respond to this situation by providing different mechanisms for initializing the ORB depending on whether the program is an applet or an application.

Access of the classes. An application accesses CORBA and application-specific classes from the local file system, for example, as specified by the environment variable `CLASSPATH`. Applets and the CORBA classes they require are loaded into a Web browser via a network or from the file system. Netscape browsers (4.0 and later) have CORBA classes (Visibroker for Java) built in.

Figures 9.3 to 9.6 illustrate our graphical user interfaces for both applet and application clients in various stages of their use. They aid understanding of the code in the following subsections.

Figure 9.3 shows the initial state of a client which is viewing a booking system containing four bookings made previously by other clients. This figure shows the applet client.

Figure 9.4 shows the action that takes place after the user has clicked a button labeled "Book" for the Training Room's 9 A.M. time slot. The user has entered the relevant data into the text fields. This is a view of the Java application version of the client.

Figure 9.5 shows the application after the booking is made.

Figure 9.6 shows the form produced by clicking the "View" button for the same meeting slot.

We have separated the parts of a client that are independent of the kind of client into a class `RoomBookingClient` which is implemented in section 6.3. That leaves the tasks of creating an object of the class `RoomBookingClient` and catching and processing user events in the applet or application class. In section 6.1 we look at the applet class and in section 6.2 we look at the Java application class.

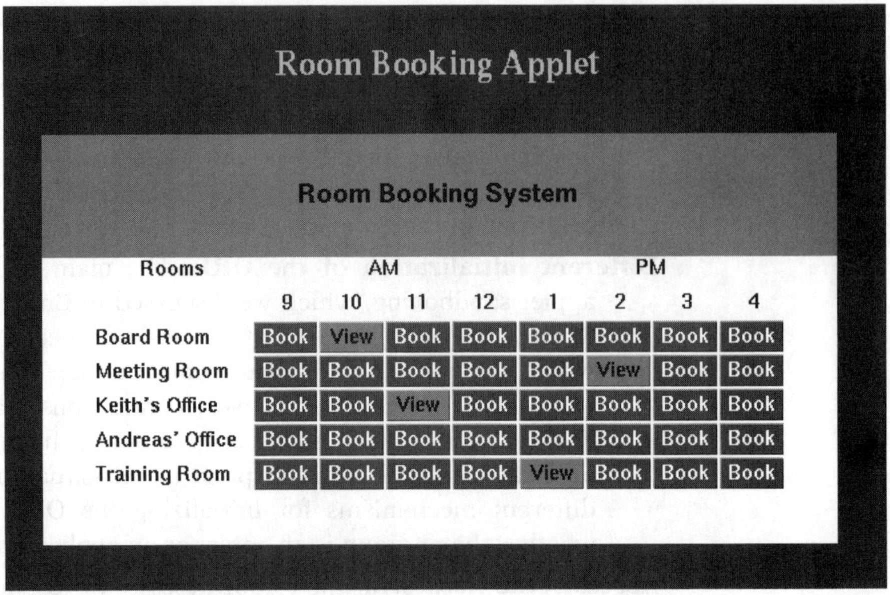

FIGURE 9.3 Applet—initial state.

6.1 Client as Applet

The first thing we have to do to develop the applet is to write an HTML page that anchors it. We give the page a title and a header and put the applet in the middle of the page. The applet class is RoomBookingApplet and we reserve a display area of 600 by 300.

```
<html><header>
<title>
Room Booking Applet
</title>
<BODY BGCOLOR=15085A TEXT=FFD700 LINK==FFFFFF VLINK=FFFFFF
ALINK=FFFFFF>
<center>

<h1>
Room Booking Applet
</h1>

<applet

code=com/wiley/compbooks/vogel/chapter9/RoomBookingImpl/RoomBoo
kingApplet.class
    width=600 height=300>
    <param name=org.omg.CORBA.ORBClass
value=com.visigenic.vbroker.orb.ORB >
```

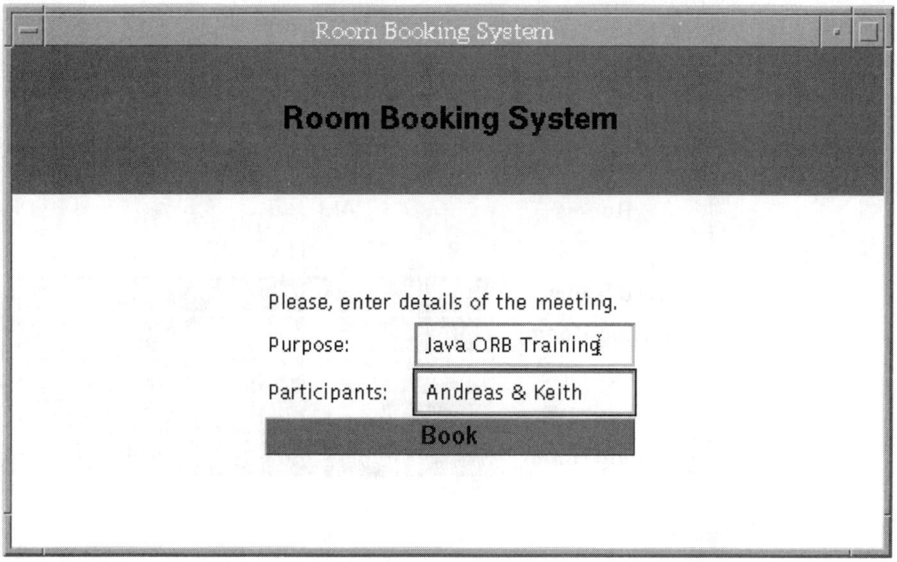

FIGURE 9.4 Application—booking form.

```
    <param name=ORBgatekeeperIOR

value=http://www.wiley.com/compbook/vogel/gatekeeper.ior>
    <param name=ORBservices value=CosNaming >
    <param name=SVCnameroot value=ROOT >

</applet>

</center>
</body></html>
```

The structure of an applet is based on the structure of its base class java.applet.Applet. We override the method init() of the applet base class. We declare a variable as a reference to an object of the class RoomBookingClient. Then we create the object within the method init(). We have two constructors for the class RoomBookingClient which are similar to the two kinds of constructors for the ORB: one to be used by applets, the other by applications. As you will see later on, these constructors use the appropriate ORB constructor and get a root context of the Naming Service using the class EasyNaming, which we introduced in Chapter 8.

We initialize the GUI with method init_GUI() on the object client of class RoomBookingClient. To do this we have to provide an object of class java.awt.Container. The Applet class extends the Container class.

We start by calling the method init_from_ns() on the client object which obtains the Meeting Factory and Room naming context references

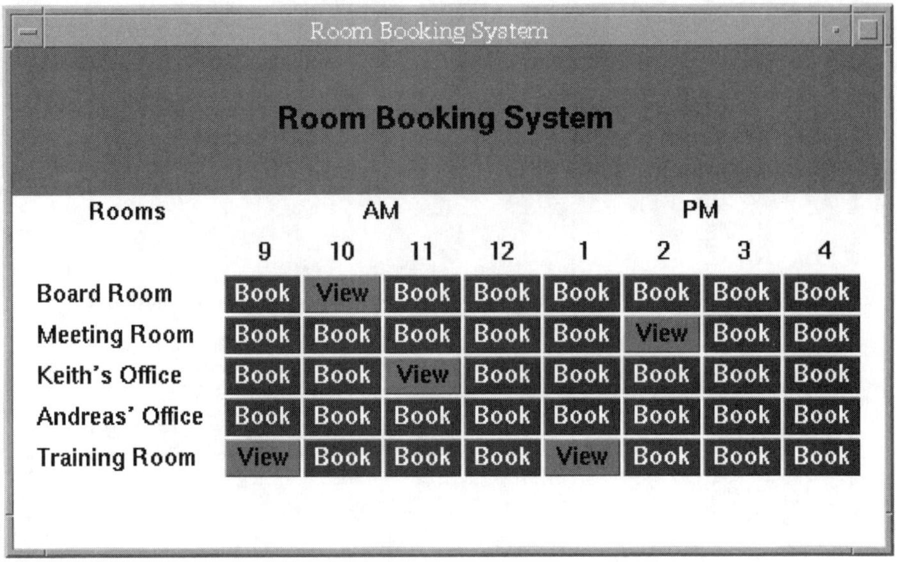

FIGURE 9.5 Application—view after booking.

from the Naming Service. Then we invoke the method `view()` which obtains the available rooms from the Naming Service and invokes the operation View() on each of these Room objects.

```
package com.wiley.compbooks.vogel.chapter9.RoomBookingImpl;

import java.awt.*;
import java.awt.event.*;
import org.omg.CORBA.*;
import com.wiley.compbooks.vogel.chapter9.RoomBooking.*;
import
com.wiley.compbooks.vogel.chapter9.RoomBooking.RoomPackage.*;

public class RoomBookingClientApplet
    extends java.applet.Applet {

    private RoomBookingClient client;

    // override init method of Class Applet
    public void init() {

        // create a RoomBookingClient client -
        // using the applet constructor
        client = new RoomBookingClient( this );

        // initialise the GUI
        client.init_GUI( this );
```

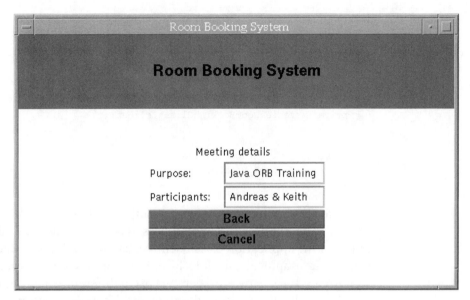

FIGURE 9.6 Application—cancel form.

```
        // initialise the Naming Service
        client.init_from_ns();

        // view existing bookings
        client.view();
    }


}
```

6.2 Client as Application

To make the Room Booking System client a Java application we implement a class RoomBookingClientApplication. This class extends java.awt.Frame, a specialization of the class java.awt.Component. The application class also implements the Java interface java.awt.WindowListener.

The implementation of the constructor of the RoomBookingClient-Application class invokes the constructor of the superclass (java.awt.Frame). Its only parameter sets the title of the corresponding window. We pass the string "Room Booking System" to the constructor (see Figure 9.4).

```
package com.wiley.compbooks.vogel.chapter9.RoomBookingImpl;

import java.awt.*;
import org.omg.CORBA.*;
import com.wiley.compbooks.vogel.chapter9.RoomBooking.*;
```

```
import
com.wiley.compbooks.vogel.chapter9.RoomBooking.RoomPackage.*;

public class RoomBookingClientApplication
    extends Frame
    implements Runnable {

    private static RoomBookingClient client;

    // constructor
    RoomBookingClientApplication() {
        super( "Room Booking System" );
    }
```

We also implement the `main()` method of the class, which is similar to the `init()` method of the applet class. The `main()` method must create an object of the application class itself. We call this object `gui` since it plays the role of our graphical user interface. We again create an object of the class `RoomBookingClient`. However, here we use a different constructor that is suitable for applications rather than applets. Then we again initialize the GUI and obtain some object references from the Naming Service by calling `init_from_ns()` on the client object. Then we invoke the method `view()` to get the booking information from each Room.

```
public static void main( String args[]) {

        // create an object of its own class
        RoomBookingClientApplication gui =
            new RoomBookingClientApplication();

        // create a RoomBookingClient object -
        // using the application constructor
        client = new RoomBookingClient();

        // initialise the GUI
        client.init_GUI( gui );

        // initialise the Naming Service
        client.init_from_ns();

        // view existing bookings
        client.view();
    }
}
```

6.3   Client-Type Independent Code

In this subsection we explain the client code which is independent of the applet or application details, that is, the client code that makes calls to the various object implementations. This code is encapsulated in a class

`RoomBookingClient`. The code of the class is rather voluminous, mainly due to the necessity of managing the graphical user interface. We will partition the code to aid understanding.

6.3.1 Overview of Methods

The class `RoomBookingClient` implements the following methods:

```
public void init_GUI( java.awt.Container gui )
```

initializes the graphical user interface.

```
public void init_from_ns()
```

gets the room context from the root context and obtains a reference to the Meeting Factory by resolving it from a predefined name.

```
public boolean view()
```

queries all rooms and displays the result at the user interface.

```
public boolean cancel()
```

cancels a selected booking.

```
public boolean process_slot(int selected_room, int selected_slot)
```

processes the event of clicking a button to book or view a meeting. It decides if the room is free and a booking can be made or if the booking details should be displayed.

```
public boolean meeting_details()
```

queries and displays the details of a meeting. The method deals mainly with GUI programming; the code is shown in the Appendix on the companion website.

```
public void booking_form()
```

produces a booking form for a user to enter meeting details. As this is pure GUI programming, we have omitted its explanation in the following text. The complete code is in the Appendix on the companion website.

```
public boolean book()
```

creates a meeting and books it into a selected slot.

```
public boolean actionPerformed()
```

catches and processes user events.

6.3.2 Variable Declarations

We start the implementation of the class with a number of local variables. The buttons are defined as `public` because they are used by the applet and application objects.

```
package com.wiley.compbooks.vogel.chapter9.RoomBookingImpl;

import java.awt.*;
import java.awt.event.*;
import org.omg.CORBA.*;
import org.omg.CosNaming.*;
import com.wiley.compbooks.vogel.chapter8.naming.*;
import com.wiley.compbooks.vogel.chapter9.RoomBooking.*;
import
com.wiley.compbooks.vogel.chapter9.RoomBooking.RoomPackage.*;

public class RoomBookingClient implements ActionListener {

    public Button viewButton;
    public Button bookButton;
    public Button cancelButton;
    public Button[][] slotButton;

    private TextField participants_tf;
    private TextField purpose_tf;

    private Panel mainPanel;
    private Panel titlePanel;

    private boolean[][] booked;

    private int selected_room;

    private int selected_slot;

    private ORB orb;
    private NamingContext room_context;
    private EasyNaming easy_naming;

    private MeetingFactory meeting_factory;
    private Room[] rooms;
    private Meeting[] meetings;
    private String ior;

    Color green = new Color( 0, 94, 86 );
    Color red = new Color( 255, 61, 61 );
```

6.3.3 Constructors

The class `RoomBookingClient` has two constructors, one each for applets and applications.

Constructor for applets. The constructor for applets has a single parameter of type `java.applet.Applet`. It initializes the ORB in a way that is convenient for applets.

```
// constructor for applets
  RoomBookingClient( java.applet.Applet applet ) {

      try {
          // initialize the ORB
          orb = ORB.init( applet );
          easy_naming = new EasyNaming( orb );
      }
      catch(SystemException system_exception ) {
          System.err.println( "constructor RoomBookingClient:
"         system_exception );
      }
  }
```

Constructor for applications. The constructor for Java applications initializes the ORB in the default way.

```
// constructor for applications
  // using a stringified IOR to get a root context
  RoomBookingClient() {

      try {
          // initialize the ORB
          orb = ORB.init();

          easy_naming = new EasyNaming( orb );
      }
      catch(SystemException system_exception ) {
          System.err.println( "constructor RoomBookingClient:
"         system_exception );
      }
  }
```

6.3.4   *init_GUI()*

The method `init_GUI()` defines the principal layout of our graphical user interface. It takes one argument, which is of type `java.awt.Container`. Depending on where we call the method from, we supply either an object of type `Applet` or of type `Frame` which are both extensions of the `Container` class. The relationships between these classes are shown in Figure 9.7.

After setting the background and creating some button objects, we create two panels, one for the title and another one where we display information from the Room Booking system. For the layout we use the Java layout manager and a `BorderLayout`.

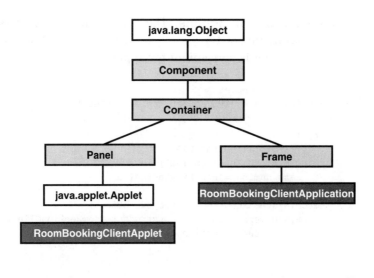

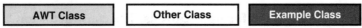

FIGURE 9.7 GUI class relationships.

```java
public void init_GUI( java.awt.Container gui ) {

        // initialize widgets

        gui.setBackground( Color.white );

        viewButton = new Button("Back");
        viewButton.setFont(new Font("Helvetica", Font.BOLD,
14));
        viewButton.setBackground( red );
        viewButton.setActionCommand("View");
        viewButton.addActionListener( (ActionListener) this );

        bookButton = new Button("Book");
        bookButton.setFont(new Font("Helvetica", Font.BOLD,
14));
        bookButton.setBackground( red );
        bookButton.setActionCommand("Book");
        bookButton.addActionListener( (ActionListener) this );

        cancelButton = new Button("Cancel");
        cancelButton.setFont(new Font("Helvetica", Font.BOLD,
14));
        cancelButton.setBackground( red );
        cancelButton.setActionCommand("Cancel");
        cancelButton.addActionListener( (ActionListener) this
);
```

```
        mainPanel = new Panel();
        titlePanel = new Panel();

        titlePanel.setLayout( new GridLayout(3,1));
        titlePanel.setFont(new Font("Helvetica", Font.BOLD,
20));
        titlePanel.setBackground( red );
        titlePanel.add( new Label("", Label.CENTER) );
        titlePanel.add( new Label("Room Booking System", Label.CENTER) );
        titlePanel.add( new Label("", Label.CENTER) );

        gui.setLayout(new BorderLayout());
        gui.add( "North", titlePanel );
        gui.add( "Center", mainPanel );
        gui.validate();
    }
```

6.3.5 *init_from_ns()*

We have decided on a naming convention for the Room Booking system illustrated in Figure 9.2. Room objects are bound to names in the context `"/BuildingApplications/Rooms"` and the Meeting Factory object is bound to the name `"/BuildingApplications/MeetingFactories/MeetingFactory"`. The method `init_from_ns()` resolves the "Rooms" context and obtains an object reference to the Meeting Factory using methods from the class `EasyNaming`, which we introduced in Chapter 8.

```
public void init_from_ns() {

        // initialize from Naming Service
        try {
            // get room context
            room_context = NamingContextHelper.narrow(
                easy_naming.resolve_from_string(
                "/BuildingApplications/Rooms" ) );
            if( room_context == null ) {
                System.err.println( "Room context is null," );
                System.err.println( "exiting ..." );
                System.exit( 1 );
            }
            // get MeetingFactory from Naming Service
            meeting_factory = MeetingFactoryHelper.narrow(
                easy_naming.resolve_from_string(
"/BuildingApplications/MeetingFactories/MeetingFactory") );
            if( meeting_factory == null ) {
                System.err.println(
                    "No Meeting Factory registred at Naming
Service" );
                System.err.println( "exiting ..." );
```

```
                System.exit( 1 );
            }
        }
        catch(SystemException system_exception ) {
            System.err.println( "Initialise ORB: " +
system_exception );
        }
        catch(UserException naming_exception) {
            System.err.println( "Initialise ORB: " +
naming_exception );
        }
    }
```

6.3.6 view()

The method view() displays information about the current availability of rooms. Therefore it has to find out about all existing rooms and call the View() operation on each of them.

Object references for the available rooms can be obtained from the Naming Service. We have already initialized a room context in which, according to our convention, room objects are bound.

We query the room context by using the operation list() defined in the interface CosNaming::NamingContext. As explained in Chapter 8, the operation list() has three parameters:

- ◆ in long length—the maximum length of the list returned by the second parameter, which is an int in Java.
- ◆ out CosNaming::BindingList—a sequence of names. Since it is an out parameter we use a Holder object in the Java language binding.
- ◆ out CosNaming::BindingIterator—a binding iterator, that is, an object from which further names can be obtained. It is also an out parameter and so we use a holder object.

In our implementation, we demonstrate the use of the list as well as the iterator. We create a temporary Vector in which we store the room objects we obtain from the naming service. We obtain those references from the room context via the resolve() operation. We then narrow the resulting object to the right type. We go through the binding list as well as through the binding iterator. Once we have obtained all the rooms and temporarily stored them in the room vector, we convert the vector into an array of rooms.

```
public boolean view() {
        try {
            // list rooms
            // initialize binding list and binding iterator
            // Holder objects for out parameter
```

```
                BindingListHolder blHolder = new
BindingListHolder();
                BindingIteratorHolder biHolder = new
BindingIteratorHolder();
                BindingHolder bHolder = new BindingHolder();
                Vector roomVector = new Vector();
                Room aRoom;

                // we are 2 rooms via the room list
                // more rooms are available from the binding
iterator
                room_context.list( 2, blHolder, biHolder );

                // get rooms from Room context of the Naming
Service
                // and put them into the roomVector
                for( i = 0; i < blHolder.value.length; i++ ) {
                   aRoom = RoomHelper.narrow(
                      room_context.resolve(
blHolder.value[i].binding_name ));
                      roomVector.addElement( aRoom );
                }
                // get remaining rooms from the iterator
                if( biHolder.value != null ) {
                   while( biHolder.value.next_one( bHolder ) ) {
                      aRoom = RoomHelper.narrow(
                         room_context.resolve(
bHolder.value.binding_name ) );
                         if( aRoom != null ) {
                            roomVector.addElement( aRoom );
                      }
                   }
                }

                // convert the roomVector into a room array
                rooms = new Room[ roomVector.size() ];
                roomVector.copyInto( rooms );

                // be fiendly with system resources
                if( biHolder.value != null )
                   biHolder.value.destroy();
```

We create an array of labels, one for each room, that is eventually used to display the names of the rooms. We also create an array of type `boolean` for internal use, to store information about whether each slot is already booked or not.

```
                // create labels and slots according to the number
of rooms
                Label[] r_label = new Label[rooms.length];
                slotButton =
                   new Button[rooms.length][MaxSlots.value];
```

```
    booked =
        new boolean[rooms.length][MaxSlots.value];
    mainPanel.removeAll();
```

Then we define the layout of the rest of the table.

```
    // define layout for the table
    GridBagLayout gridbag = new GridBagLayout();
    GridBagConstraints c = new GridBagConstraints();
    mainPanel.setLayout(gridbag);

    c.fill = GridBagConstraints.BOTH;

    c.gridwidth = 2;
    c.gridheight = 1;
    Label room_label = new Label("Rooms", Label.CENTER
);
    room_label.setFont(new Font("Helvetica", Font.BOLD,
14));
    gridbag.setConstraints( room_label, c);
    mainPanel.add( room_label );

    // and so on for the header of the table
```

Next we initialize the elements of the label array by creating objects of type java.awt.Label. The constructor we use takes a string argument, which we set to the name of a room. We obtain the name by invoking the accessor method for the attribute name of the interface Room.

```
    // show the label with the room name
    for( int i = 0; i < rooms.length; i++ ) {
        c.gridwidth = 2;
        c.gridheight = 1;
        r_label[i] = new Label( rooms[i].name() );
        r_label[i].setFont(new Font("Helvetica",
Font.BOLD, 14));
        gridbag.setConstraints( r_label[i], c);
        mainPanel.add( r_label[i] );
```

For each of the rooms we invoke the operation View(), which returns an array of Meeting objects. For such arrays a valid object reference identifies a Meeting object which is booked into the indexed slot, while a nil object reference means an empty slot. We go through the array and create either a green or red button depending on whether the slot is empty or not.

```
    // call view operation on the i-th room object
and
    // create book or free button
    meetings = rooms[i].View();
    c.gridheight = 1;
```

```
                    for( int j = 0; j < meetings.length; j++ ) {
                        if( j == meetings.length - 1 )
                            c.gridwidth =
GridBagConstraints.REMAINDER;
                        else
                            c.gridwidth = 1;
                        if( meetings[j] == null ) {
                            // slot is free
                            slotButton[i][j] = new Button("Book");
                            slotButton[i][j].setBackground( green
);
                            slotButton[i][j].setForeground(
Color.white );
                            slotButton[i][j].setFont(new
Font("Helvetica",
                                Font.BOLD, 14));
slotButton[i][j].setActionCommand("Slot"+i+j);
                            slotButton[i][j].addActionListener(
(ActionListener) this );
                            booked[i][j] = false;
                        }
                        else {
                            // slot is booked - view or cancel
                            slotButton[i][j] = new Button("View");
                            slotButton[i][j].setBackground( red );
                            slotButton[i][j].setFont(new
Font("Helvetica",
                                Font.BOLD, 14));
slotButton[i][j].setActionCommand("Slot"+i+j);
                            slotButton[i][j].addActionListener(
(ActionListener) this );
                            booked[i][j] = true;
                        }
                        gridbag.setConstraints( slotButton[i][j],
c);
                        mainPanel.add( slotButton[i][j] );
                    }
                }

            // some more laying out

            mainPanel.validate();
        }

        catch(SystemException system_exception) {
            System.err.println("View: " + system_exception);
        }
        catch(UserException naming_exception) {
            System.err.println("View: " + naming_exception);
        }
        return true;
    }
```

6.3.7 cancel()

To cancel a meeting, the method cancel() invokes the operation Cancel() on the appropriate room, providing the selected slot as an argument. If the selected slot does not contain a Meeting object reference the operation Cancel() raises an exception of type NoMeetingInThisSlot. This can only happen when there are multiple clients running which attempt to cancel the same meeting in overlapping time intervals. A more sophisticated approach would be to use the CORBA Transaction Service.

```
public boolean cancel() {
      try {
          rooms[selected_room].Cancel(
              Slot.from_int(selected_slot) );
      }
      catch(NoMeetingInThisSlot no_meeting ) {
          System.err.println("Cancel :" + no_meeting );
      }
      catch(SystemException system_exception) {
          System.err.println("Cancel :" + system_exception);
      }

      // show bookings of all rooms
      return view();
  }
```

The method process_slot() sets state variables and determines whether a red or a green button has been pressed and how to proceed in each case. If a green button was pressed it invokes the method booking_form(), allowing the user to enter meeting details. If a red button was pressed it invokes the method booking_details(), which displays the meeting details of the selected meeting and provides buttons to cancel the meeting or to return to the main view. The implementation of both methods is omitted, but the complete code is in the Appendix on the website.

```
public boolean process_slot( int selected_room, int
selected_slot ) {
      this.selected_room = selected_room;
      this.selected_slot = selected_slot;

      if( booked[selected_room][selected_slot] ) {
          // view the meeting details, potentially cancel
          meeting_details();
      }
      else {
          // get meeting details and book
          booking_form();
      }
      return true;
  }
```

6.3.8 book()

The booking of a meeting, managed by the method book(), involves two tasks: creation of the appropriate Meeting object and booking of the selected meeting. We create the Meeting object using the Meeting Factory. This is done by invoking the operation CreateMeeting(). Its two parameters are obtained from two text fields.

The newly created meeting is then booked by calling the operation Book() on the selected room object. It is again possible that someone else has booked the slot in the meantime. If so, we catch an exception of type SlotAlreadyTaken.

```
public boolean book() {
        try {
            Meeting meeting =
                meeting_factory.CreateMeeting(
                    purpose_tf.getText(),
                    participants_tf.getText() );
            System.out.println( "meeting created" );
            String p = meeting.purpose();
            System.out.println("Purpose: "+p);
            rooms[selected_room].Book(
                Slot.from_int(selected_slot), meeting );
            System.out.println( "room is booked" );
        }
        catch(SlotAlreadyTaken already_taken ) {
            System.out.println( "book :" + already_taken );
        }
        catch(SystemException system_exception ) {
            System.out.println( "book :" + system_exception );
        }

        // show bookings of all rooms
        return view();
    }
```

6.3.9 actionPerformed()

The method actionPerformed() is defined in the interface ActionListener which the class RoomBookingClient implements. We check if an event that occurred relates to one of the actions we have defined for the buttons we introduced in the GUI. If this is the case we invoke the appropriate method.

```
// catch and process events
    public void actionPerformed( ActionEvent ev ) {

        if(ev.getActionCommand().equals("View"))
            view();
        if(ev.getActionCommand().equals("Book"))
            book();
```

```
if(ev.getActionCommand().equals("Cancel"))
    cancel();

// look for free/book button pressed
for( int i = 0; i < no_of_rooms(); i++ ) {
    for( int j = 0; j < MaxSlots.value; j++ ) {
        if( ev.getActionCommand().equals("Slot"+i+j) )
{
            process_slot( i, j );
        }
    }
}
}
```

7 Extensions to the Example Application

The example can be extended to include various other CORBA services. We outline possible extensions.

The Trading Service can be used as an alternative to the Naming Service for locating objects. The server classes would *register* objects with the Trading Service and a client would *query* the Trading Service to search for Room and Meeting Factory objects.

The Transaction Service could be used to ensure ACID properties to booking and cancel operations. In the current implementation we do not explicitly roll back the creation of a Meeting object when it cannot be booked into a particular slot.

The Security Service could be used to authenticate users and to authorize a user to execute certain operations. For example, only a user who booked a meeting originally should be allowed to cancel it. We explain approaches to authentication and authorization with CORBA in Chapter 12.

The Event Service could be used to notify certain users that a meeting in which they are participating is now starting. The Event Service is introduced and explained in Chapter 11.

We revisit the room booking application in Chapter 13 when we explain design approaches for scalability.

10

Advanced Features

In this chapter we explain and give examples of how to use some advanced CORBA features. The features explained in detail here have already been introduced in Chapters 6 and 7: TypeCodes, Anys, Interface Repository (IR), Dynamic Invocation Interface (DII), Dynamic Skeleton Interface (DSI), Applet Servers, and the Tie approach.

To demonstrate these advanced features we will adapt the extended Hello World example from Chapter 5. For the implementation of objects in applets we present a more appropriate example.

1   The Any Type and TypeCodes

In this section we demonstrate the use of Anys as parameters of IDL-defined operations. We use a variant of the extended Hello World example in Chapter 5.

1.1 Interface Specification

In this IDL, although we have changed the signature of the interface specification, we retain the semantics of the hello() operation. Both the result of the operation and the only parameter are of type Any. As before, the operation will return the location of the object implementation as a string, this time contained in an Any. This is an example of the use of a predefined data type within an Any.

The any_time parameter is an example of passing a user-defined data type in an Any. The parameter will contain a structure with two fields, both short integers, representing the minute and hour of the local time at the object implementation. Although this structure is not directly used in the specification of the operation, its definition needs to be available to the client and the server. Hence we define the Time structure within the module.

```
module com {
  . . .
module chapter10 {
module any {
module HelloWorld {

    struct Time {
        short hour;
        short minute;
    };

    interface GoodDay {
        any hello( out any any_time );
    };
};  . . . };
```

1.2 Object Implementation

The object implementation class GoodDayImpl extends the servant base class _GoodDayImplBase which is generated by the IDL compiler. We also keep the same private variable any_location and the constructor.

```
package com.wiley.compbooks.vogel.chapter10.any.HelloWorldImpl;

import java.util.Date;
import org.omg.CORBA.*;
import com.wiley.compbooks.vogel.chapter10.any.HelloWorld.*;

class GoodDayImpl extends _GoodDayBaseImpl {

    private String location;
```

```
// constructor
GoodDayImpl( String location ) {
    this.location = location;
}
```

The signature of the method `hello()` corresponds to the IDL mapping for Anys, as explained in Chapter 6. We have an Any for the result and declare a variable of type `AnyHolder` for the `out` parameter.

We create a `date` object, as in the original example. In the next step we create an object of the class `Time`, which is the Java representation of the IDL type definition `struct Time`. We use the default constructor of this class, which takes two parameters corresponding to the fields of the structure. We provide values for the parameters by invoking methods on the object `date` to obtain the current time in hours and minutes. Again we have to cast the integer values to type `short`.

Objects of type Any are created by the ORB, by calling `create_any()` on *the ORB object*. Now we have to insert the value of the time variable into the Any. We do this using the `insert()` methods which are generated in the helper class by the IDL compiler. Now the Any object `any_time` contains the value of `struct_time`. Figure 10.1 illustrates the object `any_time`.

```
// method
public Any hello( AnyHolder any_time)
    throws SystemException {
      // get location time of the server
      Date date = new Date();

      // create time-structure assign hour and minute to it
      Time struct_time = new Time(
          (short) date.getHours(),
          (short) date.getMinutes() );

      // create an any and shuffle structure into it
      any_time.value = _orb().create_any();
      TimeHelper.insert( any_time.value, struct_time );

      // create an any and shuffle location into it
      Any any_location = _orb().create_any();
      any_location.insert_string( location );
```

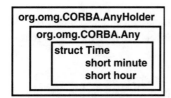

FIGURE 10.1 AnyHolder object.

```
            return any_location;
        }
    }
```

The operation result is stored in the variable `any_location`, an Any holding a string value. Once again we obtain an Any object from the ORB. Since string is a predefined IDL type, we insert the value of `location` by calling the method `insert_string()` on the Any object. There are similar methods, listed in Chapter 6, defined in the class `CORBA.Any` for the other predefined data types.

The last task of the implementation is to return the Any `any_location`.

The server class implementation is the same as in Chapter 5. It is *also* called `server`, but it is defined in a different package.

1.3 Client Implementation

The client implementation follows the same structure that we used before.

1.3.1 *Initialization and Invocation*

We declare two variables `any_location` and `any_time` of type `Any` and `AnyHolder` for the method's result and its parameter, respectively.

```
package com.wiley.compbooks.vogel.chapter10.any.HelloWorldImpl;

import java.util.*;
import java.io.*;
import org.omg.CORBA.*;
import com.wiley.compbooks.vogel.chapter10.any.HelloWorld.*;

public class Client {

    public static void main(String args[]) {

        AnyHolder any_time = new AnyHolder();
        Any any_location;
        // get stringified IOR from command line
        String ior = new String( args[0] );

        try {
            // initialize the ORB.
            ORB orb = ORB.init(args,null);

            // get object reference . .
            org.omg.CORBA.Object obj = orb.string_to_object(
ior );

            // and narrowed it to GoodDay
            GoodDay goodDay = GoodDayHelper.narrow( obj );
```

```
if( goodDay == null )
    System.exit( 1 );

// invoke the operation
any_location = goodDay.hello( any_time );
```

We initialize the *ORB, convert* the command-line argument into an object reference, and narrow it to the right type. Then we invoke the method `hello()` with the argument `any_time` and assign the result to `any_location`.

1.3.2   *Obtaining TypeCodes*

TypeCodes are a run-time representation of IDL types. They are explained in detail in Chapter 7. In the following example we obtain type information about the values contained in the Anys. First we declare a variable `tc` of type `TypeCode`. Then we obtain the TypeCode of the value held in the container variable `any_time`. The container object's public variable `value` stores the Any which was returned as an `out` parameter. The Any object referred to by `value` has a method `type()`, which returns the TypeCode of the stored value. In this example the value is a Java object representing an IDL struct.

A TypeCode represents an attributed type tree. It provides various methods to obtain the values of the attributes. For example, we query the Interface Repository identifier of the type by calling the method `id()` on the TypeCode object. Similarly we get the name of the type by invoking the method `name()`.

Since we are expecting the Any to contain an IDL structure, we need to traverse the type tree to obtain type information about the fields of the struct. The method `member_count()` returns the number of fields and `member_name()` returns the name of the indexed field.

Since type definitions differ in their structure, operations on TypeCode objects are only valid for particular kinds of TypeCodes. If an inappropriate method is invoked, the exception `BadKind` is raised. The method `member_name()` raises the exception `Bounds` when the index is out of bounds.

```
            // declare a type code object
            TypeCode tc;

            // get type of any_time.value and print type
information
            tc = any_time.value.type();
            try {
                System.out.println("IfRepId of any_time: " +
tc.id() );
                System.out.println("Type code of any_time: " +
tc.name() );
                for( int i = 0; i < tc.member_count(); i++ )
```

```
                            System.out.println("\tname: " +
tc.member_name(i) );
                }
                catch(org.omg.CORBA.TypeCodePackage.BadKind ex_bk)
{
                    System.err.println("any_time: " + ex_bk);
                }
                catch(org.omg.CORBA.TypeCodePackage.Bounds ex_b) {
                    System.err.println("any_time: " + ex_b);
                }
```

In the following code, we check if the value of `any_location` is of the expected kind, `TCKind.tk_string`, and if so we query for its length. Note that the length refers to the type definition and not the current value. The method `length()` returns the maximum size of a bounded string, sequence, or array. If the type is unbounded it returns zero. We must again catch the exception `BadKind`.

```
                // get length any_location.value
                tc = any_location.type();
                try {
                    if( tc.kind() == TCKind.tk_string )
                        System.out.println( "length of
any_location: "
                                + tc.length() );
                    else
                        System.out.println("any_location does NOT
contain a string.");
                }
                catch(org.omg.CORBA.TypeCodePackage.BadKind ex_bt)
{
                    System.err.println("any_location: " + ex_bt);
                }
```

When executing the client, the code above will produce the following result:

```
IfRepId of any_time: IDL:HelloWorld/Time:1.0

Type code of any_time: Time

        name: hour
        name: minute

length of any_location: 0
```

1.3.3   Unpacking the Results

Now we proceed to the normal behavior of the client; that is, we obtain the results and print them. We can either print the Anys directly by using their predefined toString() method or we can obtain the contained value and can print it in a customized manner. We show both possibilities.

First we print the Anys any_location and any_time.value in the default format. Then we obtain the string from any_location by invoking the extract_string() method. To get the time object from the Any any_time.value we call the extract method provided by the helper class, which takes an Any as an argument. Once we have the values in variables of basic types we print the message in the same way as in the original example.

```java
// get String from any_locality
String locality = any_locality.extract_string();

// get struct from any_time
Time time = TimeHelper.extract( any_time.value );

// print results to stdout
System.out.println("Print Anys:");
System.out.println("any_locality: ");
System.out.println( any_locality );
System.out.println("time:");
System.out.println( any_time.value );

// print results to stdout
System.out.println("Hello World!");
if( time.minute < 10 )
    System.out.println("The local time in " +
        locality +
        " is " + time.hour + ":0" +
        time.minute + "." );
else
    System.out.println("The local time in " +
        locality +
        " is " + time.hour + ":" +
        time.minute + "." );
}
```

When the client is invoked, it prints the results in the following form:

```
Print Anys:

any_location:
"Brisbane"

time:
struct Time{short hour=12/ort minute=23;}

Hello World!
The local time in Brisbane is 12:23.
```

2 *Interface Repository and Dynamic Invocation Interface*

In this section we present a client that is capable of invoking operations on an object whose type was unknown to the client at compile time. So far, clients have used stub code generated by an IDL compiler to create a proxy object on which they have invoked methods corresponding to each operation. The structure of the example is

- ♦ Initialize the ORB (section 2.1)
- ♦ Browse the Interface Repository (section 2.2)
- ♦ Unparse and print the type information obtained from the Interface Repository (section 2.3)
- ♦ Create a Request object (sections 2.4–2.6)
- ♦ Invoke an operation using the Dynamic Invocation Interface (section 2.7)
- ♦ Obtain and print results (section 2.8)

To make invocations on objects without having access to IDL-generated code we have to obtain information about the interface type of the object and invoke a method without an IDL-generated client-side proxy class. The first task is carried out using the Interface Repository, which contains type information about interfaces. Typically the Interface Repository is populated by the IDL compiler. Our client will query the Interface Repository using a standard method on the object reference, defined in CORBA::Object. This returns a reference to an Interface Repository object that represents the target object's interface type. The object is part of a type tree which the client can traverse.

The second task is carried out using the Dynamic Invocation Interface (DII). It provides a Request object that can be used for the invocation of methods on arbitrary objects. The DII's interface Request is defined in the CORBA module using pseudo-IDL. It is the programmer's responsibility to initialize a Request pseudo-object with all the necessary information (a target object reference, an operation name, argument types and values) in order to make an invocation.

Figure 10.2 illustrates the process by which interface information is obtained and used to invoke the object implementation. The IDL compiler creates the skeleton code for the server side as usual and populates the Interface Repository with the types specified in the IDL file. The client can then query the Interface Repository about the type of Any object reference it obtains.

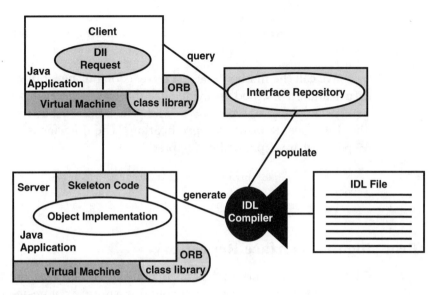

FIGURE 10.2 DII client.

2.1 Initializing the ORB

The client obtains an object reference from, for example, a stringified object reference or from the Naming or Trading Service. For simplicity, we use stringified object references in our example. Note that we cannot narrow the object reference to its particular interface type because we do not know its type and do not have access to the narrow method, which is part of the code generated by the IDL compiler.

```
package com.wiley.compbooks.vogel.chapter10.dii;

import java.io.*;
import org.omg.CORBA.*;
import org.omg.CORBA.InterfaceDefPackage.*;

public class DiiClient {

    public static void main(String args[]) {

        // get stringified IOR from command line
        String ior = new String( args[0] );

        try {
            // initialize the ORB
            ORB orb = ORB.init();
```

```
                // get object reference
                org.omg.CORBA.Object obj = orb.string_to_object(
        ior );
```

We call the method _get_interface() on our new object reference. This is a standard method, provided by the class org.omg.CORBA.Object, which returns an object of type InterfaceDef. The InterfaceDef interface is defined in the Interface Repository specification. The interfaces of the Interface Repository are explained in Chapter 2.

```
                // get interface definition from Interface
        Repository
                InterfaceDef if_def = obj._get_interface();
```

2.2   Browsing the Interface Repository

The InterfaceDef interface has an operation describe_interface() that returns a structure FullInterfaceDescription. It contains a number of nested structures that represent the operations and attributes contained in the interface. One of the nested structures, OperationDescription, describing an operation, also contains nested structures describing the operation's parameters.

The structure FullInterfaceDescription represents a flattening of the objects in the Interface Repository to provide all the necessary type information in a single data structure without the need to make further calls to Interface Repository objects to query their types. Alternatively, traversal of the Interface Repository can be done by obtaining object references to OperationDef objects and AttributeDef objects that can be queried to discover their component definitions.

```
            // using the Interface Repository
            // get full interface description
            FullInterfaceDescription full_if_desc =
                if_def.describe_interface();
```

In our client we store the interface description in a variable full_if_desc. The type is defined in IDL as the following struct. We only show the type definitions we use in the example.

```
typedef string Identifier;
typedef sequence <OperationDescription> OpDescriptionSeq;

struct FullInterfaceDescription {
    Identifier  name;
    RepositoryId       id;
    RepositoryId       defined_in;
    VersionSpec        version;
    OpDescriptionSeq  operations;
```

```
        AttrDescriptionSeq attributes;
        RepositoryIdSeq    base_interfaces;
        TypeCode           type;
    }
```

We use the members name and operations which is a sequence of OperationDescription structs:

```
    typedef sequence < ParameterDescription > ParDescriptionSeq;
    typedef sequence < ExceptionDescription > ExcDescriptionSeq;

    struct OperationDescription {
        Identifier name;
        RepositoryId id;
        RepositoryId defined_in;
        VersionSpec version;
        TypeCode result;
        OperationMode mode;
        ContextIdSeq contexts;
        ParDescriptionSeq parameters;
        ExcDescriptionSeq exceptions;
    };
```

In turn, parameters and exceptions that are part of an operation are described by structures.

2.3   A Simple Unparser

The following code traverses the nested structures and prints all operations of the interface in a simplified version of OMG IDL syntax. We go through all the operations defined in the interface, obtaining the result type in the form of a TypeCode, the operation name which is a string, and the parameters. The method `toString()` is available on TypeCode objects and prints them in IDL syntax.

```
    int no_of_parameters;

    // print various information
    System.out.println("Querying the Interface Repository\n");
    System.out.println("interface " + full_if_desc.name + "
{\n" );

    for( int i = 0; i < full_if_desc.operations.length; i++ ) {

        no_of_parameters =
full_if_desc.operations[i].parameters.length;
        System.out.println(" " +

        // print the type code of the operation's result
        full_if_desc.operations[i].result + " " +
```

```
        // print the name of the operation
        full_if_desc.operations[i].name + " ("
);
```

The parameters are described by a sequence of structures of type ParamDescription:

```
enum ParameterMode { PARAM_IN, PARAM_OUT, PARAM_INOUT };

struct ParamDescription {
    Identifier      name;
    TypeCode        type;
    IDLType         type_def;
    ParameterMode   mode;
};
```

The parameter's type member is of type TypeCode and its name is an Identifier, which is an alias of string. The parameter mode is an integer and its values are defined in the enumerated type ParameterMode. We have to convert the mode value into strings.

```
        // define and initialize text representations
        // for parameter modes
        String mode, in, inout, out;
        in = new String("in");
        inout = new String("inout");
        out = new String("out");
        char last_char = ',';

        // print parameters of the operations
        for( int j = 0; j < no_of_parameters; j++ ) {

                // set the right text for the parameter mode
                switch
(full_if_desc.operations[i].parameters[j].mode.value() ) {
                        case ParameterMode._PARAM_IN:
                                mode = in; break;
                        case ParameterMode._PARAM_INOUT:
                                mode = inout; break;
                        case ParameterMode._PARAM_OUT:
                                mode = out; break;
                        default:
                                mode = new String("unknown mode");
                }

                // deal with separating commas
                if( j == no_of_parameters - 1 )
                                last_char = ' ';

                // print mode, type and name of the parameter
                System.out.println("          " +
```

```
                    mode + " " +
                    full_if_desc.operations[i].parameters[j].type + " "
                    full_if_desc.operations[i].parameters[j].name +
last_char
                );
        }
        System.out.println(" );\n};\n");
```

2.4   Initializing Requests

Now that we have discovered the type of the object, we want to invoke an operation on it. We will need the DII to do this. This requires the creation of a Request object, as illustrated in Figure 10.3. A Request has three components:

- ◆ string—carries the name of the operation to be invoked
- ◆ NamedValue—carries the type and value of the operation's result
- ◆ NVList—carries the mode, type, and value of the operation's parameters

2.5   Creating Supporting Objects

We now create and initialize the Named Value for the result and the NVList containing the arguments to the operation. A Named Value is a data type defined in pseudo-IDL in the module CORBA. It is a triple of a name of type String, a typed value of type Any, and a mode of type int. Appropriate constants are defined in the class org.omg.CORBA.ParameterMode.

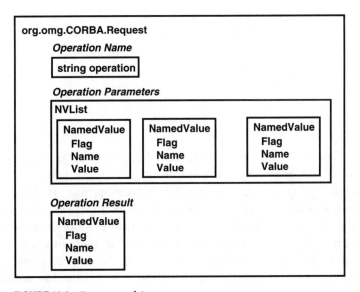

FIGURE 10.3   Request object.

An NVList is an object containing a list of Named Value objects. See Chapter 7 for details.

To initialize an operation result we only need to set the type we expect by initializing the value with a dummy value of the right type. After the invocation, the value will hold the result of the operation.

There are no operations to create and manage Named Value objects directly. Instead we create an NVList result_list of length one and insert a single element later using the method add_value(). This method has three parameters, one for each of the components of a Named Value.

The tricky part is to create an Any that carries the type and the value of an argument. For out parameters we only need to put the type information into the Any. The class Any provides methods to get and set the TypeCode of an Any object (see Chapter 6). So we just create a new Any object and set the type using the set method. We have this encapsulated in a class called DiiAnySupport:

```
package com.wiley.compbooks.vogel.chapter10.dii;

import org.omg.CORBA.*;

public class DiiAnySupport {

    private ORB orb;

    DiiAnySupport() {
        orb = ORB.init();
    }

    // creates an Any and sets the type
    Any TC2Any( TypeCode tc, int mode ) {

        Any resAny = orb.create_any();
        resAny.type( tc );
        return resAny;
    }

}
```

The class deals only with setting the types of Any objects but not their values. This is needed for parameters which are tagged as in or inout. The portability layer defined in the IDL/Java mapping provides us with output streams as a mechanism to solve this problem. If you look at the code generated for IDL-defined types you will find examples of the use of output streams. The following code shows the implementation of the method insert() defined in the class TimeHelper which has been generated by the IDL compiler. It is the Helper class for the struct Time that we defined for the example above.

```
public static void insert(
    org.omg.CORBA.Any any,
    com.wiley.compbooks.vogel.chapter10.any.HelloWorld.Time
value) {
    org.omg.CORBA.portable.OutputStream output =
        any.create_output_stream();
    write(output, value);
    any.read_value(output.create_input_stream(), type());
}
```

The method `insert()` creates an output stream and writes the values into it. Then it inserts the output stream into the Any, providing a TypeCode to ensure the type safety of the insertion. The filling of the output stream is delegated to a method `write()` which is shown here:

```
public static void write(
    org.omg.CORBA.portable.OutputStream _output,
    com.wiley.compbooks.vogel.chapter10.any.HelloWorld.Time
value) {

    _output.write_short(value.hour);
    _output.write_short(value.minute);
}
```

The method takes the two fields of the struct and writes them into the output stream using methods of the output stream class. To write output streams for arbitrary data types you would need to traverse the type tree and write the leaves of this tree, which are values of predefined IDL types, to the stream using the corresponding methods provided by the output stream class.

2.6   Using the Supporting Objects

We now return to our DII client class. For simplicity we have chosen to invoke the first operation of the interface specification, `full if desc.operations[0]`. This is the interface specification for the object whose object reference we obtained from a string when initializing the client.

We create an instance of the DiiAnySupport class that we introduced above. Then we create two Name Value lists, one for the operation result, `result list`, and the other for the operation's parameter list, `arg_list`.

For the operation result, we only have to set the type which we expect the operation to return. We get an Any object of the right type for the result by calling the method `TC2Any()` on the DiiAnySupport object. The list is populated using the `NVList` method `add value()`.

```
// DiiClient.java
            // using the DII to make an invocation
            System.out.println("Make a DII call\n");
```

```
                // create a support object

                DiiAnySupport dii_any_support = new

DiiAnySupport();

                // create and initialize result
                NVList result_list = orb.create_list( 0 );

                result_list.add_value( "",
                    dii_any_support.TC2Any(
                        full_if_desc.operations[0].result,
                        ParameterMode._PARAM_OUT ),
                    0 );

                // create and initialize arg_list

                NVList arg_list = orb.create_list( 0 );

                no_of_parameters =
full_if_desc.operations[0].parameters.length;
                for( int i = 0; i < no_of_parameters; i++ ) {

                    arg_list.add_value(

full_if_desc.operations[0].parameters[i].name,
                        dii_any_support.TC2Any(

full_if_desc.operations[0].parameters[i].type,

full_if_desc.operations[0].parameters[i].mode.value() ),

full_if_desc.operations[0].parameters[i].mode.value() + 1 );
                }
```

For the argument list we use a for loop over the parameter specifications from the interface description and add corresponding values for each argument with the add value() method. The values are Any objects of the right type obtained from the DiiAnySupport object by calling the TC2Any() method. The argument list must contain values for in and inout arguments. Note that this method only deals properly with out parameters.

2.7   Creating and Invoking a Request Object

Once we have initialized the result and the arguments we can create and initialize a Request object by calling _create_request() on the object reference on which we want to invoke the operation. The method _create_request() has the following parameters:

♦ A context—which we do not use and hence initialize to a `null` object reference
♦ The operation's name—which we obtain from the interface description
♦ The arguments—which we have created in NVList `arg_list`
♦ The result—which is the first element of the NVList `result_list`

```
// create request
        Request request = obj._create_request(
            null,                            // context - not used
            full_if_desc.operations[0].name, // operation name
            arg_list,                        // NVList with arguments
            result_list.item(0)              // NamedValue for result
        );

        // invoke request
        request.invoke();
```

Now we can call the method `invoke()` on the Request object. This results in an invocation on the object reference from which we obtained the Request. Once the call is completed the Request object will place the result of the operation and the values for the inout and out parameters into the NVLists provided to its constructor.

2.8   Getting Results

Next we print the value of the result and the values of the out parameters of the operation. We use the `toString()` method on the Any objects, which allows us to print the value of Any objects directly using `System.out.println()`, as shown here.

```
        // get result
        System.out.println("result:\n " +
request.result().value() );

        // get out parameters
        CORBA.NVList nv_list = request.arguments();
        for( int i = 0; i < no_of_parameters; i++ )
            System.out.println( nv_list.item( i ).name() +
                ":\n " + nv_list.item( i ).value() );
    }
    // catch CORBA system exceptions
    catch(CORBA.SystemException ex) {
        System.err.println(ex);
    }
    }
}
```

2.9   Executing the Client

When executing the DII client we can invoke operations on arbitrary objects. In our example we invoke the first operation defined in the interface. The following output is produced when the object reference used refers to an object supporting the extended Hello World interface introduced in Chapter 5.

```
.../dii > java DiiClient
IOR:000000000000001b49444c3a48656c6c6c...

Querying the Interface Repository

interface GoodDay {

    string hello (
        out short hour,
        out short minute
    );
};

Make a DII call

result:
    any[string=Brisbane, Queensland, Australia]
hour:
    any[short=13]
minute:
    any[short=47]
```

As another example we use the DII client program to invoke the AnyHelloWorld object we implemented in section 1. Again the client queries the Interface Repository and prints the interface specification in OMG IDL syntax. As in the previous section, the interface GoodDay again provides an operation hello(). However, this time the result and the only parameter are both of type Any. The client creates the corresponding Request object and invokes it.

```
.../dii > java DiiClient
IOR:000000000000001e49444c3a48656c6c6c...

Querying the Interface Repository

interface GoodDay {

    any hello (
        out any any_time
    );
};
```

```
Make a DII call

result:
    any[any=any[string=Brisbane, Queensland, Australia]]
any_time:
    any[any=any[struct Time{short hour=14/ort minute=28;}]]
```

There is a tool called Universal CORBA Client which improves the client outlined previously by providing a good graphical user interface for selecting operations and entering and displaying parameters. This tool was implemented by Gerald Vogt during his time with the authors at DSTC in Brisbane, Australia, in 1996. The implementation uses Java and Visibroker for Java. The combination of portability provided by Java and interoperability through IIOP make the tool almost universally usable. Figure 10.4 shows the Universal CORBA Client at work.

3   *Dynamic Skeleton Interface*

Similar to the DII on the client side, the Dynamic Skeleton Interface (DSI) provides an interface on the server side that allows the invocation of methods on objects without compiler-generated skeletons. We introduced the CORBA specification of the DSI in Chapter 2 and explained its mapping to

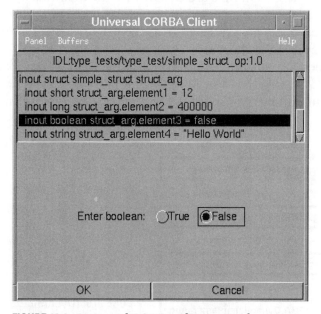

FIGURE 10.4   Universal CORBA Client at work.

Java in Chapter 7. In this section we demonstrate how to program with the DSI. Once again we use a modified Hello World example to illustrate it.

The implementation of the server class is the same as before, only we provide a different implementation of the GoodDay interface. The interface is implemented by a Java class called GoodDayImpl, but of course it is located in a separate package.

```
package com.wiley.compbooks.vogel.chapter10.dsi;

import java.io.*;
import java.util.Date;
import org.omg.CORBA.*;
class GoodDayImpl extends DynamicImplementation {
```

The implementation class extends the class DynamicImplementation. The full inheritance path is shown in Figure 10.5. As with the static implementation class we declare a private field location.

The constructor of the class calls the constructor of the superclass. Here we have to use a different constructor than in the static case. We have to provide the type information for the interface—this information is usually contained in the generated skeleton class. The constructor needs this information to create valid object reference for the object, which must contain the object's type information.

We describe the interface type in the form of an Interface Repository identifier. These identifiers are strings with the following syntax (in EBNF): "IDL:" {*module_name*"/"} *interface_name*":" *major*"." *minor*. The major/minor pair are currently always 1 and 0, as the use of versioning in the Interface Repository is not well defined.

Repository identifiers can be easily created. In our example we just hard code one into the class. More flexible and sophisticated solutions could look them up from the Interface Repository or receive them from a third party.

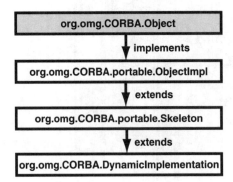

FIGURE 10.5 DynamicImplementation inheritance.

```
private String location;
    // constructor
    GoodDayImpl( String location ) {
        super( location,
```

```
"IDL:com/wiley/compbooks/vogel/chapter10/dsi/HelloWorldImpl/Goo
dDay:1.0" );
        this.location = location;
    }
```

Note that the IDL module and interface are identical to those implemented using the skeleton method; this is just another way of implementing the same interface type.

The class `DynamicImplementation` defines an abstract method `invoke()`. This method is called whenever an invocation is made on the dynamic implementation object. The method has one parameter that is of class `ServerRequest`, which is very similar to the corresponding class `Request` in the DII in structure, but different in signature. The class `ServerRequest` is defined in Java as

```
public abstract class org.omg.CORBA.ServerRequest
    extends java.lang.Object {

    public java.lang.String op_name();
    public org.omg.CORBA.Context ctx();
    public void params(org.omg.CORBA.NVList);
    public void result(org.omg.CORBA.Any);
    public void except(org.omg.CORBA.Any);
}
```

Within the implementation of the method `invoke()` we need to analyze the server request object to determine which operation has been invoked. The DSI is usually used to dynamically delegate incoming requests for operations that were not defined at the time the server was written. Of course the server must be able to interpret the semantics of the request or forward the request somewhere where it is understood. Examples of this sort of behavior can be found in generic wrappers whose clients define IDL in a particular pattern that is understood by the server, which identifies the corresponding legacy functionality to perform the required task and in bridges that simply pass on the request uninterpreted.

In our example we only provide one operation as a demonstration of dealing with the ServerRequest. This is implemented directly in the `invoke()` method. If the operation name of an incoming request is not "hello" we throw the CORBA system exception BAD_OPERATION.

```
// method
public void invoke( ServerRequest request ) {
```

```
if( !request.op_name().equals("hello") ) {
    throw new BAD_OPERATION();
}
```

Otherwise we proceed with the implementation of the hello() operation by creating a date object and getting the current time. To return the result and the out parameters we have to wrap the values in Any objects and put them into the Server Request object. This needs to be done earlier when we are expecting some arguments to our operation, as the ServerRequest requires us to pass an NVList with all the parameter names and types initialized, into which it places the values that came from the client. In our case, we are only passing out parameters, so we can create the NVList after the processing is done.

We create the Any objects in the usual way and insert our values using the appropriate insert methods on the Any object. For user-defined data types we would use output streams as described in the previous section.

```
// get local time of the server
Date date = new Date();

// create anys for hour and minute and location
Any location_any = _orb().create_any();
location_any.insert_string( location );

Any hour_any = _orb().create_any();
hour_any.insert_short( (short) date.getHours() );

Any minute_any = _orb().create_any();
minute_any.insert_short( (short) date.getMinutes() );
```

We now create a Name Value list for the arguments to which we add two elements: the two Any objects we created for the out parameters. Then we set the parameters and the result of the ServerRequest object.

```
        NVList parameters = _orb().create_list(0);
        parameters.add_value("hour", hour_any, ARG_OUT.value );
        parameters.add_value("minute", minute_any,
ARG_OUT.value );

        request.params( parameters );

        request.result( location_any );
    }
}
```

When a client invokes methods on an object implemented with the DSI, it does not notice any difference to invoking an object implemented with an IDL-generated skeleton.

4 *Tie Mechanism*

So far we have constructed statically typed object implementations by inheritance of skeleton classes generated by the IDL compiler. These skeletons implement the network management, marshaling, and incoming request delegation of the CORBA object. They are then extended to provide methods that support the operations in the IDL interface. The inheritance approach, however, has the following shortcomings.

Java single inheritance. Since Java only supports single class inheritance, an object implementation cannot extend any application-specific class as it already extends the skeleton class.

One implementation object for multiple interfaces. There are occasions where it makes sense for one Java object to implement multiple IDL interfaces, for example, an application-specific interface and a general management interface. This cannot be achieved via Java extension because the implementation object needs to extend two or more skeletons.

A solution to these problems is to use delegation instead of inheritance. This is achieved by generating a *pseudo-implementation* or *Tie class* which inherits the skeleton. However, rather than implementing the operations, this pseudo-implementation class calls methods on another object that actually implements the operations' semantics. Figure 10.6 compares the inheritance approach with the delegation approach. The delegation approach is also known as the Tie mechanism.

We use the Hello World example as introduced in Chapter 5 to demonstrate the Tie approach. We have to modify both the server class and the object implementation class and introduce the pseudo-implementation class.

Let's start with the implementation class. The only difference to the inheritance approach is in the declaration of class GoodDayImpl.

```
package com.wiley.compbooks.vogel.chapter10.tie.HelloWorldImpl;
```

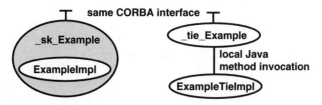

FIGURE 10.6 Inheritance versus delegation.

```
import java.util.Date;
import org.omg.CORBA.*;
import com.wiley.compbooks.vogel.chapter10.tie.HelloWorld.*;

public class GoodDayImpl implements GoodDayOperations {

    // implementation as before

}
```

While the implementation class extends the skeleton class in the inheritance approach, in the Tie approach it implements the interface GoodDayOperations. This implementation class could inherit another, application-specific class.

The interface GoodDayOperations is the same as the interface GoodDay, without extending org.omg.CORBA.Object. It simply declares the signature of the methods corresponding to the IDL operations, and because this class is generated it ensures a type-safe implementation class.

```
package com.wiley.compbooks.vogel.chapter10.tie.HelloWorld;

public interface GoodDayOperations {
  public java.lang.String hello(
    org.omg.CORBA.ShortHolder hour,
    org.omg.CORBA.ShortHolder minute
  );
}
```

Within the server class, we initialize the ORB and the BOA. Then we create the implementation object goodDayImpl and supply it as a parameter to the constructor of the Tie object goodDayPseudoImpl. Finally, we notify the BOA that the object goodDayPseudoImpl is ready. Figure 10.7 shows the various interfaces and classes of both approaches and illustrates their relationships.

```
package com.wiley.compbooks.vogel.chapter10.tie.HelloWorldImpl;

import org.omg.CORBA.*;
import com.wiley.compbooks.vogel.chapter10.tie.HelloWorld.*;
import
com.wiley.compbooks.vogel.chapter10.tie.HelloWorldImpl.*;

public class Server {

    public static void main(String[] args) {
        try {
            //init orb
            ORB orb = ORB.init(args,null);
            //init basic object adapter
            BOA boa = orb.BOA_init();
```

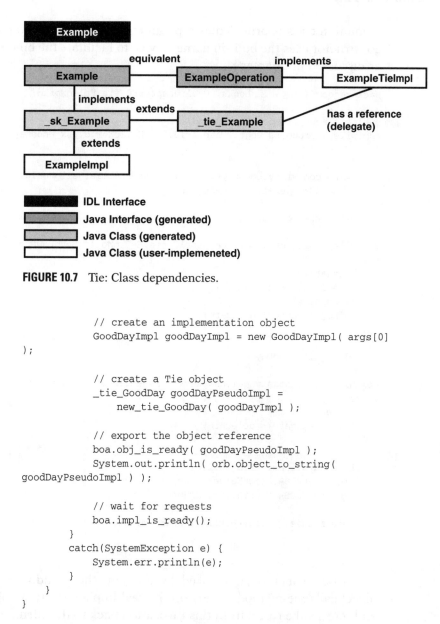

FIGURE 10.7 Tie: Class dependencies.

```
        // create an implementation object
        GoodDayImpl goodDayImpl = new GoodDayImpl( args[0]
);

        // create a Tie object
        _tie_GoodDay goodDayPseudoImpl =
            new_tie_GoodDay( goodDayImpl );

        // export the object reference
        boa.obj_is_ready( goodDayPseudoImpl );
        System.out.println( orb.object_to_string(
goodDayPseudoImpl ) );

        // wait for requests
        boa.impl_is_ready();
    }
    catch(SystemException e) {
        System.err.println(e);
    }
  }
}
```

To understand what is happening behind the scenes, let's have a look at the class `tie_GoodDay`. This is the Tie or pseudo-implementation class.

The Tie class extends the skeleton class, which connects it with the ORB run-time system and provides the marshaling and unmarshaling routines. The class has a private variable, an object reference of type `GoodDayOperations` called `delegate`. This variable will be initialized by each of the constructors. As has already been shown in the server class, the implementation class is provided as a parameter to the constructor. The second constructor uses the built-in name service to facilitate the bind mechanism, as discussed in Chapter 8.

```
package com.wiley.compbooks.vogel.chapter10.tie.HelloWorld;

public class _tie_GoodDay extends
com.wiley.compbooks.vogel.chapter10.tie.HelloWorld._sk_GoodDay
{

  private com.wiley.compbooks.vogel.chapter10.tie.HelloWorld.
      GoodDayOperations _delegate;

  public _tie_GoodDay

com.wiley.compbooks.vogel.chapter10.tie.HelloWorld.GoodDayOpera
tions
    delegate,
    java.lang.String name) {
    super(name);
    this._delegate = delegate;
  }

  public _tie_GoodDay(

com.wiley.compbooks.vogel.chapter10.tie.HelloWorld.GoodDayOpera
tions
    delegate) {
    this._delegate = delegate;
  }

  public java.lang.String hello(
    org.omg.CORBA.ShortHolder hour,
    org.omg.CORBA.ShortHolder minute
  ) {
    return this._delegate.hello( hour, minute );
  }
}
```

Once a method is invoked by a client, the pseudo-implementation object calls the method `hello()` on the real implementation object `delegate` and returns the result from this invocation back to the client. Note that the out parameter is also set by the delegate.

5   Applet Server

So far we have only considered cases where applets invoke objects but do not provide object implementations of their own. In this section we show how a CORBA server can be implemented as an applet:

♦ Introduction of the application and interface specification (sections 5.1 and 5.2)
♦ Overview of implementation classes (section 5.3)
♦ Object implementation (section 5.4)
♦ Applet implementation (section 5.5)

The main motivation to have CORBA objects hosted by applets is the ability to make callbacks into the applet, but there can also be cases where we might want to have interapplet communication, as in the following example.

5.1   The Application

Since none of the examples introduced previously fits this case, we will use a fresh one called AppletTalk. It is based on two applets that can interact with each other by sending messages. Figure 10.8 illustrates this.

For simplicity we only consider two-party talk, although the implementation is easily extensible to support multiparty talks. The talking applets are instances of the same class. This class acts as a speaker, a client sending some text by invoking an operation offered by an object reference. It also acts as a listener, offering an object to receive messages.

Although Figure 10.8 shows direct connections between the two applets, this would only be the case when using signed applets and setting the browser security level so that it allows requests to connect to and receive connection requests from arbitrary machines on the net. More likely the

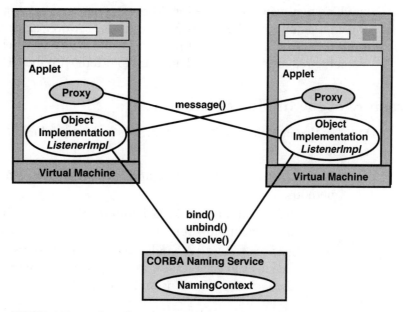

FIGURE 10.8   AppletTalk.

communication would be routed via an IIOP gateway residing on the host from where the applets have been downloaded.

Applets register themselves with the CORBA Naming Service using the name context's bind() operation. Interested parties can establish connections by resolving the name of the potential partner to an object reference. Once a party decides to quit the system it simply deregisters its name from the Naming Service using the unbind() method.

5.2 The Interface Specification

As we see in the IDL specification, the interface Listener provides an operation message. The applet will host an object of this interface type. The operation has an in parameter which is a string. This is a message sent from the other party. The interface is defined inside a module, Talk.

```
module com {
...
module appletServer {
module Talk {
    interface Listener {
        void message( in string msg );
    };
}; ... };
```

The IDL specification is rather simple and so is the implementation. All the complexity is taken care of by the ORB. There seems to be the problem of handling two event loops: one for CORBA events, that is, incoming requests, and another one for GUI events from the user. However, since Java ORBs are multithreaded, this is taken care of. The ORB has its own thread to listen for incoming requests. This thread does not interfere with the GUI event loop.

5.3 Structure of the Implementation

Let's go through the implementation. We have the following implementation classes:

◆ AppletServer—extends the Java applet class. We override the following methods:

init()—initializes the GUI and the ORB. It also instantiates the implementation objects.

actionPerformed()—handles user-initiated events. We implement the Java interface ActionListener to catch events caused when the user clicks buttons in the GUI.

register()—registers the object implementation with the Naming Service.

resolve()—connects an applet (client) to another applet (server) by resolving a name into an object reference.

display()—displays a string in a particular text field. This method is used by the implementation object ListenerImpl to display the message received through a method invocation.

◆ ListenerImpl—the implementation of the IDL-defined interface.

5.4 Object Implementation

The implementation of the interface Listener follows the same pattern as we have used before. We define a class ListenerImpl which extends the servant base class _ListenerImplBase. The constructor of the implementation class has a parameter of type AppletServer. We store this reference in a private variable talkApplet. This reference is used to eventually display incoming messages in a text area controlled by the applet.

```
package
com.wiley.compbooks.vogel.chapter10.appletServer.TalkImpl;

import java.awt.*;
import java.awt.event.*;
import org.omg.CORBA.*;
import com.wiley.compbooks.vogel.chapter8.naming.*;
import com.wiley.compbooks.vogel.chapter10.appletServer.Talk.*;

class ListenerImpl extends _ListenerImplBase {

    private AppletServer talkApplet;

    // constructor
    ListenerImpl( AppletServer applet ) {
        talkApplet = applet;
    }
    // method
    public void message( String msg ) {

        talkApplet.display( msg );
        return;
    }
}
```

The implementation of the method message() is quite simple. We invoke the method display() on the applet talkApplet, which in turn displays the message in a text area of the applet (see section 5.5).

5.5 Applet Implementation

The implementation of the applet AppletServer has the typical applet structure. First, we declare a number of private variables which determine the state of the applet. There are three variables for CORBA-related objects, orb, listener, and listenerImpl, and one for the convenience class easyNaming. The others are for various GUI elements.

```
public class AppletServer
    extends java.applet.Applet
    implements ActionListener {

    private ORB orb;
    private EasyNaming easyNaming;
    private Listener remoteListener;
    private ListenerImpl myListener;
    private Panel namePanel;
    private Panel buttonPanel;
    private Panel textPanel;
    private Button registerButton;
    private Button resolveButton;
    private Button sendButton;
    private Button deregisterButton;
    private Label nameLabel;
    private TextField nameField;
    private TextArea inArea;
    private TextArea outArea;
    private String myName;
```

The implementation of the init() method has two parts. The first part initializes the GUI components. The second part initializes the ORB and creates and connects the object.

5.5.1 Initializing the GUI

In the first part we initialize the various GUI components. We create text areas for the incoming messages inArea, outgoing messages outArea, and a text field nameField to enter the string of an object/applet you want to talk to. There are also four buttons:

◆ registerButton—to register the applet's listener object with the Naming Service

◆ resolveButton—to resolve the listener object of another applet

◆ sendButton—to send a message to the listener object obtained from the Naming Service

◆ deregisterButton—to deregister the applet's listener object from the Naming Service

```java
public void init() {

        registerButton = new Button("register");
        registerButton.setFont(new Font("Helvetica", Font.BOLD, 20));
        registerButton.setActionCommand("register");
        registerButton.addActionListener( (ActionListener) this );

        resolveButton = new Button("resolve");
        resolveButton.setFont(new Font("Helvetica", Font.BOLD, 20));
        resolveButton.setActionCommand("resolve");
        resolveButton.addActionListener( (ActionListener) this );

        sendButton = new Button("send");
        sendButton.setFont(new Font("Helvetica", Font.BOLD, 20));
        sendButton.setActionCommand("send");
        sendButton.addActionListener( (ActionListener) this );

        deregisterButton = new Button("deregister");
        deregisterButton.setFont(new Font("Helvetica", Font.BOLD, 20));

        deregisterButton.setActionCommand("deregister");
        deregisterButton.addActionListener( (ActionListener) this );

        nameLabel = new Label("Enter name: ");
        nameLabel.setFont(new Font("Helvetica", Font.BOLD, 14));

        nameField = new TextField();
        nameField.setFont(new Font("Helvetica", Font.BOLD, 14));

        inArea = new TextArea("Write here:\n", 40, 5);
        inArea.setFont(new Font("Helvetica", Font.BOLD, 14));
        outArea = new TextArea("Read here:\n", 40, 5 );
        outArea.setEditable(false);
        outArea.setFont(new Font("Helvetica", Font.BOLD, 14));

        namePanel = new Panel();
        buttonPanel = new Panel();
        textPanel = new Panel();

        namePanel.setLayout( new GridLayout(1,2));
        namePanel.add( nameLabel );
        namePanel.add( nameField );

        buttonPanel.setLayout( new GridLayout(1,4));
        buttonPanel.add( registerButton );
        buttonPanel.add( resolveButton );
        buttonPanel.add( sendButton );
        buttonPanel.add( deregisterButton );

        textPanel.setLayout( new GridLayout(2,1));
        textPanel.add( inArea );
        textPanel.add( outArea );
```

```
setLayout( new BorderLayout());
add( "North", namePanel );
add( "Center", textPanel );
add( "South", buttonPanel );
```

We choose a layout for our GUI elements by using the layout manager class `BorderLayout` for the panels and `GridLayout` for the buttons, label and text fields, and text area. The effect is shown in the screen shots in Figures 10.9 and 10.10.

5.5.2 *Initializing the ORB and Object Creation*

In the second part of the implementation of the `init()` method we initialize the ORB. Then we create the implementation object `listenerImpl` by calling its constructor `ListenerImpl()` and passing it to a reference to the applet (`this`). We also create an instance of the class `EasyNaming` for the use of the Naming Service, as already explained in Chapters 8 and 9.

```
try {
        //init ORB
        orb = ORB.init( this );
        // create a Listener object
        myListener = new ListenerImpl( this );
```

We use an object of the class `EasyNaming` to obtain an initial naming context and to query the Naming Service. The implementation of this class is shown in Chapter 8.

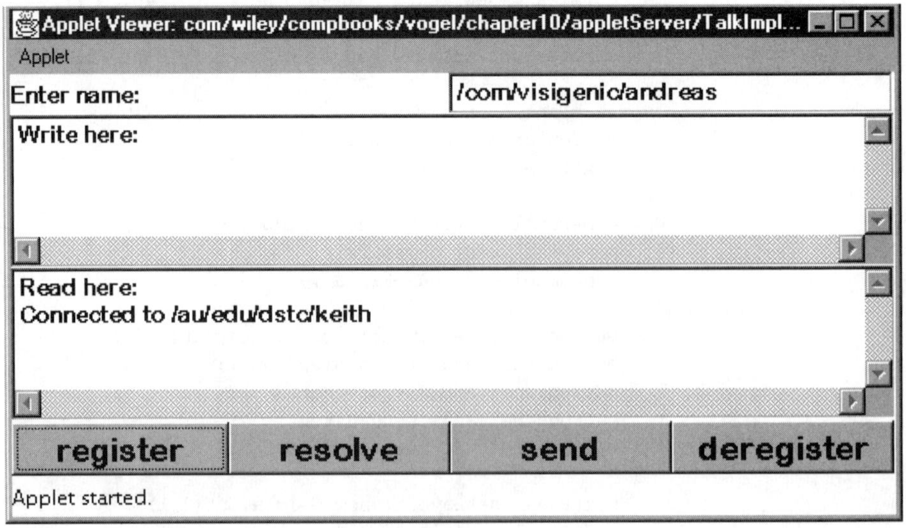

FIGURE 10.9 AppletTalk: establishing a session.

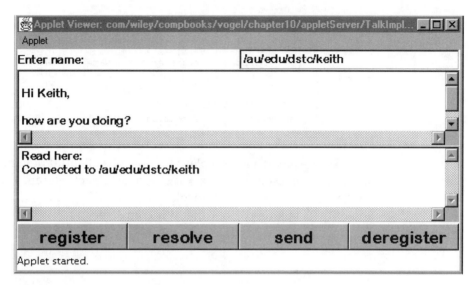

FIGURE 10.10 AppletTalk: sending a message.

```
        easyNaming = new EasyNaming( orb );
```

Once the implementation object is created we connect it to the ORB by calling

```
connect().
        orb.connect( myListener );

    }
    catch(SystemException e) {
        System.err.println(e);
        System.exit( 0 );
    }
  }
```

In the other examples we have seen so far, the last statement in a server's main routine was an infinite loop such as `impl_is_ready()`. There is, however, no need for a special loop. In this case the applet already provides its own event loop.

Now we have a look at the additional methods we have declared in the class. The method `register()` gets a name from the `nameField` and registers the object implementation `myListener` under this name with the Naming Service.

```
public void register() {
        try {
            myName = nameField.getText();
```

```
                    easyNaming.bind_from_string( myName, myListener );
        }
        catch(UserException ue) {
            outArea.append( "register " + myName + " failed: "
+ ue );
        }
        catch(SystemException se) {
            outArea.append( "Exception: " + se );
        }
    }
```

The `resolve()` method plays the role of a client. It obtains a name from the `nameField`, resolves it via `EasyNaming` to an object reference, and narrows it to the type `Listener`. It then invokes the method `message()` on the new object to notify its talking partner that it is connected.

```
public void resolve() {

        try {

            //resolve name and narrow it to Listener
            remoteListener = ListenerHelper.narrow(
                easyNaming.resolve_from_string(
nameField.getText() ) );

            // send initial message
            remoteListener.message( "Connected to " + myName );
        }

        // catch exceptions
        catch(UserException ue) {
            outArea.append( "resolve failed: " + ue );
        }
        catch(SystemException se) {
            outArea.append( "Exception: " + se );
        }
        return;
    }
```

The method `deregister()` deregisters a listener from the Naming Service.

```
public void deregister() {

        try {
            easyNaming.unbind_from_string( myName );
        }
        catch(UserException ue) {
            System.err.println(ue);
        }
        catch(SystemException se) {
```

```
                    System.err.println(se);
        }
    }
```

The `display()` method displays a string in the applet's text field `outArea`. It is used by the `Listener` implementation object to display incoming messages.

```
public void display( String msg ) {

    outArea.append( msg );
    return;
}
```

Finally, we implement the method `actionPerformed()`. It watches for events caused by clicking one of the four buttons we have declared and created earlier. For each of the buttons we invoke an appropriate method.

```
public void actionPerformed(ActionEvent ev) {

        // catch and process events
        if(ev.getActionCommand().equals("resolve") ) {

            resolve();
        }

        if(ev.getActionCommand().equals("register") ) {

            register();
        }

        if(ev.getActionCommand().equals("deregister") ) {

            deregister();

        }

        if(ev.getActionCommand().equals("send") ) {

            try {
                remoteListener.message( inArea.getText() );
            }
            // catch exceptions
            catch(SystemException ex) {
                outArea.append( "Exception: " + ex );
            }
        }
    }
}
```

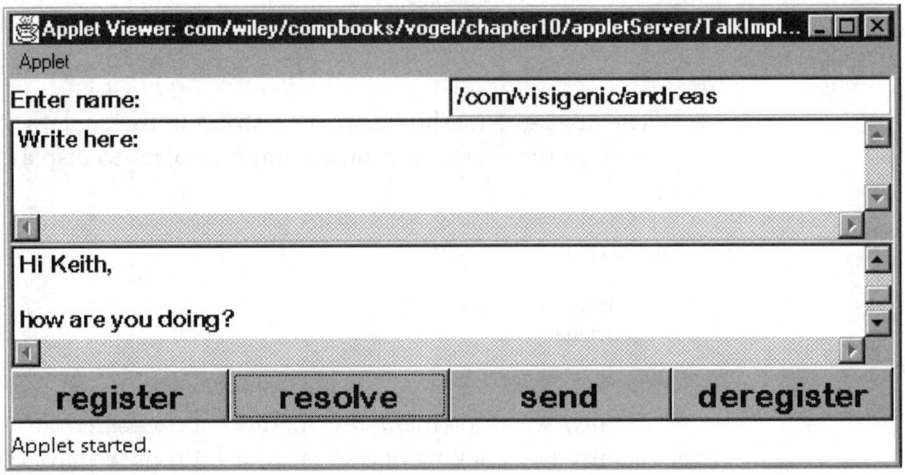

FIGURE 10.11   AppletTalk: receiving a message.

5.6   Executing the Application

Once the classes are compiled, we can start our AppletTalk example. We have two instances of our class `AppletServer`. Figure 10.9 shows the applet after is has been registered with the Naming Services under the name "/com/visigenic/andreas" and another party, under the name of "/au/edu/dstc/keith" has established contact with it.

Figure 10.10 shows one applet server with a message which is ready to be sent and Figure 10.11 shows the other applet server once it has received the message.

Events

In this chapter we explain events in the Java/CORBA world. The concept of events is quite overloaded, so to clarify we distinguish between events and event delivering mechanisms. More specifically we address

+ CORBA Event Service concepts (section 1)
+ The interfaces of the CORBA Event Service (section 2)
+ ORB events (section 3)
+ An example which uses the CORBA Event Service to deliver ORB events (section 4)
+ How the JavaBean Event Model relates to CORBA (section 5)

1   CORBA Event Service Concepts

The CORBA Event Service provides a way of distributing data about an occurrence in a distributed application to a number of interested parties without requiring the originator of the event data to know the receivers and to make several calls to specific objects. The Event Service's *event channel* takes event data from a *supplier* of events and delivers that data to one or more event *consumers*. The channel may act as a client to the supplier, *pulling* the event data from the supplier, or it may provide an object interface that allows the supplier to *push* the event data into the channel. When the data is to be delivered to consumers, the same options are available: the channel may push the event data to the consumer, or it may wait until the consumer pulls the event data from the channel. Channels may also use a combination of the push and pull approaches with different clients.

The specification defines the communication interfaces used to push and pull event data to and from suppliers and consumers. It then defines the Event Channel in terms of proxy suppliers and consumers. That is, the channel is an intermediary object between a supplier and a consumer, and it acts toward a supplier as a *proxy consumer* and toward a consumer as a *proxy supplier.*

The event channel provides administration interfaces that allow clients to choose whether to act as a supplier or consumer, and then to choose the appropriate interface for either push or pull model communication. The final step in beginning communications with an event channel is to connect to the channel, supplying any necessary callback object references (for example, to allow the channel to call a pull operation at an event supplier).

1.1 Push Model Communications

As we have already noted, the event service acts as a proxy that receives an event communication on behalf of event consumers and then passes the event data to the consumers on the supplier's behalf. It is as if the supplier directly called an interface at the consumer to push some event by invoking a push() operation that the consumer supplies. See Figure 11.1 for a diagram representing this interaction.

The interface for this invocation when an event channel is involved in the interaction is the same, but the invocation happens twice, once by the supplier at the event channel, and once by the channel at the consumer. This is shown in Figure 11.2.

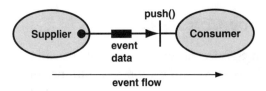

FIGURE 11.1 Direct push.

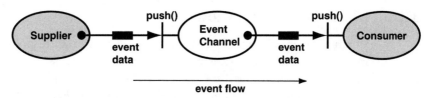

FIGURE 11.2 Event channel push.

1.2 Pull Model Communications

When a consumer wishes to be the active party in event data transmission, it must invoke a pull() operation on an object reference supplied by the event supplier. In some cases the consumer may not wish to make a blocking operation invocation that must wait until an event is generated. In this case another operation, try_pull(), must be supported by the supplier. This operation returns immediately with an event, if one is available, or with no event if none is available. Figure 11.3 represents an interaction between a pull model consumer and supplier.

As with push model communications, an event channel can be interposed between the supplier and consumer. The channel will call pull() or try_pull() at the supplier's interface and then store the event until the consumer calls pull() or try_pull() at the identical interface offered by the channel, as depicted in Figure 11.4.

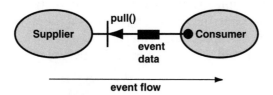

FIGURE 11.3 Direct pull.

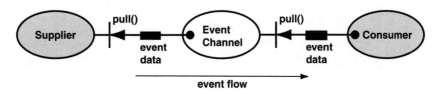

FIGURE 11.4 Event channel pull.

1.3   Mixed Mode Communications

When an event channel is used, not only can multiple suppliers place events into the channel for transmission to multiple consumers, but the model chosen by the suppliers to deliver the event data can be either push or pull, regardless of the model chosen by the consumers. Figure 11.5 depicts a mixture of push and pull model suppliers and consumers.

The Event Service specification does not prescribe the semantics of event delivery to be implemented by event channels. An event channel could keep track of what event data has been transmitted to which consumers and store data until it is delivered to every consumer. On the other hand, the semantics might be that each event supplied need only be forwarded to one of the consumers connected to the channel. Most implementations of the Event Service assume the former semantics, and some can be configured to provide different semantics or various qualities of service.

1.4   Federated Event Channels

Because event channels implement the same interfaces as the suppliers and consumers using them, it is possible to connect event channels together simply by making one channel act as the supplier to another. This configuration can be used to provide alternative paths of delivery for fault tolerance by running different event channels on different hosts and connecting them together in a federation. Then consumers can connect to more than one channel in case a host becomes unavailable.

Using the event service as it is currently specified, consumers would have to deal with multiple instances of the same data. However, the OMG is specifying an extension to the Event Service, called the Notification Service. This will provide more sophisticated mechanisms for dealing with this situation. A specification will be adopted in early 1998.

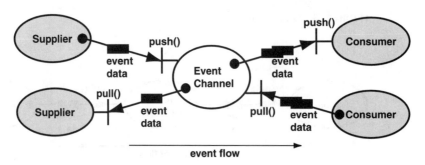

FIGURE 11.5 Mixed mode communications.

1.5   Event Types

So that we can define generic interfaces for event communications, the data transmitted by the push and pull operations must be wrapped in an Any. This means that there is an extra layer of unmarshaling before an event consumer can access the data it receives, and the TypeCode for the data must also be transmitted.

The Event Service accounts for this problem by defining a mechanism for typed event communication. That is, an operation which includes parameters of particular types can be defined for use in place of the push and pull operations which have an Any as a parameter. Because it is not known what types of applications we'll wish to use, the specification defines operations that return references of the type Object, which must be narrowed at run time to produce an agreed interface type that has an operation (or operations) with typed parameters. The Typed Event Service specification is not implemented commercially, but it is used in some projects.

Typed Event Services can be implemented to suit a particular application and recognize a limited number of typed communication interfaces. Alternatively, Event Service implementations that use the Dynamic Server Interface and the Interface Repository to accept any invocation could also implement this functionality. This would allow applications to use agreed interfaces for type-specific invocations for ease of programming.

2   Interface Specifications

Let's have a look at the interfaces that provide the Event Service functionality. First we will provide the definitions for the interfaces that facilitate the push and pull communications (section 2.1). Then the interfaces that the event channel offers to provide proxy consumers and suppliers are shown in section 2.2. The Administration interfaces are given in section 2.3. Finally, we present the Typed Event Channel interfaces in section 2.4.

2.1   Module CosEventComm

The interfaces supporting the push and pull operations used to transmit event data are all defined in the CosEventComm module. These interfaces use a notion of being *connected* while event data is being transmitted, and *disconnected* when either party decides not to continue transmitting or receiving event data. The operations for connecting to an event channel are defined in another module. The following is the declaration of the module and of an exception to deal with the case when event transmission is attempted after one of the parties has disconnected.

```
module CosEventComm {
  exception Disconnected{};
```

2.1.1 Push Model

Now let's look at the IDL for the first of two pairs of interfaces: PushConsumer and PushSupplier.

```
interface PushConsumer {
  void push (in any data) raises(Disconnected);
  void disconnect_push_consumer();
};
```

This interface is supported by the consumer of events to allow suppliers (including an event channel) to push event data using the push() operation. The supplier may decide to terminate the connection by calling disconnect_ push_consumer().push() will raise the Disconnected exception if its supplier client has already called disconnect_push_consumer(). It is assumed that the consumer has an object reference to a reciprocal interface supported by the supplier so that it may also disconnect. This interface is called PushSupplier.

```
interface PushSupplier {
  void disconnect_push_supplier();
};
```

Note that PushSupplier supports a disconnect operation but no communications operations. This is because in the push model the consumer is passive and must wait until the supplier is ready to send it event data. In the next section we will show how the consumer and supplier become connected (swap object references to each other's interfaces).

2.1.2 Pull Model

In pull model communications it is the supplier that is passive, offering an interface that the consumer may call at any time. This interface is called PullSupplier.

```
interface PullSupplier {
  any pull () raises(Disconnected);
  any try_pull (out boolean has_event)
    raises(Disconnected);
  void disconnect_pull_supplier();
};
```

The pull consumer that calls these operations cannot be sure that any new event data will be waiting for it at the supplier, so it has a choice between two pull operations. A call to pull() will block until some data is ready.

Whereas a call to try_pull() will return immediately with data if there is any, or with an undefined result if there is none. Its out parameter has_event will be TRUE if there is a valid result, or FALSE otherwise. The disconnect_push _consumer() operation allows the consumer to signal that it will no longer pull any event data.

Once again there is a reciprocal interface that allows the supplier to disconnect. Its definition is as follows:

```
interface PullConsumer {
    void disconnect_pull_consumer();
};
}; // CosEventComm
```

2.2 Module CosEventChannelAdmin

The interfaces defined in CosEventComm can be implemented for use in any context as a pattern for transmitting event data, and they are inherited for use by event channels. The IDL for event channel interfaces is in the module CosEventChannelAdmin. This module facilitates the connection of suppliers and consumers to the consumer and supplier proxy interfaces of an event channel. An exception, AlreadyConnected, is raised when a connection to a channel is attempted after a connection is already established. See section 2.2.1 for details of its use.

```
module CosEventChannelAdmin {
    exception AlreadyConnected {};
    exception TypeError {};
```

The TypeError exception is used by the interfaces for typed event communication. Its use will be explained in section 2.4.

2.2.1 Proxy Interfaces

The event channel supports proxy consumers that event suppliers connect to and communicate with using the inherited push and pull operations from the CosEventComm interfaces. They also support proxy suppliers that event consumers connect to in order to receive events via the same push and pull operations inherited into other interfaces. We will describe all four combinations of push and pull models with consumer and supplier roles.

Proxy Push Consumer. The first interface defined is ProxyPushConsumer. It inherits from PushConsumer and supports one additional operation called con-nect_push_supplier(), which takes a PushSupplier object reference that the channel will use when it wishes to disconnect from the supplier.

```
interface ProxyPushConsumer: CosEventComm::PushConsumer {
    void connect_push_supplier(
            in CosEventComm::PushSupplier push_supplier)
        raises(AlreadyConnected);
};
```

Once the supplier has provided its callback interface to the connect_ push_supplier() operation, it may begin calling the push() operation that the proxy interface inherits from PushConsumer. Any further calls to connect_push_supplier() will raise the AlreadyConnected exception. The PushSupplier interface provided by the supplier contains only a disconnect operation, and is therefore not essential to transmitting event data. For this reason some event channels will accept a nil object reference as an argument to connect_push_supplier().

When the supplier is finished providing event data it will call the disconnect_push_consumer() operation which is also inherited from PushConsumer. See Figure 11.6 for a graphical representation of the life cycle of a connection to an event channel.

Each of the other proxy interfaces work in essentially the same way, although the operations they inherit from their corresponding CosEventComm interfaces will be different.

Proxy Pull Supplier. The ProxyPullSupplier interface is for use by pull model consumers. The inherited operations are pull(), try_pull(), and a disconnect operation.

```
interface ProxyPullSupplier: CosEventComm::PullSupplier {
    void connect_pull_consumer(
            in CosEventComm::PullConsumer pull_consumer)
        raises(AlreadyConnected);
};
```

Once again the PullConsumer interface type supplied as a parameter to the connect operation contains only a disconnect operation, and nil object references may be acceptable to some event channels.

Proxy Pull Consumer. The ProxyPullConsumer interface supports the connect_pull_supplier() operation, which takes a callback object reference parame-

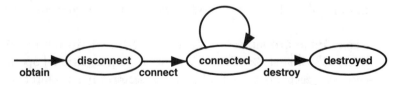

FIGURE 11.6 Life cycle of a connection.

ter of type PullSupplier. The event channel will use this callback to invoke the supplier's pull() and try_pull() operations.

```
interface ProxyPullConsumer: CosEventComm::PullConsumer {
    void connect_pull_supplier(
            in CosEventComm::PullSupplier pull_supplier)
        raises(AlreadyConnected,TypeError);
};
```

The connect_pull_supplier() operation may raise a TypeError exception as well as the usual AlreadyConnected. This is to allow typed event channels to narrow the argument they receive to a derived interface which supports extra operations. If the object reference passed will not narrow then TypeError will be raised. See section 2.4 for the details of typed event channels.

Proxy Push Supplier. The final proxy interface is ProxyPushSupplier, which is used by consumers that supply a PushConsumer callback object reference argument to the connect_push_consumer() operation so that the event channel can use the callback's push() operation to transmit event data to the consumer.

```
interface ProxyPushSupplier: CosEventComm::PushSupplier {
    void connect_push_consumer(
            in CosEventComm::PushConsumer push_consumer)
        raises(AlreadyConnected, TypeError);
};
```

The exceptions declared on the connect_push_consumer() operation are raised in the same circumstances as described previously.

2.3   Obtaining a Proxy

The EventChannelAdmin module also provides interfaces that allow suppliers and consumers to obtain object references to the proxies described previously. The ConsumerAdmin interface is used by consumers to obtain references to supplier proxies.

```
interface ConsumerAdmin {
        ProxyPushSupplier obtain_push_supplier();
        ProxyPullSupplier obtain_pull_supplier();
};
```

The SupplierAdmin interface allows suppliers to obtain references to the channel's consumer proxies.

```
interface SupplierAdmin {
    ProxyPushConsumer obtain_push_consumer();
    ProxyPullConsumer obtain_pull_consumer();
};
```

Finally, the EventChannel interface represents the "front door" to an Event Service implementation. Its operations for_consumers() and for_suppliers() give consumers and suppliers references to the Admin interfaces described above.

```
interface EventChannel {
    ConsumerAdmin for_consumers();
    SupplierAdmin for_suppliers();
    void destroy();
};
```

The destroy() operation is provided to complete the life cycle of an event channel. However, there is no standard factory interface defined to create new event channels. Visibroker's implementation of the Event Service provides a channel factory with the following interface. This implementation also allows you to create event channels in the same JVM as the other parts of your application and hence to optimize the communication for sending or receiving events.

```
interface EventChannelFactory {

    exception AlreadyExists {};
    exception ChannelsExist {};

    EventChannel create();

    EventChannel create_by_name(in string name) raises(AlreadyExists);

    EventChannel lookup_by_name(in string name);

    void destroy() raises(ChannelsExist);

};
```

2.4   Typed Event Communication

The Event Service specification allows for the use of typed operations to transmit event data instead of the generic push and pull operations defined in CosEventComm. This is a part of the specification that is not implemented by any commercially availble CORBA Event Service. Two new interfaces that inherit from the CosEventComm interfaces supporting push and pull operations are defined in the module CosTypedEventComm. These interfaces are TypedPushConsumer and TypedPullSupplier.

Typed event communication reuses the ProxyPullConsumer and Proxy-PushSupplier interfaces, but it expects that subtypes of the parameters to their connect operations will be passed by the channel's clients so that they can be narrowed to an agreed interface type that provides typed operations. Hence the declaration of the TypeError exception to be raised by the connect operations in these interfaces.

```
module CosTypedEventComm {

    interface TypedPushConsumer : CosEventComm::PushConsumer {
        Object get_typed_consumer();
    };
```

The TypedPushConsumer interface supports all of the functionality of the generic PushConsumer interface, but implementations may implement the generic operations by returning a NO_IMPLEMENT system exception. Instead of a connect operation, the typed push consumer interface supports the operation get_typed_consumer(). Its return type is Object, but the supplier must narrow the returned object reference to an agreed interface type. This narrowed interface type must support operations with only in parameters and no return values, as event data travels in only one direction. The mechanism for choosing this interface type is provided by the TypedSupplierAdmin and TypedConsumerAdmin interfaces explained in section 2.4.3.

The TypedPullSupplier interface works in the same manner as the TypedPushConsumer interface.

```
    interface TypedPullSupplier : CosEventComm::PullSupplier {
        Object get_typed_supplier();
    };
};
```

The interface returned from get_typed_supplier() can be made equivalent to a typed push model interface X by defining an interface PullX. The PullX interface must contain an operation pull_op() for each operation op in X. The parameters of pull_op() must be equivalent to those in op, but tagged as out parameters instead of in parameters. PullX should also support another operation for each op in X, called try_op(), each of which must return a boolean. A return value of true indicates that the values in the out parameters are valid event data; that is, there was an event waiting to be pulled.

2.4.1 Typed Event Types

The typed event channel administration interfaces offer the same functionality as the generic event channel. That is, they offer interfaces to obtain appropriate proxies for supplier and consumer, for push and pull model communications. One extra feature is provided: the ability to specify which type of interface to use for typed communication. This will be the type of object reference returned from the get_typed_supplier() and get_typed_consumer() operations defined earlier.

```
module CosTypedEventChannelAdmin {

    exception InterfaceNotSupported {};
    exception NoSuchImplementation {};
    typedef string Key;
```

The CosTypedEventChannelAdmin module introduces two new exceptions to deal with two error cases:

- ♦ InterfaceNotSupported is raised when the event channel cannot support the typed interface required by its clients.
- ♦ NoSuchImplementation is raised when the event channel cannot make invocations on an interface type.

It also defines a string type, Key, that is used to nominate the interface type required, or offered, by the client.

2.4.2 The Typed Proxy Interfaces

The TypedProxyPushConsumer interface has all of the operations of the equivalent generic proxy, as well as those of the new TypedPushConsumer interface we defined.

```
interface TypedProxyPushConsumer :
        CosEventChannelAdmin::ProxyPushConsumer,
        CosTypedEventComm::TypedPushConsumer {};
```

Likewise, the TypedProxyPullSupplier interface inherits from both the generic proxy and the new TypedPullSupplier interface.

```
interface TypedProxyPullSupplier:
        CosEventChannelAdmin::ProxyPullSupplier,
        CosTypedEventComm::TypedPullSupplier {};
```

Each object returned by a typed event channel will also implement the operations of an additional interface or be capable of calling the operations of an additional interface that is implemented at its client. The bootstrap operations described in the next section provide the mechanism for the channel and its client to agree on the type of that interface.

2.4.3 The Typed Admin Interfaces

The interface TypedSupplierAdmin is used by typed event suppliers to obtain proxies that support typed event transmission operations, while the Typed-1ConsumerAdmin interface is used by typed event consumers to obtain proxies that support similar operations.

TypedSupplierAdmin. This interface is an extension of the untyped event channel's supplier administration interface and has operations for push and pull model event transmission.

```
interface TypedSupplierAdmin :
        CosEventChannelAdmin::SupplierAdmin {
    TypedProxyPushConsumer obtain_typed_push_consumer(
        in Key supported_interface)
    raises(InterfaceNotSupported);
```

The obtain_typed_push_consumer() operation takes a Key parameter which the supplier uses to specify which interface type it wishes to use for typed communications. The supplier will then call the get_typed_consumer() operation on the returned TypedProxyPushConsumer object reference. The resulting Object return type can then be narrowed to the type given as the Key parameter. However if the channel cannot supply an object reference of this interface type it will raise an InterfaceNotSupported exception from obtain_typed_push_consumer().

```
    ProxyPullConsumer obtain_typed_pull_consumer (
        in Key uses_interface)
    raises(NoSuchImplementation);
}; //TypedSupplierAdmin
```

The obtain_typed_pull_consumer() operation returns an ordinary Proxy-PullConsumer interface. If the channel cannot make calls to the interface type specified in the uses_interface parameter it will raise the NoSuch-Implementation exception.

Once the ProxyPullConsumer is obtained, the supplier must use its connect_pull_supplier() operation, passing it an interface that supports PullSupplier (the argument type), as well as PullX, where X is the interface type specified in the uses_interface parameter of the operation above. The connect_pull_supplier() operation will raise the TypeError exception if it cannot narrow the object reference supplied to type PullX.

TypedConsumerAdmin. This interface behaves in a similar way to its supplier counterpart, and is used by consumers to obtain typed proxy supplier object references.

```
interface TypedConsumerAdmin :
        CosEventChannelAdmin::ConsumerAdmin {
    TypedProxyPullSupplier obtain_typed_pull_supplier(
        in Key supported_interface)
    raises (InterfaceNotSupported);
```

The obtain_typed_pull_supplier() operation returns a TypedProxyPullSupplier object reference. The consumer will call the get_typed_supplier() operation on this reference, which will return an object reference that can be narrowed to the interface type specified in the supported_interface parameter. The channel raises the InterfaceNotSupported exception from the call to obtain_typed_pull_supplier() if it cannot supply a reference of the type specified in Key.

```
ProxyPushSupplier obtain_typed_push_supplier(
        in Key uses_interface)
        raises(NoSuchImplementation);
};
```

The obtain_typed_push_supplier() operation returns an ordinary ProxyPush-Supplier object reference, which the consumer must connect to. It does this by supplying a subtype of the PushConsumer interface that also supports the interface type the consumer specified in the uses_interface parameter. Like its supplier counterpart, the operation will raise the NoSuchImplementation exception if it cannot use this interface type. The returned ProxyPushSupplier's connect operation will raise the TypeError exception if the consumer's object reference does not support the interface type it specified.

TypedEventChannel.　The TypedEventChannel interface acts as a bootstrap for all kinds of typed Event Service clients. It offers similar operations to generic event channels to gain access to the Admin interfaces we described.

```
interface TypedEventChannel {
    TypedConsumerAdmin for_consumers();
    TypedSupplierAdmin for_suppliers();
    void destroy ();
};
}; // module TypedEventChannelAdmin
```

3 ORB Events

ORB events are events produced by an ORB. Typically they are notifications about state changes in the ORB. They play an important role when building industrial-strength applications, as we explain in more detail in Chapter 13. ORB events are independent of any event delivery mechanism. ORB events are not specified by CORBA, but are ORB specific. Examples of mechanisms which expose ORB events to programmers are Orbix Filters and Visibroker Interceptors. The examples in this chapter will be based on Visibroker Event Handlers, which are implemented as a layer on top of Interceptors.

Visibroker's Event Handler mechanism produces notifications about state changes in client stubs and the object adapter. The events are fired when certain actions occur. Some examples are a client binds to an object, an operation is invoked, a response to an invocation is received, or the connection from the client or the server is dropped.

Event handlers are provided to the programmer as Java interfaces, one for the client and one for the server. Each method in the interfaces corresponds to a different kind of event. You can implement the methods corresponding to the events that you are interested in. Once an event handler implementation is instantiated and registered with the ORB, the ORB invokes the methods corresponding to the events that occur.

The IDL struct ConnectionInfo describes a connection in the form of a host name and a port number. It is used by both client and server event handlers. It is mapped to Java in the standard way.

```
public class com.visigenic.vbroker.interceptor.ConnectionInfo
    extends java.lang.Object {

    public java.lang.String hostname;
    public int port;
}
```

The client-side event handler is defined in the Java interface ClientEventHandler:

```
interface ClientEventHandler {

    void bind_succeeded(in Object obj, in ConnectionIno info);

    void bind_failed( in Object obj );

    void server_aborted( in Object obj );

    void rebind_succeeded( in Object obj, in ConnectionIno info);

    void rebind_failed( in Object obj );
};
```

The methods have the following meaning:

- ♦ bind_succeeded()—a client successfully bound (established a connection) to an object
- ♦ bind_failed()—a client failed to bind to an object
- ♦ server_aborted()—the server program is no longer running
- ♦ rebind_succeeded()—a client lost the connection to an object and successfully rebound, most likely to a replica of the original object

♦ rebind_failed()—a client lost the connection to an object and could not rebind

The server-side event handler is defined in the Java interface ImplEventHandler:

```
interface ImplEventhandler {

    void bind( in ConnectionInfo info, in Principal, in Object obj );

    void unbind( in ConnectionInfo info,in Principal, in Object obj );

    void client_aborted( in ConnectionInfo info, in Object obj );

    void pre_method( in ConnectionInfo info, in Principal,
        in string operation_name, in Object obj );

    void post_method( in ConnectionInfo info, in Principal,
        in string operation_name, in Object obj );

    void post_method_exception( in ConnectionInfo info, in Principal,
        in string operation_name, in string exception_name,
        in Object obj );
```

The methods have the following meaning:

♦ bind()—a new connection has been established to this server
♦ unbind()—a connection has been terminated
♦ client_aborted()—a client disappeared
♦ pre_method()—a request has arrived at the server
♦ post_method()—a response is about to be sent to the client
♦ post_method_exception()—an exception is about to be sent as a response to the client

To activate an event handler object you have to obtain a registry from the ORB and register your event handler with the registry. The APIs and details are explained later in this section when we show how to register the event handlers for our example.

4   An Example

The example demonstrating the use of the Event Service and ORB events is a visualization tool for ORB events which we call the *monitor*. The monitor allows you to watch which objects are available in your application and which interactions take place.

The ORB events we are interested in occur when an operation implementation method is about to be called and when a method has returned its result to the ORB. These are signaled by the `pre_method()` and `post_method()` events in the server event handler, respectively. Additionally, we want to be aware when objects are created and destroyed. Some ORBs other than Visibroker have similar interfaces that give programmers access to such event hooks, but any CORBA application may be instrumented by adding code to the application to create events at the beginning and end of each operation implementation method. The benefit of using event handler hooks is that the code is decoupled from the application-specific code and can be easily added and removed without recompilation.

We use the CORBA Event Service as the event delivery mechanism. We use the push-push model, which means that the client and server are event producers that push their events into a dedicated event channel. The monitor itself is a Java application that provides visual representation of the clients, the servers, and their interactions. The monitor consumes events from the same event channel. Figure 11.7 illustrates a scenario with multiple objects and clients, an event channel, and the monitor.

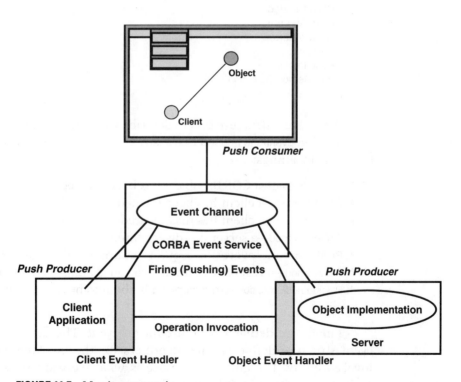

FIGURE 11.7 Monitor scenario.

4.1 Event Data Types

As we explained earlier, the events transmitted by the CORBA Event Service are of type Any. We define some IDL data types representing the events we monitor, so that data of these types can be placed into Anys for transmission.

```
module com {
...
module chapter11 {
module MonitorType {

struct Date {
  long year;
  long month;
  long day;
  long hour;
  long minute;
  long second;
};

enum EventKind {
  ObjectCreated,
  ClientCreated,
  ClientAborted,
  ServerAborted,
  PreMethod,
  PostMethod,
  PostMethodException
};
```

We define a structure Date to describe when an event has occurred. The enumeration EventKind is used to classify events. The different kinds have the following meanings:

- ObjectCreated—a CORBA object has been created
- ClientCreated—a client has been created
- ClientAborted—a client has disappeared
- Server Aborted—a server has disappeared
- PreMethod—an invocation request has arrived at the object adapter
- PostMethod—a response to an invocation is about to be sent to the client
- PostMethodException—an exception is about to be sent as a response to the client

Finally, we define a structure for an event. The first two fields of the event structure define unique identifiers for the invoking entity and the invoked entity. The question we face is what we want to consider as an entity for visualizing a CORBA system.

We choose CORBA objects for invoked entities. Another useful way to identify invoking entities is a combination of the object's identity and that of its server (or JVM). In our example we identify servers by the port they listen on, which can be obtained from a server or an object reference.

On the client side, things are less obvious. Although every client has a proxy object for the CORBA object, proxies are too fine-grained for our visualization purposes. The next level of granularity is the JVM which executes the client code. A *pure client* does not contain any CORBA objects, but when invocations are made from servers, we are interested in whether the invocation is made from inside one of its CORBA objects. To satisfy these requirements we came up with a hybrid solution: if the invocation is made from a CORBA object we use the object's identifier, otherwise we use the JVM's identifier.

The next issue is the identifier. CORBA does not define a standard unique object identifier. An IOR may not be unique as it describes exactly one object, but there could be many IORs pointing to the same object. Even if we had a way to uniquely identify objects, that would not be sufficient for our example because we also need to identify client programs. Hence we define our own unique identifiers which we can apply to CORBA objects as well as to client programs.

```
struct Event {
    string clientUuid;
    string serverUuid;
    EventKind kind;
    Date dateStamp;
    string hostname;
    long port;
    string operationName;
    string exceptionName;
    CORBA::Object obj;
};
};};};};};
```

We compile this IDL and get a number of Java files containing class definitions for the IDL data types as well as holder and helper classes. The helper classes are most useful for our purposes because we need to convert Event structs into Any objects for transmission by an Event Channel. The helper class contains convenience methods to insert events into and extract them from Any objects. The generated code is shown here.

```
package com.wiley.compbooks.vogel.chapter11.MonitorType;

abstract public class EventHelper {
    ...
    public static void insert(
```

```
        org.omg.CORBA.Any any,
        com.wiley.compbooks.vogel.chapter11.MonitorType.Event value) {

        org.omg.CORBA.portable.OutputStream output =
            any.create_output_stream();
        write(output, value);
        any.read_value(output.create_input_stream(), type());
    }

    public static com.wiley.compbooks.vogel.chapter11.MonitorType.Event
extract(
        org.omg.CORBA.Any any) {

    if(!any.type().equal(type())) {
        throw new org.omg.CORBA.BAD_TYPECODE();
    }
    return read(any.create_input_stream());
    }
...
}
```

4.2   Identity

We implement a class Identity which creates and contains a unique identifier. In the constructor of the class we create a unique identifier id by concatenating string representations of the host name, the current time, and a random number.

```
package com.wiley.compbooks.vogel.chapter11.MonitorImpl;

import java.util.*;
import java.net.*;

public class Identity {

    public String id;

    public Identity() {

        StringBuffer buf = new StringBuffer();
        InetAddress adr;
        Date d = new Date();
        Random r = new Random();
        try {
            adr = InetAddress.getLocalHost();
            buf.append( adr.toString() );
        }
        catch( UnknownHostException ex ) {
            System.err.println( ex );
            buf.append("LocalHost");
```

```
        }
        buf.append( d.getTime() );
        buf.append( r.nextInt() );
        id = new String( buf );
    }
}
```

4.3   Event Producers

Now that we have defined the structure and meaning of an Event, we must create events when certain ORB actions occur. As discussed, Visibroker's Event Handlers provide a good mechanism to decouple the application code from the monitoring code. We simply implement the Java interfaces for client and object implementation handlers and then register our event handlers with the clients and servers, respectively.

4.3.1   *Client Event Handler*

We implement our client event handler in the class MonitorClientEvent-Handler. It provides the methods for the operations defined in the CORBA Event Service PushSupplier interface, and hence extends the skeleton class generated by the IDL compiler. It also implements the Java interface Client-EventHandler which is defined in Visibroker's interceptor package. Figure 11.8 illustrates the relationship between the various interfaces, classes, and objects.

```
package com.wiley.compbooks.vogel.chapter11.MonitorImpl;

import org.omg.CosEventComm.*;
import org.omg.CosEventChannelAdmin.*;
```

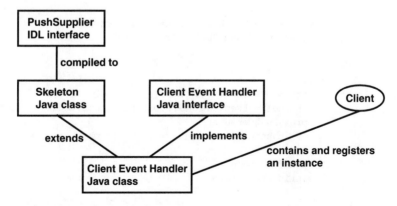

FIGURE 11.8   Client event handler.

```
import org.omg.CORBA.*;
import com.visigenic.vbroker.interceptor.*;
import com.wiley.compbooks.vogel.chapter11.MonitorType.*;

public class MonitorClientEventHandler
    extends _sk_PushSupplier
    implements ClientEventHandler {

    private EventChannel channel = null;
    private ProxyPushConsumer proxyPushConsumer = null;
    private String uuid;
    private String client_name;
    private org.omg.CORBA.Object obj;
    private org.omg.CORBA.ORB orb;
    private java.util.Date d;
    private String hostname;
```

After we declare a number of private variables, we implement the constructor of the class. The constructor has string parameters for the event channel's object id, the client's identifier, the client's name, and an IOR in the case that the client is a CORBA object.

We then obtain an IOR for the event channel using Visibroker's `bind()` method. From the event channel we obtain a proxy push consumer object.

```
public MonitorClientEventHandler(
    String channel_name, String id,
    String client_name, org.omg.CORBA.Object obj ) {

    uuid = id;
    this.obj = obj;
    this.client_name = client_name;
    d = new java.util.Date();
    try {
        hostname = java.net.InetAddress.getLocalHost().getHostName();
    }
    catch( java.net.UnknownHostException ex ) {
        hostname = new String("localhost");
    }

    try {
        orb = ORB.init(args, null);
        channel = EventChannelHelper.bind( orb, channel_name );
        proxyPushConsumer =
            channel.for_suppliers().obtain_push_consumer();
    }
    catch(Exception e) {
        e.printStackTrace();
    }
}
```

The method `connect()` is called by the client to connect our push consumer, which is an instance of the class `MonitorClientEventHandler` to the Event Service. It invokes the method `connect_push_supplier()` on the `Proxy-PushConsumer` we obtained from the event channel in the constructor. We also call the method `client_created()` which creates an event indicating that this client was created.

```
public void connect() {

    try {
       proxyPushConsumer.connect_push_supplier( this );
       client_created();
    }
    catch(Exception e) {
       e.printStackTrace();
    }
}
```

The IDL interface PushSupplier defines the operation disconnect_push_supplier() to allow the Event Channel to disconnect when it shuts down. We have to implement the equivalent method `disconnect_push_supplier()`, which deactivates the object.

```
public void disconnect_push_supplier() {
    System.out.println("disconnect_push_supplier()");
    try {
       _boa().deactivate_obj(this);
    }
    catch(SystemException e) {
       e.printStackTrace();
    }
}
```

Then we implement a `push()` method that takes an event in the form of an Any object and calls the push() operation on the proxy push consumer object we obtained from the event channel.

```
public void push( Any event ) {
    try {
        proxyPushConsumer.push( event );
    }
    catch(Disconnected e) {
        System.out.println("Disconnected");
    }
    catch(SystemException e) {
        System.out.println( e );
    }
}
```

The method `client_created()`, which we called from the constructor, now creates an event for the first time. We create a Java object for an IDL struct Date and then another Java object event which corresponds to the IDL struct Event. We initialize the Java Event object with values mostly obtained in the constructor. We also set the event kind to `EventKind.ClientCreated`. Then we obtain an Any object `any_event` from the ORB and insert the Event object into `any_event` using the `insert()` method provided by the helper class. Finally, we invoke the `push()` method with `any_event` as its argument.

```
public void client_created() {

    Date date = new Date(
        d.getYear(), d.getMonth(), d.getDay(),
        d.getHours(), d.getMinutes(), d.getSeconds() );
    Event event = new Event(
        uuid,
        uuid,
        EventKind.ClientCreated,
        date,
        hostname,
        0, // port
        client_name,
        new String(""), // exception name
        obj );

    try {
        Any any_event = _orb().create_any();
        EventHelper.insert( any_event, event );
        push( any_event );
    }
    catch( SystemException se ) {
        System.out.println( se );
    }

}
```

The method `server_aborted()` indicates that a server to which the client had a connection has disappeared. Its implementation follows the same pattern as `client_created()`.

```
public void server_aborted(org.omg.CORBA.Object obj) {

    d = new java.util.Date();
    date = new Date(
        d.getYear(), d.getMonth(), d.getDay(),
        d.getHours(), d.getMinutes(), d.getSeconds()
    );
    Event event = new Event (
        uuid,
```

```
                    uuid,
                    EventKind.ServerAborted,
                    date,
                    hostname,
                    0, // port
                    new String("server aborted"),
                    new String(""), // exception name
                    obj );

            try {
                Any any_event = _orb().create_any();
                EventHelper.insert( any_event, event );
                push( any_event );
            }
            catch( SystemException se ) {
                System.out.println( se );
            }
    }
}
```

Finally, we provide dummy implementations for the methods corresponding to the ORB events we don't want to handle.

```
    public void bind_succeeded(org.omg.CORBA.Object obj,
        ConnectionInfo info ) { ; }

    public void rebind_succeeded(org.omg.CORBA.Object obj,
        ConnectionInfo info ) { ; }

    public void bind_failed(org.omg.CORBA.Object obj) { ; }

    public void rebind_failed(org.omg.CORBA.Object obj) { ; }
}
```

4.3.2   *Implementation Event Handler*

The structure of our implementation event handler for objects that make invocations is the same as the handler for pure clients. It is illustrated in Figure 11.9. The class MonitorImplEventHandler implements the IDL interface **PushSupplier** and the Java interceptor ImplEventHandler. The implementation is very similar to MonitorClientEventHandler; the differences are in the ORB events handled and the data inserted into the Event object.

```
package com.wiley.compbooks.vogel.chapter11.MonitorImpl;

import org.omg.CosEventComm.*;
import org.omg.CosEventChannelAdmin.*;
import org.omg.CORBA.*;
import com.visigenic.vbroker.interceptor.*;
import com.wiley.compbooks.vogel.chapter11.MonitorType.*
```

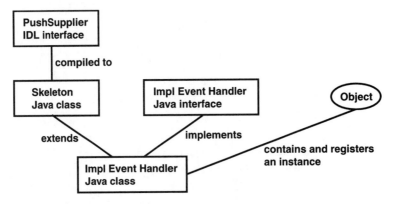

FIGURE 11.9 Implementation Event Handler.

```
class MonitorImplEventHandler
        extends _sk_PushSupplier
        implements ImplEventHandler {

    ...

    MonitorImplEventHandler( String channel_name, String id,

    String obj_name, org.omg.CORBA.Object obj ) {

        ...

}

public void disconnect_push_supplier() {
    ...
}

public void push( Any event ) {
    ...
}
```

Instead of the method `client_created()`, we have a method `object_cre-`
`ated()`. The differences between the two methods are that we supply a new
`EventKind` as an argument to the constructor of the `Event` object, as well as a
reference to the created object.

```
public void object_created() {
    ...
    Event event = new Event (
            uuid,
            uuid,
            EventKind.ObjectCreated,
```

```
                    date,
                    hostname,
                    0, // port
                    obj_name,
                    new String(""), // exception name
                    obj );
      ...
}
```

Now we have to implement all the methods defined in the interface ImplEventHandler. We only provide real implementations for the methods that correspond to the ORB events we are interested in. These are client_aborted(), pre_method(), post_method(), and post_method_exception().

As an example implementation we show the method pre_method(). This method is invoked by the ORB which supplies its arguments. After we have set the date in the usual manner, we get the identifier of the client from the Principal pseudo-object, which the ORB initializes with a name set by the caller. The Principal's name method returns a byte array that we convert to a string. We explain how to set information in the Principal at the client side when we discuss the sample client. We get the host name and the port number from the connection information parameter info, as well as the operation name from the operation_name parameter.

```
public void pre_method(
        ConnectionInfo info,
        Principal principal,
        java.lang.String operation_name,
        org.omg.CORBA.Object obj) {
        d = new java.util.Date();
        Date date = new Date(
                d.getYear(), d.getMonth(), d.getDay(),
                d.getHours(), d.getMinutes(), d.getSeconds()
                );
        String client_uuid = new String( principal.name() );
        Event event = new Event (
                client_uuid,
                uuid,
                EventKind.PreMethod,
                date,
                info.hostname,
                info.port,
                operation_name,
                new String(""), // exception name
                obj );

        try {
                Any any_event = _orb().create_any();
                EventHelper.insert( any_event, event );
                push( any_event );
```

```
        }
        catch( SystemException se ) {
            System.out.println( se );
        }
    }
}
```

Finally, we create an Any object, insert the Event object, and push the event into the event channel.

4.4   Event Consumer

In our example the event consumer is the monitor, a Java application with a GUI front end. The monitor watches a CORBA system by obtaining event objects from an event channel and then creates a visual representation of them on the screen. The monitor is implemented in a class Monitor which extends the class Frame and implements the Java interface WindowListener. We declare private object variables of type MonitorSubscriber and Monitor-Display, which receive events and display a representation of them, respectively. We also declare a private variable for the ORB pseudo-object.

```
package com.wiley.compbooks.vogel.chapter11.MonitorImpl;

import java.awt.*;
import java.awt.event.*;
import org.omg.CORBA.*;

public class Monitor
    extends Frame
    implements WindowListener {

    private MonitorDisplay monitor_display;
    private MonitorSubscriber monitor_subscriber;
    private ORB orb;
```

Within the constructor we call the constructor of the Frame class and set the name of the frame to "CORBA Monitor". We also register the monitor object as a WindowListener and set the layout and the size of the frame. Then we initialize the ORB and create an instance of the class MonitorDisplay which manages the visualization of events. We add monitor_display to the frame. Now we create an instance of the class MonitorSubscriber, to which we pass the first command-line argument determining the object id of the event channel and the monitor_display object. We connect the monitor_subscriber object to the ORB to make it invokable by clients. Finally, we call connect() on the monitor_subscriber which connects it to the event channel.

```
public Monitor( String channelName ) {

    super( "CORBA Monitor" );
    addWindowListener(this);
    setLayout( new GridLayout(1,1));
    setSize( 350, 250 );

    try {
        orb = ORB.init(args,null);
        monitor_display = new MonitorDisplay( 10 );
        add( monitor_display );

        monitor_subscriber =
            new MonitorSubscriber( channelName, monitor_display );
        orb.connect( monitor_subscriber );
        monitor_subscriber.connect();
    }
    // catch CORBA system exceptions
    catch(SystemException ex) {
        System.err.println(ex);
    }
}
```

We skip over the default implementation of the methods of the Java interface WindowListener. In the main() method we check if there is an argument for a channel name, and if so we create an instance of Monitor object.

```
// default implementation of the interface WindowListener

public static void main(String args[]) {

    if( args.length != 1 ) {
        System.out.println(
            "Usage: java com.wiley.compbooks.vogel.chapter11." +
            "MonitorImpl.Monitor <channel>");
        System.exit( 1 );
    }
    Monitor m = new Monitor();
    m.setVisible(true);
}
}
```

The class MonitorSubscriber is an implementation of the CORBA Event Service's PushConsumer IDL interface and hence it extends the implementation base class _PushConsumerImplBase.

```
package com.wiley.compbooks.vogel.chapter11.MonitorImpl;
```

```
import org.omg.CORBA.*;
import org.omg.CosEventComm.*;
import org.omg.CosEventChannelAdmin.*;
import com.wiley.compbooks.vogel.chapter11.MonitorType.*;
public class MonitorSubscriber extends _PushConsumerImplBase {

   private EventChannel channel = null;
   private ProxyPushSupplier proxyPushSupplier = null;
   private MonitorDisplay monitor_display;
   private ORB orb;
```

In the constructor of the class we obtain an object reference to an event channel using the `bind()` method provided by Visibroker. From the event channel we obtain a reference to a proxy push supplier interface.

```
public MonitorSubscriber( String channelName, MonitorDisplay md ) {

   monitor_display = md;
   try {
      orb = ORB.init();
      channel = EventChannelHelper.bind( orb, channelName );
      proxyPushSupplier =
         channel.for_consumers().obtain_push_supplier();
   }
   catch(Exception e) {
      e.printStackTrace();
   }
}
```

The method `connect()` connects our push consumer object to the event channel.

```
public void connect() {

   try {
      proxyPushSupplier.connect_push_consumer( this );
   }
   catch(Exception e) {
      e.printStackTrace();
   }
}
```

Now we implement the method `push()`, which is called by the event channel when it receives an event. The method has one parameter that contains an `Event` in the form of an Any object. We extract the `Event` object from the argument using the `extract()` method provided by the `EventHelper` class. Then we decide which method to call on the `monitor_display`, based on the kind of event. This results in the event being depicted on the screen.

```
public void push(Any any_event) throws Disconnected {

    int value = 0;
    try {
        Event event = EventHelper.extract( any_event );
        switch( event.kind.value() ) {
            case EventKind._ClientCreated:
                monitor_display.create_client( event.clientUuid,
                    event.operationName, event.obj);
                break;

            case EventKind._ObjectCreated:
                monitor_display.create_object( event.serverUuid,
                    event.operationName, event.obj);
                break;

            case EventKind._PreMethod:
                monitor_display.invoke( event.clientUuid,
                    event.serverUuid, event.hostname, event.port,
                    event.operationName, event.obj);
                break;

            case EventKind._PostMethod:
                monitor_display.respond( event.clientUuid,
                    event.serverUuid,event.hostname, event.port,
                    event.operationName, event.obj);
                break;

            case EventKind._PostMethodException:
                monitor_display.exception( event.clientUuid,
                    event.serverUuid, event.hostname, event.port,
                    event.operationName, event.exceptionName,
                    event.obj);
                break;

            default: ;
        }

    }
    catch( Exception e ) {
        System.out.println( e );
    }
}
```

We provide a dummy implementation for the PushConsumer interface's operation disconnect_push_consumer().

```
public void disconnect_push_consumer() {
    System.out.println("disconnect_push_consumer");
}
}
```

4.5   Visualizing Events

Our object `monitor_display` of class `MonitorDisplay` draws a visualization of each kind of event. We omit the explanation of the code because it is ordinary Java graphics programming, which has no relationship to CORBA. We have seen the relevant methods of the `MonitorDisplay` class in the case statement of the `push()` method. The complete code of the class `MonitorDisplay` is on the website.

4.6   Instrumenting an Application

Now that we have the mechanisms in place to monitor a CORBA application, we can take the steps necessary to instrument an application. We have chosen our trusty Hello World application to demonstrate this. We have placed the application code in a different package, `com.wiley.compbooks.vogel` `.chapter11.MonitorExample`.

Instrumenting the application consists of creating and registering the event handler objects which we implemented above. For our example this means installing an instance of `MonitorClientHandler` at the client and an instance of `MonitorImpEventHandler` at the server. We also have to provide identifiers to the various components. On the client side we set the Principal name to a unique identifier. The client's Principal pseudo-object is automatically transmitted with every invocation and can be accessed by the event handlers, as we saw earlier in the implementation of the class `MonitorImp-EventHandler`.

In the server we give the object implementation a unique identifier that we also pass to the constructor of `MonitorImpEventHandler`.

4.6.1   Instrumenting the Client

The client is implemented in a class Client. In the `main()` method we initialize the ORB, creating the client's identity object. Then we create an instance of the `MonitorClientEventHandler` class which we initialize with the name of the event channel, the client's identity, and its name. We connect the client event handler to the ORB. Finally we invoke the method `connect()` on the client event handler object which connects the event handler to the event channel.

```
package com.wiley.compbooks.vogel.chapter11.MonitorExample;

import java.io.*;
import org.omg.CORBA.*;
import com.visigenic.vbroker.interceptor.*;
import com.wiley.compbooks.vogel.chapter5.simple.HelloWorld.*;
```

```
import com.wiley.compbooks.vogel.chapter11.MonitorImpl.*;

public class Client {

   public static void main(String args[]) {

   GoodDay goodDay;

      try {
         ORB orb = ORB.init();

         Identity identity = new Identity();
         // create MonitorClientEventHandler object
         MonitorClientEventHandler clientHandler =
            new MonitorClientEventHandler("monitor", identity.id,
            "TestClient", null);
         orb.connect( clientHandler );
         clientHandler.connect();
```

To activate an event handler we have to register it with a handler registry. We obtain an instance of the registry from the ORB by calling `resolve_initial_references()` on the ORB pseudo-object with the keyword `"HandlerRegistry"` as its argument. After we have narrowed the returned object reference to the right type, we can register our event handler object by calling `reg_glob_client_handler()` on the registry object.

```
// get reference to a handler registry
HandlerRegistry registry = HandlerRegistryHelper.narrow(
    orb.resolve_initial_references("HandlerRegistry") );

// register our event handler
try {
    registry.reg_glob_client_handler( clientHandler );
}
catch(Exception e) {
    System.err.println(e);
}
```

We now proceed with getting an object reference for our GoodDay object using the `bind()` method. We obtain the `Principal` pseudo-object from the ORB by calling `default_principal()` and set its name to our client identifier (in a byte array representation). Now every time we make an invocation, the Principal we initialized is transmitted with the invocation.

```
goodDay = GoodDayHelper.bind( orb );

// set principal to id
orb.default_principal().name( id.getBytes() );
```

```
        for(;;) {
            // invoke the operation and print the result
            System.out.println( goodDay.hello() );
            Thread.sleep( 3000 );
        }
    }
    catch(Exception ex) {
        System.err.println(ex);
    }
  }
}
```

For demonstration purposes we keep the client running, making an invocation on the goodDay object every three seconds.

4.6.2 *Instrumenting the Server*

On the server side we make a slight modification to the object implementation, delaying the response to an invocation by half a second. This is only done to get better visual effects when running the demonstration and is totally independent of reporting events.

```
public String hello() throws SystemException {

    try {
            Thread.sleep( 500 );
    }
    catch(java.lang.InterruptedException ex) {
        System.err.println(ex);
    }
    return "Hello World, from " + location;
  }
}
```

The server class implements the usual main() method where we declare the variables implHandler and handlerRegistry. In the try block we initialize the ORB and the BOA and create an Identity object. The next step is to create an instance of the GoodDayImpl class and notify the BOA about the object's existence.

```
package com.wiley.compbooks.vogel.chapter11.MonitorExample;

import org.omg.CORBA.*;
import com.wiley.compbooks.vogel.chapter11.MonitorImpl.*;
import com.visigenic.vbroker.interceptor.*;

public class Server {

  public static void main(String[] args) {
```

```
MonitorImplEventHandler implHandler;
HandlerRegistry registry;

...

try {

    // init ORB

    ORB orb = ORB.init(args,null);

    // init Basic Object Adapter
    BOA boa = orb.BOA_init();

    // create Identity object
    Identity identity = new Identity();

    // create a GoodDay object
    GoodDayImpl goodDay = new GoodDayImpl( args[0] );

    // export the object reference

    boa.obj_is_ready( goodDay );
```

Now we create an instance of `MonitorEventHandler` that we initialize with the event channel name, and the `GoodDay` object's identity, its name, and a reference to the object itself. As in the client, we obtain a registry via the ORB by calling `resolve_initial_references()` on it providing the keyword `"HandlerRegistry"` as argument. Then we register our event handler with the registry. We register this event handler specifically for this object. Alternatively you can register an event handler for all objects in a server, but this would be inappropriate in this case since we have individual object identities.

```
// create TestHandler object
implHandler = new MonitorImplEventHandler( args[1], identity.id,
    args[0], (org.omg.CORBA.Object)goodDay );

// get reference to a handler registry
registry = HandlerRegistryHelper.narrow(
    orb.resolve_initial_references("HandlerRegistry") );

// register our event handler
registry.reg_obj_impl_handler( goodDay, implHandler );

implHandler.object_created();

// print stringified object reference
System.out.println( orb.object_to_string( goodDay ) );
```

```
        // wait for requests
        boa.impl_is_ready();
    }
    catch(Exception e) {
        System.err.println(e);
    }
    }
}
```

Finally, we call the method `object_created()` on our event handler, which sends an initial event to the event channel.

4.7   Monitoring Events

We now run the Hello World server and client, and the monitor. To start the monitored application in the right order we execute the following steps:

1. Start the Event Service (here we use Visibroker's implementation).

```
java com.visigenic.vbroker.services.CosEvent.Channel monitor
```

2. Start the monitor.

```
java com.wiley.compbooks.vogel.chapter11.MonitorImpl.Monitor monitor
```

3. Start a server.

```
java com.wiley.compbooks.vogel.chapter11.MonitorExample.Server Brisbane
monitor
```

4. Start a client.

```
java com.wiley.compbooks.vogel.chapter11.MonitorExample.Client monitor
```

The more clients and servers you start the more interesting the output of the monitor becomes. Figure 11.10 shows two servers and three clients communicating with each other.

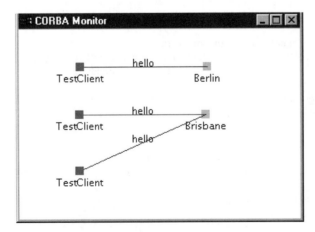

FIGURE 11.10   Monitor at work.

4.8 Extensions to the Example

You can modify and extend this example in various ways. First, you can use other mechanisms instead of Visibroker's Event Handlers. Two options are Visibroker Interceptors or OrbixWeb Filters. Another alternative is to create events directly in the application code. You could still separate the event generation from the application code, for example, by using the Tie approach. You would extend the Tie class with the event code and keep the implementation class application specific.

You can extend the example by generating more events. For example, you could create events occurring within transactions, such as waiting for a lock, or events related to back-end systems, for example, indicating that an object has consumed a resource such as a database connection. We made the Event type fairly generic; you may think of further information to be included.

There could be also other event consumers. Obvious candidates are programs dealing with logging, auditing, performance measurement, and distributed application management. We have a closer look at patterns for these issues in Chapter 13.

You could also make the event delivery infrastructure smarter. A first step would be to have a sequence of linked event channels. Downstream event channels would receive the events from all the other channels, and additional events from other Event Handlers. Consumers would connect to a channel that pushed the kinds of events that they were interested in. A more sophisticated infrastructure could deal with filtering and composition of events. Events could be combined using rules that create a new event with composite semantics. For example, most ATM machines handle the event of three consecutive invalid authentication attempts quite differently from a single one. We discuss approaches to event filtering at the end of the chapter.

5   Java Beans Events and CORBA

So far we have only looked at events from the CORBA perspective. But Java also has events, specifically the event model defined as part of the Java Beans specification. These Java events rely on Java method invocations. There is another more generic Java event mechanism that is part of the Beans component model. This is known as InfoBus. InfoBus events are self-describing data objects. The delivery of an event is controlled by its type and value. In this section we investigate how these concepts fit into the CORBA world.

5.1 JavaBeans Events

One of the core features of JavaBeans are events. The event model is based on JDK 1.1 extensions to the package `java.util`. These extensions are the class `EventObject`, the interface `EventListener`, and the exception `TooMany-ListenersException`:

```
public class EventObject extends Object {
    // constructor - source is the object the event occurred in
    public EventObject( Object source );

    // getSource() returns the object the event occurred initially upon
    public Object getSource()
}
```

JavaBeans provides events as a convenient mechanism to propagate state change notifications from a source object to a set of listener objects. JavaBeans events are mainly focused on but not limited to events occurring in the context of user interfaces, for example, mouse events, keyboard actions, etc.

A source object creates and "fires" an event to a number of event listeners. The event itself is an object and its class should extend the class `EventObject`, which is the abstract base class for all Beans events. The listener objects implement the interface `EventListener`. Firing the event results in the source objects invoking a method on each of the listener objects.

The event object encapsulates the data associated with the event and provides methods to access this data. The event targets implement a method that has an event object as its parameter. This method is invoked by an event source object on all the event targets it wants to notify. Figure 11.11 illustrates the firing of an event. Java events work only within the boundaries of a JVM.

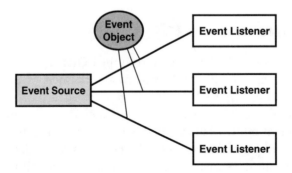

FIGURE 11.11 JavaBeans events.

We have used the JavaBeans event model in all the examples in this book that include GUI components. Typically, we have one class that implemented the interface `ActionListener` which is an extension of the interface `EventListener`. We have other objects such as buttons that are the event sources. We then invoke `addActionListener()` on the event source object to register the event listener. The implementations of the `ActionListener` interface contain the method `actionPerformed()` which is invoked when one of the event sources fires an event. The events `ActionListeners` deal with are of the type `ActionEvent` which is an extension of the class `EventObject` (indirectly via the class `AWTEvent`).

5.2   InfoBus

InfoBus is an extended Java event mechanism for JavaBeans. InfoBus enables components to exchange data asynchronously. It differs from the basic Java event model in two major ways:

- ♦ Event producers and event consumers are decoupled; they only have to know a common InfoBus.
- ♦ The delivery of an event is determined by a name convention for data items.

InfoBus is also designed for communication between components running in the same JVM.

InfoBus was originally developed by Lotus and is under review for inclusion in JDK, probably in time for the JDK 1.3 release. InfoBus has the following major activities: establishing membership of the InfoBus, listening for InfoBus events, rendezvous with event consumers, and access to data items.

5.2.1   *Membership*

A Java component connects to the InfoBus. This requires the programmer to implement the Java interface `InfoBusMember`, obtain an instance of an `InfoBus` object and associate the `InfoBusMember` with the `InfoBus`. The last step is also known as *joining*.

The `InfoBus` class has the following static methods to create an instance of the InfoBus:

```
public static synchronized InfoBus open( Component c );
public static synchronized InfoBus open( String busname );
```

Once you have implemented and created an `InfoBusMember` object, you call `join()` on the `InfoBus` object to associate the member with the bus. This is shown in Figure 11.12.

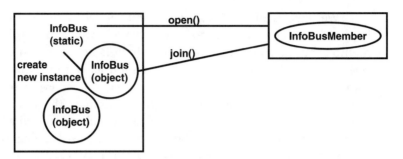

FIGURE 11.12 Establish InfoBus connections.

```
public synchronized void join( InfoBusMember member );
```

5.2.2 Listening for InfoBus Events

Once an object that is an InfoBus member has joined an InfoBus, the member can listen to InfoBus events via the normal Java event model. There are two kinds of events, one for data consumers and one for data producers. Of course, a component can be a data producer as well as a data consumer. There are listener classes and methods to add those listeners for each kind of event. The interface InfoBus defines the following methods for adding and removing listeners:

```
public class InfoBus {
    public void addDataProducer( InfoBusDataProducer producer );
    public void addDataConsumer( InfoBusDataConsumer consumer );
    public void removeDataProducer( InfoBusDataProducer producer );
    public void removeDataConsumer( InfoBusDataConsumer consumer );
}
```

The two interfaces InfoBusDataProducer and InfoBusDataConsumer are extensions of the class InfoBusEventListener, which add methods specific to producers and consumers, respectively. We have a closer look at these interfaces below.

5.2.3 Rendezvous

The rendezvous has three phases. A producer *announces* the availability of a data item. A consumer is sent this announcement. Alternatively, a consumer may ask about certain data, for example, when it has just started up and has not been able to listen to announcements. In either case, the consumer finds out about the availability of a data item and requests it. The code below demonstrates these three phases.

A producer calls the method `fireItemAvailable()` on the InfoBus:

```
public class InfoBus {
   public void fireItemAvailable( String dataItemName,
      InfoBusDataProducer producer );
}
```

This method creates an event of type `InfoBusItemAvailableEvent` and the InfoBus sends it to all registered data consumers.

Sending the event means that InfoBus invokes the method `dataItemReceived()` on each registered `InfoBusDataConsumer`.

```
public interface InfoBusDataConsumer extends InfoBusEventListener {

   public void dataItemAvailable( InfoBusItemAvailableEvent e );
}
```

The `InfoBusDataConsumer` interface must be implemented by an application programmer. The implementation of the method `dataItemReceived()` handles the event. Typically that would involve checking whether the announced data item is of interest to the consumer. If so, the consumer requests the data item by calling `requestDataItem()` on the object `InfoBusItemAvailableEvent`.

```
public interface InfoBusItemAvailableEvent extends InfoBusEvent {

   public DateItem requestDataItem( string itemName,
      InfoBusDataConsumer consumer );
   }
```

Alternatively, a consumer can ask the InfoBus for the availability of a certain data item by calling one of the following methods on the InfoBus class.

```
public class InfoBus {
   public DataItem findDataItem( String dataItemName,
      InfoBusDataConsumer consumer );
   public DataItem findDataItem( String dataItemName,
      InfoBusDataConsumer consumer,
      InfoBusDataProducer producer );
   public DataItem[] findMultipleDataItems( String dataItemName,
      InfoBusDataConsumer consumer );
}
```

The InfoBus creates and fires an event object of type `InfoBusItemRequestEvent`.

```
public interface InfoBusItemRequestEvent extends InfoBusEvent {
```

```
        InfoBusItemRequestEvent( string itemName,
          InfoBusDataConsumer consumer );
        public void setDataItem( DataItem item );
        public DateItem getDataItem();
   }
```

Firing the event means invoking the method `dataItemRequested()` on all data producers registered with the InfoBus.

```
public interface InfoBusDataProducer extends InfoBusEventListener {

      public void dataItemRequested( InfoBusItemRequestEvent e );
      ...
}
```

Either way, at the end the consumer has obtained a data item it can now access, as shown in Figure 11.13.

5.2.4 Access to Data Items

A data access object implements the interface `DataItem`. This interface is implemented by all data items. It provides some generic methods, for example, for firing events about changes to a data item. Methods to manipulate the data in a data item are provided by various subclasses and depend on the kind of data they contain.

The interface `ImmediateAccess` gives access to the item in the form of a string or an object. It also allows the programmer to set the value of the data item. The difference between `getValueAsString()` and `getPresentationString()` is that the former returns the raw data, while the latter returns the data in a formatted way, for example, a string representing currency data may include the characters "$", "." and ",".

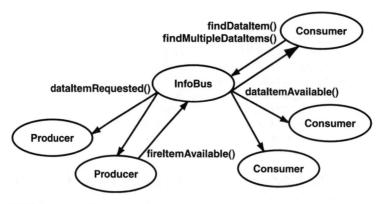

FIGURE 11.13 InfoBus rendezvous.

```
public interface ImmediateAccess extends DataItem {

   public String getValueAsString();
   public Object getValueAsObject();
   public String getPresentationString();
   public void setValue(ImmediateAccess newValue )
      throws InfoBusAccessException;
}
```

The interface CollectionAccess gives access to data that is a collection of items. This interface is extended by the interface ArrayAccess or KeyedAccess depending on the type of the collection. The interface ArrayAccess is intended for array-like collections, while the interface KeyedAccess is for hash tables and dictionaries.

The interface RowSetAccess is provided for data items corresponding to tables in relational databases. The interface provides methods for accessing meta-data, for example, to obtain the number of columns, the name and type of a column, etc. There are also methods to access rows and columns and to retrieve, insert, delete, and update rows.

Finally, the interface DbAccess gives a consumer more control of a data item. It allows a consumer to directly query a database.

5.3   Comparison of the Various Event Models

The event delivery mechanisms we have looked at so far can be categorized by various aspects of the communication model. The communication can be local, that is, within the same JVM, or distributed, that is, across JVM boundaries. We can also distinguish between communication mechanisms:

- ♦ Tightly coupled—The event producer knows all the event consumers directly.
- ♦ Decoupled—The event producer does not know the consumers; they both only know about an intermediate object, for example, an event channel or an InfoBus.
- ♦ Filtering—Consumers receive selected events depending on their name, type, and/or value.

Table 11.1 shows a summary of the various event models we have looked at and puts them into various categories. It does not include Event Handlers because these are a particular kind of event source but not an event delivery mechanism.

TABLE 11.1 Overview and Comparison of Event Models and Mechanisms

Communication	*Local*	*Distributed*
Tightly coupled	JavaBeans events	Sending events as CORBA invocations
Decoupled	JavaBeans over InfoBus	CORBA Event Service
Filtering	JavaBeans over InfoBus	CORBA Notification Service

5.4   Integrating the Various Event Models and Mechanisms

There are plenty of possibilities for integrating the various event models. We concentrate on the following combinations: distributing Java events using CORBA, and distributing Java events using the CORBA Event Service.

5.4.1   Distributing JavaBeans Events with CORBA

This integration model puts the JavaBeans event approach on top of the CORBA communication model, allowing event data to cross JVM boundaries. The interfaces and conventions of the JavaBeans framework are kept wherever possible. Figure 11.14 illustrates this approach.

We define some IDL that corresponds to the JavaBeans classes and interfaces used for transmitting events. The Event IDL struct corresponds to the data part of the EventObject class. This struct is mapped to a Java interface by the IDL compiler. The IDL interface EventListener corresponds to the JavaBeans interface EventListener and the IDL interface EventSource provides management operations corresponding to those of the class EventObject.

```
module com {
...
module chapter11 {
module JavaEventType {

    exception ListenerAlreadyKnown{};
    exception UnknownListener{};
```

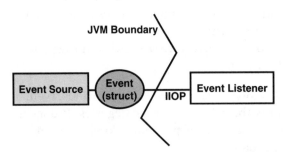

FIGURE 11.14   Distributing JavaBeans events with CORBA.

```
struct Event {
   Object source;
   string str;
};
  interface EventListener {

   void handle_event( in Event event );
  };

  interface EventSource {

   void addEventListener( in EventListener listener )
      raises(ListenerAlreadyKnown);

   void removeEventListener( in EventListener listener )
      raises(UnknownListener);
};};};};};};
```

Whenever the event source creates an event it notifies the registered listeners by invoking the IDL operation handle_event(). The object reference of the source is now a CORBA interoperable object reference instead of the Java object reference.

Instead of remodeling the Java event class as a CORBA struct, you can directly deliver Java event objects in an RMI or Caffeine-like fashion. Caffeine is an extension of Visibroker that offers a Java-to-IDL/IIOP mapping including the object-by-value feature. Once OMG's object-by-value specification has been adopted and implementations become available the same functionality will be available for CORBA objects.

5.4.2 *Distributing JavaBeans Events with the CORBA Event Service*

The event source can avoid having to manage event listeners by using a decoupled communication paradigm, which is provided by the CORBA Event Service as explained in sections 1 and 2. The event sources publish events to an event channel and the event listeners consume the events from the channel, as shown in Figure 11.15. Event producers and consumers can use the push model or the pull model.

The CORBA Event Service uses the IDL type Any for events. The Helper class generated for the IDL Event struct shown above contains methods for the insertion of an event into an Any and for the extraction of an event from an Any.

```
public class EventHelper {

  // insertion of the event into an any and issuing of the event
  public static void insert(
```

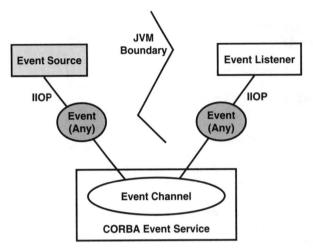

FIGURE 11.15 Distributing JavaBeans events with CORBA event channels.

```
       org.omg.CORBA.Any any, TestEvent.Event value ) {
         ...
       }

       // receiving the event and extraction of the event from the any
       public static TestEvent.Event extract(org.omg.CORBA.Any any) {
         ...
       }
     }
```

This model can be further refined by using the forthcoming CORBA Notification Service. This service will allow delivery of events to be based on their contents in a manner similar to the InfoBus, but with distributed capabilities. The RFP for this service has been issued by the Telecommunications Domain Task Force; the resulting specification is expected to be usable in a wide range of applications. The final specification submissions are scheduled for early 1998.

An event source publishes events as before, but the listeners subscribe to events of a certain type and content. The event selection is controlled by filter objects. Listeners can provide references to filter objects when subscribing to an event channel or they can use a constraint language to express their filter requirements.

Another possible model is to extend the InfoBus event type with the Java class generated from the IDL Event struct. You need to provide fields for references to CORBA objects that provide or request data. The data is obtained by making CORBA operation invocations. This leads to a distributed InfoBus implementation.

C　H　A　P　T　E　R

12

Security

Security is an important issue for most distributed applications, in particular when deployed over the Internet. Security is not a well-defined concept, but stands for a collection of issues. For this chapter we have selected the following topics: applet security restrictions (section 1), firewalls (section 2), IIOP over Secure Socket Layer (section 3), CORBA Security Service (section 4), design pattern for authentication and authorization (section 5), and a login CORBA Bean (section 6).

1　Applet Security Issues

Java virtual machines included in web browsers that execute applet byte code are restricted in their capabilities compared with the full JVM specification. The restrictions are in access to local resources, in particular the local file system, but also printers and other devices as well as networking. Applets are only allowed to open network connections to the host where they were downloaded from. These restrictions are known as *applet sandboxing*.

From a **CORBA** point of view, the network restrictions create a major problem. CORBA provides location transparency, which means that as long as a client holds an **IOR** it can invoke operations on the object that it denotes, regardless of its location. Applet sandboxing breaks CORBA location transparency.

A solution to this problem is to put a forwarder on the web server, as shown in Figure 12.1. This forwarder program is also known as IIOP gateway. All CORBA-enabled applets loaded from this web server will invoke operations on the IIOP gateway instead of an actual object. The IIOP gateway acts as a proxy for the object, sending the invocation to the object and passing the reply back to the applet.

The concept of an IIOP gateway is implemented by the leading Java ORB vendors. Visigenic's Gatekeeper provides IIOP gateway functionality (among other things) as does Iona's Wonderwall.

Another approach to overcoming applet sandboxing is to use signed applets. If users agree to grant the applet the requested privileges, the applet can open direct connections to servers. Signed applets could also grant privileges to applets for printing and accessing the local file system.

2 *Firewalls*

Firewalls restrict network traffic to and from certain hosts. The restrictions can be based on the origin or destination of the traffic, the type of protocol, or they can be application specific.

Firewalls create a complex problem for CORBA applications deployed on the Internet. A typical scenario is illustrated in Figure 12.2. The server-side objects are protected by a server-side firewall and clients can be behind a client-side firewall.

The problem is complex because there are very few standards for firewall products, and an application provider may not have control over client-

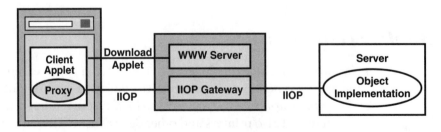

FIGURE 12.1 Restoring CORBA location transparency using an IIOP gateway.

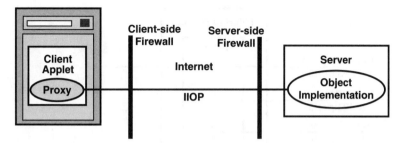

FIGURE 12.2 Generic firewall scenario.

side firewalls. We investigate this topic by looking into several aspects of the firewall problem. First we look at the different types of firewalls and then at client-side and server-side firewalls.

2.1 Types of Firewalls

Firewalls operate using different mechanisms. The most common mechanisms are the filtering of packets based on their origin and/or destination, filtering based on the protocol, and filtering for a specific application. We explain each of these mechanisms in the following subsections. Note that firewall products typically provide combinations of the different types.

2.1.1 Origin/Destination Filtering

Firewalls that filter packets based on their origin and destination are closely coupled with routers. To implement a particluar policy, the firewall sets restrictions on the router. The origin and destination of IP packets can be described in terms of the IP addresses of individual hosts and/or subnets, or in terms of port numbers. We refer to these firewalls as *filtering firewalls*. Figure 12.3 illustrates the mechanism of a filtering firewall. Typically such firewalls allow policies stated in rules such as these:

◆ Allow all kinds of packets, but only to this IP address and this port.
◆ Allow incoming traffic only from the specified IP subnets.

To enable cooperation between a CORBA application and a filtering firewall, it is important that the ORB allows CORBA servers to run on specific ports. Visibroker, for example, allows servers to start with the option -DOAport, which makes the server listen on the specified port. This forces all client connections to the server to use this port.

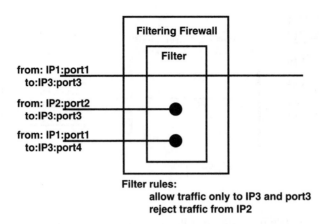

FIGURE 12.3 Origin/destination filtering firewalls.

2.1.2 Gateway Firewalls

Gateway firewalls are typically based on a dual-homed bastion host as shown in Figure 12.4. A dual-homed machine is one that has two network cards with separate IP addresses. Typically one address, the external one, is accessible from the Internet; the other address, the internal one, is connected to the protected intranet. Such a configuration physically blocks the Internet traffic directed to IP addresses in the protected domain. We refer to this kind of firewall as a *gateway firewall*.

The only way to access machines on the protected subnet is to run a gateway on the bastion host which forwards incoming traffic to the internal machines. These gateways can be protocol specific or application specific. Typically, gateway firewall products come with HTTP (web), FTP (file transfer), NNTP (news), and SMTP (e-mail) gateways.

There are also IIOP gateways including Visigenic's Gatekeeper and Iona's Wonderwall, but there is no standard for IIOP gateways at the time of

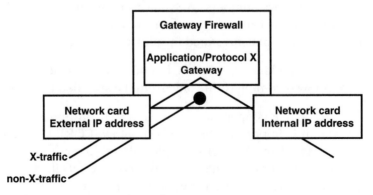

FIGURE 12.4 Gateways firewalls.

writing. However, the OMG is expecting submissions to an RFP on IIOP gateways. We expect a standard to be adopted in mid-1998 and compliant products to be available shortly thereafter. IIOP gateways are not yet integrated into firewall vendors' offerings, and it is unclear how quickly IIOP gateways will become widely available.

2.2   Client-side Firewalls

A client-side firewall is typically put into place by a company to restrict employee access to the Internet and to protect the company's intranet from outside attacks. Internet service providers also have firewalls in place in some cases. These usually restrict the Internet access of their subscribers to certain protocols, for example, HTTP and NNTP. Some further restrictions may also apply, for example, an NNTP gateway that only allows access to selected news groups.

2.2.1   *Controlled Client-side Firewalls*

When the clients of an application are in the same organization as the application provider then the provider can negotiate a security policy for the client-side firewall with systems administrators. This can extend to situations where organizations have clients in multiple locations and use the Internet for communication between them. Other organizations providing a service to a finite set of known customers can require that these customers modify their client-side firewall policy.

Depending on the type of the client-side firewall, it can be made permeable for the traffic related to a CORBA application. Destination IP addresses and port numbers can be enabled on filtering firewalls, and IIOP gateways can be installed on bastion machines with gateway firewalls. Most gateway firewalls can also operate in filtering mode.

2.2.2   *Unknown Client-side Firewalls*

CORBA-enabled applets that are available over the Internet to arbitrary clients cannot expect that a client firewall will be configured according to their needs. If the firewall does not allow IIOP traffic to pass, the applet is stuck.

A common technique for overcoming this problem is HTTP tunneling. HTTP tunneling means that an IIOP request is enclosed into an HTTP envelope and sent via the HTTP protocol. The receiving HTTP server must be able to understand these special HTTP requests. It takes the IIOP request out of the HTTP envelope and makes the real IIOP request on the target objects. Figure 12.5 illustrates the idea behind HTTP tunneling. In this way,

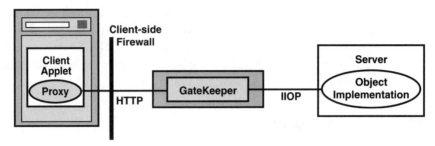

FIGURE 12.5 HTTP tunneling with Gatekeeper.

any client that can load a CORBA applet using HTTP can make invocations using HTTP calls to the same machine.

Visibroker and OrbixWeb support HTTP tunneling in the ORB's applet library. Their respective gateways, Gatekeeper and Wonderwall, act as special HTTP servers.

HTTP tunneling suffers all the shortcomings of HTTP which we discussed in Chapter 1. Also HTTP tunneling disables callbacks into the applet. This is because there is no HTTP/IIOP gateway installed on the client side that can respond to an HTTP request by extracting an IIOP request and forwarding it to the callback object.

One other attempt can be made to overcome client-side firewalls without using HTTP tunneling. If the firewall is only blocking requests to certain ports (for example, all ports but 80—the HTTP port—or 443—the SSL port), the gateway can be configured to listen on port 80. This prevents an ordinary HTTP server from running on the same machine. However, the applet needs to be loaded from this machine.

Figure 12.6 shows a solution to this dilemma. There are two hosts. One provides normal web services. The other machine hosts the Visibroker Gatekeeper listening on port 80. Since the Gatekeeper is a functionally complete HTTP server, the applet can be loaded via the Gatekeeper. Similarly, port 443 could be used for IIOP traffic, in particular when using IIOP over SSL, as explained later in this chapter.

We consider that the only acceptable, complete solution to the problem is for client-side firewalls to implement the IIOP gateway standard expected to be published by the OMG.

2.3 Server-side Firewalls

On the server side, the variety of firewall configurations is even larger, but solutions are more easily achievable since the application provider usually has control over the policies enforced by server-side firewalls. We identify several server-side firewall scenarios in the next section.

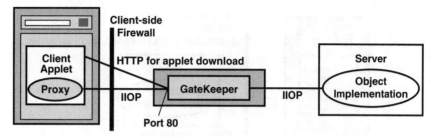

FIGURE 12.6 IIOP via port 80.

2.3.1 Filtering Firewalls

Filtering firewalls constrain traffic based on origin and target IP addresses and ports. To enable invocation on CORBA applications' objects you have to allow traffic through the firewall that is destined for any port on any host that the applications' servers are listening on.

If the clients to the applications are applets, the scenario becomes very simple. In most cases applets require an IIOP gateway, which is the single point of access. The IP address and port number of the gateway are known, for example, Visibroker's Gatekeeper uses port 15000 by default, although it can be configured to listen on other ports. To enable access to your applications you simply have to allow TCP/IP access to a single port through the firewall. This scenario is shown in Figure 12.7.

If there is no IIOP gateway available, or the firewall is placed between the gateway and the application servers, the same mechanism applies. You have to make sure that your servers always start on the same port. Visibroker allows you to set the port on which a server is listening with the option -DOAport. Firewalls would now need to allow traffic through to all the ports used by the servers. This scenario is illustrated in Figure 12.8.

Note that you have to enable UDP traffic when using Visibroker's OSAgent. However, allowing UDP traffic through firewalls is considered a security threat, and hence other bootstrap mechanisms are explained in

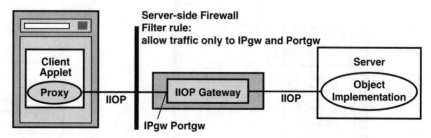

FIGURE 12.7 Filtering firewalls with an IIOP gateway.

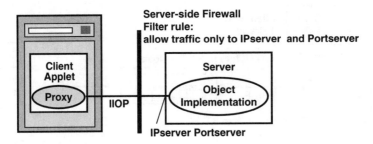

FIGURE 12.8 Filtering firewalls without an IIOP gateway.

Chapter 8. Similar issues may apply when using other ORBs' proprietary bootstrapping mechanisms.

2.3.2 Gateway Firewalls

A gateway firewall physically blocks all traffic unless a protocol-specific or application-specific gateway is installed on the bastion host which forwards the traffic. IIOP gateways are provided by ORB vendors, for example, by Visigenic (Gatekeeper) or Iona (Wonderwall). You just have to install an IIOP gateway on the bastion host. You have to start the IIOP gateway so that it listens on the external network card and forwards to the internal network. Such a configuration is shown in Figure 12.9.

Visigenic's Gatekeeper, for example, provides you with the following options that allow you to configure it properly when using multihomed bastion hosts:

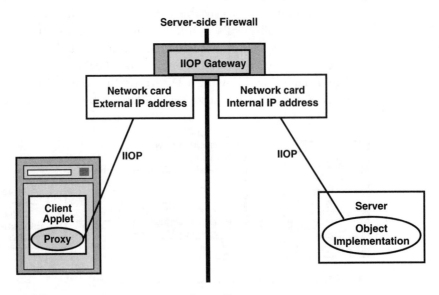

FIGURE 12.9 Server-side gateway firewalls.

♦ `-exIP`—determines the IP address of the external network card
♦ `-inIP`—determines the IP address of the internal network card

There are further options for more fine-grained control.

2.3.3 Multiple Server-side Firewalls

In many cases there are multiple firewalls on the server side. A typical scenario is a *demilitarized zone* which is shielded from the Internet by a firewall. It hosts web servers and IIOP gateways. The IIOP gateway forwards the CORBA invocations to the application's objects, which again are protected by a firewall. Figure 12.10 shows such a firewall scenario.

If both firewalls are of the filtering kind, the setup is straightforward. You open the ports for the Web server and the IIOP gateways on the first firewall, and enable traffic to the ports on which your application servers are listening on the second firewall.

If one of the firewalls is of the gateway type, the IIOP gateway needs to be located on the bastion host that represents the gateway firewall. If both firewalls are of the gateway kind, IIOP gateways available at the time of writing cannot handle the situation because they do not recursively support the forwarding of IIOP requests.

3 IIOP over Secure Socket Layer

Secure Socket Layer (SSL) is a security protocol that sits directly on top of the TCP/IP transport protocol. It has become popular in the context of the Web as the underlying protocol for Secure HTTP (SHTTP). The OMG recognized this popularity and issued an RFP soliciting a specification for IIOP over SSL as a simple alternative to the CORBA Security specification. The OMG adopted the specification resulting from the RFP process in mid-1997 and implementations of the specification became available shortly thereafter. In this section we explain the concepts of SSL, the specification of

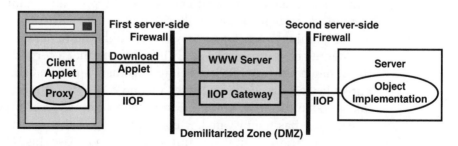

FIGURE 12.10 Demilitarized zone.

IIOP over SSL, and the interfaces provided by Visibroker for Java. Finally, we show an SSL-secured Hello World example.

3.1 SSL

SSL is a protocol on top of TCP/IP which adds security capabilities. The SSL API is an extension to the TCP/IP socket API. SSL's security capabilities include encryption of the messages sent through an SSL communication channel, authentication of the server based on digital certificates and signatures, and optional authentication of the client. Note that we use the terms client and server differently in this context. In SSL the client is the program that initiates an SSL connection and the server is the program that accepts the connection. The client and server participating in an SSL connection are also known as *peers*.

SSL authentication is based on public key cryptography. Public key technology uses a pair of asymmetric keys for encryption and decryption. This means that a message encrypted with one key can only be decrypted using the other key of the pair. If you keep the *private key* secret and distribute the *public key*, anyone can encrypt messages using the public key that only you can decrypt (using your private key). Furthermore, messages that are encrypted with the private key can only be decrypted with the corresponding public key. Assuming that the other party obtained your public key from a trusted place, this provides proof that the message was from you. If two parties exchange their public keys they can establish a two-way encrypted communication.

Authentication means establishing that the identity of a party is what it claims to be. In SSL this is based on digital certificates. A digital certificate is issued by a certificate authority. The certificate contains the name of the certificate authority, the name of the party who owns the certificate (and which is identified by it), the public key of this party, and time stamps. All this data is *signed* by the certificate authority, which means that the certificate cannot be modified without this being noticed. Security is always based on trust. In order to establish an identity you have to trust someone. If you don't trust a particular certificate authority, you can obtain its certificate and authenticate it with an authority that you do trust.

Obtaining a certificate, however, is only the first step in establishing the identity of your peer. The only information that a certificate gives you is that a name and a public key belong together. Given that the name and the public key are public knowledge, anyone can obtain this information and fake an identity. What you need to prove is that whoever presents the certificate also has the private key corresponding to the public one contained by the certificate. Digital signatures are used to prove this. The mechanism behind the digital signature involves creating a random message and encrypting it with the private key. If the server wishes to authenticate itself with the client who holds its certificate, the server sends the message in clear text as well as the encrypted message to the client. The client can compare the clear text message with the result of decrypting the encrypted message using the public key it obtained from the certificate. If they match, the client knows that the public and private key of the server match and has finally established the identity of the server.

SSL also provides data integrity using a message authentication code (MAC). This allows you to detect if someone in the transmission path has corrupted the message. MAC encryption is based on the private key and a part of the message itself.

Although asymmetric encryption technology can be used for encrypting the data once the SSL connection is established, a symmetric encryption mechanism is typically used. Symmetric algorithms are less computationally complex than asymmetric ones. Symmetric mechanisms work by having the two parties share a secret code that is used to encrypt and decrypt messages going in either direction. Once the server is authenticated, it can send the client a secret code encrypted with the client's public key and at that point both parties use this secret code for encrypting messages.

SSL is based on certificates defined in the ISO standard X.509. There are various options for the encryption mechanism and MAC algorithm. SSL contains a handshake protocol to establish the algorithms used for a particular session.

Finally, to use SSL to secure your CORBA communications you need at least a digital certificate for the server. At the time of writing, the supporting infrastructure is quite rudimentary. You can obtain certificates from certificate authorities such as Verisign, but there is little support for storing them and integrating them with directory servers. However, companies like Netscape, Microsoft, Oracle, and Novell are working on solutions.

3.2   Specification

OMG's document orbos/97-02-04, which contains the IIOP over SSL specification, is, in contrast to almost every other CORBA specification, a very thin document and the specification itself fills only one and a half pages. The specification addresses two issues: the encoding of an IOR when using IIOP over SSL and the protocol itself.

The specification defines a *profile* for IORs when using IIOP over SSL. This allows for future integration of SSL security with the CORBA Security Service. The definition of the profile is only of interest to ORB implementers and does not concern the application programmer.

We explain the protocol by quoting the specification: "As SSL provides a secure transport layer over TCP/IP. The CORBA SECIOP protocol is not required when using SSL. Instead the connection rules of IIOP (PTC/96-3-93 12.7.1.) are applied to SSL (which itself uses TCP/IP)."

The specification does not define an extension of the interface to the ORB which is needed for using IIOP over SSL. In the next section we will explain Visibroker's APIs for using IIOP over SSL. It was the only Java ORB providing SSL security at the time of writing.

3.3 Visibroker Interfaces

When using IIOP over SSL, you need APIs to

♦ Ensure that a server accepts only SSL connections
♦ Ensure that a client initiates SSL connections
♦ Set the certificate for the server, and optionally for the client
♦ Obtain the SSL connection attributes
♦ Obtain the certificate of a peer

The API for such operations has not been defined in the IIOP over SSL specification and hence it is left to the ORB implementers to define such interfaces. In this section we explain Visibroker's API. Visibroker places all the interfaces dealing with SSL in the package com.visigenic.vbroker.ssl.

The most important interfaces are to the certificate manager, the certificate chain, and the SSL Current pseudo-object. You must also initialize the ORB and the BOA differently, as we explain in the next example.

3.3.1 Certificate Manager

The certificate manager allows you to determine the attributes of an SSL connection. The certificate manager API is defined as the Java interface CertificateManager:

```
public interface com.visigenic.vbroker.ssl.CertificateManager
    extends java.lang.Object
    implements org.omg.CORBA.Object
```

It offers the following methods:

♦ public void setProtocolVersion(

com.visigenic.vbroker.ssl.SetProtocolVersion);

—sets the SSL version. Versions currently available are Version_20 and Version_30. The BOA will only accept connections from a peer that has the same version number.

◆ `public void requestClientCertificate();`

> —enforces the client authentication. If you don't invoke the method, the SSL handshake protocol does not request a client certificate.

◆ `public void setCertificateChain(byte[][]);`

> —sets the certificate chain. The certificate chain starts with the user's (or entity's) certificate followed by the hierarchy of certificates of certificate authorities. Each certificate is supplied as an array of bytes and the certificate chain is an array of certificates.

◆ `public void addTrustedCertificate(byte[], int);`

> —allows you to certify a certificate as being trusted. For example, you may trust a company's certificate or a certificate authority's certificate.

◆ `public void setClearPrivateKey(byte[]);`

> —sets a *clear* private key. The certificate together with the private key will allow the ORB to establish the identity of an entity. Private keys can be password protected or clear. This method and the next deal with clear private keys. There is another pair of methods that set password-protected private keys.

◆ `public void setClearExportPrivateKey(byte[]);`

> —sets a clear private key, of a shorter length, that is allowed to be exported under U.S. federal regulations.

◆ `public void setEncryptedPrivateKey(byte[], java.lang.String);`

> —sets a password-protected private key.

◆ `public void setEncryptedExportPrivateKey(byte[], java.lang.String);`

> —sets a password-protected, exportable private key.

◆ `public byte decodeBase64(java.lang.String)[];`

> —decodes a stringified version of a certificate or a private key into a byte array.

3.3.2 Certificate Chain

The certificate chain API is provided by the class `X509CertificateChain`:

```
public final synchronized class
    com.visigenic.vbroker.ssl.X509CertificateChain
    extends java.lang.Object
```

We explain only some of its methods, as others are not interesting for the application programmer:

◆ `public byte[] berEncoding();`

> —returns the byte array format of a single certificate.

♦ `public java.lang.String distinguishedName();`

> —returns the distinguished name of the certificate holder. A distinguished name is a hierarchical name as defined in the ISO standard X.500.

♦ `public java.lang.String toString();`

> —creates a string representation of the certificate.

3.3.3   SSL Current

Current objects provide shared context between the client and server. They are used by services such as the CORBA Security Service (see section 4) and the Transaction Service. The SSL Current psuedo-object is defined by the following interface:

```
public interface com.visigenic.vbroker.ssl.Current
    extends java.lang.Object
```

> It provides the following methods:

♦ `public abstract com.visigenic.vbroker.ssl.ProtocolVersion`
  `getProtocolVersion(org.omg.CORBA.Object);`

> —returns the version of the SSL protocol. Available values are `Version_20` and `Version_30`.

♦ `public abstract short getNegotiatedCipher(org.omg.CORBA.Object);`

> —returns the negotiated cipher for the SSL connection as constant. There are currently 28 different values for the cipher. The cipher describes the type of certificate (for example, RSA or DH), the encryption technology for the data transfer (for example, symmetric versus asymmetric encryption), the key length, and the MAC.

♦ `public abstract com.visigenic.vbroker.ssl.X509CertificateChain`
  `getPeerCertificateChain(org.omg.CORBA.Object);`

> —returns the peer's X509 certificate chain.

3.4   Example

We again use the simple Hello World example from Chapter 5. The interfaces and the functionality are exactly the same as in the original example. But now the client and server have to provide a certificate to authenticate themselves and the communication is encrypted.

3.4.1   Client Implementation

The SSL-enabled client imports the package `com.visigenic.vbroker.ssl` which contains Visibroker's SSL interfaces. Within the client class we have static strings that contain the base-64 encoded representations of a client certificate, the certificate authority's certificate, and the client's private key, respectively. Obviously the hard-coding of this information is not appropriate, but we have already pointed out that there is currently a lack of security infrastructure that would provide interfaces to obtain certificates and keys. You only need provide certificates and keys in the client implementation when you want to use client-side authentication, that is, that the server can obtain the client's certificate and check the client's identity.

```
package com.wiley.compbooks.vogel.chapter12.ssl.HelloWorldImpl;

import java.io.*;
import org.omg.CORBA.*;
import org.omg.CORBA.ORBPackage.*;
import com.visigenic.vbroker.ssl.*;
import com.wiley.compbooks.vogel.chapter5.simple.HelloWorld.*;

public class Client {
    final private static String testCert_base64 =
    "MIICZzCCAfECAQIwDQYJKoZIhvcNAQEEBQAwgaQxCzAJBgNVBAYTAlVTMRMwEQYD\n" +
...
    "I4KxIDdjSY5rxpvhKG5GQ7+m2pq3fAtnbtB2ppC5sHjXe66duZYD33hi7A==\n";

    final private static String caCert_base64 =
    "MIICdDCCAf4CAQEwDQYJKoZIhvcNAQEEBQAwgaQxCzAJBgNVBAYTAlVTMRMwEQYD\n" +
...
    "rGzloIlCRQI=\n";

    final private static String encryptedPrivateKey_base64 =
    "MIICCDAaBgkqhkiG9w0BBQMwDQQIWr2kNRXj9qECAQUEggHohb32URya32YuRW8t" +
...
    "eJcUsro3/SwApSwQK+cCd9BuRR958ajKRJQ1FJdNTFEjdnD/yW5ba5/bUnc=";
```

In the `main()` method we initialize the ORB. This time we use the version of ORB's `init()` method which takes Java properties as a second argument. This requires us to create a Java `Properties` object and insert our desired property. We set the property `ORBservices` to the value `com.visigenic.vbroker.ssl`. This makes the ORB SSL aware. We then proceed as usual by obtaining a stringified object reference, converting it to a live one, and narrowing it to the `GoodDay` interface type.

```
public static void main(String args[]) {

    try {
        // Create a property list specifying SSL.
        java.util.Properties orbProps = new java.util.Properties();
        orbProps.put("ORBservices", "com.visigenic.vbroker.ssl");

        // Initialize the ORB.
        org.omg.CORBA.ORB orb = org.omg.CORBA.ORB.init(args, orbProps);
```

```
// get object reference from command-line argument
org.omg.CORBA.Object obj = orb.string_to_object( args[0] );

// and narrowed it to HelloWorld.GoodDay
GoodDay goodDay = GoodDayHelper.narrow( obj );
if( goodDay == null ) {
    System.err.println(
        "stringified object reference is of wrong type");
    System.exit( -1 );
}
```

The following two code segments are again optional. You only need to include them if you want to implement client authentication. To set a certificate you must obtain a certificate manager, which you get from the ORB via the method resolve_initial_references(). Since we set the property ORBservices to refer to the SSL package, which includes the certificate manager class, the ORB can load the class and create an instance of the certificate manager.

The certificate manager provides the method decodeBase64() which allows us to convert the stringified certificates into a certificate chain, which is a two-dimensional byte array. We the set this certificate chain at the certificate manager.

```
// Get the certificate manager
CertificateManager certificateManager =
    CertificateManagerHelper.narrow
    (orb.resolve_initial_references("SSLCertificateManager"));

// Set my certificate chain, ordered from user to CA.
byte[][] certificates = {
  certificateManager.decodeBase64(testCert_base64),
  certificateManager.decodeBase64(caCert_base64)
};
certificateManager.setCertificateChain(certificates);
```

We proceed in the same way to set the private key. We convert the stringified version into a byte array and set it at the certificate manager. Once again, the password is hard-coded for simplicity. A real application would ask the user for a password.

```
// Set my private key, given the specified password.
byte[] encryptedPrivateKey =
    certificateManager.decodeBase64(encryptedPrivateKey_base64);
certificateManager.setEncryptedPrivateKey
    (encryptedPrivateKey, "password");
```

We obtain an instance of an SSL Current pseudo-object from the ORB. The SSL Current allows us to look at negotiated values: the cipher and the protocol version. It also enables us to investigate the server's certificate. We explain the returned values later when we look at the running example.

```
// Get the SSL current
Current current = CurrentHelper.narrow
    (orb.resolve_initial_references("SSLCurrent"));

// Check the cipher
System.out.println("Negotiated Cipher: " + "\n\t" +
    CipherSuite.toString(current.getNegotiatedCipher(goodDay))
    + "\n");

// Check the protocol version
System.out.println("Protocol Version: " + "\n\t" +
    current.getProtocolVersion(goodDay) + "\n");

// Check the peer's distinguished name
System.out.println("goodDay's distinguished name: " + "\n\t" +
    current.getPeerCertificateChain(goodDay).distinguishedName()
    + "\n");
```

Finally, we invoke the `hello()` method in the usual way.

```
        // invoke the operation and print the result
        System.out.println( goodDay.hello() );
    }

    // catch CORBA system exceptions
    catch(Exception ex) {
        System.err.println(ex);
    }

  }
}
```

3.4.2 Server Implementation

The server uses the same API as the client to set its certificate and private key. On the server side, the setting of the certificate is mandatory.

```
package com.wiley.compbooks.vogel.chapter12.ssl.HelloWorldImpl;

import java.io.*;
import org.omg.CORBA.*;
import com.visigenic.vbroker.ssl.*;
import com.wiley.compbooks.vogel.chapter5.simple.HelloWorld.*;

public class Server {

  final private static String testCert_base64 =
  "MIICZzCCAfECAQIwDQYJKoZIhvcNAQEEBQAwgaQxCzAJBgNVBAYTAlVTMRMwEQYD\n" +
```

```
...
"I4KxIDdjSY5rxpvhKG5GQ7+m2pq3fAtnbtB2ppC5sHjXe66duZYD33hi7A==\n";

final private static String caCert_base64 =
"MIICdDCCAf4CAQEwDQYJKoZIhvcNAQEEBQAwgaQxCzAJBgNVBAYTAlVTMRMwEQYD\n" +
...
"rGzloIlCRQI=\n";

final private static String encryptedPrivateKey_base64 =
"MIICCDAaBgkqhkiG9w0BBQMwDQQIWr2kNRXj9qECAQUEggHohb32URya32YuRW8t" +
...
"eJcUsro3/SwApSwQK+cCd9BuRR958ajKRJQ1FJdNTFEjdnD/yW5ba5/bUnc=";
```

We again initialize the ORB with property `ORBservices` set to Visibroker's SSL package. We obtain the certificate manager and set the certificate chain and the private key as in the client code.

```
public static void main(String[] args) {

    if( args.length != 1 ) {
        System.out.println(
            "Usage: vbj com.wiley.compbooks.vogel.chapter12." +
            "ssl.HelloWorldImpl.Server <location>");
        System.exit( 1 );
    }

    try {
        // Create a property list specifying ssl
        java.util.Properties props = new java.util.Properties();
        props.put("ORBservices", "com.visigenic.vbroker.ssl");
        // Initialize the ORB.
        org.omg.CORBA.ORB orb = org.omg.CORBA.ORB.init(args, props);

        // Get the certificate manager
        CertificateManager certificateManager =
            CertificateManagerHelper.narrow
            (orb.resolve_initial_references("SSLCertificateManager"));

        // Set my certificate chain, ordered from user to CA.
        byte[][] certificates = {
            certificateManager.decodeBase64(testCert_base64),
            certificateManager.decodeBase64(caCert_base64)
        };
        certificateManager.setCertificateChain(certificates);
        // Set my private key, given the specified password.
        byte[] encryptedPrivateKey =
            certificateManager.decodeBase64(encryptedPrivateKey_base64);
        certificateManager.setEncryptedPrivateKey
            (encryptedPrivateKey, "password");

        // As for the client's certificates, for client authentication.
        certificateManager.requestClientCertificate();
```

We initialize the BOA with the value `SSLTSession` which instructs the BOA to accept only SSL connections. The BOA negotiates the setup for an SSL connection with any clients attempting to use our objects. We proceed as usual by creating the object and calling `obj_is_ready()` and `impl_is_ready()` on the BOA.

```
        // Initialize the BOA with SSL
        org.omg.CORBA.BOA boa = orb.BOA_init("SSLTSession", null);

        // create a GoodDay object
        GoodDayImpl goodDayImpl = new GoodDayImpl( args[0] );

        // export the object reference
        boa.obj_is_ready( goodDayImpl );

        // print stringified object reference
        System.out.println( orb.object_to_string( goodDayImpl ) );

        boa.impl_is_ready();
    }
    catch(Exception e) {
        System.err.println(e);
    }
  }
}
```

3.4.3 Object Implementation

The class `GoodDayImpl` implements the IDL interface GoodDay that we specified in Chapter 5. It is functionally equivalent to the implementation in the Chapter 5 package. However, we add some code to inspect the SSL Current and to check the client's certificate.

```
package com.wiley.compbooks.vogel.chapter12.ssl.HelloWorldImpl;

import org.omg.CORBA.*;
import org.omg.CORBA.ORBPackage.*;
import com.visigenic.vbroker.ssl.*;
import com.wiley.compbooks.vogel.chapter5.simple.HelloWorld.*;

public class GoodDayImpl extends _GoodDayImplBase {

    private String location;

    // constructor
    GoodDayImpl( String location ) {
        super( location );
    // initialize location
        this.location = location;
}
```

```
// method
public String hello() {
```

Here we obtain the SSL Current pseudo-object, as already seen in the client. We then check the cipher and the protocol version. If the client has set a certificate, we obtain the distinguished name from it and print it.

```
try {
    Current current = CurrentHelper.narrow
      (_orb().resolve_initial_references("SSLCurrent"));
    System.out.println("Negotiated Cipher: " + "\n\t" +
        CipherSuite.toString(current.getNegotiatedCipher(this))
        + "\n");
    System.out.println("Protocol Version: " + "\n\t" +
        current.getProtocolVersion(this) + "\n");

    if(current.getPeerCertificateChain(this) != null ) {
        System.out.println("Peer's distinguished name: " + "\n\t" +
        current.getPeerCertificateChain(this).distinguishedName()
        + "\n");
    }
}
catch(InvalidName e) {
        System.err.println(e);
}
return "Hello World, from " + location;
    }
}
```

3.4.4 *Example at Work*

When we start the server it prints out the stringified IOR. Once a client has established an SSL connection to the server and invokes an operation on the GoodDay object, the SSL Current is obtained and the negotiated cipher and protocol version are printed. We also obtain the client's certificate, get the distinguished name from it, and print it. As you see, in this example we are using a certificate issued by the Consensus Development Corporation for testing only.

```
IOR:000000000000001b49444c3a4...

Negotiated Cipher:
        RSA_WITH_3DES_EDE_CBC_SHA

Protocol Version:
        Version_30

Peer's distinguished name:
        C=US, ST=California, O=Consensus Development Corporation, OU=SSL
Plus TESTING AND EVALUATION ONLY, CN=*.consensus.com
```

The distinguished name is a hierarchical name as defined in the ISO standard X.500. Its fields have the following meanings:

- ◆ C: country
- ◆ ST: state
- ◆ O: organization
- ◆ OU: division or unit within the organization

The client similarly prints the results of the SSL handshaking process once it has established an SSL connection with the server. As you can see, the negotiated cipher matches the one printed by the server above and so does the protocol version.

```
Negotiated Cipher:
        RSA_WITH_3DES_EDE_CBC_SHA

Protocol Version:
        Version_30

goodDay's distingushed name:
        C=US, ST=California, O=Consensus Development Corporation, OU=SSL
Plus TESTING AND EVALUATION ONLY, CN=*.consensus.com

Hello World, from Berlin
```

Next we print the server's distinguished name which is the same as the client's name. This is, of course, not the normal case, but due to the lack of other certificates we used the Consensus test certificate in the client and the server. Finally we see the normal printout from the hello() operation.

3.5 Applets and SSL

There are few issues which make the use of SSL with applets different from its use in Java applications. If you want to use certificates for client authentication, an applet needs to access a certificate from a source local to the browser, for example, the local file system, a local certificate server, or from the browser itself. Unless you use signed applets and the browser user gives the applet the capabilities to access local resources, there is no way that an applet can obtain the client's certificate. The currently available API requires access to the private key and would enable applets to steal identities by obtaining the certificate and the private key of a client. The only solution is that the browser (or its JVM) provides an API to access the browser user's credentials without giving its private key to the applet.

Typically an IIOP gateway is used when using applets. Visigenic's Gatekeeper allows you to use IIOP over SSL between the applet and Gatekeeper.

You can also force Gatekeeper to use IIOP over SSL to the server. Whether or not you want to do this depends on your firewall configuration. If Gatekeeper is already behind the firewall then there is probably no need to encrypt the IIOP messages between the gatekeeper and the application servers. However, this depends on your security policies.

At the time writing, the Visibroker SSL implementation relies on C code libraries for cryptographic functions. It is expected that a pure Java implementation will be available in 1998.

4   Overview of the CORBA Security Service

The CORBA Security Service defines a framework for the use of many different underlying security technologies to secure CORBA applications. It provides interfaces that are generic enough to allow the use of any of these technologies. However, this means that not all of the functionality that the interfaces provide will be supported by all of the technologies that implement security.

4.1   Overview of Security Goals and Terminology

In this subsection we provide an overview of the aims of a secure object system and a summary of the security features that are specified in the Security Service. Lastly, we discuss the levels of conformance to this specification.

4.1.1   Aims of Security

There are several different aims of providing a secure object invocation environment. These can be divided into the following broad classifications:

- ◆ Confidentiality—Information is only available to those it is intended for.
- ◆ Integrity—Information is only modified by those authorized to do so and is transferred without interference or corruption.
- ◆ Accountability—Users' security actions are recorded so that they can be held accountable for them.
- ◆ Availability—Authorized users cannot be maliciously denied service.

4.1.2   Threats to Security

There are several ways in which security can be breached, and an adequate security system should be able either to detect and stop or prevent the occurrence of

- An authorized user gaining access to information or services they are not permitted to access
- A user pretending to be someone else and using this false identity to access information or services that they would otherwise not be able to access
- A user finding a way to bypass the security system to access information or services that should be secured
- Monitoring communications channels for confidential messages intended for others
- Modifying, deleting, or replaying messages on communications channels
- A user performing untraceable malicious actions, even if they are authorized to do so

4.1.3 *Features of the Security Service*

The CORBA Security specification defines the following functionality to provide safeguards against the possible breaches mentioned:

Identification and authentication. The provision of identities to principals (human users and objects which require their own identity) and the ability to verify that the principals are who they claim to be.

Authorization and access control. A way of deciding whether a principal is allowed to access an object. This includes the ways in which administrators can specify which principals (or groups of principals) may access particular objects and how applications may decide whether to grant access to a principal.

Auditing. Keeping records of which principals perform which invocations on secured objects. The specification also defines the means of deciding which actions to audit and which to ignore.

Communications security. This may include several actions: authentication of the client to its target object, (optionally) authentication of the target object by the client, protecting the integrity of messages transmitted, and (optionally) protecting the confidentiality of messages transmitted.

Nonrepudiation. Creation, transmission, and storage of irrefutable evidence that a principal performed an action so that it can be retrieved later in case of a dispute. This may include evidence of creation of objects and the sending or receipt of messages.

Administration of security policy. Interfaces that apply security to a domain, including many objects and applications regardless of whether or not the applications are security aware.

4.1.4 Security Conformance Levels

The Security Service can be implemented to conform to one of two levels of security, with a single optional facility: nonrepudiation. There are also ways of implementing ORBs to make them security ready without actually providing a security mechanism underneath.

Security Level 1 is designed to allow ORB security to be applied to applications that are not security aware. It provides for user authentication and for this authentication to be available to the applications run by the users. It will then apply the security policies specified to the objects in the secure ORB's domain. This includes provision of message integrity (and confidentiality where required), as well as access control as specified by administration policy. It will also allow for auditing of certain security events.

Security Level 2 provides all of the facilities of Level 1, as well as some enhanced integrity, trust, and auditing. It also provides interfaces to applications so that they can find out about the domain's policies and their own privileges and decide how to apply them.

The security specification also defines three ways in which ORBs can implement security so that the mechanism they use can be replaced. These are only of interest to ORB implementers.

4.2 Security Model

The model of security in an ORB system uses the notions of clients, target objects, and operation invocations, as specified in CORBA. The process of building a request, transmitting it to the target object over a network, and then executing an operation and sending a reply are all augmented by security procedures that ensure that the security policies of the domain are enforced. This model is very general, as it aims to include all of the possible security functions that may be required in any application, and it expresses them in generic terms that can describe the behavior of many different underlying security mechanisms. The subsections that follow explain principals and their security attributes, how a secure invocation is made, how security information can be delegated to other objects, how nonrepudiation works, and what kinds of security domains the security specification defines.

4.2.1 Principals and Security Attributes

In the security model the users and some of the applications are called principals, and are given authenticated identities. Sometimes a principal will have more than one identity. For example, a user may have an access identity which they use to log on to a system, and an audit identity, which is known only to the system administrator, and is associated with the principal at log-on time.

Authentication usually requires the principal to have a *security name,* which is then used along with some authentication information (such as a password, or some bytes on a smart card) to produce some *privilege attributes.* These are stored along with the principal's identity attributes and some public information in a *credential* (shown in Figure 12.11).

Without explaining the use of specific interfaces and operations, the security specification explains the high-level concepts for making a secure operation invocation. Some of the actions explained may be performed by the application, if it is security aware. If the application is not security aware, then all of the actions are performed by the Security Service, using context information where necessary.

A secure invocation is made using the following steps:

Establish a *security association* between the client and target object. This means that a satisfactory level of trust in the identity of the other must be reached between the client and target object. Often the client trusts that it received a reliable object reference, and only the target object needs to perform an authentication of the client's identity. This is done by establishing a *binding* between the client and the target object. This allows them to share security information that the Security Service provides in their *current execution context.* This context is represented by an object called *Current,* which provides operations and attributes that allow client and target to set their own security attributes and access those of the other party.

Using the Current object, the target object (or the Security Service) decides whether, based on the authenticated identity and privileges of the client, the requested invocation is permitted. This can be done by looking at Access Control Lists, or at policies about what group membership, role, security clearance, or the like that

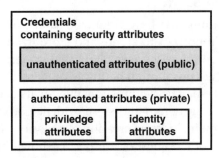

FIGURE 12.11 A credential.

the client principal must have in order to be granted access. It may be performed without any intervention from the application at all, as the security administrator can specify policy about access that is automatically enforced by the Security Service.

If security policy dictates that auditing is required, the appropriate information about the invocation must be sent to an *audit channel*. This can be done by the application, or automatically by the Security Service, based on policy determined by the security administrator.

Depending on the *quality of protection* required by both parties, the messages passed between client and target object may be protected against eavesdropping and modification.

Often in a peer-to-peer model like CORBA, a target object will be client to other target objects in the application. If a target is to make invocations, it may need the privileges of the client principal in order to have permission to do so. To facilitate this, the security system must allow a principal's privileges to be delegated to other principals (called *intermediate objects*) to allow them to perform a task.

In the security model there are a number of schemes that can be used to delegate privileges.

♦ The intermediate target object may use its own privileges to make further calls.

♦ The intermediate target object may use the privileges of the calling principal to make further calls.

♦ The privileges of the caller and the intermediate target object may be combined to make calls in two ways: the two sets of privileges may both be used or they may be combined into a single new set of credentials.

The scheme that is used may be limited by the capabilities of the security mechanism. The style of delegation used by particular objects will be determined by the security administrator who will set delegation policies.

4.2.2 *Nonrepudiation Services*

When clients perform actions that have financial, safety, or confidentiality consequences it may be important to create and store irrefutable evidence of these actions. Nonrepudiation services allow this evidence to be generated and later verified when proof of an action is requested so that a client principal (or target object) may be held responsible for its actions.

It may be necessary to generate and store evidence of various sorts of actions. These actions might include the creation of a new object, the creation of a request, or the receipt of a request or a reply. As shown in Figure 12.12,

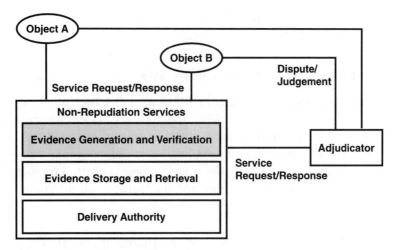

FIGURE 12.12 Nonrepudiation service.

nonrepudiation services support interfaces to service components that perform evidence generation and verification and evidence storage and retrieval.

There may be two other independent agents involved in a nonrepudiation service. A *delivery authority* is responsible for the delivery of evidence between the objects taking part in the application. It also delivers evidence to an independent *adjudicator* which is consulted when there is a dispute about the actions that have taken place in the system.

4.2.3   Security Domains

A domain is a scope within which common characteristics are exhibited and common rules can be applied. In terms of security, there can be several types of domains. A *security technology domain* is the scope within which a single security technology is applied.

In a secure distributed object environment, only some applications are aware of security, even though all applications may take advantage of security services. The way that security unaware applications are secured is by placing the application within one or more *security policy domains*. Access to the applications is then mediated by the security policies of the domains that enclose them.

Policy domains can be organized in hierarchies, with the inner subdomains overriding policies or providing additional policies to their parent domains. An application's objects are subject to the policies of the innermost subdomain which encloses them. However, domains may simply overlap, and policies relating to different aspects of security (for example, auditing and access control) may have different scopes. Often the use of a particular security technology means that a particular arrangement of security policy domains must be used.

4.3   Security Model Seen by Applications

The Security Service specification explains the interfaces to be used by application developers, ORB implementers, Security Service implementers, and security administrators. In this section we present the interfaces to security components that application developers may use to develop security aware applications. The specification is written to allow the use of any underlying security mechanism, and thus not all interfaces will be applicable to all mechanisms.

4.3.1   Finding the Security Features of an ORB

The ORB interface has been extended to add a new operation to the ORB pseudo-object. It is called `get_service_information()`. This operation returns details of the security facilities and mechanisms available within this ORB.

4.3.2   Authentication of a User Principal

Often a user will be authenticated outside the ORB security system, for example, by a security log-on. In this case the credentials that the user is given are available through the Current object. The Current object is associated with a client's binding to a target object that the client will use to make a secure invocation on the target object. The user may use Current to choose which privileges to associate with the secure invocation.

If the user is not authenticated by an external mechanism, then it must use a PrincipalAuthenticator object to authenticate itself and acquire credentials for use in secure invocations.

4.3.3   Selecting Privileges

A client can use the Credentials object that it obtains through either the Current object or directly from a PrincipalAuthenticator to select from the privileges available to it. It may also obtain information about the security features that are implemented in the system and about the security policies that apply to it in the current domain.

The Credentials object supports operations called set_privileges() and set_security_features() that allow the client to select the types of security and the privileges that will be used for secure invocations from the client. Clients can also make copies of the credentials using the copy() operation on their Credentials object so that they can customize the copies for use with different targets.

The Current object has operations get_credentials() and set_credentials() that allow the default credentials object used for invocations to be inspected and changed. Target object references to secure objects support operations override_default_QOP() and override_default_credentials() that allow clients to choose the quality of protection and the credentials that will be used to make invocations on those references.

4.3.4   Making a Secure Invocation

A binding must be established between the client and the target object so that they can share security information. The binding conveys the user principal's credentials to the target object, where they can be used to determine whether the principal is allowed access to the target object or to particular operations on the object. Audit and nonrepudiation policies may also be applied using information about the client's credentials obtained via the Current object at the target. This is done using the operation get_attributes() supported by both the Current object and the Credentials object it refers to.

When a target object must make other invocations in order to complete the current request, it must apply the delegation policy that is set by the security administrator. This may allow it to use the client's credentials that it has received or to combine its own credentials with the client's. It creates or selects appropriate credentials by using the same operations on the Current and Credentials objects that the client used in order to select the privileges for the initial invocation.

When the target object processes the incoming request, it must decide whether or not to audit the invocation. It does this by first checking the policy for auditing that it inherits from the security domain by supplying an audit policy argument to the get_policy() operation on the Current object. It may also decide autonomously to do its own auditing, and for this it uses an AuditDecision object, which has an operation called audit_needed(). If an audit is required then the AuditDecision object will return an appropriate audit channel from its audit_channel() operation.

4.3.5   Nonrepudiation

If nonrepudiation is supported by the security service then the user can obtain an NRCredentials object from its Current object and set this as its default Credentials object using set_credentials(). The NRCredentials object has operations called get_NR_features() and set_NR_features() which allow the user to choose the type of evidence generation and select other nonrepudiation features.

A number of calls to the NRCredentials object are required to generate evidence of an invocation. Which of these are required depends on the implementation of the nonrepudiation service.

- ♦ generate_token()—creates an unforgeable token to be used in the evidence
- ♦ verify_evidence()—can be used to check if evidence is valid

Some nonrepudiation services require evidence generation to be done in multiple steps and so another operation is provided:

- ♦ form_complete_evidence()—uses the original token to generate further evidence, such as time stamps.

4.4   Overview of Application Security Interfaces

A number of the security interfaces defined in the Security Service are designed to provide a layer of abstraction for ORB security implementers so that they can replace underlying security mechansims with a minimum of effort. We will only look at the interfaces designed for use by security-aware applications. Note that applications need not have any awareness of security in order to be protected by the Security Service. These applications can be made secure by the security administrator, which sets security policy to be enforced by the ORB without the need for the application developer to do any security programming.

4.4.1   Common Security Types

The Security module defines the data types and constants that are used within the modules SecurityLevel1 and SecurityLevel2. The definitions in the Security module depend on the Time Service module, Time. This is because reliable distributed time stamps are needed to avoid several kinds of attacks on secure systems, as well as for the creation of evidence for nonrepudiation and logs for auditing.

The types defined here include a number of integers and opaque types because the data types to be used by the underlying security service are unknown to the specifiers of this service. The use of *family* identifiers is also widespread. A family is a unique identifier representing a concept in the Security Service, for example, identity or privilege. All features of security services, known as *security attributes*, are qualified by which family they belong to.

```
typedef sequence<octet> Opaque;
struct ExtensibleFamily {
        unsigned short family_definer;
        unsigned short family;
};
typedef unsigned long SecurityAttributeType;
struct AttributeType {
        ExtensibleFamily attribute_family;
```

```
                SecurityAttributeType attribute_type;
    };
    typedefsequence<AttributeType> AttributeTypeList;
    struct SecAttribute{
            AttributeType attribute_type;
            Opaque defining_authority;
            Opaque value;
    };
    typedef sequence <SecAttribute> AttributeList;
```

This module also defines a number of standard SecurityAttributeTypes, which are given as constants relative to a family, for example,

```
    // identity attributes; family=0
    const SecurityAttributeType AuditId = 1;
    const SecurityAttributeType AccountingId = 2;
    const SecurityAttributeType NonRepudiationId = 3;
```

These are used in Attribute structures along with a family identifier. The type is named ExtensibleFamily because it is anticipated that new families and corresponding attribute types will be defined when new kinds of underlying security services are used with these interfaces.

Many other types are defined for use in all of the other security interfaces. We have provided only enough definitions to show the flavor of the specification and to show the single signature needed for Security Level 1 in the following section.

4.4.2   Security Level 1

The first level of conformance to the Security Service does not allow principals in applications to choose the privileges they will apply or allow objects to enforce their own security policies. However, the Current object defined in the module SecurityLevel1 allows an application to find out which security attributes are defined in the domains within which it operates.

```
    interface Current:CORBA::Current { // PIDL
            Security::AttributeListget_attributes(
                    in Security::AttributeTypeList attributes
            );
    };
```

The get_attributes() operation returns the values associated with all of the attribute types provided in the list argument.

4.4.3   Security Level 2

The second conformance level defines all the interfaces that are used in security-aware applications, as well as the interfaces used by ORB security implementers to allow replaceability of security mechanisms. The applications use the interfaces called Current, RequiredRights, PrincipalAuthenticator, Credentials, and Object. We will provide a brief explanation of the operations supported by these interfaces, but the signatures of the operations will not be shown because they contain too much detail for an introduction to security.

4.4.4 *Current*

The Current interface specifies operations and attributes that are available to both clients and target objects. The attributes are references to other objects specified in the Security Service. The operations are all applicable to both client and target unless otherwise stated.

In the SecurityLevel2 module, the Current interface inherits the Current interface from SecurityLevel1. It extends this functionality with read-only attributes that return object references to the following objects: RequiredRights and PrincipalAuthenticator. It also gives access to Credentials objects that have been initialized outside of the ORB (i.e., by some means other than using a PrincipalAuthenticator object).

Current has operations to set and get the credentials object used by default for invocations in a client context. They are get_credentials(), which returns the current default Credentials object, and set_credentials(), which allows modified Credentials to be used for invocations.

It also has read-only attributes for use by a target object which allow it to inspect the security features and credentials received from the principal initiating an invocation. These are called received_security_features and received_credentials. They may be used by the target to enforce its own security policy.

4.4.5 *RequiredRights*

The RequiredRights interface offers two operations, one for use by a client principal to discover what rights it needs in order to make an invocation on a particular operation on a particular object reference, and the other for use by a target object to set the rights required on its operations. The use of this interface assumes that access to operations on objects is granted on the basis of policy specified in terms of principal groups given the rights to perform certain kinds of actions. This is much like file modification privileges under UNIX.

> get_required_rights()—returns the set of rights that a client principal must have in order to use an operation. It can be thought of as "Is -1" in UNIX file terms, which reveals read, write, and execute permissions on files.

set_required_rights()—used to set the rights required to invoke an operation. It is much like the "chmod" command used to change per-
missions on files in UNIX.

4.4.6 *PrincipalAuthenticator*

This interface provides only two operations: authenticate() and continue_
authentication(). These are used by a principal to obtain a reference to a
Credentials object for later use in making secure invocations. Some underlying authentication services will allow the user to provide its security
name and authentication data (such as a password) and will return the
credentials required in one step using the authenticate() operation. Other
authentication services, however, require more than one interaction.
Rather than returning a reference to a Credentials object, they will return
some *continuation data* which must be supplied to the continue_authentica-
tion() operation with some *response data* in order to obtain either credentials
or additional continuation data. Eventually, assuming that the responses
are satisfactory to the authenticator, the principal will have obtained some
valid credentials.

4.4.7 *Credentials*

The Credentials interface allows a principal to choose from the security features and privileges available to it after authentication. This interface is
used by both clients and object implementations awaiting invocations. The
Credentials pseudo-object can be copied so that different available features
and privileges can be set on different object references (on the client side) or
for use with different incoming requests (on the target object side).

- ◆ copy()—provides a duplicate set of Credentials.
- ◆ get_security_features()—allows a principal to find out which security features are available. The return value is a sequence of security features
  such as authentication of the other party, confidentiality, auditing, and
  nonrepudiation.
- ◆ set_security_features()—allows the features required by the principal to be
  selected.
- ◆ get_attributes()—allows a principal to discover a set of security attributes,
  such as its identity or privileges.
- ◆ set_privileges()—to update the set of privileges that a client wishes to use.
  The client passes a sequence of attributes belonging to a privileges family as a parameter.

There are two other operations on Credentials that relate to the expira-
tion of credentials after a time limit within some security mechanisms.

- is_valid()—returns a boolean indicating whether or not the credentials are still valid, as well as a time when they are expected to expire.
- refresh()—allows the application to update the credentials in the Credentials object that have expired. It returns a boolean to indicate whether or not the update was successful.

4.4.8 Object

The Object pseudo-IDL interface provided by the CORBA module is extended in the security service. A set of operations is provided to allow security information to be accessed. Other operations allow clients with secure object references to change to security information associated with those references.

- get_security_features()—returns a list of the security features supported by the security service for this object.
- get_security_names()—returns the list of security names that the target object uses within the security system.
- get_security_mechansims()—returns a list of the underlying security mechanisms that can be used with this object reference.
- override_default_security_mechanism()—used to change the mechanism used for secure invocations on this object.

A secure object reference obtains a set of credentials from the client's current execution context, but these can be overridden using the operations override_default_credentials(), which takes a new Credentials object as a parameter, or get_active_credentials(), which returns the Credentials object currently in use for invocations on this object. One other operation is provided to allow a client to customize the security protection used when making invocations on an object: override_default_QOP(), which allows the user to strengthen or weaken the level of protection associated with messages sent to the target object, for example, to add the requirement that message replay detection be included.

4.5 Secure IIOP

The problem of interoperability between ORBs with security implementations was tackled by the 1996 RFP on Secure Interoperation. It asked for an extension to the current IIOP standard that could establish secure connections between clients and servers implemented using different ORBs. These ORBs would, of course, need to use the same security mechanism.

The resulting specification has become an additional chapter in the Security Service. It defines extensions to the definition of IORs and of the types of messages that are transmitted using IIOP.

The protocol uses the General Inter-ORB Protocol (GIOP), which is a definition of message formats for invocations, and places an extra layer between it and IIOP, which defines how GIOP is used over TCP/IP.

IORs that support SECIOP contain extra information, known as tags, to indicate which security mechanisms the object's server supports. They also contain the security identity of the target object, so that it can be authenticated by the client during a connection, and some security policy attributes so that the client can determine if the security policy in its domain is compatible.

The rest of the SECIOP specification provides details of additional security message types that need to be transmitted to share the security context between client and target. This is how the Current object can contain the same information on both sides. There are also tags defined for object references to objects that support the DCE interoperability protocol so that different vendors can use one another's objects.

5   A Simple Authentication and Authorization Mechanism

In this section we explain a lightweight mechanism for authentication and authorization that is independent of the CORBA Security Service. The approach is based on the CORBA Principal pseudo-object and Visibroker's interceptors, and allows the implementation of an access control mechanism independently of the application code. The idea is that a client obtains a session identifier, or ticket, when it logs in to an application session by providing its user ID and password. Logging in implies being authenticated by an authentication object. The ticket that is issued contains the user ID in some encrypted form. The client sets this ticket as its Principal's name. The Principal pseudo-object is then sent by the ORB with the request each time the client makes an invocation on an object. When the call arrives at the server side, the invocation is intercepted and the Principal is checked to see if the client is allowed to make the invocation. The check is done by a similar authorization object based on the client's ticket, the object being invoked, and the operation name. Figure 12.13 illustrates this scenario. This pattern is only secure when used with IIOP over SSL as the underlying transport. SSL features are needed to secure the described authentication and authorization approach.

5.1   Specification of the Services

The first step is to define the data types and interfaces of the basic security service which will handle authentication and authorization. We define a

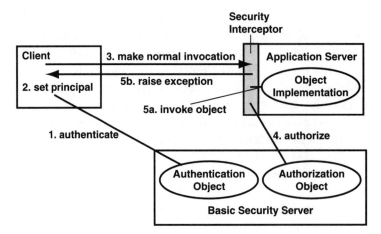

FIGURE 12.13 Simple authorization mechanism.

Ticket as a sequence of octets, which fits nicely with the type of the Principal's name. Then we declare two exceptions, NotAuthenticated and NotAuthorized, which have the obvious meanings.

```
module com {
module wiley {
module compbooks {
module vogel {
module chapter12 {
module security {

    typedef sequence<octet>Ticket;
    exception NotAuthenticated{};
    exception NotAuthorized{};
    interface Authentication {

        Ticket authenticate(
            in string userId,
            in string passWord )
        raises( NotAuthenticated );
};
    interface Authorization {

        void authorize(
            in Ticket clientTicket,
            in Object targetObject,
            in string operationName )
        raises( NotAuthorized );
};

    interface BasicSecurity: Authentication, Authorization {};
};};};};};};
```

We define an interface for each of the security functions we want to provide: Authentication and Authorization. Each interface provides an operation for the corresponding security function. Authentication is based on a user name and a password. Authorization controls access to operations on objects based on the ticket (which contains the client's user ID), the object, and the operation a client wants to invoke. The algorithm that implements access control can vary from implementation to implementation.

Finally, we declare the interface BasicSecurity which inherits the interfaces Authentication and Authorization.

The IDL here only defines the essential functionality for authentication and authorization. To make the security interfaces fully operational you need to add administrative operations, for example, to add users, to change passwords, and to set and modify capabilities.

5.2 Implementing Access Control

We implement access control in an interceptor. Interceptors are a Visibroker feature that allow you to intercept IIOP requests and responses on the client and server sides. Interceptors are a more basic form of Visibroker's Event Handlers, which provide more fine-grained control. Interceptors provide access to the complete IIOP request and allow modifications on the address information as well as the data buffer. This makes interceptors very powerful and they should be used with caution as they can dramatically alter the behavior of the ORB. OrbixWeb provides a similar mechanism known as Filters.

5.2.1 Interceptors

Visibroker provides three different kinds of interceptor: for clients, for servers, and for bind calls. Interceptors are Java interfaces that define methods for various interaction points. Once an invocation passes an interaction point, the ORB invokes the corresponding method on installed interceptor implementations. As an example, we show the interface for a server-side interceptor here.

```
public interface com.visigenic.vbroker.interceptor.ServerInterceptor
    extends java.lang.Object {

    public abstract com.visigenic.vbroker.IOP.IOR locate(
        int,
        byte[],
        com.visigenic.vbroker.interceptor.Closure);

    public abstract void locate_succeeded(
        int,
        com.visigenic.vbroker.interceptor.Closure);
```

```
public abstract void locate_forwarded(
    int,
    com.visigenic.vbroker.IOP.IORHolder,
    com.visigenic.vbroker.interceptor.Closure);

public abstract com.visigenic.vbroker.IOP.IOR locate_failed(
    int,
    byte[],
    com.visigenic.vbroker.interceptor.Closure);
```

The first four methods deal with locating an object. The method `receive_request()` is triggered when an IIOP request is received by the server.

```
public abstract org.omg.CORBA.portable.InputStream receive_request(
    com.visigenic.vbroker.GIOP.RequestHeader,
    org.omg.CORBA.ObjectHolder,
    org.omg.CORBA.portable.InputStream,
    com.visigenic.vbroker.interceptor.Closure);
```

There are four methods invoked during an IIOP response. The first two are triggered when a reply is prepared and sent. The last two are triggered by successful or failed delivery of the IIOP response, respectively.

```
public abstract void prepare_reply(
    com.visigenic.vbroker.GIOP.RequestHeader,
    com.visigenic.vbroker.GIOP.ReplyHeaderHolder,
    org.omg.CORBA.Object,
    com.visigenic.vbroker.interceptor.Closure);

public abstract org.omg.CORBA.portable.OutputStream send_reply(
    com.visigenic.vbroker.GIOP.RequestHeader,
    com.visigenic.vbroker.GIOP.ReplyHeader,
    org.omg.CORBA.Object,
    org.omg.CORBA.portable.OutputStream,
    org.omg.CORBA.Environment,
    com.visigenic.vbroker.interceptor.Closure);

public abstract void send_reply_failed(
    com.visigenic.vbroker.GIOP.RequestHeader,
    com.visigenic.vbroker.GIOP.ReplyHeader,
    org.omg.CORBA.Object,
    org.omg.CORBA.Environment,
    com.visigenic.vbroker.interceptor.Closure);

public abstract void request_completed(
    com.visigenic.vbroker.GIOP.RequestHeader,
    org.omg.CORBA.Object,
    com.visigenic.vbroker.interceptor.Closure);
```

The ORB invokes the `shutdown()` method when a connection is terminated. This can be caused by the client, the server, or the network.

Disregarding network failure, a connection can be closed due to connection management at the client or the server.

```
public abstract void shutdown(
    com.visigenic.vbroker.interceptor.
    ServerInterceptorPackage.ShutdownReason);
```

Interceptors can be chained, which means that you can have multiple interceptors that are called one after the other. If one of the interceptors raises an exception, interceptions further down the chain won't be invoked, the ORB invokes the method exception_occurred() instead.

```
public abstract void exception_occurred(
    com.visigenic.vbroker.GIOP.RequestHeader,
    org.omg.CORBA.Environment,
    com.visigenic.vbroker.interceptor.Closure);
}
```

5.2.2 Access Control Interceptor

We now implement an interceptor, called SecurityServerInterceptor, that controls access to objects by authorizing a client using the basic security service which we have specified. The implementation is based on the assumption that a client uses the authentication provided by the basic security service and sets the Principal to contain the ticket returned from the authenticate() operation.

```
package com.wiley.compbooks.vogel.chapter12.securityInterceptor;

import com.visigenic.vbroker.interceptor.*;
import com.visigenic.vbroker.IOP.*;
import com.visigenic.vbroker.GIOP.*;
import org.omg.CORBA.*;
import org.omg.CORBA.portable.*;
import com.wiley.compbooks.vogel.chapter12.security.*;

public class SecurityServerInterceptor implements ServerInterceptor {

    private BasicSecurity basicSecurity;
```

In the constructor of the security interceptor we obtain a reference to a basic security object using Visibroker's bind() method and store it in a private variable. If we cannot locate one, we exit the program.

```
public SecurityServerInterceptor() {
    ORB orb = ORB.init(args,null);
    try {
        basicSecurity = BasicSecurityHelper.bind( orb );
    }
```

```
        catch(Exception e) {
            System.err.println(
                "Security Interceptor cannot bind" +
                " to Basic Security Server");
            System.err.println(
                "Existing ... ");
            System.exit(1);
        }
    }
}
```

The only method we really implement is receive_request(). All other methods in the Java interface are given dummy implementations. We obtain the data we need for the authorization from the IIOP request. We extract the Principal and the operation name from the request header, and the target object reference from its holder object. We provide these values as arguments to the authorize() operation which we invoke on the basic security object.

```
public InputStream receive_request(
    RequestHeader hdr,
    org.omg.CORBA.ObjectHolder target,
    InputStream buf,
    Closure closure){

    try {
        basicSecurity.authorize(
            hdr.requesting_principal,
            target.value,
            hdr.operation );
        return null;
    }
    catch( NotAuthorized na ) {
            System.err.println("not authorized");
            throw new NO_PERMISSION();
    }
}


...
}
```

If the authorization succeeds, we just return and the operation is subsequently invoked on the target object. If not, we throw the CORBA system exception NO_PERMISSION. In this case, the invocation on the target object never happens.

One more class is required to allow interceptors (or a single intecpetor) to be installed at the server at run time. It is a factory which creates instances of interceptor classes. Visibroker defines the interface ServerInterceptor-Factory which we must implement. It has a single method create() which must return an instance of a ServerInterceptor.

Our class `SecurityServerInterceptorFactory` implements the `Server-InterceptorFactory` interface. The implementation is straightforward, we use a single interceptor instance for all our security needs. Our factory keeps a private reference `_server` to a `SecurityServerInterceptor`. In our implementation of the `create()` method we check to see if we already have an instance of the interceptor, and if not we create one.

```
package com.wiley.compbooks.vogel.chapter12.securityInterceptor;
import com.visigenic.vbroker.interceptor.*;

public class SecurityServerInterceptorFactory
    implements ServerInterceptorFactory {

    private SecurityServerInterceptor _server = null;

    public ServerInterceptor create(
        com.visigenic.vbroker.IOP.TaggedProfile profile) {

        if (_server == null)
        {
            _server = new SecurityServerInterceptor();
        }
        return _server;
    }
}
```

5.3   Implementing the Basic Security Interface

The implementation of the basic security interface is rather simple and is only included to complete the example. We use a file in a simple format to store user names, passwords, and access rights. This file has a line for each user in the following format:

               <user name> ":" <password> ":" <allowed object name> " " <allowed object name> . . .

More sophisticated implementations of the services could use existing password files, directory, or security services.

The implementation class of the basic security interface follows the normal pattern for implementation using the BOA with the inheritance approach: the implementation extends the skeleton class. We declare two hash tables: one for the users and their passwords, and another for the access control list.

```
package com.wiley.compbooks.vogel.chapter12.securityImpl;

import java.util.*;
import java.io.*;
```

```java
import org.omg.CORBA.*;
import com.wiley.compbooks.vogel.chapter12.security.*;

public class BasicSecurityImpl extends _sk_BasicSecurity {

    private Hashtable userTable;
    private Hashtable accessControlList;
    private String star;

    BasicSecurityImpl( String name, String fileName ) {

        super( name );

        userTable = new Hashtable( 50 );
        accessControlList = new Hashtable( 100 );
        star = new String("*");
        try {
            RandomAccessFile file;
            String line;
            String user, passwd, acDesc;
            int userIndex, passwdIndex, acDescIndex;

            file = new RandomAccessFile( fileName, "r" );

            while( ( line = file.readLine() ) != null ) {

                userIndex = line.indexOf(':', 0);
                if( userIndex > -1 ) {
                    user = line.substring( 0, userIndex );
                    passwdIndex = line.indexOf(':', userIndex+1);
                    if( passwdIndex > -1 ) {
                        passwd = line.substring( userIndex+1, passwdIndex );
                        userTable.put( user, passwd );

                        acDesc = line.substring( passwdIndex+1 );
                        if( acDesc !=null ) {
                            accessControlList.put( user, acDesc );
                        }
                        else {
                            System.err.println( "user " + user +
                                " has no access rights" );
                        }
                    }
                    else {
                        System.err.println( "user " + user +
                            " has no password - file format error?" );
                    }
                }
                else {
                    System.err.println( "line " + line +
                        " has no user - file format error?" );
```

```
                }
            }
        }
        catch ( IOException ioex ) {
            System.err.println( "file " + fileName + " not found" );
            System.exit( 1 );
        }
    }
```

The constructor registers the object with the OSAgent and creates and initializes the hash tables by reading a file containing the security information in the format we described. The wildcard character "*" means that a user is allowed to access any object.

```
public byte[] authenticate( String userId, String passWord )
      throws NotAuthenticated {

  if( userTable.containsKey( userId ) &&

     userTable.get( userId ).equals( passWord ) ) {

     // create a simple ticket
        return encrypt( userId );
     }
     else {
        throw new NotAuthenticated();
     }
  }
```

The implementation of the authenticate() method has a user ID and password as arguments. It looks up the password for the user ID in the user hash table. If this matches the supplied password we create a ticket by encrypting the user ID and return it to the client. Otherwise we throw the exception NotAuthenticated.

```
public byte[] encrypt( String userId ) {

     return userId.getBytes();
  }

  public String decrypt( byte[] ticket ) {

     return new String( ticket );
  }
```

Our algorithm for creating a ticket is overly simple; we just convert the user ID to a byte array. A more realistic implementation would add a time stamp and really encrypt the ticket. You can use a symmetric encryption technology since the only entity that needs to decrypt the ticket again is this basic security service when it authorizes an invocation.

```
public void authorize( byte[] ticket, org.omg.CORBA.Object object,
        String operationName )
    throws NotAuthorized {

        String userId = decrypt( ticket );
        System.err.println( "authorize: " + userId );
        String objectId = object._object_name();

        if( objectId == null ) {
            System.err.println( "authorize: non-name object" );
            return;
        }

        if( accessControlList.containsKey( userId )) {
            String allowedObjects =
                (String) accessControlList.get( userId );
            if( allowedObjects.regionMatches( 0, "*", 0, 1 ) ) {
                return;
            }
            if( allowedObjects.
                regionMatches( 0, objectId, 0, objectId.length() ) ) {
                return;
            }
        }
    throw new NotAuthorized();
    }
}
```

The method authorize() has three parameters: a ticket, the object which the client wants to access, and the name of the operation to invoke. We get the object's name from the object and the user ID from the ticket. Then we use the accessControlList hash table to obtain a string that contains the names of objects the user may invoke. If the name of the object the client wants to invoke is among these, we return and allow the invocation to proceed. We do the same if the object is not named or the user has global privileges. Otherwise we throw the exception NotAuthorized.

The access policies that can be implemented with this approach are based on the object name only. This has the limitation that it only works with named objects. Transient objects may not be able to be named, and in any case, an administrator would have to update the access control file when each transient object was created. Alternatively, you could use the interface name instead of the object name, but that would not allow you to distinguish between different implementations and instances of the same interface type.

5.4   Implementing the Secure Client

We again use the Hello World example to demonstrate authentication and authorization. The client code below is very similar to that in Chapter 5. We extend it by using the basic security service. First, we obtain a reference to a basic security object. Then the client logs into the system by calling authenticate() on the basic security object. The user ID and the password are expected as command-line arguments. If the authentication succeeds, a ticket is returned.

The next step is to obtain the default Principal from the ORB and set it to include the ticket. The ticket will thereafter implicitly be sent with each invocation.

```
package com.wiley.compbooks.vogel.chapter12.securityExample;

import java.io.*;
import org.omg.CORBA.*;
import com.wiley.compbooks.vogel.chapter5.simple.HelloWorld.*;
import com.wiley.compbooks.vogel.chapter12.security.*;
public class Client {

    public static void main(String args[]) {
        ...
        try {
            // initiliaze the ORB.
            ORB orb = ORB.init(args, null);

            BasicSecurity basicSecurity = BasicSecurityHelper.bind( orb );

            byte[] ticket = basicSecurity.authenticate( args[0], args[1] );

            orb.default_principal().name( ticket );

            GoodDay goodDay = GoodDayHelper.bind( orb );

            // invoke the operation and print the result
            System.out.println( goodDay.hello() );
        }

        // catch user defined exceptions
        catch(NotAuthenticated na) {
            System.err.println("User not authenticated.");
            System.err.println(na);
        }
        catch(NO_PERMISSION np) {
            System.err.println(
                "User not authorized to invoke operation on object.");
            System.err.println(np);
        }
```

```
        // catch CORBA system exceptions
        catch(SystemException ex) {
            System.err.println(ex);
        }
    }
}
```

As well as catching CORBA system exceptions, we explicitly catch the user-defined exception NotAuthenticated raised by the operation authenticate() and the CORBA system exception NO_PERMISSION, which can be thrown by the access control interceptor.

5.5   Installing the Interceptor

To activate the access control interceptor we have to register it with the server. There are two ways to do this. We can either explicitly create and register the interceptor in the server in the same way as we registered the event handler in Chapter 11 or we can register the interceptor when we start the server with a command-line option.

The Visibroker for Java code execution program, vbj, takes command-line arguments that configure the ORB. For example, the option

```
-DORBservices=<package_name>
```

makes the ORB look for the named package. Then it uses the following naming convention: when it finds the package, it loads the Init class in this package, and calls its init() method. This means that we don't have to make any modifications to the server code to enable the security interceptor.

In the securityInterceptor package we implement an Init class. The purpose of this class is to provide an init() method that installs our security interceptor factory. To do this we have to obtain a reference to a ChainServer-InterceptorFactory. This factory is the registry for server interceptor factories. It supports a method add(), which allows new interceptor factories to be added to a chain of factories that are used to obtain the interceptors to be called at each point in an invocation request.

Chain interceptor factories are one of Visibroker's initial services, and hence can be obtained via resolve_initial_references() from the ORB. Once we have obtained the reference to the Chain Factory and narrowed it to the type ChainServerInterceptorFactory, we can use it to add an instance of our security interceptor to the chain of interceptors used by the server by calling its add() method.

```
package com.wiley.compbooks.vogel.chapter12.securityInterceptor;

import java.util.*;
import com.visigenic.vbroker.interceptor.*;
```

```
public class Init extends com.visigenic.vbroker.orb.ServiceInit
{
    public void init(org.omg.CORBA.ORB orb, Properties properties)
    {
        System.out.println("Installing Security Interceptors");

        // install server interceptor factory
        try
        {
            ChainServerInterceptorFactory serverFactory =
                ChainServerInterceptorFactoryHelper.narrow(
                orb.resolve_initial_references(
                "ChainServerInterceptorFactory"));

            serverFactory.add(new SecurityServerInterceptorFactory());
        }
        catch(org.omg.CORBA.ORBPackage.InvalidName e)
        {
            throw new org.omg.CORBA.INITIALIZE(
                "Server interceptor factory is not installed: " + e);
        }
    }
}
```

To ensure that our initialization code is invoked we start the Hello World server with the following command:

```
$ vbj -DORBservices=com.wiley.compbooks.vogel.
chapter12.securityInterceptor
  com.wiley.compbooks.vogel.chapter5.simple.HelloWorld.Server
```

5.6 Running the Example

To run the example, you have to first start the basic security service:

```
$vbj com.wiley.compbooks.vogel.chapter12.securityImpl.Server
BasicSecurityServer sec.data
```

The file `sec.data` contains the following users, passwords, and access rights:

```
admin:admin:*
keith:duddy:Brisbane
andreas:vogel:Berlin
```

Then we start the security-enabled application server:

```
$vbj -DORBservices=com.wiley.compbooks.vogel.chapter12.securityInterceptor
com.wiley.compbooks.vogel.chapter5.simple.HelloWorldImpl.Server Brisbane
```

Now we run clients with various user IDs and passwords. In the first two cases, the client is authenticated and authorized. In the third case the client is authenticated but not authorized, and in the fourth case the client is not even authenticated.

```
$ vbj com.wiley.compbooks.vogel.chapter12.securityExample.Client admin admin
Hello World, from Brisbane

$ vbj com.wiley.compbooks.vogel.chapter12.securityExample.Client keith duddy
Hello World, from Brisbane

$ vbj com.wiley.compbooks.vogel.chapter12.securityExample.Client andreas
vogel
User not authorized to invoke operation on object.
org.omg.CORBA.NO_PERMISSION[completed=MAYBE]

$ vbj com.wiley.compbooks.vogel.chapter12.securityExample.Client john smith
User not authenticated.
exception NotAuthenticated{}
```

5.7 Alternative Approaches and Extentions

We have already discussed variations in the implementation of the basic security service. However, there are a number of approaches that modify and/or extend these.

5.7.1 Authorization per Server

If it is sufficient to authorize clients on a more coarse-grained basis, for example, to give them access to all the objects in a server, then the overhead introduced by the access control mechanism can be reduced. In case of server-level access control, it is sufficient to check the principal's access rights when the connection is established, since there is typically only one connection between a client and a server. This could be implemented by using a bind interceptor, which allows you to authorize the client when the connection to the server is established, rather than a server interceptor.

5.7.2 Location Restriction

An alternative to identification and subsequent authorization based on tickets is to use the client's host name/IP address as identification and authorize based on this. This would eliminate the need for an explicit login, but restricts clients to a physical location rather than using a logical identity.

5.7.3 Access Control at the IIOP Gateway

Access control at an IIOP gateway makes sense for two major reasons. First, it is easy to manage since the gateway is typically a single point of access.

Second, in many cases, there is a firewall between the gateway and the application servers.

Checking access at the gateway prevents the penetration of the protected network by unauthorized users. A drawback is that IIOP gateways are already potential performance bottlenecks, and an extension of their function would further decrease their performance. Another problem could be access to the security service. Locating the security service on the bastion host with the gateway can be a security risk in certain firewall configurations. However, if the security service is behind the firewall, then access control checks could be become expensive due to firewall-crossing remote calls.

5.7.4 *Performance Tuning*

The basic security service configuration shown above leads to a remote call for every authorization. Performance can be improved by running the application server and the basic security service in the same JVM. Additionally, the security service could cache the user and access control lists. A master server that controls the database can notify the other service instances about updates in the database using some event model.

6 *Login CORBA Bean*

In this section we implement a client to the authentication object we introduced in section 5 as a JavaBean. The JavaBeans specification defines a JavaBean as a reusable software component. The client to the authentication service seems to be a very suitable example. Many applications have a need for a password-based login mechanism and so motivate the implementation of a login bean.

In Chapter 3 we distinguished between visible and invisible CORBA client beans. In this section we implement a visible bean. Our bean will implement the following characteristics of a JavaBean:

> **Introspection.** Introspection is provided by JDK versions 1.1 and later. Our bean implementation follows the bean naming conventions. We do not implement an additional BeanInfo class, as such a class deals only with the customization of introspection, which has no direct relevance to CORBA.
>
> **Properties.** Our bean implementation has properties for the appearance of the bean as well as CORBA-related properties.
>
> **Events.** We define an event object which we fire when a user has successfully logged into the system. We also provide a corresponding login event listener interface.

Persistence. Our bean is made persistent by implementing the Java interface `java.io.Serializable`.

Figure 12.14 shows the various classes and interfaces that belong to our login bean. There is a class `Login`, which is the bean itself, a class `LoginEventObject`, which is the event the bean fires when a user has successfully logged in, and the interface `LoginEventListener`, which needs to be implemented by other beans interested in login events.

6.1 Login Bean Implementation

The login bean is implemented in the class `Login` which belongs to the package `com.wiley.compbooks.vogel.chapter12.loginBean`. As we mentioned before, there is no special bean base class that all JavaBeans extend or bean interface that all beans implement. Instead we extend the class `java.awt.Panel` and implement the Java interfaces `Serializable` and `ActionListener`.

Implementing the interface `Serializable` makes our login bean persistent. In fact, we do not have to implement specific methods. The default behavior is that all fields are saved. Exceptions to this rule are fields which are declared transient or static. As you will see, we have declared a few fields transient because we do not consider them as properties of the bean.

We also implement the interface `ActionListener` so that the components of the bean can communicate with each other via Java events using the

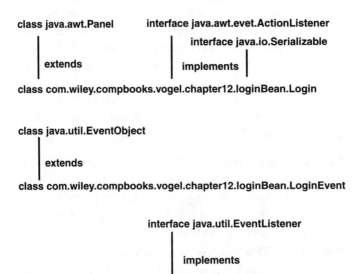

class java.awt.Panel   **interface java.awt.evet.ActionListener**

   interface java.io.Serializable

  | extends | implements

class com.wiley.compbooks.vogel.chapter12.loginBean.Login

class java.util.EventObject

  | extends

class com.wiley.compbooks.vogel.chapter12.loginBean.LoginEvent

   interface java.util.EventListener

   | implements

interface com.wiley.compbooks.vogel.chapter12.loginBean.LoginEventListener

FIGURE 12.14 Login bean and login event.

beans event model. Note that this is just for communication within the bean, the event for interbean communication is introduced later.

```
package com.wiley.compbooks.vogel.chapter12.loginBean;

import java.io.*;
import java.util.*;
import java.awt.*;
import java.awt.event.*;
import java.beans.*;
import org.omg.CORBA.*;
import com.wiley.compbooks.vogel.chapter12.security.*;

public class Login
    extends Panel
    implements Serializable, ActionListener {

    // GUI related properties
    private String welcomeString;
    private String rejectString;
    private String acceptString;
    private String failureString;
    private String idLabelString;
    private String passwdLabelString;
    private String loginButtonString;

    // CORBA related properties
    private String authenticationName;
    private String authenticationHost;

    // other state variables
    private transient Label messageLabel;
    private transient Label idLabel;
    private transient Label passwdLabel;
    private transient TextField idTextField;
    private transient TextField passwdTextField;
    private transient Button loginButton;
    private transient PropertyChangeSupport changes;
    private transient Vector loginEventListeners;
    private transient Authentication authentication;
```

In the constructor of the bean class, we initialize the various aspects of the bean including:

- ♦ Initializing the properties of the bean with default values
- ♦ Initializing the GUI objects, creating a layout, and displaying them
- ♦ Initializing bean-specific objects
- ♦ Initializing the ORB and binding to the CORBA server which hosts the Authentication object

The default values of the bean are mainly strings that we display on labels and buttons. We set them to some initial values that can be customized by a programmer who uses the bean. For example, the initial strings like `"Please login"` could be translated to other languages.

We also have to set properties that are CORBA related. The strings `authenticationName` and `authenticationHost` control the bind process to the server.

```
public Login() {

    loginButtonString = new String("login");
    welcomeString = new String("Please login");
    rejectString = new String("Not authenticated, please try again!");
    acceptString = new String("Authenticated!");
    failureString = new String("Security server not available, " +
        "please try again later");
    idLabelString = new String("User id: ");
    passwdLabelString = new String("Password: ");
    authenticationName = new String("");
    authenticationHost = new String("");
```

We initialize the GUI by creating and initializing all of our GUI objects, labels, buttons, and text fields. We create a `Gridbag` layout and compose our objects in this layout. Figure 12.15 shows the result of the code here.

```
// create GUI objects
loginButton = new Button( loginButtonString );
loginButton.setActionCommand("login");
loginButton.addActionListener( (ActionListener) this );

idLabel = new Label( idLabelString );
passwdLabel = new Label( passwdLabelString );
idLabel = new Label( idLabelString );
passwdLabel = new Label( passwdLabelString );
messageLabel = new Label( welcomeString, Label.CENTER );

idTextField = new TextField( 20 );
idTextField.setFont(new Font("Helvetica", Font.BOLD, 14));
passwdTextField = new TextField( 20 );
passwdTextField.setEchoChar('*');
passwdTextField.setFont(new Font("Helvetica", Font.BOLD, 14));

// layout

GridBagLayout gridbag = new GridBagLayout();
GridBagConstraints c = new GridBagConstraints();
this.setLayout(gridbag);
c.fill = GridBagConstraints.BOTH;
c.gridheight = 1;
```

```
c.gridwidth = GridBagConstraints.REMAINDER;
gridbag.setConstraints( messageLabel, c);
this.add( messageLabel );

c.gridwidth = 1;
gridbag.setConstraints( idLabel, c);
this.add( idLabel );
c.gridwidth = GridBagConstraints.REMAINDER;
gridbag.setConstraints( idTextField, c);
this.add( idTextField );

c.gridwidth = 1;
gridbag.setConstraints( passwdLabel, c);
this.add( passwdLabel );
c.gridwidth = GridBagConstraints.REMAINDER;
gridbag.setConstraints( passwdTextField, c);
this.add( passwdTextField );

c.gridwidth = GridBagConstraints.REMAINDER;
gridbag.setConstraints( loginButton, c);
this.add( loginButton );
this.validate();
```

We define the properties of the bean as *bound properties,* which means that the bean fires an event when the value of a property changes. To enable this feature we need a `PropertyChangeSupport` object, which we create below.

We also have to keep track of the listeners to the login event which the bean fires. We create the vector object `loginEventListeners` for this purpose.

```
changes = new PropertyChangeSupport(this);
loginEventListeners = new Vector();
```

Initializing the ORB and binding to the authentication object works in the usual manner. Depending on the values of the properties for the object name and the server's host name, we use different flavors of the Visibroker `bind()` call. If we cannot bind to the authentication object, we display the value of the property `failureString` in the bean's GUI.

```
try {

    // initialize the ORB
    ORB orb = ORB.init(args, null);

    // initialize authentication
    if( authenticationName.equals("") &&
        authenticationHost.equals("") ) {
        authentication = AuthenticationHelper.bind( orb );
    }
    else if( !authenticationName.equals("") ) {
```

```
            authentication = AuthenticationHelper.bind( orb,
                authenticationName );
        }
        else {
            authentication = AuthenticationHelper.bind( orb,
                authenticationName, authenticationHost, null );
        }
    }
    // catch CORBA system exceptions
    catch(SystemException ex) {
        messageLabel.setText( failureString );
    }
}
```

The method `login()` provides the core functionality of the bean. It invokes the method `authenticate()` on the authentication object reference. For the purposes of the login bean, we ignore the ticket returned by the `authenticate()` operation. We display the appropriate message on the GUI and clear the password text field. Then we create a new login event. The implementation of the `Login` object is explained below. Then we fire the event, which results in invoking the method `handleLoginEvent()` on all registered login event listeners. The methods to register and deregister event listeners are shown here.

The operation authenticate() can raise either a CORBA system exception or the user-defined exception NotAuthenticated. We display the string `failureString` if the CORBA exception is raised, or we display `rejectString` if the user fails authentication.

```
public void login( String id, String passwd ) {

    try {

    byte[] ticket = authentication.authenticate( id, passwd );

        messageLabel.setText( acceptString );

        passwdTextField.setText( "" );

        // fire event
        LoginEventObject loginEvent = new LoginEventObject( this, id );
        LoginEventListener 1;
        for( int i = 0; i < loginEventListeners.size(); i++ ) {
            1 = (LoginEventListener) loginEventListeners.elementAt( i );
            1.handleLoginEvent( loginEvent );
        }
    }

    // catch user defined exceptions
    catch(NotAuthenticated na) {
```

```
                 messageLabel.setText( rejectString );
        }
        // catch CORBA system exceptions
        catch(SystemException ex) {
                 messageLabel.setText( failureString );
        }


}
```

The method `actionPerformed()` handles the events (of type `ActionEvent`) that the bean receives. The only event we fire internally is when the `loginButton` is pressed. If this is the case, we invoke the method `login()` with arguments we obtain from the text fields.

```
public void actionPerformed( ActionEvent e ) {
    if( e.getActionCommand().equals("login") )
        login( idTextField.getText(), passwdTextField.getText() );
}
```

We implement methods to add and remove login event listeners. Those methods are invoked by other beans when they want to communicate with our login bean. We add or remove the specified listener to our listener vector `loginEventListeners`.

```
public void addLoginEventListener( LoginEventListener listener ) {
    loginEventListeners.addElement( listener );
}

public void removeLoginEventListener( LoginEventListener listener ) {
    loginEventListeners.removeElement( listener );
}
```

Similarly we implement a pair of methods to add and remove listeners to property change events.

```
public void addPropertyChangeListener( PropertyChangeListener l ) {
    changes.addPropertyChangeListener( l );
}

public void removePropertyChangeListener( PropertyChangeListener l ) {
    changes.removePropertyChangeListener( l );
}
```

Finally, we have a pair of methods for each of the bean's properties to set and get the value of the property. As an example we show the methods for the property `idLabelString`. According to Java Bean's naming convention, the set and get methods are called `setIdLabelString()` and `getIdLabelString()`, respectively. Bean-aware environments such as the Beanbox and other component builders acquire semantic information based on this naming convention.

Within the set method we fire a property change event to notify other beans about the changed property value. We also display the new value in the corresponding idLabel.

```
public void setIdLabelString( String newValue ) {
    changes.firePropertyChange("idLabelString",
        idLabelString, newValue);
    idLabelString = newValue;
    idLabel.setText( idLabelString );
}

public String getIdLabelString() {
    return idLabelString;
}
}
```

6.2   Login Event Object and Event Listener

Now we will have a closer look at the class LoginEventObject and the interface LoginEventListener. The class LoginEventObject extends the event base class java.util.EventObject. The constructor of our event stores the identifier of the user who has successfully logged in. The method getId() allows access to this value from an event object.

```
package com.wiley.compbooks.vogel.chapter12.loginBean;

import java.util.*;

public class LoginEventObject extends EventObject {

    private String id;

    public LoginEventObject( Object source, String id ) {

        super( source );
        this.id = id;
    };

    public String getId() {

        return id;
    }
}
```

The interface LoginEventListener needs to be implemented by other beans that want to be notified of login events. Those beans have to implement the method `handleLoginEvent()`, which is invoked by the login bean on all registered listeners.

```
package com.wiley.compbooks.vogel.chapter12.loginBean;

import java.util.*;

public interface LoginEventListener extends EventListener {

    public void handleLoginEvent( LoginEventObject ev );
}
```

6.3   Login Jar File

Finally, we have to compose all class files belonging to the login bean into a jar file. We also have to create a *manifest file,* which describes the classes contained in the jar file. The manifest file lists all classes and indicates whether or not a class is a bean. Here we see the contents of the file `Login.manifest` which describes our bean and the related class files.

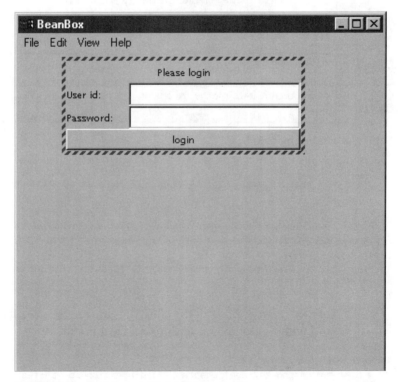

FIGURE 12.15 Starting and initializing the Beanbox.

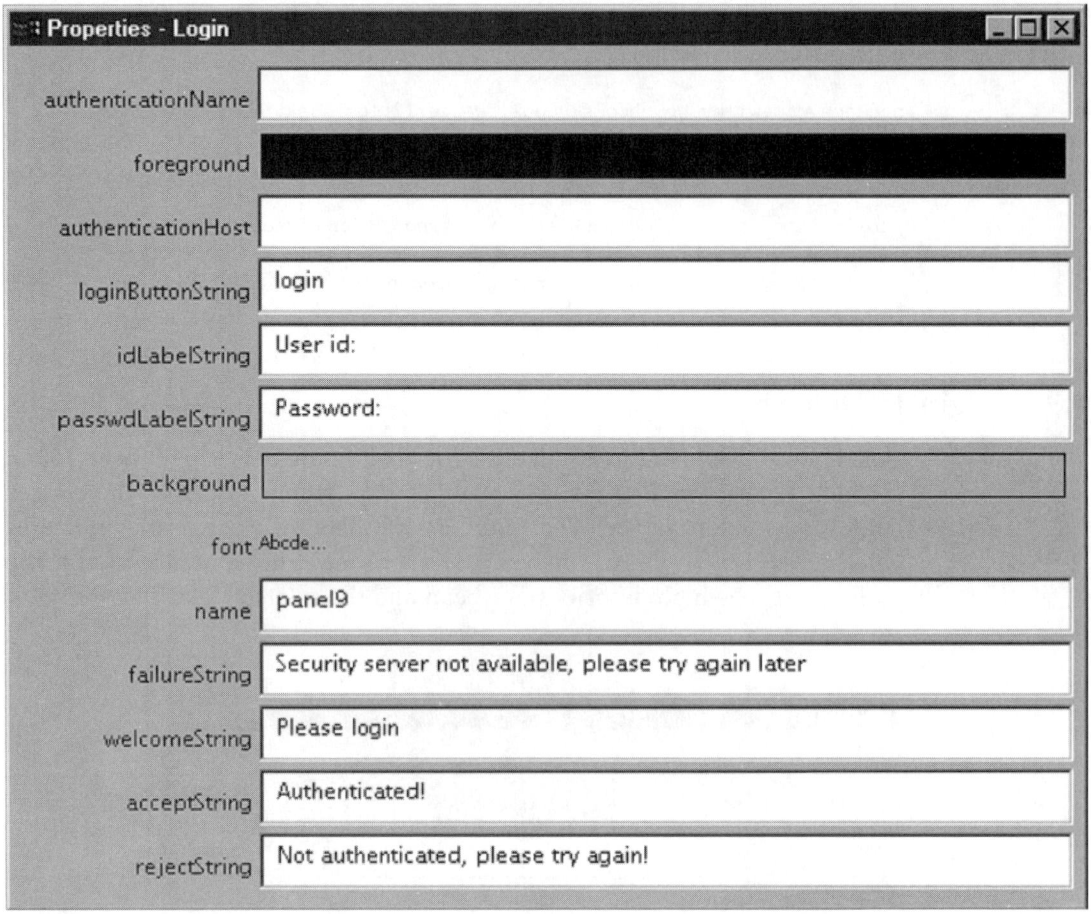

FIGURE 12.16 Setting properties in login bean.

```
Name: com/wiley/compbooks/vogel/chapter12/loginBean/Login.class
Java-Bean: True

Name: com/wiley/compbooks/vogel/chapter12/loginBean/LoginEventObject.class
Java-Bean: False

Name: com/wiley/compbooks/vogel/chapter12/loginBean/LoginEventListener.class
Java-Bean: False
```

Now we can compose all the class files into a `Login.jar` file using the `jar` command with the following options and arguments.

```
...> jar -cfm Login.jar
com/wiley/compbooks/vogel/chapter12/loginBean/Login.manifest
com/wiley/compbooks/vogel/chapter12/loginBean/Login.class
```

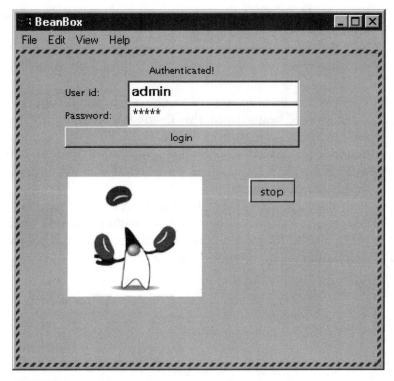

FIGURE 12.17 Composing beans into applications.

```
com/wiley/compbooks/vogel/chapter12/loginBean/LoginEventObject.class
com/wiley/compbooks/vogel/chapter12/loginBean/LoginEventListener.class
```

This finishes the creation our bean. We can now have our login bean interact with other beans.

6.4 Login Bean in the Beanbox

We use JavaSoft's Beanbox as an example of a bean composer. We start the Beanbox with the following command:

```
java sun.beanbox.BeanBoxFrame.
```

We load the `Login.jar` file via the file menu in the main Beanbox window. As a result we get an additional entry for our login bean in the Toolbox window. We drag and drop the login bean into the main Beanbox window.

This results in the creation of an instance of the login bean which tries to connect to an authenticator object. If you have a BasicSecurity server running, as described in the previous section, then you see the bean as shown in Figure 12.15. If you cannot reach the server, the value of the `failureString` property is displayed at the top of the bean's GUI.

Figure 12.16 shows the property window for the login. You can change the value of all properties which will be displayed immediately in the bean itself.

We now want to compose a new application from pre-existing beans. We add two beans from the Beanbox's samples, the `Juggler` and the `ExplicitButton`, as shown in Figure 12.17. First we change the label of the button from `press` to `stop`. Then we connect the button's button-push event with the juggler's `stopJuggling()` method. If you now press the stop button, the juggler stops juggling.

Similarly we connect the login bean's `loginEvent` with the Juggler's `startJuggling()` method. Now you can login to the new application by providing a valid ID and the corresponding password. If your login attempt is successful the juggler starts juggling again.

13

Performance, Scalability, and Maintenance

So far in this book we have explained Java ORB technology, but not how to go about using it effectively. In this chapter we explain how to use the technology successfully. When CORBA is used the wrong way, the implemented applications, although they are functionally complete, can have performance and scalability problems. Performance and scalability, however, are key factors in the successful deployment of an application. In section 1 we will look at several important techniques for gaining high performance in CORBA applications and ensuring that the performance remains acceptable when the number of clients or sever objects participating in an application increases dramatically.

Another important issue for distributed applications is their maintenance. In a centralized application there is one machine running a program or set of programs that can be controlled by an administrator using that machine. In distributed applications, especially those that support location transparency, as CORBA applications do, the objects that take part in the application may be running in many servers on many machines, some of them unknown to the administrator. Some planning is required to ensure that clients which suddenly withdraw from an application don't leave unused objects behind. Coping with this situation can be called distributed garbage collection. The other consideration is how to shut down an application gracefully. We will look at this issue in section 2.

1   Scalability Issues

In this section we show a few techniques for enhancing the performance and scalability of a Java/CORBA application:

Refining the object model (section 1.1). The design of an application's objects may not translate into an efficient implementation when the objects are implemented and distributed. This is usually due to the extra cost of making distributed invocations. When decisions about the implementation and location of objects are made, some redesign may be necessary to optimize the communication between them. In this section we look at the object model of the room booking example from Chapter 9 and optimize it for distribution.

Threading models (section 1.2). The use of threads to allow parallel processing can be employed to reduce the impact of the delays caused by remote invocations. When servers have many clients they can also employ threads to more evenly process the requests from all clients. Java builds threads into the language, and so threads are easy to use. We will look at the use of threads in clients and servers, and explain the threading models used by ORBs for delivering invocation requests.

Distributed callbacks (section 1.3). When a client makes a call to a remote object that may take some time to return, it is sometimes better to allow the object to respond asynchronously. The client can supply a callback reference for the server to invoke when it has results for the request. This allows the client's main thread to continue and delegate the task of dealing with the response to a CORBA object that it implements. We will show an example of the use of callbacks.

Iterators (section 1.4). When a result of an invocation is very large it can be delivered in smaller pieces by using an iterator. This has the advantage that clients can use a small set of results at a time and need not keep the whole set. It also allows the server to generate further results as they are required, and avoids the need to generate the entire response if the client decides not to retrieve the entire result set. We explain two models for the design and implementation of iterators, one driven by the client and the other by the server.

Client-side caching (section 1.5). Sometimes the cost of a remote call can be avoided altogether. If a particular operation is called multiple times, and always returns the same result, this result can be cached by the client and returned later instead of making a remote call. We will show a simple technique for implementing caching in a client.

Monitoring performance (section 1.6). Decisions about which parts of a distributed application to performance tune should be based on the results of testing. Identifying the bottlenecks in an application may allow these parts to be improved and provide better performance for the whole application. We show some performance monitoring code using interceptors.

1.1 Refining the Object Model

In this section we look at the implications of distributing objects that we have designed in IDL. We then redesign the object model introduced in Chapter 9 to improve the communication between clients and objects.

When we design and implement a CORBA application we use two models that mirror one another:

♦ Functional model—specifies the application or system in terms of objects. Those objects represent the logical composition of functionality and are independent of the actual distribution of the various objects.
♦ Deployment model—specifies the application or system in terms of objects associated with various run-time entities such as machines, processes, JVMs, and threads.

Typically we start with a functional model, defined in terms of OMG IDL. Then as we implement the IDL we transform the specification into implementations of classes that must be instantiated in server programs running on machines in our distributed system. However, sometimes the more concrete considerations of the deployment model have an impact on the functional model. This section looks at the considerations of implementation and deployment, and their impact on the IDL specification.

The transformation of a functional model into a deployed application is a critical factor for the scalability of the system. The most important reason not to naively implement a functional model as if it were a nondistributed application is the very nature of distributed systems. A remote operation call is functionally equivalent to a local one but it differs dramatically in its performance. Experience shows that a local invocation is in the order of microseconds, whereas a remote invocation is in the order of milliseconds, or even worse, depending on the quality of the network connection. To control the overall system performance it is important to carefully design a deployment model for distribution performance. In fact, it is not sufficient to simply distinguish between local and remote calls. In many cases remote calls run over different networks with various performance parameters. As Java/CORBA applications are often deployed on the Internet, you could, for example, distinguish between remote invocations over modem connections (0.5–7 Kbyte/sec), corporate Internet connections (10–100 Kbyte/sec), intranets (100–1000 Kbyte/sec), or FDDI, high-speed Ethernet, and ATM (> 1 Mbyte/sec). To illustrate the problem and introduce some approaches to transforming a functional model into a deployment model, we revisit the room booking application introduced in Chapter 9.

The interface specification of the room booking application we presented in Chapter 9 is a purely functional object model. Even very fine-grain objects such as the Meeting objects are defined as CORBA objects, each with an OMG IDL interface. In that chapter, we took this model and naively implemented it. Certain performance overheads are introduced by the design; this is a problem for scalability. For example, meetings are represented as objects. The access of each of a Meeting's attributes potentially results in a costly remote invocation.

Let us we revisit the specification and implementation of the room booking application, taking scalability into account. The specification of the Room interface below keeps the signatures of the operations, but it changes the specification of a meeting. Here we specify a meeting as an IDL struct. The attributes of the Meeting interface become fields in the Meeting struct. We also add an extra field to indicate whether the meeting is booked or not.

```
module com {
...
module chapter13 {
module modeling {
module RoomBooking {

  interface Room {

    struct Meeting {
       boolean booked;
       string purpose;
       string participants;
    };

    enum Slot { am9, am10, am11, pm12, pm1, pm2, pm3, pm4};

    const short MaxSlots = 8;
```

```
        typedef Meeting Meetings[ MaxSlots ];

        exception NoMeetingInThisSlot {};
        exception SlotAlreadyTaken {};

        readonly attribute string name;

        Meetings View();
        void Book( in Slot a_slot, in Meeting a_meeting)
            raises(SlotAlreadyTaken);

        void Cancel( in Slot a_slot )
            raises(NoMeetingInThisSlot);
        };
    }; ...};
```

Now the Java `Meeting` class generated by the IDL compiler no longer extends the CORBA Object base class. In some language mappings, the meeting would be represented by an even more lightweight construct, for example, the mapping to C++ would generate a struct. This is the code generated by a Java IDL compiler:

```
package
com.wiley.compbooks.vogel.chapter13.modeling.RoomBooking.RoomPackage;

final public class Meeting {

    public boolean booked;
    public java.lang.String purpose;
    public java.lang.String participants;

    public Meeting() {}

    public Meeting(
        boolean booked,
        java.lang.String purpose,
        java.lang.String participants ) {
        this.booked = booked;
        this.purpose = purpose;
        this.participants = participants;
    }
    ...
}
```

In the implementation in Chapter 9, we obtained an IOR for a CORBA meeting object, on which we invoked remote operations. Now we obtain a struct (by value) and access the fields of the local Java object implementing it.

Figure 13.1 illustrates the two different specifications and their implementation configurations. The figures show the two applications after the

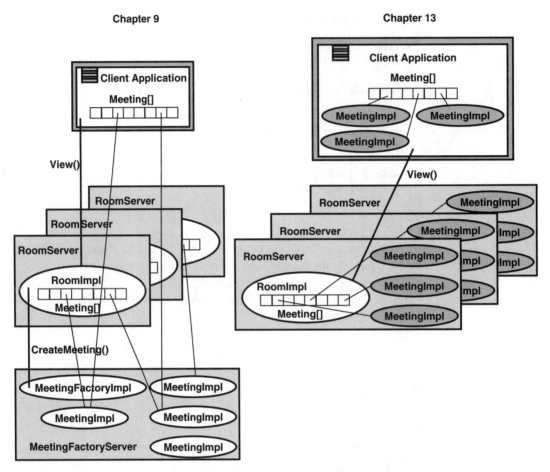

FIGURE 13.1 Comparing the two approaches to the room booking application.

View() operation has been invoked on a room object. We have omitted the Naming Service because it is used to locate Room objects in the same way in both approaches.

Let's go through the interactions step by step:

Viewing a Room's Bookings.

Chapter 9 specification

> The View() operation returns an array of CORBA object references. The size of a CORBA object reference is in the order of 100 to 400 bytes. The client now has an array of IORs to remote meeting objects.

Chapter 13 specification

> The View() operation returns an array of IDL structs represented by Java objects. The size of the Java objects is about 100 bytes, unless you have very long strings for the purpose and/or the participant fields. The client now has an array of references to local Java meeting objects.

Accessing Details of a Meeting.

Chapter 9 specification

> The client makes two CORBA invocations on a remote Meeting object.

Chapter 13 specification

> The client accesses fields of a local Java object.

Booking a Meeting.

Chapter 9 specification

> The client makes a CORBA invocation on the remote Meeting Factory object which creates a CORBA object and returns its IOR to the client. The client now makes a CORBA invocation on the remote Meeting object. The creation of a CORBA object with a transient object reference is slightly slower than the creation of a comparable Java object. Objects with persistent IORs may need much more time to be created.

Chapter 13 specification

> The client instantiates a local Meeting Java object, initializes its contents locally, and passes it as an argument to a CORBA invocation on the remote Room object.

Canceling a Meeting.

Chapter 9 specification

> The client makes a CORBA invocation on a remote Booking object which makes another CORBA invocation on the Meeting object to deactivate it. The actual invocation is likely to be quick, as the Booking and the Meeting objects are probably colocated, but the deactivation of a persistent IOR could involve a remote call to an ORB agent.

Chapter 13 specification

> The client makes a CORBA invocation on a remote Booking object which sets the booked field of its local Meeting Java object to FALSE.

In summary, the Chapter 13 specification leads to far better performance than the Chapter 9 approach. However, the performance gain doesn't come for free. One reason for the performance improvement is an implicit client-side caching by bringing all data about meetings to the client when calling the View() operation. This could lead to outdated information at the client side. If the client refreshes its cache by calling View() frequently it can loose much of the performance gain, or performance could even be worse than it was originally.

There are no magic solutions for specifying your deployment model. However, there are some rules of thumb that can be applied. As we have seen, pros and cons of a specification depend on the usage of the objects. Your functional model should be analyzed by looking at the way in which the objects it specifies are used. You need to identify what data is exchanged, how much of it there is, and how often it is transferred between particular objects. This analysis should feed back into the design of the interfaces to optimize the data exchange, and often results in respecifying your objects.

Sometimes the analysis must take the form of testing an application under load, looking for bottlenecks. We will look at this is section 1.6.

1.2   Threading Models

In this section we consider the execution of code in a single Java virtual machine. We start with a motivation for threading that is based on the user's perception of performance in an application: the reaction of the user interface to input. Improvements are demonstrated by an example of a multithreaded client. Then we look at the way in which servers can use threads to improve their performance.

1.2.1   Threading in Clients

A major factor determining the success of an application is the quality of the user interface. Possibly the most annoying thing that can happen to a user is that the GUI blocks while waiting for a response. The synchronous nature of CORBA operation invocations and the relatively long duration of remote calls make CORBA-based distributed applications particularly vulnerable to the threat of a blocking GUI.

Figure 13.2 illustrates the behavior of a CORBA client making a simple operation call on a CORBA object. The client is blocked for the duration of the call. The duration can range from microseconds, when the client and the invoked object are colocated, to seconds when a remote invocation is made over a modem. The processing performed by the method implementing the operation may also lead to delays.

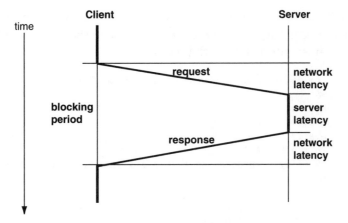

FIGURE 13.2 Behavior of a naive interaction.

The approach to avoiding a blocked user interface that we look at here is to use threading in client code. We will look at two other proven design patterns to address this problem in the next two sections, which address distributed callbacks and iterators.

1.2.2 Multithreaded Clients

We will modify the Hello World applet client we introduced in Chapter 5, as shown in Figure 13.3. We will substitute the text field with a text area to show more information on the screen. We will also add a second text area to

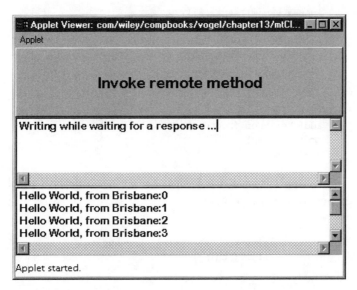

FIGURE 13.3 Modified Applet GUI.

the GUI just to demonstrate the nonblocking behavior that we can achieve using threads. The result is that you can type in the upper window while the client is busy interacting with an object.

```
package com.wiley.compbooks.vogel.chapter13.mtClient.HelloWorldImpl;

import java.awt.*;
import java.awt.event.*;
import java.io.*;
import org.omg.CORBA.*;
import com.wiley.compbooks.vogel.chapter5.simple.HelloWorld.*;

public class Applet
        extends java.applet.Applet
        implements ActionListener {

    private ORB orb;
    private GoodDay goodDay;
    private Button helloWorldButton;
    private TextArea inArea;
    private TextArea outArea;

    public void init() {

        helloWorldButton = new Button("Invoke remote method");
        helloWorldButton.setFont(new Font("Helvetica",
            Font.BOLD, 20));
        helloWorldButton.setActionCommand("invoke");
        helloWorldButton.addActionListener( (ActionListener) this );

        inArea = new TextArea();
        inArea.setFont(new Font("Helvetica", Font.BOLD, 14));

        outArea = new TextArea();
        outArea.setEditable(false);
        outArea.setFont(new Font("Helvetica", Font.BOLD, 14));

        setLayout( new GridLayout(3,1) );
        add( helloWorldButton );
        add( inArea );
        add( outArea );
```

For simplicity we use Visibroker's bind() method to obtain an object reference to a GoodDay object.

```
try {
    // initialize the ORB (using this applet)
    orb = ORB.init( this );

    // bind to object
    goodDay = GoodDayHelper.bind( orb );
```

```
    }
    // catch exceptions
    catch(SystemException ex) {
        System.err.println("ORB is not initialized");
        System.err.println(ex);
    }
}
```

Multithreaded clients spawn separate threads for each activity associated with a certain user event. In our case we create a new thread when the `hello world` button is pushed. Within this thread we will make the invocation, return the results back to the applet, and display them. The thread then terminates. As Figure 13.4 shows, the GUI will only be blocked while the new thread is created and started.

We have to add two things to the applet: a method which can be called by the thread to return the results of the operation, and the code for creating and starting a new thread. The method `setResult()` displays a string in the output area.

```
public void setResult( String str ) {

    outArea.append( str );

}
```

When the `hello world` button is pushed we create a new object of class `ThreadedProxy`, which extends `java.lang.Thread`. We initialize the new object with the reference to our applet and the reference to the CORBA object `goodDay`. Once the object is created, we start it by calling the method `start()` which is defined in the class `java.lang.Thread`.

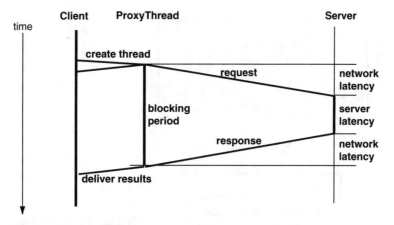

FIGURE 13.4 Multithreaded client—threading behavior.

```
public void actionPerformed( ActionEvent e ) {

    if( e.getActionCommand().equals("invoke") ) {

        // invoke the operation via threaded proxy
        try {
            ThreadedProxy threadedProxy =
                new ThreadedProxy( this, goodDay );
            threadedProxy.start();
        }

        // catch CORBA system exceptions
        catch(SystemException ex) {
            System.err.println(ex);
        }
    }
}
```

Figure 13.5 shows the various objects in the multithreaded client and how they interact. The new object is an instance of the class ThreadedProxy.

The class ThreadedProxy extends the thread class of the Java class library. In its constructor we initialize the private fields goodDay and applet with references to the applet and a GoodDay object.

```
package com.wiley.compbooks.vogel.chapter13.mtClient.HelloWorldImpl;

import org.omg.CORBA.*;
import com.wiley.compbooks.vogel.chapter5.simple.HelloWorld.*;

public class ThreadedProxy extends Thread {

    private GoodDay goodDay;
    private Applet applet;
```

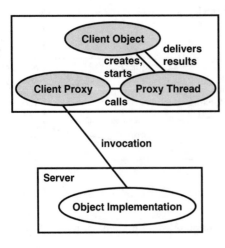

FIGURE 13.5 Multithreaded client—design.

```
public ThreadedProxy( Applet applet, GoodDay goodDay ) {

    this.applet = applet;
    this.goodDay = goodDay;

}
```

The functionality of a thread is in the implementation of the method `run()` defined by the Java thread class. We invoke the hello() operation on the CORBA object `goodDay` and display the result of the operation in the applet's output area by a calling `setResult()` on the applet.

```
public void run() {

        // invoke the operation
        try {
            applet.setResult( goodDay.hello() );
        }
        // catch CORBA system exceptions
        catch(SystemException ex) {
            System.err.println(ex);
        }
    }
}
```

As an alternative to threading, the application can make deferred operation calls using the DII. The IDL/Java mapping defines the following methods on the class `Request`:

- ♦ `public void send_deferred();`—sends an invocation request and returns immediately
- ♦ `public void get_response();`—obtains an invocation response
- ♦ `public boolean poll_response();`—polls the `Request` object to find out if the response has arrived

As we saw in Chapter 10, the DII is more complex to use than generated stubs. There is also no compile-time type checking for DII invocations. Because threads are a language feature in Java and are easy to use, they are usually a better way to do other processing while waiting for an operation invocation to complete.

You can improve the performance of threaded clients by avoiding the creation of a new thread every time a CORBA call is made. Instead of just letting a used thread go out of scope, it can be returned to a thread pool. It is then available for further use.

The overall performance of a multithreaded client also depends on the behavior of the server and, if the client is an applet, on the performance of the IIOP gateway. In the next section we explain different server-side threading models.

1.2.3 Threading in Servers

In the previous section our main purpose was to make the client responsive to the user by optimizing the communication between the client and the server. On the server side there is another problem, namely, how can a server handle hundreds or thousands of concurrent clients? Fortunately, application programmers do not have to deal with this problem explicitly because most Java ORB implementations already provide automatic mechanisms for multithreaded servers.

ORBs usually provide three threading models for server implementations: single-threaded servers, thread per connection, and thread pools or thread per request. Single-threaded servers (Figure 13.6) place incoming requests in a queue and process only one invocation at a time. The problems are obvious. This leads to poor performance, as clients making apparently quick invocations must wait until all requests in the queue have been processed, even if they require much more processing. There is also the potential of deadlocks, which can occur when an object tries to make a callback to a single-threaded client program. Typically Java ORBs (unlike C or C++ ORBs) do not offer single-threaded request processing since threads are a native concept in Java.

The thread-per-connection model uses one worker thread for each network connection, as shown in Figure 13.7. Typically all invocations originating from a single JVM to target objects which reside in the same server

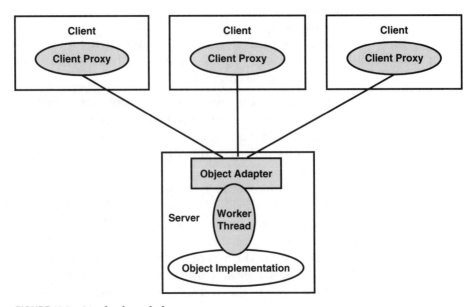

FIGURE 13.6 Single-threaded servers.

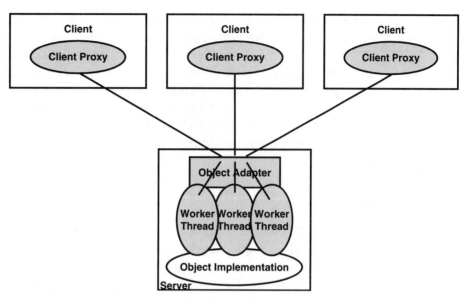

FIGURE 13.7   Thread-per-connection.

are multiplexed over the same connection. Invocations from this JVM are queued and processed sequentially by the worker thread.

Finally, the thread-per-request model creates a new worker thread for each incoming request, as illustrated in Figure 13.8. Typically there is a maximum number of threads for use in the server, and threads that have fin-

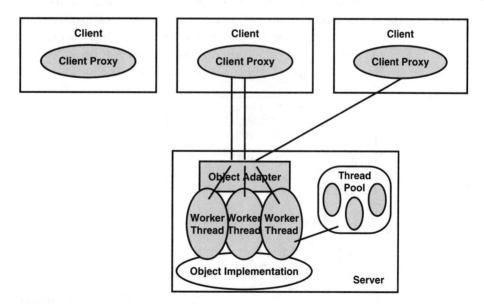

FIGURE 13.8   Thread-per-request.

ished processing a request are returned to a thread pool. This minimizes the cost associated with creating new threads. The default threading model of Visibroker for Java 3.0 is thread per request with thread pooling.

Mechanisms for multithreaded servers that are built into the ORB ease the application programmer's task. However, you have to take care with synchronizing access to shared data in the server. Standard mechanisms such as mutexes can be used to ensure safety of access, and Java allows blocks, methods, and classes to be declared `synchronized` and then automatically synchronizes their use.

1.3   Distributed Callbacks

Distributed callbacks break a synchronous call that returns some data into a pair of calls, a request and a response, as illustrated by Figure 13.9. The request call is made by the client, which supplies an object reference to accept the response. The response call is made on this object reference later by the server-side object implementation. Typically, both calls have only `in` parameters and the return type `void`. The client is then blocked only for the time it takes to transfer the request arguments, and the processing of the returned values is delegated to another object.

To allow the server-side object to call the client back, the client must host an object that implements an IDL-defined interface. The reference of this client-side object is provided as an in parameter of the request operation. As an example, we introduce a new interface in the HelloWorld IDL module and modify the hello() operation to fit the callback paradigm.

The HelloWorld module now contains two interfaces: GoodDay and Callback. The interface GoodDay now contains the operation requestHello() which has an interface of type Callback as its in parameter. The interface Callback contains the

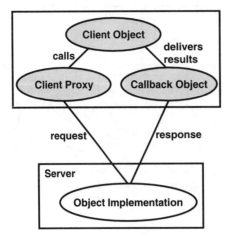

FIGURE 13.9   Distributed callbacks—design.

operation responseHello(). It has one in parameter of type string which corresponds to the return value of the hello() operation as it was originally specified.

```
module com {
...
module chapter13 {
module callback {
module HelloWorld {

   interface Callback {
      void responseHello( in string str );
   };

   interface GoodDay {
      void requestHello( in Callback cb );
   };
};... };
```

To receive the callback from the GoodDay object, our applet has to create an object that implements the interface Callback. This can be done globally for the applet (one callback object that receives all callbacks), or a separate callback object can be instantiated for each invocation. Here we have chosen to create one object in the init() method of the applet. We create the object in the usual manner and connect it to the ORB.

```
// create a callback object
callbackImpl = new CallbackImpl( this );
System.out.println("create");

// connect with ORB
orb.connect( callbackImpl );
System.out.println("connect");
```

When the hello world button is pushed we invoke the requestHello() method on the GoodDay object. We provide the object reference of the callback object created above as the argument to the operation.

```
public void actionPerformed( ActionEvent e ) {

   if( e.getActionCommand().equals("invoke") ) {

      // invoke the operation
      try {
         goodDay.requestHello( callbackImpl );
      }

      // catch CORBA system exceptions
      catch(SystemException ex) {
```

```
            System.err.println(ex);
        }
    }
}
```

The implementation of the callback object is no different from any other object implementation. The implementation class extends the servant base class. We provide a reference to the applet to the constructor so that the result can be displayed. The implementation of responseHello() takes the string argument provided by the remote object implementation and calls the setResult() method on the applet which displays the result in the output area.

```
package com.wiley.compbooks.vogel.chapter13.callback.HelloWorldImpl;

import org.omg.CORBA.*;
import com.wiley.compbooks.vogel.chapter13.callback.HelloWorld.*;

public class CallbackImpl extends _CallbackImplBase {

    private Applet applet;

    // constructor

    CallbackImpl( Applet applet ) {

        this.applet = applet;
    }

    // method
    public void responseHello( String str ) {

        applet.setResult( str );
    }
}
```

On the server side we implement the requestHello() method by delegating it to a newly created thread. Once we have started the thread, the requestHello() method returns. A new thread is created to allow the invocation to return without waiting. The allocation of requests to threads is taken care of by the object adapter.

```
public void requestHello( Callback callback ) {

    ThreadedImpl threadedImpl =
        new ThreadedImpl( callback, location+counter++ );
    threadedImpl.start();
    return;
}
```

The essential part of the class `ThreadedImpl` is the implementation of the `run()` method. First we simulate delay of the method execution by putting the thread to sleep for 10 seconds. Then we make the callback to the applet by invoking the `responseHello()` method on the callback object.

```
public void run() {

        try {
          // sleep for 10 seconds
          Thread.currentThread().sleep(10000);
        }
        catch(InterruptedException e) {
        }

        // make the callback
        try {
            callback.responseHello( "Hello World from " + location );
        }
        // catch CORBA system exceptions
        catch(SystemException ex) {
            System.err.println(ex);
        }
    }
}
```

Figure 13.10 shows the thread behavior of a distributed callback. Using callbacks also makes the client implicitly multithreaded, as the ORB creates a new thread to execute requests for the client-side callback object.

You can further improve the performance of distributed callbacks by declaring the request and response operations oneway. This has the advantage that the call returns immediately and is therefore faster. Because oneway

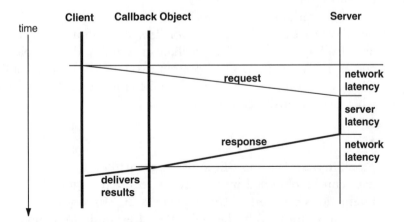

FIGURE 13.10 Distributed callbacks—threading behavior.

operations are asynchronous, you don't have to explicitly create a new thread on the server side since the client is not waiting for the completion of the ORB-generated thread. The semantics of oneway operations defined in CORBA is quite vague: it states that the call is delivered at most once. So technically, doing nothing for oneway call is a CORBA-compliant implementation. However, you can safely assume that ORBs have better implementations. In fact, oneway calls are quite reliable because they are implemented with IIOP which uses TCP to ensure that delivery is reliable.

If you want to use callbacks with applets, make sure that you never rely on HTTP tunneling for the communication, as this prevents callbacks. You also need to make sure that the IIOP gateway supports callbacks. Visibroker's Gatekeeper, for example, enables callbacks into applets when using IIOP.

1.4   Iterators

Iterators are a commonly used design pattern to handle the transmission of large amounts of data. They allow access to large amounts of data in multiple smaller packages rather than in one big chunk. Another motivation is support for the *lazy evaluation* paradigm. This means that additional values are only produced on demand. This approach can avoid allocating large amounts of memory on both the client and the server sides. Clients can process a proportion of the results and discard them before requesting more. They may also decide that they do not require the rest of the results and destroy the iterator. Servers using lazy evaluation can produce a small part of the total result at a time, either ready for the next call to the iterator or when the call is made on the iterator. When clients do not require all the results, the server can avoid the unnecessary processing required to produce the entire set.

The iterator pattern has been adopted in serveral CORBA specifications. We have already seen iterators in specifications of the CORBA Naming and Trading Services. The mechanism employed to implement iterators comes in various flavors. We present two kinds of iterator: pull and push. A client is in control when using a pull iterator and the server is in control when using a push iterator.

1.4.1   Pull Iterators

A pull iterator is a short-lived object created on the server side from which data can be obtained by a client as required. Figure 13.11 illustrates the interactions between a CORBA client, a CORBA object, and a pull iterator.

We again modify the Hello World example to demonstrate iterators. We introduce a new data type ResultSet which is an unbounded sequence of

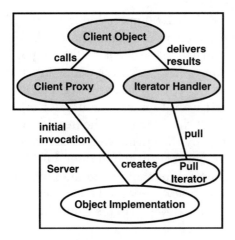

FIGURE 13.11 Pull iterator.

strings. In a real application we would probably use a sequence of some other type to represent, for example, a row in a database table. The iterator would then serve as a way of accessing the results of a query that matched a large number of rows.

```
module com {
...
module pullIterator {
module HelloWorld {

    typedef sequence<string>ResultSet;

    interface PullIterator {

        boolean nextN( in long n, out ResultSet result_set);

        void destroy();

    };

    interface GoodDay {

        ResultSet hello( in long how_many, out PullIterator pull_iterator);
    };
};};};};};};
```

The hello() operation of the GoodDay object has a new signature. It now returns a result of type ResultSet. The in parameter how_many allows the client to control the maximum length of the returned sequence. The out parameter pull_iterator is an object reference to a PullIterator which is created by the GoodDay object. After a client has made the hello() call on a GoodDay object it can query the PullIterator object for more data by calling its nextN() operation.

The boolean result of the nextN() operation indicates whether there is any data left in the iterator. A client can again control the maximum length of the ResultSet which is returned to the client via the out parameter result_set.

The destroy() operation is important for managing system resources. Although an iterator could destroy itself after it delivers all its data, a client could decide that it doesn't want to query the iterator any further, even if there is still data available. If this happened the iterator would never know that it has been abandoned by the client. Well-behaved clients will always call destroy() when they no longer want the iterator, but the iterator should have some time-out mechanism, as there is nothing but the programmer's discipline to ensure that the destroy() operation is actually invoked. In section 2 of this chapter we discuss the problem of distributed garbage collection in a more general manner.

Let's have a look at an applet that uses a pull iterator to access a large amount of data. First we declare and implement a new method on the applet. The method setResult() displays a ResultSet in the output area. The initialization of the applet is the same.

```
public void setResult( String[] resultSet ) {

    for( int i = 0; i < resultSet.length; i++ )
        outArea.append( resultSet[i] );
}
```

When the hello world button is pushed we invoke the hello() method. Before we can do this we have to create a PullIteratorHolder object for the out parameter of the hello() method. Once the hello() operation has returned we display the first result set.

```
public void actionPerformed( ActionEvent e ) {

    if( e.getActionCommand().equals("invoke") ) {

        // invoke the operation
        try {
            PullIteratorHolder pullIteratorHolder =
                new PullIteratorHolder();
            String[] resultSet = goodDay.hello( 5, pullIteratorHolder );
            outArea.append( resultSet );
            IteratorHandler iteratorHandler =
                new IteratorHandler( this, pullIteratorHolder.value );
            iteratorHandler.start();
        }

        // catch CORBA system exceptions
        catch(SystemException ex) {
```

```
                System.err.println(ex);
            }
        }
    }
```

We create a new object of type `IteratorHandler` which handles the further querying of the iterator in a separate thread. We initialize the `IteratorHandler` with references to the applet and the pull iterator. The key functionality of the class `IteratorHandler` is in the implementation of the method `run()`.

```
...
public class IteratorHandler extends Thread {
...
    public void run() {

        ResultSetHolder resultSetHolder = new ResultSetHolder();
        try {
            while( pullIterator.nextN( 5, resultSetHolder ) )
                applet.setResult( resultSetHolder.value );
        pullIterator.destroy();
    }
...
}
```

In the implementation of `run()` we create a new `ResultSetHolder` object. Then we call the `nextN()` method on the iterator and display the result set obtained in the applet by calling its `setResult()` method. We continue querying the iterator as long as it returns true, indicating that it contains more data. Finally, we destroy the iterator.

On the server side we have a new implementation of the `hello()` method provided by the `GoodDayImpl` class. We simulate a large amount of data by creating result sets on the fly. Many iterator implementations that use lazy evaluation do the same thing, although the new result sets are a meaningful response to the original call. Our response contains our standard string plus a counter so that we can watch the progress at the client side.

```
...
public class GoodDayImpl extends _sk_GoodDay {
...
    // method
    public String[] hello( int howMany, PullIteratorHolder pullIteratorHolder)
    {

        String[] resultSet = new String[ howMany ];
        for( int i = 0; i < howMany; i++ ) {
            resultSet[i] = new String(
                "Hello World, from " + location + ":" + i + "\n" );
        }
```

```
        PullIteratorImpl pullIteratorImpl =
           new PullIteratorImpl( howMany, 100, location );
        _orb().connect( pullIteratorImpl );
      pullIteratorHolder.value = pullIteratorImpl;
       return resultSet;
    }
  }
```

We create a result set of size howMany and fill it with our strings. Next we create an object of type PullIteratorImpl which we initialize with the value of the counter, the maximum number of these sets (100), and the location string. We make this object accessible to the CORBA client by connecting it with the ORB. The GoodDayImpl object acts as a PullIterator factory. Finally, we assign the object reference of the pull iterator to the value field of the holder object and return the result set created earlier.

The class PullIteratorImpl is a normal CORBA object implementation. It extends the servant base class _PullIteratorImplBase. In the implementation of the method nextN() we check first if the counter is beyond the maximum. This would mean that the iterator has done its job and delivered all the data to the client. If so, we return false.

```
...
public class PullIteratorImpl extends _PullIteratorImplBase {

    // method
    public boolean nextN( int howMany, ResultSetHolder resultSetHolder) {

        if( counter > max )
           return false;

        try {
          // sleep for 5 seconds
          Thread.currentThread().sleep(5000);
        }
        catch(InterruptedException e) {
        }

        String[] resultSet = new String[ howMany ];
        for( int i = 0; i < howMany && counter < max; i++, counter++ ) {
            resultSet[i] = new String(
                "Hello World, from " + location + ":" + counter + "\n" );
        }
        resultSetHolder.value = resultSet;
        return true;
    }
```

If we have not exceeded the maximum, we simulate a processing delay by putting the thread to sleep for 5 seconds. Once the thread comes back to life we prepare the next result set to be returned to client in the same way as in the implementation of the `hello()` method above. We then assign the result to the value field of the Holder object `resultSetHolder` and return true.

```
public void destroy() {

    _boa().deactivate_obj( this );
}
}
```

The `destroy()` method removes the only reference to the iterator which is held by the **BOA** by calling `deactivate_obj()`.

1.4.2   Push Iterators

Push iterators have the same basic characteristics as pull iterators but they differ in the delivery mechanism. Pull iterators are queried by the client, push iterators are controlled by the server. Push iterators can be understood as a combination of iterators with callbacks. The iterator controls the delivery of the remaining data by making a series of callbacks.

We will adapt our GoodDay object to use a push iterator. Figure 13.12 illustrates the behavior of a **CORBA** client, a GoodDay object, and a client object receiving callbacks from a push iterator. Again we have two interfaces defined in an IDL file. There is the GoodDay interface which provides a hello() operation, as before. However, this time the client provides an interface on which the iterator can call. This interface is called Receiver. It provides one operation, nextN(), which takes a value of type ResultSet as an in parameter. Note that the interface Receiver is not the iterator itself but the interface the iterator calls to deliver data sets.

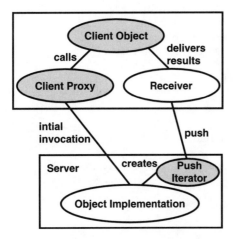

FIGURE 13.12   Push iterator.

```
module com {
...
module chapter13 {
module pushIterator {
module HelloWorld {

  typedef sequence< string > ResultSet;
  interface Receiver {
    void nextN( in ResultSet result_set);
  };

  interface GoodDay {
    ResultSet hello( in long how_many, in Receiver receiver);
  };
};};};};};};
```

We have not included a destroy() operation in the Receiver interface. Whether you do this or not depends on where the control of the application is. Typically a client that initiates an action will destroy its own receiver object if it doesn't wish to receive any further results. Sometimes the design will give the server responsibility for cleaning up receivers, in which case you need a destroy() operation. An alternative is an operation that lets the server notify the client that the delivery is finished.

On the client side, when the hello world button is pushed, the applet creates the callback object for the push iterator, receiverImpl, and connects it with the ORB. Then we invoke the hello() method on the goodDay object and supply the reference to receiverImpl as an argument. The other argument specifies an initial result set size of 5. The enclosing setResult() call will display the returned result set in the applet's output area.

```java
public void actionPerformed( ActionEvent e ) {

    if( e.getActionCommand().equals("invoke") ) {

        // create a pushIterator object
        receiverImpl = new ReceiverImpl( this );

        // connect with ORB

        orb.connect( receiverImpl );

        // invoke the operation
        try {
            setResult( goodDay.hello( 5, receiverImpl ) );
        }

        ...

}
```

The class `ReceiverImpl` is again a normal object implementation, extending the servant base class. The implementation of the method is straightforward. We call the method `setResult()` on the applet and supply the `resultSet` we get from the iterator as its argument.

```
...
public class ReceiverImpl extends _ReceiverImplBase {

...
    public void nextN( String[] resultSet ) {

        applet.setResult( resultSet );
    }
}
```

On the server side the class `GoodDayImpl` implements the `hello()` method by preparing a result set of size `howMany` in the usual manner. Then we create a new object called `pushIterator` and start the thread associated with it.

```
...
public class GoodDayImpl extends _sk_GoodDay {
...
    // method
    public String[] hello( int howMany, Receiver receiver ) {

        String[] resultSet = new String[ howMany ];
        for( int i = 0; i < howMany; i++ ) {
            resultSet[i] = new String(
                "Hello World, from " + location + ":" + i + "\n" );
        }

        PushIterator pushIterator =
            new PushIterator( receiver, howMany, 100, location );
        PushIterator.start();

        return resultSet;

    }
}
```

The push iterator is implemented in the class `PushIterator` by its `run()` method using a while loop. As long as the counter is less than the maximum, the iterator keeps pushing data sets to the applet. However, first we simulate some processing delay by putting the thread to sleep for 5 seconds. Then we prepare the result set and invoke the `nextN()` operation on the `receiver` object.

```
...
public class PushIterator extends Thread {
```

```
...
        public void run() {

            try {
                while( counter < max ) {
                    try {
                        // sleep for 5 seconds
                        Thread.currentThread().sleep(5000);
                    }
                    catch(InterruptedException e) {
                    }

                    String[] resultSet = new String[ 5 ];
                    for( int i = 0; i < 5 && counter < max; i++, counter++ ) {
                        resultSet[i] = new String(
                            "Hello World, from " + location + ":" + counter + "\n" );
                    }
                    receiver.nextN( resultSet );
                }
            }
            // catch CORBA system exceptions
            catch(SystemException ex) {
                System.err.println(ex);
            }
        }
    }
```

Again, it is an alternative to declare the nextN() operation oneway, which has the same implications as discussed for callbacks.

1.5   Client-side Caching

Another way to optimize communication is to cache data at the client side. The result of a remote invocation is kept in the client and further calls to the operation return the cached value without making a remote call. This approach is particularly useful when an attribute or operation that requires a remote call returns the same result repeatedly. There are two approaches to elegantly achieve client-side caching. The two approaches perform caching in the same way but on different abstraction levels, as shown in Figure 13.13.

You can explicitly encapsulate the IDL-generated client proxy object in a caching object. The caching object implements the Java interface that represents the IDL interface type. This is also the Java interface that the client-side proxy object implements. However, your implementation of the methods of this interface will either make a call to access the data from the remote object and keep the values in the local cache, or simply return the cached values without making a call. The condition for refreshing the cached values must be

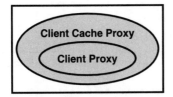 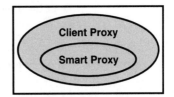

FIGURE 13.13 Client-side caching.

implemented according to some caching policy. This can be combined with callbacks indicating that the cache is invalid.

Alternatively, you can achieve the same effect by using extensions provided by some ORB implementations. Examples are Visibroker's Smart Stubs and OrbixWeb's Smart Proxies. The idea is that the application programmer has access to an additional API through which the request is passed after the client calls the object reference proxy. Smart Stubs and Smart Proxies are particularly useful for accessing cached data.

We have implemented a caching example using the explicit approach. As an example we extend the Hello World example from Chapter 5. We must implement a new client which talks to the same server. The client class becomes leaner than the original class, as we delegate most of the CORBA-related activities to the client cache class GoodDayCache.

We create an instance of the holder classes as in the original example. Then we create an instance of the caching proxy, of class GoodDayCache, which we will explain. We invoke the hello() method on the caching proxy instead of on the CORBA client proxy. Finally, we print the results as in the original example.

```
package com.wiley.compbooks.vogel.chapter13.caching.HelloWorldImpl;

import org.omg.CORBA.*;

public class Client {

    public static void main(String args[]) {

        // create Holder objects for out parameters
        ShortHolder minuteHolder = new ShortHolder();
        ShortHolder hourHolder = new ShortHolder();

        // create client caching proxy
        GoodDayCache goodDayCache = new GoodDayCache( args[0] );

        for( int i = 0; i < 20; i++ ) {
            // invoke the operation
            String location = goodDayCache.hello( hourHolder, minuteHolder );
```

```
            // print results to stdout
            System.out.println("Hello World!");
            if( minuteHolder.value < 10 )
                System.out.println("The local time in " + location + " is "
                    + hourHolder.value + ":0" + minuteHolder.value + "." );
            else
                System.out.println("The local time in " + location + " is "
                    + hourHolder.value + ":" + minuteHolder.value + "." );
            try {
                    Thread.sleep( 15000 );
            }
            catch(java.lang.InterruptedException ex) {
                System.err.println(ex);
            }
        }
    }
}
```

As a test we make 20 invocations with a pause of 15 seconds between them so that we can see when the invocation on the caching proxy results in a remote call and when it returns locally cached data.

The caching proxy class has the same signature as the CORBA client proxy. We ensure this by implementing the Java interface GoodDayOperations generated by the IDL compiler. This class is generated for use by the Tie object implementation approach, but it fits our purpose as well.

```
package com.wiley.compbooks.vogel.chapter13.caching.HelloWorldImpl;

import java.io.*;
import org.omg.CORBA.*;
import com.wiley.compbooks.vogel.chapter5.extended.HelloWorld.*;

public class GoodDayCache implements GoodDayOperations {
private GoodDay goodDay;
private String location;
private long lastTime;
private long currentTime;
private short hour;
private short minute;
```

The major parts of the class are the constructor and the method implementation. In the constructor we initialize the ORB and obtain a reference to the object implementation.

```
public GoodDayCache(String arg) {

    lastTime = 0;
try {
```

```
        // initialize the ORB
        ORB orb = ORB.init(args, null);

        // get object reference from command-line argument
        org.omg.CORBA.Object obj = orb.string_to_object( arg );

        // and narrowed it to GoodDay
        goodDay = GoodDayHelper.narrow( obj );
    }
    catch(SystemException ex) {
        System.err.println(ex);
    }
}
```

In the method implementation we implement the following caching policy: if the previous invocation was made within the last minute we return cached values, otherwise we make a remote call. This makes sense for the example as the granularity of the time value returned by the server-side object is in the order of minutes.

```
    public String hello( ShortHolder hourHolder, ShortHolder minuteHolder )
{

        currentTime = System.currentTimeMillis();

        if( currentTime - lastTime < 60000 ) {
            System.out.println("use cached data");
            hourHolder.value = hour;
            minuteHolder.value = minute;
        }
        else {
            System.out.println("make remote invocation");
            try {
                location = goodDay.hello( hourHolder, minuteHolder );
                hour = hourHolder.value;
                minute = minuteHolder.value;
                lastTime = currentTime;
            }
            catch(SystemException ex) {
                System.err.println(ex);
            }
        }
        return location;
    }
}
```

To run the example we first start the server from Chapter 5 and then our new client. Our output trace demonstrates that three out of four invocations are handled by returning cached data.

```
$ vbj com.wiley.compbooks.vogel.chapter5.extended.HelloWorldImpl.Server
Montreal > /tmp/ior

$ vbj com.wiley.compbooks.vogel.chapter13.caching.HelloWorldImpl.Client
cat /tmp/ior
```

make remote invocation
```
Hello World!
The local time in Montreal is 17:05.
```
use cached data
```
Hello World!
The local time in Montreal is 17:05.
```
use cached data
```
Hello World!
The local time in Montreal is 17:05.
```
use cached data
```
Hello World!
The local time in Montreal is 17:05.
```
make remote invocation
```
Hello World!
The local time in Montreal is 17:06.
```

1.6   Monitoring Performance

Now that we have investigated a number of ways of improving performance in clients, we still need to instrument the application to measure the performance results. Although a requirements specification would typically state that the time for a certain user-initiated action should not exceed a certain number of milliseconds or seconds, you need to instrument each component of your application to isolate any performance bottlenecks. You have to find out exactly where your application introduces delays that break the requirements.

A simple way to instrument your application is to wrap each invocation on the client and server sides into a pair of statements that take the time, calculate the difference, and log the data. However, this approach has multiple disadvantages. First, you litter the application with code that is only designed to be used during testing. Furthermore, you must be able to easily switch the performance measurement on and off; this means making all of your performance measurement code conditional. This clutters the application code even more.

ORBs provide mechanisms to decouple application logic from performance measurement. An example of such a mechanism is Visibroker's interceptor construct, which we introduced in Chapter 12. A simple implementation for performance measurement interceptors is given here. The complete implementation can be found in the Appendix on the companion website.

The two ORB events in which we are interested occur when the request is received by the server and when the response is sent. At these times the ORB calls the methods begin() and complete(), respectively. These methods are implemented in the class TimeInterceptor, which we put in the same package as the other performance instrumentation classes. The code follows and is explained.

```
package com.wiley.compbooks.vogel.chapter13.mamo.
performanceMeasurementInterceptor;

import com.visigenic.vbroker.interceptor.*;
import com.visigenic.vbroker.IOP.*;
import com.visigenic.vbroker.GIOP.*;
import org.omg.CORBA.portable.*;

public class TimerServerInterceptor
    extends TimerInterceptor
    implements ServerInterceptor {

    ...

    public InputStream receive_request( RequestHeader hdr,
        org.omg.CORBA.ObjectHolder target, InputStream buf,
        Closure closure) {

        begin(closure, hdr.operation );
        return null;
    }

    ...

    public void request_completed( RequestHeader reqHdr,
        org.omg.CORBA.Object target, Closure closure){
        complete(closure);
    }
    ...
}
```

The client-side interceptor is very similar. In the client case the relevant methods are prepare_request() and receive_reply() which are called by the ORB at the start and end of an operation invocation.

```
package com.wiley.compbooks.vogel.chapter13.mamo.
performanceMeasurementInterceptor;

import com.visigenic.vbroker.interceptor.*;
import com.visigenic.vbroker.GIOP.*;
```

```
public class TimerClientInterceptor
    extends TimerInterceptor
    implements ClientInterceptor {

    public void prepare_request(RequestHeaderHolder hdr, Closure closure) {
        begin(closure, hdr.value.operation);
    }

    ...

    public void receive_reply(ReplyHeader hdr,
        org.omg.CORBA.portable.InputStream buf,
        org.omg.CORBA.Environment env, Closure closure) {
        complete(closure);
    }
}
```

The class `TimeInterceptor` implements the methods `begin()` and `complete()` and is extended by the client and the server interceptor implementations. The method `begin()` creates a new `TimerData` object and assigns it to a *closure object.* The closure object is used to associate data with a particular interceptor thread for use by other methods in that interceptor. The `TimerData` class encapsulates its creation time and a string which we use to store the name of the operation.

```
package com.wiley.compbooks.vogel.chapter13.mamo.
performanceMeasurementInterceptor;

import com.visigenic.vbroker.interceptor.*;

public class TimerInterceptor {

    public void begin( Closure closure, String operation ) {

        closure.object = new TimerData( operation );
    }

    public void complete(Closure closure) {

        TimerData      t1 = (TimerData)closure.object;
        TimerData      t2 = new TimerData( null );
        long delta = t2.startTime - t1.startTime;

        System.out.println( t1.operation +":bst"+ delta );
    }
}
```

The `complete()` method gets the `TimeData` object from the closure object, calculates the time the operation needed to complete, and logs the performance data.

The last class required is `TimeData`, which provides public fields for the starting time, in milliseconds, and the operation name. In its constructor we set the starting time and assign the operation name from the constructor's argument to the `operation` field.

```
package com.wiley.compbooks.vogel.chapter13.mamo.
performanceMeasurementInterceptor;

public class TimerData {

    public long startTime;
    public String operation;

    public TimerData( String operation) {
      this.operation = operation;
        startTime = System.currentTimeMillis();
    }
}
```

To instrument an application using the performance measurement interceptors we simply set the property `ORBservices` to the package `com.wiley` `.compbooks.vogel.chapter13.mamo.performanceMeasurementInterceptor` which contains the classes of our performance measurement interceptor. The ORB will automatically call the `init()` method of the `Init` class in the package and initialize the interceptors.

```
$ vbj -DORBservices=com.wiley.compbooks.vogel.chapter13.mamo.
performanceMeasurementInterceptor TestedServer

$ vbj -DORBservices=com.wiley.compbooks.vogel.chapter13.mamo.
performanceMeasurementInterceptor TestClient
```

There is a set of tools accompanying Visibroker for Java that includes a full-blown performance monitor. The performance monitor produces performance data in a similar fashion to our interceptors and provides a GUI client to view the data in various forms. This tool provides a more sophisticated alternative to the approach presented here.

1.6.1 A Test Client to Drive the Application

Typically the GUI client driving your application is not useful for stress testing because it relies on human interactions and cannot simulate different loads. We suggest that you implement a stress-test client that uses the following pattern:

```
class TestClient {

    int noOfCycles;
```

```
public static void main( String args ) {

    // get a number of cycles from the command line

    noOfCycles = ...

    // obtain IOR to an initial application object
    initialApplicationObject = ...
        for( int i =0; i < noOfCycles; i++ ) {
            // simulate typical client behavior
            // could be derived from use cases
        }
    }
}
```

An implementation following this pattern can simulate various load levels. A more sophisticated implementation could be multithreaded. Alternatively, you could simulate different loads with single-threaded clients by starting multiple clients in their own JVMs. When using a multithreaded test client implementation you need to take the server-side threading model into account.

The implementation of a cycle in the test client depends on scenarios you would consider to be typical. It could be derived from use cases that may have developed as part of your analysis and design phase. This is another motivation to spend some time on the development and formalization of use cases after the design phase.

Since the test client is a command-line driven Java application, it can be used from test scripts written in UNIX shells, perl, or as batch files. This will help to create an automated and repeatable test process.

You may also consider commercial Java test tools. Their general approach is that they can capture activity on your client program and replay the captured sequences in different scenarios, simulating different loads.

1.6.2 Analysis of the Performance Data

Once we have measured the performance of our application in the manner described above, we can analyze it. The detailed measurements allow us to locate performance bottlenecks. Typically performance problems fall into one of the following categories. We also give you some hints on where to look for performance improvements.

♦ Delay problem at light load

—Delay in the communication leg. Make sure that the amount of data shipped between client and server is optimized using the techniques described in the previous sections.

—Delay in the computation leg. Double-check your code for potential performance problems. Do performance measurements for non-ORB components, for example, databases. Try to cache data in the server-side CORBA objects.

◆ Delay problem at heavy load.

—Delay in the communication leg. Make sure that you use the best threading model: thread-per-request.

—Delay in the computation leg. Make sure that enough resources are available to your objects. Resources include those provided by the operating systems such as threads, memory, CPU cycles, file descriptors, and socket connections and third-party resources, for example, available database connections. Reconfiguring and redistributing your servers is the only solution here.

2 Maintenance

There are many maintenance issues in distributed applications. We have selected two of these issues for discussion:

◆ Distributed garbage collection—cleaning up objects that are no longer required by their remote clients.
◆ Graceful shutdown—the ability to safely shut down an application without needing to be aware of where all the servers and their objects are executing.

The management approach that we take compliments the use of factory objects for starting a distributed application. Factories provide a way of easily creating new objects with the characteristics that we require, as they are needed. However, we need to consider what to do when individual objects are no longer required, especially when their client programs shut down without indicating that they no longer require the objects they are using. We also need an approach to shutting down an entire application that ensures that the current objects can terminate cleanly. They may need to save their state or to clean up other objects they are using. We will show an implementation of a simple maintenance tool that monitors the objects created and allows them to be gracefully shut down. Section 2 has the following structure:

◆ Distributed garbage collection (section 2.1)
◆ Design of a maintenance interface for graceful shutdown of a distributed application (section 2.2)
◆ Implementing a maintenance tool (section 2.3)

♦ Implementing maintained objects (section 2.4)

♦ Using the maintenance tool (section 2.5)

2.1 Distributed Garbage Collection

Distributed garbage collection means that a distributed object will be destroyed once no (remote) client holds a reference to the object. CORBA does not address this problem except in the form of explicit operations to release objects, as specified in the Life Cycle Service. The problem of cleaning up when clients just discard object references is still unsolved. This is a common occurrence in applications deployed on the Internet since applet clients are not under the application's control.

CORBA does address the memory management of client proxies and server objects. We explained the general mechanism in Chapter 2. The Java case is simpler because it allows the delegation of memory management to the Java garbage collection mechanism. This means that client proxies are garbage collected once all Java object references to the proxy go out of scope. The same applies to the server side, but here the object adapter holds a reference it obtained when the object was registered, for example, by calling `connect()` on the ORB or `obj_is_ready()` on the BOA. To release this reference you must make the matching call, `disconnect()` or `deactivate_obj()`, respectively. In order to safely deactivate an object, one should be sure that there is no client out there holding an IOR to the object. Generally the ORB cannot determine this and hence cannot automate distributed garbage collection. For example, a client passes an object reference to a third-party object which stores it without making a connection to the server. Since the server does not know about the other reference it might just deactivate the object once the original client is done with it. This, however, does not mean that you cannot solve the problem of distributed garbage collection in your application since your application can keep information about the copying or passing of references which the ORB does not have access to.

First of all, clients that request an object to be created for their exclusive use should release the object once they are done with it by calling an explicit destroy operation. The implementation of this operation will release any references to itself, including the one held by the object adapter, and so prepare the object for garbage collection by Java. You have to declare this destroy operation in the IDL interface of the object. You can declare your own destroy operation or the object can inherit the CORBA LifeCycleObject interface and implement its remove() operation (Figure 13.14).

```
exception NotRemovable { string reason; };
interface LifeCycleObject {
```

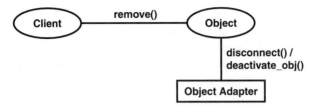

FIGURE 13.14 Explicitly destroying objects.

```
    ...
    void remove()raises( NotRemovable);
};
```

Note that the Life Cycle Service is a set of IDL interfaces intended as a design pattern you have to implement rather than as an off-the-shelf service such as the Naming or Event Services.

Another way of disposing of objects is to implement your factories as managers which control the complete life cycle of the objects they create. A client will create an object using a factory's create operations, use the object, and once a client is done it will call a destroy operation on the manager, passing the object's reference as an argument. The manager then releases the object reference held by the object adapter and removes its own reference to the object. Then, if there are no other references to the object, it is ready for disposal by the Java garbage collector. See Figure 13.15.

This leaves us with two problems. First, what happens if multiple clients use the same transient object and second, what needs to be done if a client terminates a connection abnormally, for example, due to a network failure.

The first issue can be addressed by a distributed reference counting mechanism. For example, Visibroker creates matching bind and unbind events that occur when a client proxy is created and destroyed. These events can be used by event handlers and interceptors to count the number of live references to an object. The problem with this approach is that when a con-

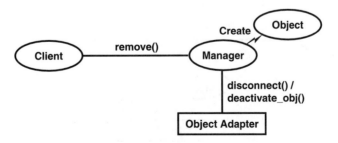

FIGURE 13.15 Destroying objects via a manager.

nection terminates abnormally, the proxy cannot signal that it is being destroyed. This is quite a frequent occurrence on the Internet.

An abnormal termination of a connection is detected by Visibroker event handlers and interceptors and they can decrement the reference count. If the counter indicates that there are now no clients using this object it will be prepared for garbage collection, and if the client recovers the connection it may find that the reference is stale. Any further invocations on this reference will raise the exception NO_IMPLEMENT.

The same problem occurs when the client passes an IOR to a third party which does not make an immediate connection to the server. You can, however, avoid this problem by forcing an immediate connection establishment, for example by calling non-existent() on the object.

Another simpler but more robust approach is to give a transient object a certain lifetime. Once the lifetime has expired, the object is deactivated and made ready for Java garbage collection. The lifetime can be absolute or relative to the last invocation of the object. This mechanism can be easily implemented by a thread which is notified by the factory when the object is created. When using a relative lifetime, the thread must be notified when the object is invoked, for example, by a Visibroker event handler or interceptor or a similar mechanism. The thread will check the elapsed time every so often, and once it passes the predetermined lifetime it will deactivate the object, as shown in Figure 13.16.

This approach has two advantages in addition those of other garbage collection mechanisms. It aids resource management in the server, cleaning up objects created for clients that have been inactive for a while, for example, while the user is on lunch break. Also, it can assist in implementing security policies that require the time out of a user session after a given time.

2.2   Design of Maintenance Interfaces

When maintaining a distributed system, we need to be able to use a client that invokes administrative operations on maintenance interfaces supported

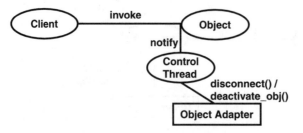

FIGURE 13.16 Transient objects with a limited lifetime.

by all the important objects in the application. The objects we need to administer must register object references to their maintenance interfaces, for example, in a Naming Service or a Trader. They may also hold references to objects they administer. In particular, factories may keep references to the objects they create. A hierarchy of administration can be set up to allow an administrator to delegate maintenance functions. In the remainder of this section we show this principle by implementing the graceful shutdown of an application by adding some maintenance interfaces to objects and creating a tool that maintains these objects.

We specify an interface called Maintained to be implemented by all objects you need to gracefully shut down. These are typically factories and manager objects, for example, session managers. Additionally there is an interface Maintainer that is implemented by a tool which you or a system operator would use to control the shutdown. Figure 13.17 illustrates the interfaces and their interactions.

As is shown in the following IDL, the interface Maintained has an operation prepareShutdown() that is called by the Maintainer object in the maintenance tool we implement in section 2.3. It provides the IOR of its implementation of the interface Maintainer as an argument. Once the prepareShutdown() method has been called, the receiving object prepares its graceful shutdown, which typically includes

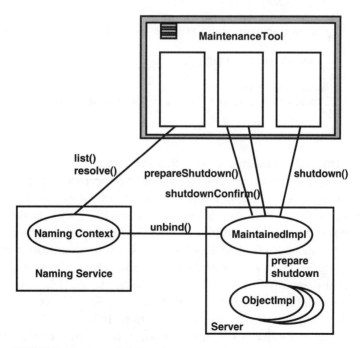

FIGURE 13.17   Graceful shutdown.

♦ The object makes itself invisible, for example, it deregisters itself from the Naming Service, Trading Service, or a proprietary directory service. Now potential clients can't find the object anymore.

♦ The object recursively shuts down the objects it controls in a graceful manner. The meaning of graceful here is a bit vague since it depends very much on the application. If, for example, the initial object is a session manager, it makes all the session objects gracefully shut down. This could mean that a session continues to be active until its client terminates the session or the session times out. All the objects controlled by the Maintained object should be deactivated. This means that the Maintained object and the objects themselves call `disconnect()` on the ORB or `deactivate()` on the BOA.

```
module com {
...
module chapter13 {
module mamo {
module maintenance {

    interface Maintainer;
    interface Maintained;

    interface Maintained {

        oneway void prepareShutdown( in Maintainer maintenanceTool );

        oneway void shutdown()
    };
    interface Maintainer {
        oneway void shutdownConfirmation( in Maintained confirmingObject );
    };
};};};};};};
```

Once the Maintained object has prepared the shutdown it notifies the Maintainer object with a call to its shutdownConformation() operation.

Once the maintainer has received the callback it can shut down the server that hosts the maintained object by calling shutdown() on the Maintained interface. There is no standard CORBA API for shutting down a server.

If you have used Visibroker's BOA implementation and in particular `impl_is_ready()` in the server, you can shut down the server by calling the method `shutdown()` on the ORB. This makes the `impl_is_ready()` return.

Special care needs to be taken when a server hosts a number of independent objects. If the `shutdown()` method is invoked on just one of those objects it shuts down the entire server. Some other objects hosted by this server might not have a chance to prepare themselves for a shutdown. To avoid this problem, there should be a primary object per server that directly or indirectly controls all the other objects on the server. This object should be the only one implementing the Maintained interface.

2.3   Implementing a Maintenance Tool

In order to monitor the objects supporting the Maintained interface, we need to have a maintenance client that is run by an administrator when the application needs to be shut down. In this section we present the implementation of such a maintenance tool.

Our tool is a client of the interface Maintained and an implementation of the interface Maintainer. We adopt a convention that maintained objects from a particular application register themselves in the same context in the Naming Service. We will see this registration in section 2.4. The tool allows users to nominate the Naming Context used by the objects they want to manage. It creates a list of all the maintained objects bound in that context and allows the user to select objects to prepare for shutdown. When the objects call back to indicate that they are ready, it will shut down the server. The tool is composed of three classes:

* `MaintenanceTool`—extends the Java `Frame` class and creates and initializes instances of the two other classes
* `MaintainerImpl`—implements the Maintainer interface
* `MaintenanceManager`—deals with all the GUI coordination

Figure 13.18 illustrates the design of the maintenance tool.

The class `MaintenanceTool` extends the class `Frame` and implements the interface `WindowListener`. Our implementation of the `WindowListener` interface is trivial and we have omitted it here because it has no relevance to CORBA.

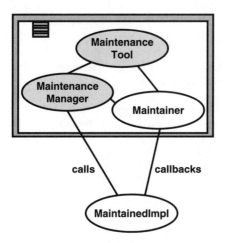

FIGURE 13.18   Design of the maintenance tool.

```
package com.wiley.compbooks.vogel.chapter13.mamo.maintenanceImpl;

import java.awt.*;
import java.awt.event.*;
import org.omg.CORBA.*;
import com.wiley.compbooks.vogel.chapter13.mamo.maintenance.*;

public class MaintenanceTool
    extends Frame
    implements WindowListener {

    private ORB orb;

    public MaintenanceTool() {

        super( "CORBA Maintenance Tool" );

        try {
            orb = ORB.init();
        }
        // catch CORBA system exceptions
        catch(SystemException ex) {
            System.err.println(ex);
        }

    addWindowListener(this);
        setSize( 450, 275 );
    }

    // default implementation of the interface WindowListener
```

In the static `main()` method of the class `MaintenanceTool` we create an instance of the class itself and make it visible on the screen. Then we create a instance of the `MaintenanceManager`, passing a reference to the `MaintenanceTool` to its constructor.

```
    public static void main( String[] args ) {

        MaintenanceTool maintenanceTool = new MaintenanceTool();
        maintenanceTool.setVisible(true);

        MaintenanceManager maintenanceManager =
            new MaintenanceManager( maintenanceTool );
        MaintainerImpl maintainer =
            new MaintainerImpl( maintenanceManager );
        maintenanceTool.orb.connect( maintainer );
        maintenanceManager.setMaintainer( maintainer );
    }
}
```

Finally, we create an instance of the implementation of Maintainer, which is used for callbacks from the maintained objects. We provide its constructor with the reference to the maintenanceManager object, which it will use to notify the tool of callbacks from maintained objects. We also provide a reference to the maintainer implementation to maintenaceManager so that it can pass it to the prepareShutdown() method of the maintained objects as a callback.

The class MaintainerImpl is a straightforward callback interface implementation. The implementation class extends the implementation base class. In the constructor it stores the maintenenceManager reference in a private variable. The implementation of the method shutdownConfirmation() calls confirm() on the maintenanceManager to update its state.

```
package com.wiley.compbooks.vogel.chapter13.mamo.maintenanceImpl;

import java.awt.*;
import org.omg.CORBA.*;
import com.wiley.compbooks.vogel.chapter13.mamo.maintenance.*;
import com.wiley.compbooks.vogel.chapter13.mamo.maintenanceImpl.*;

public class MaintainerImpl extends _MaintainerImplBase {

    private MaintenanceManager maintenanceManager;
    // constructor
    public MaintainerImpl( MaintenanceManager maintenanceManager ) {

        this.maintenanceManager = maintenanceManager;
    }

    public void shutdownConfirmation( Maintained preparedObject ) {

        maintenanceManager.confirm( preparedObject );
    }
}
```

The class MaintenanceManager is the core of the maintenace tool. It keeps the state of the maintained objects and controls the GUI. Its implementation performs the following actions to shut down an application:

- ♦ Look up objects in a specified naming context
- ♦ Select objects for shutdown
- ♦ Call prepareShutdown() on selected objects
- ♦ Wait for the callbacks that confirm the shutdown preparation
- ♦ Call shutdown() on prepared objects

Figure 13.19 shows a screen shot of the maintenance tool GUI. This helps in understanding the implementation of the MaintenanceManager class.

The class implements the `ActionListener` interface according to the JDK 1.1 event model. It declares a number of GUI components and three vectors to contain state information. The vector `candidateObjects` contains all objects found in a particular context that implement the `Maintained` interface. The vector `selectedObjects` contains the objects on which the operation `prepareShutdown()` has been invoked, and the vector `confirmedObjects` contains the objects which made the callback `shutdownConfirmation()`.

```
package com.wiley.compbooks.vogel.chapter13.mamo.maintenanceImpl;

import java.util.*;
import java.awt.*;
import java.awt.event.*;
import org.omg.CORBA.*;
import org.omg.CosNaming.*;
import com.wiley.compbooks.vogel.chapter8.naming.*;
import com.wiley.compbooks.vogel.chapter13.mamo.maintenance.*;

public class MaintenanceManager implements ActionListener {

    private Button prepareButton;
    private Button shutdownButton;
    private Button getContextButton;
    private Button quitButton;

    private TextField ncTextField;
    private TextField cbTextField;

    private Panel mainPanel;

    private java.awt.Container maintenanceTool;
```

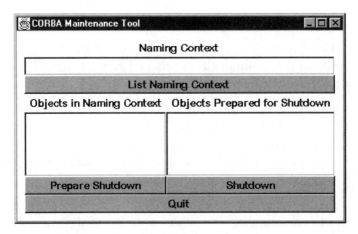

FIGURE 13.19 Maintenance tool GUI.

```
        private Maintainer maintainer;

        private Maintained maintained;

        private Vector candidateObjects;
        private Vector selectedObjects;
        private Vector confirmedObjects;

        private org.omg.CORBA.Object obj;
        private NamingContext context;
        private EasyNaming easy_naming;

private List candidateList;

private List confirmedList;
```

The constructor stores a reference to the `MaintenanceTool` object, initializes the ORB and the `EasyNaming` object, and creates new vector objects. It also creates and initializes the various GUI components, which we don't show here because it is very lengthy and does not assist in understanding CORBA concepts. The full code is on the website.

```
public MaintenanceManager( java.awt.Container maintenanceTool ) {

        this.maintenanceTool = maintenanceTool;

        ORB orb = ORB.init(args, null);
        easy_naming = new EasyNaming( orb );

        selectedObjects = new Vector();

        confirmedObjects = new Vector();

        // lots of code to create and initialize the GUI
}
```

The method `setMaintainer()` stores the object reference of the our Maintainer interface implementation in a private variable.

```
public void setMaintainer( Maintainer m ) {
    maintainer = m;
}
```

The implementation of the method `actionsPerformed()` (defined in the Java interface `ActionListener`) controls the behavior of the class. The tool is driven by events from the GUI. In this application these are action events caused by pressing one of the four buttons we have created in the `Frame`.

If the button labeled `List Naming Context` is pressed, we get the value of the text field `ncTextField` which is expected to contain a string describing a naming context. Then we obtain and display all objects bound in this naming context, as long as they are of the interface type Maintained. This behavior is encapsulated by the method selectObject().

The button labeled Prepare Shutdown leads the invocation of the method prepare(), which invokes the prepareShutdown() operation on a selected object. The button labeled Shutdown invokes the method shutdown(), which in turn invokes the operation shutdown() on a selected object. The Quit button causes the application to exit.

```
public void actionPerformed( ActionEvent ev ) {

    if(ev.getActionCommand().equals("getContext"))
        selectObject( ncTextField.getText() );

    if(ev.getActionCommand().equals("prepare"))
        prepare();

    if(ev.getActionCommand().equals("shutdown"))
        shutdown();

    if(ev.getActionCommand().equals("quit"))
        System.exit(0);
}
```

The method selectedObject() gets a string from the text field, which is expected to be a string name for a naming context using the conventions introduced in Chapter 8 by the class EasyNaming. We try to resolve the string to a naming context object. If this doesn't succeed, we print a message in the text field and return.

If a naming context is resolved, we remove all entries from the candidate list and create a new vector for candidate objects. Now we invoke the list() operation on the naming context object. Since the operation has two out parameters we have to create the appropriate Holder objects, BindingList Holder and BindingIteratorHolder.

```
public void selectObject( String contextString ) {

    try }
        // get context
        context = NamingContextHelper.narrow(
            easy_naming.resolve_from_string( contextString ) );
        if( context == null ) {
            ncTextField.setText( "context " + contextString +
                " is null, try again" );
            return;
        }
```

```
candidateList.removeAll();
candidateObjects = new Vector();

BindingListHolder blHolder = new BindingListHolder();
BindingIteratorHolder biHolder = new BindingIteratorHolder();
BindingHolder bHolder = new BindingHolder();
Maintained m;

context.list( 2, blHolder, biHolder );
```

We invoke the list() operation with the how_many parameter set to 2. This is only done to demonstrate the use of the binding iterator, even when there is a small number of objects. A production implementation would set the value far higher, since the binding list is more effective than the iterator, using one remote call rather than many. The binding iterator would be seen as an overflow mechanism.

```
for( int i = 0; i < blHolder.value.length; i++ ) {
    m = MaintainedHelper.narrow(
        context.resolve( blHolder.value[i].binding_name ) );
    if( m != null ) {
        candidateList.add( blHolder.value[i].binding_name[0].id
);
        candidateObjects.addElement( m );
    }
}
```

We process the list and then the iterator, resolving all the names they contain. Since the resolve() operation returns object references of type CORBA::Object, we try to narrow these references to objects of type Maintained. Only if we succeed (narrow() returns a nonnull reference) do we add the reference to the vector and its name to the candidate list.

```
if( biHolder.value != null ) {
    // this loop only works when the NS returns false
    //after the last binding
    while( biHolder.value.next_one( bHolder ) ) {
        m = MaintainedHelper.narrow(
            context.resolve( bHolder.value.binding_name ) );
        if( m != null ) {
            candidateList.add(
                bHolder.value.binding_name[0].id );
            candidateObjects.addElement( m );
        }
    }
}
```

When we are done with the binding iterator we call its destroy() operation. This notifies the iterator that it can clean up its resources and deactivate itself. Finally, we close the try block and catch exceptions.

```
        if( biHolder.value != null )
            biHolder.value.destroy();
}
catch(SystemException system_exception ) {
    System.err.println( system_exception.toString() );
}
catch(UserException naming_exception) {
    ncTextField.setText( "context "+contextString+
        " not found, try again" );
}
    maintenanceTool.validate();
}
```

The prepare() method starts by getting the index of the selected item from the list. If no selection has been a made, we just return. Otherwise we remove the item from the candidate list and the candidate vector. Finally, we invoke prepareShutdown() on the selected object. If a CORBA system exception is thrown, we don't do anything, since it is likely that we obtained a stale entry from the Naming Service.

```
    public void prepare() {

        int selectedIndex = candidateList.getSelectedIndex();

        if( selectedIndex == -1 ) // no selection
            return;

        candidateList.remove( selectedIndex );

        maintained = (Maintained)candidateObjects.elementAt( selectedIndex
);

        candidateObjects.removeElementAt( selectedIndex );
        selectedObjects.addElement( maintained );

        try {
            maintained.prepareShutdown( maintainer );
        }
        catch(SystemException system_exception ) {
            // don't do anything, it's likely to be stale entry
            // just remove name from the list which we do anyway
        }

        maintenanceTool.validate();
    }
```

The method `confirm()` is invoked by the implementation of the Maintainer interface when it receives a callback from a maintained object. We add the object's name to the confirmed list. We also remove the object reference from the selected vector and add it to the confirmed vector.

```
public void confirm( org.omg.CORBA.Object confirmedObject ) {

    confirmedList.add( confirmedObject._object_name() );

    selectedObjects.removeElement( (Maintained)confirmedObject );
    confirmedObjects.addElement( confirmedObject );

    maintenanceTool.validate();
}
```

The last method is `shutdown()`. Again we get the index of the selected list item and check if an item has actually been selected. We get the object that corresponds to the selected item and invoke `shutdown()` on it. If a CORBA system exception is thrown, it is most likely that the object has already been deactivated, for example, by calling `shutdown()` on another object in the same server. Anyway, since the object isn't there, we have achieved the shutdown and don't do anything.

```
public void shutdown() {

    int selectedIndex = confirmedList.getSelectedIndex();

    if( selectedIndex == -1 ) // no selection

        return;

    try {
        ((Maintained)confirmedObjects.elementAt( selectedIndex )).
        shutdown();
    }
    catch(SystemException system_exception ) {
        // don't do anything, object is already gone ...
    }

    confirmedList.remove( selectedIndex );

    confirmedObjects.removeElementAt( selectedIndex );

    maintenanceTool.validate();
    }
}
```

Finally, we remove the object's name from the list and it's reference from the vector and update the GUI.

2.4 Implementing Maintained Objects

To make the whole maintenance approach work we also have to implement the Maintained interface at selected objects for the shutdown of their host server. As an example, we have selected the Room object from the application we introduced in Chapter 9. We create an interface called MaintainedRoom which inherits the Room interface as well as the Maintained interface:

```
#include "RoomBooking.idl"
#include "maintenance.idl"

module com{
...
module chapter13{
module mamo{
module maintenanceExample{

  interface MaintainedRoom:
    com::wiley::compbooks::vogel::chapter9::RoomBooking::Room,
    com::wiley::compbooks::vogel::chapter13::mamo::maintenance::Maintained
  {};

};};};};};};
```

The implementation of the interface is very similar to the original Room implementation. We have only modified the constructor and added methods for the implementation of the operations of the Maintained interface. Besides the room name, the constructor also has a reference to an EasyNaming object. We create an EasyNaming object in the server and pass it to the constructor.

```
package com.wiley.compbooks.vogel.chapter13.mamo.maintenanceExampleImpl;

import org.omg.CORBA.*;
import com.wiley.compbooks.vogel.chapter8.naming.*;
import com.wiley.compbooks.vogel.chapter9.RoomBooking.*;
import com.wiley.compbooks.vogel.chapter19.RoomBooking.RoomPackage.*;
import com.wiley.compbooks.vogel.chapter13.mamo.maintenance.*;
import com.wiley.compbooks.vogel.chapter13.mamo.maintenanceExample.*;

class MaintainedRoomImpl extends _sk_MaintainedRoom {
    private String name;
    private Meeting[] meetings;
    private Maintainer mt;
    private EasyNaming easyNaming;

    // constructor

    MaintainedRoomImpl( String name, EasyNaming easyNaming ) {

        super( name );
```

```
        this.name = name;

        this.easyNaming = easyNaming;

        meetings = new Meeting[ MaxSlots ];

    }
```

In the implementation of the `prepareShutdown()` method, we unbind the object from the Naming Service so that it becomes invisible to potential new clients. Because of the simplicity of the room server, we don't have to do any other preparation to shut down, so we immediately make the callback to the maintainer object.

```
// Maintained operations
public void prepareShutdown( Maintainer mt ) {

    this.mt = mt;
    try {
        easyNaming.unbind_from_string(
            "/BuildingApplications/Rooms/"+name );
    }
    catch(UserException ue) {
        System.err.println(ue);
    }
    mt.shutdownConfirmation( (Maintained)this );
}
```

The Maintained Room's `shutdown()` method invokes the `shutdown()` method on the ORB which makes `impl_is_ready()` return, allowing the server to clean up and exit. The implementation of the Room interface's attribute and

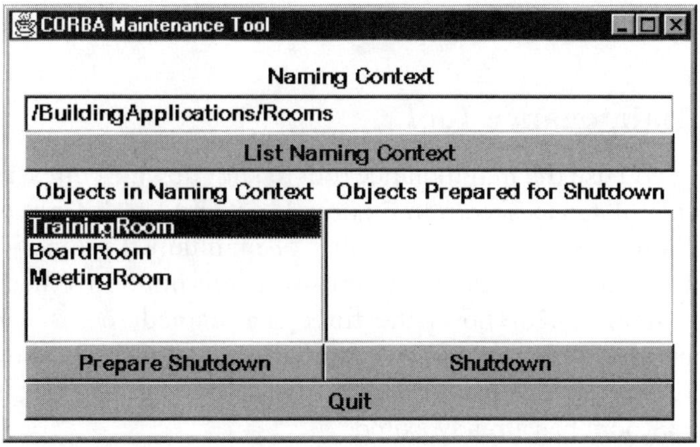

FIGURE 13.20 Objects selected for preparing to shut down.

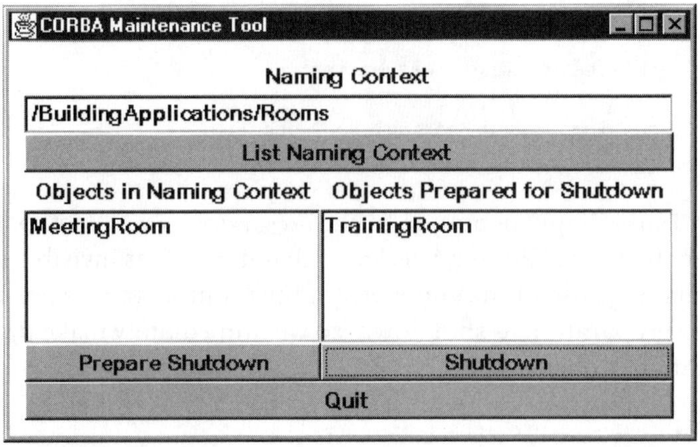

FIGURE 13.21   Objects selected for shut down.

operations is the same as before. If we had used the Tie approach in the application in Chapter 9 we could have simply extended the Room implementation class because we wouldn't need to extend the skeleton class. However, we will also use the inheritance approach for the Room object, which prevents us from inheriting the existing Room implementation class.

```
public void shutdown() {
    _orb().shutdown();
}

// Room attribute and operations
}
```

The server implementation is nearly the same as in Chapter 9, it just instantiates MaintainedRoom objects instead of Room objects and prints a message after `impl_is_ready()` saying that the server is exiting.

2.5   Using the Maintenance Tool

When you use the maintenance tool to shut down Room servers you see the GUI populated as shown in Figures 13.20 and 13.21. Once you have started the Naming Service and a number of maintained rooms—Training Room, Meeting Room, and Board Room—you can shut down their servers.

Figure 13.20 shows the three maintained rooms with the Training Room selected for shutdown preparation. Figure 13.21 shows the situation where we have called `prepareShutdown()` on the Training Room, and the Board Room has already exited.

G L O S S A R Y

Acronyms

AB: Architecture Board.

API: Application Programming Interface.

BOA: Basic Object Adapter.

CGI: Common Gateway Interface.

CORBA: Common Object Request Broker Architecture.

DCE: Distributed Computing Environment.

DCE-CIOP: DCE Common Inter-ORB Protocol.

DII: Dynamic Invocation Interface.

DIS: Draft International Standard.

DSI: Dynamic Skeleton Interface.

DTC: Domain Technology Committee.

ESIOP: Environment-Specific Inter-ORB Protocols.

EUSIG: End User Special Interest Group.

FDTF: Financial Domain Task Force.

GIOP: General Inter-ORB Protocol.

IDL: Interface Definition Language.

IIOP: Internet Inter-ORB Protocol.

IMCDTF: Interactive Multimedia and Electronic Commerce Domain Task Force.

IOR: Interoperable Object Reference.

IR: Interface Repository.

ISIG: Internet Special Interest Group.

ISO: International Standards Organization.

JSIG: Japan Special Interest Group.

MDTF: Manufacturing Domain Task Force.

ODP: Open Distributed Processing.

OMA: Object Management Architecture.

OMG: Object Management Group.

ORB: Object Request Broker.

PIDL: Pseudo-IDL.

POA: Portable Object Adapter.

PTC: Platform Technology Committee.

RFI: Request For Information.

RFP: Request For Proposal.

RMI: Remote Method Invocation.

RTSIG: Real Time Special Interest Group.

SIG: Special Interest Group.

SSL: Secure Socket Layer.

TSIG: Transportation Special Interest Group.

UUID: Universal Unique Identifier.

Terms

Any: Pre-defined data type in OMG IDL which can contain self-describing values of *any* type.

Architecture Board: An OMG board that reviews proposals and technology for conformance to the OMA.

Auditing: Keeping records of which principals perform which invocations on secured objects.

Authentication: Verifing that principals are who they claim to be.

Basic Object Adapter: The first specification of an object adapter in the CORBA standard. Its interface is considered incomplete, and ORB vendors have used divergent implementations to complete its functionality.

Byte-code: Intermediate representation of programming language code. The Java byte-code is very popular and virtual machines which can execute Java byte-code are available for most hardware platforms and operating systems.

Common Facilities: See CORBA facilities.

Common Gateway Interface: Interface at HTTP servers which allows access to resources, e.g. databases or programs outside the server.

Common Object Request Broker Architecture: Architecture for distributed object systems defined by the OMG.

Common Object Services: See CORBA services.

CORBAfacilities: A set of published specifications for application-level object services that are applicable across industry domains, e.g. Printing Facility, Systems Management Facility.

CORBAnet: Permanent showcase to demonstrate IIOP-based ORB interoperability sponsored by the OMG and most ORB vendors. CORBAnet is hosted by the Distributed Systems Technology Centre in Brisbane, Australia. CORBAnet can be accessed at http://www.corba.net.

CORBAservices: Set of published specifications for fundamental services assisting all object implementations, e.g. Naming Service, Event Service, Object Trading Service.

Core Object Model: The fundamental object-oriented model in the OMA which defines the basic concepts on which CORBA is based.

Credential: An encapsulation of a principal's identity and security attributes.

DCE Common Inter-ORB Protocol. Environment Specific Interoperability Protocol based on DCE. The first ESIOP adopted by the OMG.

Distributed Computing Environment. Distributed middleware developed under the control of the Open Group, formerly Open Software Foundation (OSF).

Domain Task Force: Group in the OMG responsible for specifying technologies relevant to a particular industry sector. They report to the Domain Technical Committee.

Domain Technology Committee: OMG Committee which supervises several Domain Task Forces concerned with technology specification for particular domains.

Draft International Standard: ISO defines phases through which a potential International Standard must pass. Draft International Standard is the penultimate phase.

Dynamic Invocation Interface: Interface defined in CORBA which allows the invocation of operations on object references without compile-time knowledge of the objects' interface types.

Dynamic Skeleton Interface: Interface defined in CORBA which allows servers to dynamically interpret incoming invocation requests of arbitrary operations.

Environment-Specific Inter-ORB Protocols: CORBA interoperability protocols which use data formats other than the ones specified in the GIOP. See also DCE ESIOP.

Firewall: Networking software that prevents certain types of network connections and traffic for security reasons.

General Inter-ORB Protocol: Protocol which belongs to the mandatory CORBA Interoperability protocol specifications. It defines the format of the protocol data units which can be sent via any transport. Currently there is only one transport protocol defined, namely, IIOP.

Interface Definition Language: Language to specify interfaces of objects independent of particular programming language representations. OMG has defined OMG IDL.

Interface Repository. Component of CORBA which stores type information and makes it available through standard interfaces at run time. Typically, an Interface Repository is populated by an IDL compiler when processing IDL specifications.

Interoperable Object Reference: Object reference which identifies objects independent of the ORB environment in which they have been created.

JavaBean: A Java class that supports certain conventions to allow it to be inspected and used as a component by visual application builder environments.

Marshal: Conversion of data into a programming-language and architecture-independent format.

Non-repudiation: Creation, transmission, and storage of irrefutable evidence that a principal performed an action.

Object Adapter: The ORB component which at invocation time locates the correct method in the correct programming language object based on an object reference. It is also informed by servers when objects are ready to be invoked.

Object Management Architecture: This is the overall architecture and roadmap of the OMG, of which CORBA forms a part.

Object Management Group: An international industry consortium with over 600 members which specifies an object-oriented framework for distributed computing, including CORBA.

Object Reference: Opaque data structure which identifies a single CORBA object, and enables clients to invoke operations on it, regardless of the object's location. Objects can have multiple object references.

Object Request Broker: The central component of the OMA which transmits operation invocation requests to distributed objects and returns the results to the requester.

Object Services: See CORBAservices.

OMA Reference Model: The structural model defining roles for the various components taking part in the OMA. It identifies five groups of objects to be specified: Object Request Broker, Object Services, Common Facilities, Domain Objects and Application Objects.

Open Distributed Processing: Group within ISO which is concerned with the standardization of open distributed systems.

Platform Technology Committee: OMG Committee which supervises several Task Forces concerned with specifying the ORB platform infrastructure.

Portable Object Adapter: An object adapter with standard interfaces to associate CORBA object references to programming language object instances. It is considered to be a replacement for the Basic Object Adapter.

Principal: A user or system component with a verifiable identity.

Pseudo-IDL: Interface definitions for components of ORB infrastructure that will not be implemented as CORBA objects.

Request For Information: A formal request from an OMG body for submissions of information relating to a specific technology area.

Request For Proposal: A formal request from an OMG body for a submission of a technology specification in IDL with English semantics.

Secure IIOP: An extension of the IIOP protocol that includes security information and provides optional encryption of request data.

Secure Socket Layer: A protocol that extends TCP/IP sockets by providing authentication and encryption of communications.

Special Interest Group: Member group in the OMG that has a topic of interest in common. These groups report findings to Committees within the OMG, or the Architecture Board.

TypeCode: A run-time representation of an IDL type.

Universal Unique Identifier. Used in DCE to identify an entity.

Unmarshal: The inverse of marshaling.

I N D E X